Russian Culture
in Modern Times

Christianity and the Eastern Slavs
in three volumes

Editorial Board

Boris Gasparov
Robert P. Hughes
Irina Paperno
Olga Raevsky-Hughes
Nicholas Ríasanovsky
Theodore Taranovsky
Donald W. Treadgold

Contents of the Volumes

Volume I
Slavic Cultures in the Middle Ages
Edited by Boris Gasparov and Olga Raevsky-Hughes

Volume II
Russian Culture in Modern Times
Edited by Robert P. Hughes and Irina Paperno

Volume III
Russian Literature in Modern Times
Edited by Boris Gasparov, Robert P. Hughes,
Irina Paperno, and Olga Raevsky-Hughes

Christianity
and the
Eastern Slavs

VOLUME II

Russian Culture in Modern Times

Edited by

Robert P. Hughes and Irina Paperno

UNIVERSITY OF CALIFORNIA PRESS

Berkeley   Los Angeles   London

University of California Press
Berkeley and Los Angeles, California

University of California Press, Ltd.
London, England

© 1994 by
The Regents of the University of California

Library of Congress Cataloging-in-Publication Data

Christianity and the Eastern Slavs.

   p.   cm. — (California Slavic studies; 17)

   Based on papers delivered at two international conferences held in May 1988 at the University of California–Berkeley and the Kennan Institute for Advanced Russian Studies to commemorate the millennium of the Christianization of Kievan Rus'.

   Includes bibliographical references and index.

   Contents: v. 2. Russian Culture in Modern Times / edited by Robert P. Hughes and Irina Paperno.

   ISBN: 978-0-520-30248-8 (pbk. : alk. paper)

   1. Russia—Intellectual life—1801–1917—Congresses. 2. Russia—Intellectual life—18th century—Congresses. 3. Russia—Religious life and customs—Congresses. 4. Orthodox Eastern Church—Russia—History—Congresses. 5. Russkaia pravo-slavnaia tserkov'—History—Congresses. 6. Russia—Church history—Congresses. I. Hughes, Robert P. II. Paperno, Irina. III. Series: California Slavic studies ; 17.

DK4.C33 vol. 17

[DK189.2]
947 s—dc20
[306.6'0947]   93–25779
                                                 CIP

CONTENTS

ACKNOWLEDGMENTS

This volume is the second of a three-volume collection based on papers delivered at two international conferences held in May 1988 at the University of California–Berkeley and the Kennan Institute for Advanced Russian Studies (Washington, D.C.) to commemorate the millennium of the adoption of Christianity in Rus'. Volume I, *Slavic Cultures in the Middle Ages,* edited by Boris Gasparov and Olga Raevsky-Hughes, appeared in 1993. It contains a general introduction to the whole collection by Boris Gasparov.

A debt of gratitude is owed the following funding organizations: the National Endowment for the Humanities; the Kennan Institute for Advanced Russian Studies; the I. V. Koulaieff Educational Foundation (San Francisco); the Center for Slavic and East European Studies (University of California–Berkeley).

We gratefully acknowledge the assistance of Keith Goeringer, Catherine Gordis, David Mayberry, William Nickell, Anthony Vanchu, Glen and Irina Worthey, G. Patton Wright, and the compositor, Gareth Perkins. Vail Palomino was the coordinator of our efforts, and we wish to express our thanks to her.

We are especially grateful to Hugh McLean, Nicholas Riasanovsky, Theodore Taranovsky, and Donald W. Treadgold for reading the manuscripts and for their numerous editorial suggestions.

A note on transliteration is due. The main text of each article retains the orthography of Russian proper names chosen by the author. In some cases we have preferred the traditionally accepted transliteration of names over the Library of Congress variant (e.g., Tolstoy, Dostoevsky). However, Russian proper names in the endnotes and index are transliterated according to the Library of Congress system. (An exception is made in the case of well-established names of historical figures.)

B.G.
R.P.H.
I.P.
O.R.-H.

PART I

Institutions, Cultural Life, Mass Culture

Faith and Secularity in Eighteenth-Century Russian Literacy, 1700–1775

GARY MARKER

About twenty years ago a handful of unusually provocative new studies set off a remarkably creative "marvelous decade," to use Annenkov's famous expression, in eighteenth-century Russian studies. Books such as Marc Raeff's *Origins of the Russian Intelligentsia,* the 1964 symposium *Absoliutizm v Rossii,* the sociological works of S. M. Troitskii, and the literary studies of P. N. Berkov generated lively controversies about the nature of eighteenth-century Russian culture and society around which arose several stimulating critiques and amplifications of the ideas that had been put forth.

When one compares this ferment with the situation in eighteenth-century Russian studies today, one cannot help but be struck by the contrast. Much good work continues to appear, of course, but one would be hard pressed to identify a single raging debate about fundamental questions of analysis or conceptualization in the current literature. The reasons for this quietude are difficult to fathom, since none of the issues of social status and psychology that so exercised the passions in the 1960s and early 1970s was ever resolved to any general satisfaction. Nowadays, however, these discussions linger largely as legacies of a livelier and increasingly distant past. The separate subspecialties do still hold to their own, frequently divergent, assumptions about the nature of eighteenth-century life, but these rarely emerge as explicit controversies.

Most historians of ideas, for example, hold fast to the idea that the eighteenth century was essentially a period of transition from the relatively isolated and faith-centered world of Muscovite letters to a more cosmopolitan, lay, and increasingly secular culture, symbolized by St. Petersburg and characterized by new academies, journals, circles, and publishing ventures. It was an Age of Reason, and although the Enlightenment was by no means a monolithic culture, its proponents proceeded on the basis of a common worldview and rhetoric, and their efforts to remake Russian culture in their own image represented a coherent and philosophically consistent set of actions. Some intellectual historians, indeed, look upon the eighteenth century as the last time in Russian history when the government and educated public shared a common general outlook.[1]

Cultural and social historians, however, tend to see matters quite differently. Although they do not directly confront the notion of a harmonious Enlightenment Weltanschauung, their studies depict a society marked by fragmentation, social struggle, psychological alienation or anomie, and unresolved conflicts among radically different perspectives of culture, the individual, national identity, and legitimate authority.

Over the past three decades, the most provocative exponents of many of these views have been the brilliant Soviet semioticians Iurii Lotman and Boris Uspenskii, who have elaborated a series of "dual models" that describe eighteenth-century Russian culture as being characterized by unresolved oppositions of faith and Enlightenment, memory and construct, tradition and nature.[2] In their view the vaunted inexorable march of secular progress is largely a myth that ignores the complexity, the unpredictability, and the paradox of cultural upheavals. They argue that eighteenth-century rulers and thinkers who struggled so hard to deny their links with the past, to "erase" their memory, as it were, instead unwittingly relied upon ancient symbols of authority and fell back into older patterns of discourse. Thus the Renaissance-like counterpoint of ancients and moderns that so typifies eighteenth-century Russian thought was itself deeply rooted in the old Russian duality of *starina* and *novizna*, albeit with important modern characteristics.

Lotman and Uspenskii's methods and their remarkable erudition have proven to be enormously attractive to recent literary historians. Semiotics, however, often seems to lack the element of sociological mechanism that might explain how and why these dualisms ultimately took the form that they did, when they did. At a more pedantic level, we are often left to wonder for whom these "dialogues" among competing systems had meaning other than for eighteenth-century intellectuals and twentieth-century scholars. In other words, we are never completely certain whether the semiotics of culture is essentially a heuristic device that is helpful in conceptualizing holistically the tensions inherent in Russian culture, or whether it describes an active process (a "real" dialogue) that engaged the consciousnesses of specific groups of people.

In a recent monograph, the German literary scholar Hans Rothe applies the concept of dualism to the realm of Russian literary activity in a manner that is not particularly semiotic, but that retains a sense of cultural discourse and addresses some important questions concerning the mentalities of discreet groups that the semioticians do not. He pointedly accepts the picture of a culture built around faith-centered and lay-centered alternatives, but he locates that duality exclusively in the creative life of the most educated clergy and laity. His primary concern is the relationship between the printed literary and poetic activity of the educated laity of mid- and late eighteenth century ("the Academy") and what he terms the old Russian manuscript culture of the monasteries.

Rothe demonstrates that both cultures remained vibrant and productive during the eighteenth century and, significantly, that they were engaged in a constant and creative dialogue with each other. He does not use the language of contradiction to describe this duality; instead we see examples of acknowledged influence and inspiration.[3] By contrast, Lotman and Uspenskii describe continuing mutuality and adaptation as having been largely unconscious and paradoxical. Still, all of them paint a picture of a rapidly changing culture, constructed around the two quite different, if not entirely contradictory, alternatives of religion and secularity.

Modern social historians tend to be uncomfortable with such overarching characterizations of an entire culture; nevertheless, they share an interest in questions of social discourse. Their legacy to this discussion has been to highlight fragmentation and alienation as increasingly important features of eighteenth-century Russian life. Within Soviet scholarship this fragmentation emerges as a class struggle that set the privileged world of the court and gentry against the unfree and oppressed world of the lower classes.[4] Between the two a chasm of such magnitude and enmity came to exist during the eighteenth century that no dialogue was possible except in those exceptional circumstances when "progressive" or "democratic" writers produced works that drew appreciative audiences from the literate elements of the common people. The language of faith, according to this view, was increasingly anachronistic and entirely oppressive, and only secular communications held even a glimmer of a possibility for positive social dialogue between writers and the people.[5]

Few Western scholars have endorsed the class-struggle argument, but they too have concluded that during the eighteenth century social discourse had grown increasingly strained. For them cultural disharmony resulted largely from the ever-increasing importance of social standing (*soslovie*) in so many features of life, including legal status, service, and education. Much of this literature has concentrated rather specifically on the changing lives and psychological disaffection of the service nobility, but recent studies of other groups have come to similar conclusions.[6] Class conflict may not have been what was going on, but the breakdown of dialogue was every bit as pronounced.

In the last analysis, notwithstanding their divergent interests and perspectives, most authors have come to accept the counterpoint of a sometimes backward-looking, faith-centered tradition and a state-driven, consciously modernizing secularity as being particularly relevant to eighteenth-century Russia. Written texts, it is further acknowledged, were central to the active engagement of the two, whether as cultural artifacts or as agents of learning and socialization. Where scholars implicitly disagree is on the possibilities for dialogue across social and educational boundaries that inhered in eighteenth-century life and culture. Perhaps, then, by addressing this subject, we can revive what has become a near-dormant discourse on the nature of eighteenth-century Russian society.

Methods and sources for the history of communications are not always easy to come by, and this essay makes no pretense to having found a way out of the methodological dilemma.[7] It does, however, accept some of the insights that have come out of literary criticism, most particularly the awareness of the multiplicity of meanings that a given text or set of texts might elicit from different audiences. From this perspective language, style, appearance, and context had as important a bearing on how—or whether— a text was understood as did the didactic meaning that the author intended. Lotman's famous essay on how a particular peasant reader endowed Karamzin's "Poor Liza" with an eccentric interpretation, to give just one example, demonstrates the great distance that sometimes separated intended and received meanings.[8]

Most of Karamzin's countrymen had neither read nor heard of "Poor Liza," however. The vast majority were illiterate, and most of those who could read did not have access to literary texts. Without minimizing the significance of studying the mental worlds of individual readers, we must recognize that concepts of social discourse that are to include the majority of Russian people must also look at texts that literate people did tend to read. It was these that most often got passed along verbally to the illiterate majority, and it was these, consequently, that had the greatest chance of being incorporated somehow into a more popular cosmology.

Obviously, the publications that lent themselves to this process came mostly from the large institutional typographies, rather than from the pens of lay literati. Reaching audiences, however, depended upon more than just the capacity to print a lot of books. Rulers could—and did—command the presses to print and distribute texts in large numbers, but they could not successfully command large numbers of people to read them, a point that is compellingly made by the experiences of the state publishing houses under Peter the Great.[9] If, as often happened, a text was left unread, it could not be incorporated in any way into popular culture.

Looking at communications in this way endows the literate minority with an enormous power as the primary recipients of the written word and as its exclusive transmitters. Russia's reading class, though, was far from being either socially or intellectually unified during the eighteenth century. Indeed, the increasingly heterogeneous nature of Russian education is often seen as a prime culprit in creating so much cultural separateness.[10] Who, then, was communicating with whom, and was anyone reaching the illiterate masses with any effectiveness?

The current study addresses the possibilities and limitations of discourse in the eighteenth century from the specific perspective of the comprehensibility of the written language, an issue that logically takes precedence over the understanding of the ideas that the written language conveyed. The primacy of language over contents had a particular significance in eighteenth-century Russia, moreover, because written culture at that time was characterized by the existence of two related but distinct and vital written languages, civil Russian and Slavonic.[11]

The fact of bilingualism (or diglossia) is widely mentioned in the scholarly literature, but it is not commonly treated as a defining characteristic of Russian culture. Yet a clear linguistic duality arose during the eighteenth century in which the government and the literati relied primarily on formal Russian and the civil script, whereas the language of liturgy and prayer remained, by and large, Slavonic. Church books were printed in the pre-Petrine orthography, which by 1720 was uniformly referred to as the "church script" (*tserkovnyi shrift* or *tserkovnye litery*).[12] Surely the fact that this division by language or script corresponded to a significant degree to the dichotomy between antiquity (including faith) and modernity (including secularity) ought to suggest that bilingualism deserves serious attention in understanding how communications developed.

The particular focus of this study relates to the possible bearing of bilingualism on literacy, specifically on learning to read, during the first three quarters of the eighteenth century. How did Russian schooling accommodate itself to the presence of two languages and two scripts? Which script and written language did literate Russians tend to learn, or did they learn both? Did the script in which literacy was first achieved significantly affect how people related to the written language later on? Finally, how did the language of literacy color cultural and social discourse?

By January 1708, the new letters of Peter's reformed alphabet and the first new printing presses had arrived from Amsterdam. Although the new orthography was widely employed, Slavonic and the old script remained the language of not only virtually all prayer books, but also many educational books and even some laws and public notices.[13] All of these volumes were printed in the very type fonts (e.g., *arsen'evskie* and *nikitenskie*) that the Russian Orthodox typographies had been employing since the early seventeenth century.[14] Visually, therefore, they appeared as familiar links to the Muscovite past.

The printed civil script, by contrast, looked very new. Paleographers are undecided about the organic connection between the reformed alphabet and the business orthography (*delovoe pis'mo*) of the late Muscovite and early Petrine period.[15] But most literate people never saw the business hand of intragovernmental communications, and, as the century progressed, the two printed scripts came clearly to be affixed to separate languages. The older script led almost invariably to prayers and Slavonic, and the new one led to the newly-formalized style and grammar of civil Russian, the language of state and academy. Neither of these formal languages stood particularly close to everyday speech, but neither were they entirely unrelated to it.[16] In short, bilingualism raised the possibility of two competing and largely incompatible literacies in written languages that had ever less in common with each other as the eighteenth century progressed.

People could and did learn both languages, of course, and the graduates of the seminaries, gymnasia, and cadet academies almost certainly had facility in both. So, too, did any well-trained scribe. The vast majority of students were not so well educated, however. In fact, the published documents and descriptive histories of primary schools from most of the eighteenth century reveal two transcendent patterns: most students dropped out long before graduation, and relatively few managed to get beyond the initial course of language instruction.[17] The next level of schooling, whether it called for Latin, mathematics, history, or grammar, consistently witnessed the biggest dropoff in enrollment. Put simply, institutional primary education succeeded reasonably well at getting students through the first course of literacy books, but not at anything else. What, then, had these children learned?

Muscovites had come to recognize separate Russian and Slavonic words and expressions in everyday speech, but there was essentially only one written native language—and certainly only one alphabet, and there existed a single accepted method of teaching children how to read, the so-called primer method that was supposed to proceed from the primer to the breviary to the psalter. Students learned through constant repetition of sounds, words, and phrases; and mastery came when the student had memorized an entire text. Those whose education ended at this point had assimilated a mechanical and highly ritualized reading, but they had developed little or no facility to read for understanding. Although this system was cumbersome and tedious, it at least introduced children to the living language.[18]

The primer system also remained in force throughout the eighteenth century, but, without substantial modifications, such a ladder could not accommodate itself to the reformed alphabet. If students were going to learn the new script, the primer had to change and the subsequent pedagogy had to generate alternatives to the Slavonic breviary and psalter. This dilemma perplexed the reformers of the Petrine era and beyond: since most primary education remained either outside of formal schools or outside of effective centralized direction, literacy instruction was relatively impervious to curricular reforms. As before, how well one learned depended on the knowledge and inclinations of one's teacher, but in the wake of the reformed alphabet, the very language of literacy hinged on the script of the books that the teacher or school chose to employ. Higher governmental authorities could pass decrees and develop curricula, but interceding locally in the process of primary education proved to be exceedingly difficult, practically speaking, except by controlling the available texts. Such an environment ensured that whoever succeeded in cornering the primer market, to put it crudely, gained a tremendous advantage in guiding the eyes of children and in influencing how they responded to the lures of the written word.[19]

The state's first alternative text was a scholastic civil abecedarium (*grazhdanskaia uchebnaia azbuka*) printed in Moscow around 1710.[20] Between that time and the death of Peter the Great in 1725, there were probably only five printings of civil scholastic abecedaria, the initial Moscow imprint and four that came out as appendices to editions of the *Iunosti chestnoe zertsalo*, the well-known Petrine etiquette book for young nobles.[21] By contrast, Feofan Prokopovich's primer and catechism, *Pervoe uchenie otrokom*, went through twelve Petrine printings, mostly in unknown press runs. For all of Feofan's commitment to civic virtue and obedience to civil authorities, ideals that are clearly expressed in his primer, the *Uchenie* taught only the church script, and it directed students to the breviary and psalter for their next instruction, rather than to the *Zertsalo* or any other "civil" text.[22]

Exactly how many copies of Feofan's primer ultimately went to school children is not certain, since by official decree it was meant to be read aloud in the churches several times a year, a function that was entirely separate from teaching literacy. Between the 1720s and the 1770s, moreover, one finds numerous references to children at various levels of education being tutored in Feofan's catechism well after they had learned to read.[23]

No such questions surround the use of the church-script *azbuka ucheb-naia,* an abecedarium that appears to have been the standard literacy text during the entire second half of the seventeenth century and that continued to fulfill that function in Peter's reign. Archival records show that at least 115,000 copies of this booklet (and possibly tens of thousands more) were printed between 1708 and 1725. By comparison, Peter's typographies produced only 3500 incontrovertibly civil primers.[24] Thus, whatever the exact figure was, the church primer clearly maintained its hegemony in the publishing history of Petrine literacy texts.

All of the sources on primary education confirm the exclusive use of the church texts in teaching literacy, even in the various new "state" schools.[25] Peter did propose that writing be introduced earlier in the course of instruction than had been the case in Muscovy, and it is possible that the students who learned how to write their letters during primary schooling were taught the civil alphabet. Let us note, though, that there is no evidence of any civil primers being interposed into primary education during Peter's reign. Copies of the *Zertsalo* did circulate, but not, so far as one can tell, to students who were learning to read.[26]

To summarize, Peter's educated subjects learned their literacy through church primers and prayer books. Most of them never studied the civil script, and they never saw a civil-script textbook. This circumstance was in fact thoroughly consistent with what Peter actually said about education. The insistence upon teaching useful subjects was certainly ubiquitous in his writing, but these were meant to come only after a faith-centered literacy had been achieved. Throughout his reign Peter was emphatic on the necessity of using education to train churchmen to perform their sacraments properly and to develop a truer understanding of the church's teachings. Similar convictions also typified his discussions of lay education: at the primary level the requirements of faith were at least as important as was practical knowledge in creating the kinds of useful citizens that Peter demanded.[27] In every instance, the vehicles for instilling faith were the literacy texts.

The duality of faith and instrumentality also had a major bearing on the subsequent evolution of Russian literacy. Scholars rightly see his reign as providing the first big step in the direction of secularity, and, in particular, toward the new ideas and forms of behavior that Russia's serving men had to assimilate. Most then suggest that the subsequent thirty years saw a retreat from many of those initiatives that enabled the church to regain control over primary education.[28] In practice, however, clerical control had never been surrendered in the first place. The fact that this control was used, with the full consent of the government, to teach prayer reading in a church alphabet raises serious doubts about literacy's supposed role in helping to socialize people to the new secular world.

Indeed, between 1726 and 1755, civil typographies printed only four new editions of the *Zertsalo* with the civil abecedarium and no other civil primers of any sort. These printings were produced expressly for students at the Academy's gymnasia (and possibly those of the new Corps of Cadets) rather than for primary-school children. During these same three decades the Synod's Moscow Typography printed nearly 300,000 church primers of various sorts, and, by all accounts, it was the Moscow primers that made their way to primary schools and teachers.[29] As before, the follow-up texts were the breviary and the psalter, although some schools interposed Feofan's *Uchenie* between the *azbuka uchebnaia* and the breviary.[30]

But if students of literacy studied only the church script, the question arises whether the initial language and script of instruction necessarily directed reading toward church literacy rather than civil. Was it not possible to pick up the new script simply by seeing it or using it? Obviously, such on-the-job training did take place, since some graduates of the garrison schools and diocesan schools, among others, went on to useful and even distinguished careers in service. The available evidence suggests, however, that most pupils could not read a text printed in the civil script. Even the increasingly educated parish clergy, so critical from the state's perspective in governing village society and in disseminating the word of the state, were typically illiterate in civil Russian.

The *Dukhovnyi reglament* of 1721 mandated that all parish clergy were required to go to school prior to beginning their clerical service. They also were obliged to keep parish records and to read aloud the copies of laws and official announcements that would be supplied to them by the government. These important duties, which were to constitute the new civic side of clerical service to go along with their traditional sacramental ones, clearly anticipated that priests would be fully literate in both Russian scripts.[31] Nevertheless, most priests either did not or could not carry out these responsibilities. Few unordained clergy attended seminaries, and their exposure to literacy was consequently limited to the traditional curriculum that prevailed in most diocesan schools and in the more widespread informal teaching cir-

cumstances. Many ordained priests also appear not to have learned the civil
script during literacy training, and most did not see a printed book in civil
Russian until after they had been in school for several years, if then. Typically, clerical children studied Latin long before they began to read civil
Russian, at least after 1737.[32] Since the vast majority of those who entered
the seminary left well before graduation, most never made it to texts in the
civil script.

Church documents show that as late as the 1780s the Synod had determined that most parish priests could not read the civil script and that they
were consequently unable to perform their mandated civic duties.[33] This state
of affairs is often ascribed to bad teachers or to the well-documented harsh
seminary regimen that was so notoriously unconducive to learning. But it
would seem more fundamentally to have been the logical outcome of the
education that clerical children received. Having been trained to read only
prayer books, and to read them ritually and formulaically, they could not
be expected to carry out responsibilities that required a completely different
kind of learning.

The importance of such one-sided literacy among the majority of the
parish clergy cannot be emphasized enough. Their widespread inability to
read civil-type books simply eliminated a very large portion of Russia's
literate minority from the ranks of possible audiences for the books and
journals of the civil culture.[34] Beyond that, the fact that for much of the
countryside the clergy constituted the only literate presence meant that they
were often the only ones who were deemed capable of transmitting the official pronouncements of church and state. Several recent studies have demonstrated that most of the Russian countryside was profoundly undergoverned
by any regularly constituted state institution during the eighteenth century.[35]
Thus the rural parish priest was not just the main source of literacy, but a
primary—albeit highly problematic—source of external authority. If all he
could do was to broadcast the prayers, if indeed his literacy training obliged
him to filter out governmental publications, it is difficult to imagine how
clerical literacy, notwithstanding its significant growth during the eighteenth
century, could have been a vehicle for disseminating secular ideas or civil
information.

The church, of course, had long since accepted the hegemony of civil
authority in temporal matters, but much of the church's own writing on
temporal matters seems to have been lost at the parish level. Certainly the
ecclesiastical authorities produced numerous publications in celebration of
state power, as well as treatises emphasizing that the road to salvation

necessarily passed through obedience to secular authority. Most of these works were printed in civil Russian, however, or occasionally in simultaneous church and civil-script editions, and these generally came out in minuscule print runs of a few hundred copies each.[36] Clearly, this opus was directed essentially at a cosmopolitan, or at least an educated, audience. The rural parish clergy, who in any event were generally discouraged from preaching or sermonizing for fear of stirring the emotions and heresy, rarely saw it and still more rarely transmitted it to the flock.

The literacy of parish clergy, therefore, was by both training and practice almost exclusively an instrument of prayer and sacraments during most of the eighteenth century. But what about lay literacy? Here one would expect that the government's manifest and burgeoning need for capable servitors would have succeeded in allowing civil Russian to prevail. Surprisingly, however, church literacy remained the rule here as well. Students from the garrison schools (by far the largest of the state networks) learned their ABCs according to the church primer method, and only after they completed these books did they learn other subjects. Before they were sent on either to higher schooling or to military assignments, they had to receive certification as having successfully proceeded through the course of instruction.[37]

By most accounts, although a relatively small percentage of entering students graduated from the garrison schools, the students did receive some literacy training. Yet even the graduates often could not read anything of use to a military or technical career, and many were deemed illiterate by their first commanding officers even though they had been literate in school. Their incapacity, like that of the parish clergy, had less to do with incompetent teachers and examiners than with the inapplicability of church literacy to technical books in the civil script. Yet because of their inability to read military manuals, most garrison school students accepted apprenticeships in skills that did not require reading and writing.[38]

Similar circumstances also marked the education of students at nearly all of the other formal primary schools, including those who attended the mining schools that V. N. Tatishchev helped to organize.[39] Tatishchev wrote several famous essays on the subject of education during the 1730s, including a spirited full-length treatise in defense of civil learning (*grazhdanskaia nauka*), and his interest in primary education is well known.[40] Much, in particular, has been made of his suggestions that students at the Ural schools learn writing simultaneously with reading and that they study reading first with Feofan's *Uchenie* and then with the *Zertsalo*.[41] The focus on writing, we now know, was not new, but the proposal to combine religious and civil literacy in a single course of study was an intriguing, if improbable, innovation. As several scholars have shown, however, the Ural students did not receive copies of the *Zertsalo,* and instead they studied according to a familiar four-text sequence that began with the church *azbuka* and proceeded to the *Uchenie,* the breviary, and then the psalter.[42]

But if most primary school students did not learn to read civil Russian, who did? Institutional histories of the Cadet Corps recount that a significant percentage of their entering students during the 1730s and 1740s had received no prior education at all.[43] This circumstance is usually characterized as a transitional consequence of the large number of students who were in their early twenties and who had missed out on the new educational opportunities of the Petrine era prior to their enrolling in the Corps. Other evidence, though, indicates that, irrespective of generations and ages of initial enroll-ment, entering cadets were not equipped to read civil books.

The very first book printed in the Infantry Cadet Press in 1757 was a civil *azbuka* entitled *Probnaia kniga rossiiskim literam,* subsequently entitled *Ros-siiskaia azbuka sposobstvuiushchaia chteniiu grazhdanskoi pechati,* the ex-pressed purpose of which was to enable the cadets to understand the civil script so that they could read the textbooks that were used in their classes.[44] This book apparently was intended for use by all cadets rather than by an unlettered few, because over the next ten years the Infantry Academy pro-duced four printings with a total run of 2000 copies—approximately the number of students who had begun instruction at the Academy during that time—as well as two other civil primers. These students came from the nobility, and many of those who entered the Corps at ages eight through twelve—it was possible to begin at age six—had likely received some prior tutoring. Yet they required either remediation or basic instruction in reading the civil script as part of their formal school curriculum.

This example raises the strong possibility that literacy and reading civil Russian were considered separate and distinct skills during the eighteenth century, with the latter being associated with secondary education or possi-bly with the transition from primary to secondary education. In this regard it bears noting that Russia's scholastic presses began to produce a regular supply of civil primers during the 1760s and 1770s. How and where these texts were used is not altogether certain, but most indicators point to an audience of secondary school, and largely noble, students.

Between 1766 and the early 1780s, Moscow University and the Academy of Sciences published several editions of two primers, *Bukvar' dlia upotreble-niia rossiiskogo iunoshestva* and *Bukvar' rossiiskoi tserkovnymi i grazhdanskimi literami dlia upotrebleniia rossiiskogo iunoshestva.*[45] Although a few other civil primers appeared during this time, these two became standard texts, with eight printings of the first primer appearing between 1766 and 1786 (Moscow University: 1768, 1773, 1780; Academy of Sciences: 1766, 1768, 1773, 1778, 1780) and three of the second (Moscow University: 1770, 1782, 1786). The press runs of the Moscow imprints are not known, but most of the Academy editions had modest runs of 400 to 1200 copies per printing. Figures such as these far exceeded the very modest enrollments in the Academy's own gymnasium, but they do not begin to compare to the massive printing of church primers during this period, an indication that the market for the scholastic primers, regardless of whether it consisted mostly of primary or secondary schools, constituted only a tiny percentage of Russia's students.

Interestingly, the publishing figures for civil primers do approximate the production during the comparable years of the two Russian grammars that were most widely used in the lower classes of the Moscow University, Cadet Corps, and Academy of Sciences gymnasia, Mikhail Lomonosov's *Rossiiskaia grammatika* (which came out in 1757 [1200 copies], 1765 [1200 copies], 1772 [600 copies], 1777 [1000 copies], 1785 [612 copies], 1788, and 1799, all from the Academy of Sciences Press but with many copies being sent to Moscow); and *Kratkiia pravila rossiiskoi grammatiki,* which Moscow University published expressly for students at the University's gymnasia ("v pol'zu obuchaiushchegosia iunoshestva v gimnaziiakh Imp. Moskovskogo universiteta" was printed on the title page) in 1773, 1780, 1782, 1783, 1784, 1786, 1793, and 1797.[46] This symmetry suggests that the civil primers and Russian grammars may have been used sequentially as part of a single curriculum.

Several other small facts reinforce the impression of secondary school usage. The titles identify the primers as being directed at *iunoshestvo* ("dlia upotrebleniia rossiiskogo iunoshestva"), a word that usually referred specifically to adolescents, generally twelve- to sixteen-year-olds. This is hardly decisive evidence, to be sure, since *iunoshestvo* could also mean "youth in general," but the relevant laws and the writings of most eighteenth-century pedagogues, including officials at the University and the Academy, usually made a point of distinguishing *iunoshestvo* from *otrok* or *mladenets,* words that always referred to very young children. Thus, when a textbook indicated in its title that it was directed at *"iunoshestvo,"* we can, in the absence of any indications to the contrary, assume that the desired audience rather specifically comprised adolescents. The issue, then, is not one of beginning students versus older ones, but rather at what *middle* point in their ongoing education elite students were expected to start learning civil Russian.

Answers to this question, unfortunately, are difficult to come by. Lomonosov's famous polemic maintained that the gymnasium's students were being
asked to study foreign languages before they were competent in their own.[47]
He concentrated most of his attention on grammatical structure, style, and
rhetoric, but, along with several other educators of the 1760s and 1770s, he
expressed misgivings that the beginning gymnasium students were often entirely unequipped temperamentally, financially, and linguistically to pursue
their course of study. These concerns convinced administrators at both institutions to require that entering students be certified in reading and writing
Russian before they could go on to other subjects.[48] If they could not demonstrate facility in their native language, apparently a common outcome of
these inquiries, students had to enroll in a remedial Russian class (or "Russian school"), a course that taught civil Russian exclusively. There was no
formal Russian examination, however, and we therefore have no way of de-
termining precisely what the students knew when they arrived or what they
had to do in order to proceed with their studies.

Civil primers do not appear on the few surviving lists of books ordered
for specific classes (nor, for that matter, do the Russian grammars), and they
could easily have been meant for use either prior to gymnasium enrollment
or as the first text in the gymnasium Russian class.[49] In either case the intended users had almost certainly received some prior education before they
received their civil primers. The widespread need to employ such basic books
as civil primers and elementary grammars among these students, moreover,
suggests that those who had not learned civil Russian at home (or in a pen-
sion) could not yet use it when they arrived at the gymnasium.

Civil primers could, of course, be bought on the open market, and it is
entirely possible that some individual families or private schools used them
to teach basic literacy. The scholastic primers do not seem to have found
their way into primary school curricula, however, until the latter part of the
eighteenth century, and there are some indications that civil primers were
simply not conceived of as suitable primary school fare until the 1770s at the
very earliest.

An example of this mentality surfaced when a commission established to
organize public schools in Novgorod *guberniia* apparently decided to introduce civil primers into the primary schools during the mid-1770s. After
concluding that no appropriate ones were available, the commission convinced the Synod to compose a special civil abecedarium, *Grazhdanskaia
azbuka s kratkim katikhizisom i molitvami,* in 1776 exclusively for use in
schools in Novgorod, Pskov, and Tver.[50] This imprint deserves particular

attention for its use of a catechism and prayers, texts that had long been deemed appropriate for teaching reading to young children and that were consequently a common feature of many eighteenth-century church primers. Never before, however, had they comprised the basic reading texts in an exclusively civil primer. The combination was apparently so unusual that the private publishing firm of Weitbrecht and Schnoor printed a pirate copy— which the police soon confiscated—the very next year.[51]

This episode reveals a great deal about the generally understood meaning of literacy and literacy training in the 1770s. First, it strengthens the impression that school children in the 1770s did not normally receive civil primers when they first learned to read and that extraordinary measures were necessary in order to procure them. Second, the fact that none of the easily available civil primers from the scholastic typographies was deemed suitable is particularly revealing. Since the main difference between the scholastic primers and this one lay in their different choices of reading texts, one can infer that the inappropriateness of the former was seen to be the failure to include prayers or catechisms for reading. The relevant officials simply took for granted the virtue of maintaining the unity of literacy and faith in teaching reading to young children, a unity that ceased to be as important for the secondary school civil primers.

All of the available evidence, then, indicates that the approximately thirty printings of Russian civil primers which appeared between the first edition of the *Iunosti chestnoe zertsalo* in 1717 and the mid-1770s went to a very small and mostly privileged proportion of Russia's students, most of whom had already passed through the course of instruction of church literacy books. Without the civil primers, students appear to have been unable to read civil texts, as a result of which virtually the entire opus of secular and civil-type texts, which were pouring out of Moscow's and St. Petersburg's burgeoning typographies by the 1760s, simply lay out of the reach of the vast majority of literate people.

By contrast, devotional texts would have been relatively more accessible or at least more familiar. Through its control over textbooks and their use, therefore, the church maintained its status as the overseer of primary education and literacy. This control guaranteed that the rapidly increasing number of Russian youth who began instruction during the first three quarters of the eighteenth century had to pass through prayer and the language of the faith before they were given any introduction to the written word of secularity, an introduction that, for most students, never came.

As a consequence, the whole of educated government and civil society, notwithstanding its own rapid internal growth and the common rhetoric that enabled its members to communicate effectively among themselves, faced almost insuperable linguistic obstacles, largely of their own making, in addressing anybody else. In spite of the fact that Catherinean intellectuals still read church books, they had all but ceased to rely on Slavonic or the church script, which most of them considered to be archaic and unsuited to modern thought and literature, to express themselves in print. Such a disavowal may have made sense for translating or composing new literature, but it necessarily reinforced the exclusivity of their audience.

The irony of this state of affairs for the course of secularization must by now be manifest. A reform of the alphabet that was meant to facilitate secular learning instead achieved largely the opposite. The primer system, which had had universal applicability in Muscovy to all forms of Slavonic/Russian texts, became with the reformed alphabet a palpable symbol of faith and a specific instrument of a parochial, but still hegemonous, church literacy. Those who wished to proceed from basic education alone to useful service to the post-Petrine state found themselves to be ill equipped for that job, but well equipped to read their prayers, a perverse state of affairs indeed.

As a postscript to this paper, it should be pointed out that during the last quarter of the eighteenth century some initial steps were finally taken to address the asymmetry between church literacy and a secular *raison d'état*. How and why these strides toward civil literacy were initiated constitute a completely separate chapter in the history of Russian education. Certainly the endeavors of Catherine the Great, the new Public School Commission, and several intellectuals to revise the basic curricula of primary schools are well known. But notwithstanding the unprecedented attention that civil society showered on literacy instruction during the 1780s and 1790s, the church continued to be the dominant force. The new public primary schools, Catherine's civil *azbuka,* and the 100,000 copies of Jankovic's civil *Rossiiskii bukvar'* were indeed very important. But, in the last analysis, the church's decision in the early 1770s to replace the *azbuka uchebnaia* as the basic literacy text with Archbishop Platon's dual-script *Nachal'noe uchenie chelovekom* and its decision to print nearly a million copies of it over the next thirty years loom far larger.[52] Whether the new primer truly taught literacy in both scripts or whether it provided only a bare introduction to the civil language remains an open question. But it is clear that the church continued to be by far the largest educator of young children well into the nineteenth century. As the keeper of the gate, it was able to ensure that the primacy of faith over civil instrumentality remained the cornerstone of Russian literacy.

Notes

1. Among those who emphasize the unity of eighteenth-century thought are Hans Rogger, *National Consciousness in Eighteenth-Century Russia* (Cambridge, Mass., 1960); J. L. Black, *Citizens for the Fatherland: Education, Educators, and Pedagogical Ideals in Eighteenth-Century Russia* (New York, 1979); Nicholas V. Riasanovsky, *A Parting of Ways: Government and the Educated Public in Russia 1801–1855* (Oxford, 1976) 3–100; and Andrzej Walicki, *A History of Russian Thought from the Enlightenment to Marxism* (Stanford, 1979).

2. Lotman and Uspenskii's bibliography of eighteenth-century studies is enormous, and several of their better-known works have been translated into English. See, for example, Iu. M. Lotman and B. A. Uspenskii, *The Semiotics of Russian Culture* (Ann Arbor, 1984), which contains the important essay "The Role of Dual Models in the Dynamics of Russian Culture (Up to the End of the Eighteenth Century)" as well as several other articles that deal with the eighteenth century. See, inter alia, Daniel P. Lucid, ed., *Soviet Semiotics, An Anthology* (Baltimore, 1977); A. D. and A. S. Nakhimovsky, eds., *The Semiotics of Russian Cultural History* (1985).

3. Hans Rothe, *Religion und Kultur in den Regionen des russischen Reiches im 18. Jahrhundert* (Dusseldorf, 1984) 15–37, 70–110.

4. The list of works that would fit this characterization runs to the hundreds. Among the better-known examples are: M. M. Shtrange, *Demokraticheskaia intelligentsiia Rossii v XVIII veke* (Moscow, 1965) 3 ff.; M. T. Beliavskii, *Krest'ianskii vopros v Rossii nakanune vosstaniia E. I. Pugacheva* (Moscow, 1965), especially sect. 1; V. A. Aleksandrov et al., eds., *Ocherki russkoi kul'tury XVIII veka*, pt. 1 (Moscow, 1985) 5–8; V. V. Mavrodin, *Klassovaia bor'ba i obshchestvenno-politicheskaia mysl' v Rossii v XVIII v. (1725–1773 gg.)* (Leningrad, 1964).

5. B. I. Krasnobaev, *Russkaia kul'tura vtoroi poloviny XVII–nachala XIX v.* (Moscow, 1983) 58, 167–188; Shtrange 269–275; Beliavskii 351–355.

6. The contemporary literature on nobles begins with Marc Raeff, *Origins of the Russian Intelligentsia, The Eighteenth-Century Nobility* (New York, 1966) and the numerous essays and books that were written in its wake. See, for example, Arcadius Kahan, "The Costs of Westernization in Russia: The Gentry and the Economy in the Eighteenth Century," *Slavic Review* 35, no. 1 (1966): 40–66; Robert Jones, *The Emancipation of the Russian Nobility, 1762–1785* (Princeton, 1973); John P. LeDonne, *Ruling Russia: Politics and Administration in the Age of Absolutism, 1762–1796* (Princeton, 1984); Robert Givens, "Servitors or Seigneurs: The Nobility and the Eighteenth-Century Russian State," Unpublished PhD dissertation, University of California, Berkeley (Berkeley, 1975); Brenda Meehan-Waters, *Autocracy and Aristocracy: The Russian Service Elite of 1730* (New Brunswick, 1982); Robert Crummey, *Aristocrats and Servitors: The Boyar Elite in Russia, 1613–1689* (Princeton, 1983).

For groups other than the nobility, see Gregory Freeze, *The Russian Levites: Parish Clergy in the Eighteenth Century,* (Cambridge, Mass., 1977); Elise Kimerling, "Soldiers' Children, 1719–1856: A Study in Social Engineering in Imperial Russia," *Forschungen zur Osteuropäischen Geschichte* (Berlin, 1982), 30: 61–136; Max Okenfuss, *The Discovery of Childhood in Russia: The Evidence of the Slavic Primer* (Newton-

ville, Mass., 1980) 66–80; David Griffiths, "Eighteenth-Century Perceptions of Back-
wardness: Projects for the Creation of a Third Estate in Catherinean Russia,"
Canadian American Slavic Studies 13, no. 4 (Winter, 1979): 452–472.

7. In recent years Dominick LaCapra has become the leading advocate of inte-
grating the methods of poststructuralism into the history of ideas. See in particular
his effort to come to terms with the competing options in his essay "Rethinking
Intellectual History and Reading Texts," *History and Theory* 19 (1980): 245–276. See
also LaCapra's essays in *History and Criticism* (Ithaca, 1985); Umberto Eco, *The
Role of the Reader: Explorations in the Semiotics of Texts* (Bloomington, 1979) 3–40;
Carlo Ginzburg, *The Cheese and the Worms: The Cosmos of a Sixteenth-Century
Miller* (Middlesex, 1982); Robert C. Holub, *Reception Theory: A Critical Introduction*
(New York, 1984).

8. Iu. M. Lotman, "Ob odnom chitatel'skom vospriiatii 'Bednoi Lizy' N. M.
Karamzina. (K strukture massovogo soznaniia XVIII v.)," *XVIII vek* (Moscow,
1966), 7:280–285.

9. On the chasm that separated what was printed in Peter's reign from what was
apparently read, see Gary Marker, *Publishing, Printing and the Origins of Intellectual
Life in Russia, 1700–1800* (Princeton, 1985) 32–40.

10. On the impact of education see, inter alia, Freeze 82–106 and Okenfuss 78–79.

11. For the difference between bilingualism and diglossia, see Boris A. Uspenskii,
"The Language Situation and Linguistic Consciousness in Muscovite Rus': The Perception of Church Slavic and Russian," in Henrik Birnbaum and Michael S. Flier,
eds., *Medieval Russian Culture,* California Slavic Studies, vol. 12 (Berkeley, 1984)
365–367.

12. Concerning the thematic differences between church-type and civil-type books,
see T. A. Afanas'eva, "Svetskaia kirillicheskaia kniga v Rossii v XVIII veke (Problemy izdaniia, repertuara, rasprostraneniia, chteniia)," Candidate's Dissertation completed at the N. K. Krupskaia Institute of Culture (Leningrad, 1983); *Svodnyi katalog
russkoi knigi grazhdanskoi pechati XVIII veka, 1725–1800,* 6 vols. (Moscow, 1962–
1975); A. S. Zernova, *Svodnyi katalog russkoi knigi kirillovskoi pechati XVIII veka*
(Moscow, 1968). Zernova's catalogue, it should be noted, is missing literally hundreds of titles that were printed in the church script during the eighteenth century,
and a more comprehensive catalogue is apparently under preparation.

13. Afanas'eva 16–24.

14. The easiest method of following the continuity in typefaces is simply to compare Muscovite and eighteenth-century imprints. In the published literature the most
explicit discussion of church typefaces can be found throughout A. V. Gavrilov's
study of the St. Petersburg Synodal typography, *Ocherki istorii St. Peterburgskoi
sinodal'noi tipografii* (St. Petersburg, 1911). Otherwise, details on typefaces can be
compiled from the very extensive records concerning church publishing of the Synod
Chancellery archive (*Fond* 796 in the Tsentral'nyi gosudarstvennnyi istoricheskii
arkhiv, Leningrad (TsGIA).

15. A. G. Shitsgal has been the most persistent defender of the view that the
reformed alphabet looked very much like the business hand used by the late Muscovite *d'iaki.* For a summary of his views see his article "O rukopisnykh traditsiiakh
pervoistochnika sovremennogo russkogo tipografskogo shrifta," in A. A. Sidorov,

ed., *Rukopisnaia i pechatnaia kniga* (Moscow, 1975) 68–79. See also P. N. Berkov, "O perekhode skoropisi XVII v. v sovremennoe pis'mo," in *Trudy instituta istorii Akademii nauk SSSR, Leningradskoe otdelenie* (Moscow, 1964) 7:36–50. Recently, Shitsgal has compiled a very useful facsimile compendium of Petrine civil typefaces, a perusal of which shows just how frequently the fonts were altered during the first decade of the civil script. A. G. Shitsgal, ed., *Repertuar russkogo grazhdanskogo shrifta XVIII veka*. Pt. 1: *Grazhdanskii shrift pervoi chetverti XVIII veka 1708–1725. Reproduktsii* (Moscow, 1981).

16. A. P. Vlasto, *A Linguistic History of Russian to the End of the Eighteenth Century* (Oxford, 1986) 374–383; A. Shakhmatov, *Die kirchenslavischen Elemente in der modernen russischen Literatursprache* (Wiesbaden, 1960) 3–15; V. V. Vinogradov, *The History of the Russian Literary Language from the Seventeenth Century to the Nineteenth* (Madison, 1969) 31–54.

17. This conclusion has been derived from numerous institutional histories of individual schools or groups of schools. See as examples the following: A. A. Burov, *Peterburgskie 'russkie shkoly' i rasprostranenie gramotnosti sredi rabochikh v pervoi polovine XVIII veka* (Leningrad, 1957) 26–51; A. Likhovitskii, "Prosveshchenie v Sibiri v pervoi polovine XVIII stoletiia," *Zhurnal Ministerstva Narodnogo Prosveshcheniia* 355 (July, 1905): 19–23; S. M. Shcheglov, "Dve SPb shkoly v pervoi polovine XVIII v.," *Zhurnal Ministerstva Narodnogo Prosveshcheniia* 39 (May, 1912): 18–51; A. Kniazev, "Ocherki istorii Pskovskoi seminarii ot nachala do preobrazovaniia eia po proektu Ustava 1814 goda," *Chteniia v Imp. Obshchestve Istorii i Drevnostei Rossiiskikh pri Moskovskom Universitete* (1866), bk. 1, pp. 27–35.

18. There is an extensive descriptive literature on the Muscovite primer system. One particularly good discussion of how the system may have worked in practice is D. Izvekov, "Bukvar'naia sistema obucheniia v iskhode XVII i nachale XVIII st.," *Sem'ia i shkola* 4 (1872): 732–750. See also I. Paul'son, *Metodika gramoty po istoricheskim i teoreticheskim dannym* (St. Petersburg, 1887), and my essay "Literacy and Literacy Texts in Muscovy: A Reconsideration," *Slavic Review* 49, no. 1 (1990): 74–89.

19. There exists a considerable literature on various eighteenth-century primers, but hardly any of it confronts the particular questions of language and comparative dissemination that interest us here. An array of published and archival sources, fortunately, allows one to address this problem in some detail, although this paper can merely present a brief summary. On eighteenth-century primers see, inter alia, Okenfuss 43–65; A. I. Markushevich et al., eds., *Ot azbuki Ivana Fedorova do sovremennogo bukvaria* (Moscow, 1974) 40–63; M. I. Demkov, *Istoriia russkoi pedagogii.* Pt. 2: *Novaia russkaia pedagogiia (XVIII-i vek)* (Moscow, 1910) 60–80.

20. An earlier civil abecedarium had been printed either in 1708 or 1709, but this was not a literacy text, merely a table of letters and syllables. See a facsimile reproduction of the first part of the *azbuka* in A. G. Shitsgal, *Repertuar russkogo grazhdanskogo shrifta XVIII veka. Part 1: Grazhdanskii shrift pervoi chetverti XVIII veka 1708–1725. Reproduktsii* (Moscow, 1981); T. A. Bykova and M. M. Gurevich, *Opisanie izdanii grazhdanskoi pechati 1708–Ianvar' 1725 g.* (Moscow, 1955), nos. 18a and 32.

21. Bykova and Gurevich, nos. 226, 237, 378, 753. In addition to these, there are

some lost St. Petersburg printings of abecedaria that have been described as civil in the standard catalogue of Petrine books by Bykova and Gurevich, as well as by subsequent scholarship. A closer reading of the documentary evidence, however, suggests that these were not civil abecedaria, but church ones. On this point see my essay, "The Petrine 'Civil Primer' Reconsidered: A New Look at the Publishing History of the 'Grazhdanskaia azbuka'," *Solanus* (forthcoming). For the appropriate references to these lost imprints, see Bykova and Gurevich, nos. 137, 176, 261, 753, 879; S. P. Luppov, *Kniga v Rossii v pervoi chetverti XVIII veka* (Leningrad, 1973) 96.

22. James Cracraft, *The Church Reform of Peter the Great* (London, 1971) 276–289; P. P. Pekarskii, *Nauka i literatura v Rossii pri Petre Velikom* (St. Petersburg, 1862), 2:694.

23. Cracraft 287.

24. The relevant sources, in addition to the citations listed in Bykova and Gurevich, are Gavrilov 41 and 161, and TsGIA f. 796, op. 58, no. 43, pp. 15–24. On the primacy of the *azbuka uchebnaia* see my article, "Primers and Literacy in Muscovy: A Taxonomic Investigation," *Russian Review* 48, no. 1 (1989): 1–19.

25. See, for example, Burov 26 and 51; Shcheglov 18 and 37.

26. Luppov 135 and 145; Bykova and Gurevich 418.

27. See, for example, Peter's comments to Patriarch Adrian in 1700 on the state of Russian education, or the 1724 *ukaz* on the new Corps of Cadets in which students are ordered to study the catechism in order to learn the rules of Christian faith and to gain a general religious education. *PSZ* no. 4493; P. A. Galenkovskii, *Vospitanie iunoshestva v proshlom. Istoricheskii ocherk pedagogicheskikh sredstv pri vospitanii v voenno-uchebnykh zavedeniiakh (v period 1700–1856 gg.)* (St. Petersburg, 1904) 24; Rev. Georges Bissonnette, "Peter the Great and the Church as an Educational Institution," in John Shelton Curtiss, ed., *Essays in Russian and Soviet History in Honor of Geroid Tanquary Robinson* (New York, 1963) 5–6.

28. See, for example, Demkov 58.

29. TsGIA f. 796, op. 58, no. 43, pp. 23–39; *Svodnyi katalog russkoi knigi grazhdanskoi pechati XVIII veka,* 6 vols. (Moscow, 1962–1975) [hereafter *SK*], vol. 3, nos. 8732–8735.

30. Burov 51; S. I. Volkov, "Khoroshevskaia koniushennaia shkola v 30–40-x godakh XVIII v. (Iz istorii russkoi shkoly XVIII v.)," *Istoricheskie zapiski* 38 (1951): 278–79; I. A. Guzner, "Biblioteka uchebnykh zavedenii Sibiri v pervoi polovine XVIII veka," *Kniga v Sibiri XVII–nachala XX vv.* (Novosibirsk, 1980) 67.

31. Alexander V. Muller, ed., *The Spiritual Regulation of Peter the Great* (Seattle, 1972) 58–73.

32. Freeze 103 ff.

33. Gavrilov 317; TsGIA, f. 796, op. 62, no. 261, p. 1.

34. Freeze has argued that seminary education also failed to equip the priests to carry out pastoral responsibilities: "The seminarian did not learn how to proselytize against Old Believers and probably knew less about the religious texts than the self-taught dissenters" (105). He attributes this incapacity to the "secular curriculum" of the seminaries. But prior to about 1780, this secular curriculum was, in his own words, a pedagogical disaster, and it consisted of memorizing Latin texts, perhaps a smattering of arithmetic, and, for most of the students, little else. Whether or not

rural clergy could preach or reason theologically, they could recite the prayers, other ritual works, and the catechism, activities that reinforced the imminence of faith and the church even if they did not involve much theology or religious understanding.

35. S. Frederick Starr, *Decentralization and Self-Government in Russia, 1830–1870* (Princeton, 1972), ch. 1; Steven L. Hoch, *Serfdom and Social Control in Russia: Petrovskoe, a Village in Tambov* (Chicago, 1986), describes a peasant world in which formal governmental authority is virtually invisible.

36. TsGIA f. 796, op. 58, no. 43, pp. 27–31. See the relevant citations in *SK,* 3:127–133.

37. Kimerling 99–109.

38. Ibid. 107–110.

39. Volkov 278–280; Kniazev 25–35; Shcheglov 37–51; N. V. Nechaev, *Gornozavodskie shkoly Urala* (Moscow, 1956) 116–121; Demkov 400–401; P. Znamenskii, *Dukhovnye shkoly v Rossii do reformy 1808 g.* (Kazan, 1881) 476ff.

40. V. N. Tatishchev, "Razgovor o pol'ze nauk i uchilishch," *Chteniia v Obshchestve Istorii i Drevnostei Rossiiskikh pri Moskovskom Universitete* (1887), bk. 1, pp. 1–159; N. F. Demidova, "Instruktsiia V. N. Tatishcheva o poriadke prepodavaniia v shkolakh pri ural'skikh kazennykh zavodakh," *Istoricheskii arkhiv* 5 (1950): 167–177; Demkov 83–97.

41. Okenfuss 53–56; Black 37–42.

42. Guzner 67–72; Nechaev 120. Okenfuss surmises that the resort to the older text resulted from the fact that the *Zertsalo* had been out of print during most of the 1730s. However, old copies had remained in stock for many years after the last Petrine edition. Moreover, a new printing was in preparation at precisely the time when the Ural mining administration submitted its book order. The Academy regularly reprinted it in the 1740s, and the Ural schools could easily have procured it, had they so chosen. What was involved, then, was an explicit rejection of Tatishchev's pedagogy, either by the local administrators or by higher authorities.

43. See, for example, Petr Luzanov, *Sukhoputnyi shliakhetnyi kadetskii korpus (nyne 1-i kadetskii korpus) pri Grafe Minikhe (s 1732 po 1741). Istoricheskii ocherk* (St. Petersburg, 1907) 32–37; and Galenkovskii 22–38.

44. *SK,* vol. 6, nos. 711–713; D. D. Shamrai, "Tsenzurnyi nadzor nad tipografiei Sukhoputnogo shliakhetnogo kadetskogo korpusa," *XVIII vek* 2 (1940): 311–312.

45. *SK,* vol. 1, nos. 767–770; vol. 6, nos. 415, 417, 418; N. N. Mel'nikova, *Izdaniia napechatannye v tipografii moskovskogo universiteta, XVIII vek* (Moscow, 1966), nos. 384, 605, and 1191.

46. *SK,* vol. 2, nos. 3374–3380; Mel'nikova, nos. 618, 1230, 1422, 1519, 1600.

47. Lomonosov's views on education have been well described in the secondary literature. See Black 49–51; Demkov 129–152; D. A. Tolstoi, "Akademicheskaia gimnaziia v XVIII stoletii po rukopisnym dokumentam arkhiva Akademii nauk," *Zapiski Imperatorskoi Akademii nauk* 51 (1885): 34–35; *Istoriia Akademii nauk SSSR* 1 (1958): 300–302.

48. The decision to require certification in Russian is described in several sources. See, for example, *Dokumenty i materialy po istorii moskovskogo universiteta vtoroi poloviny XVIII veka,* vol. 3 (Moscow, 1963), pp. 41, 158.

49. Ibid., vol. 1 (Moscow, 1960), pp. 234–237; vol. 3, pp. 351–352.

50. *SK,* vol. 6, no. 454; V. A. Zapadov, "Kratkii ocherk russkoi tsenzury 60–90-x godov XVIII v.," *Uchenye zapiski Leningradskogo pedagogicheskogo instituta* 414 (1971): 108; Gavrilov 320; Robert E. Jones, *Provincial Government in Russia: Catherine II and Jacob Sievers* (New Brunswick, 1984) 76–77, 136–144.

51. *SK,* vol. 6, no. 39; TsGIA f. 796, op. 58, no. 280/22, pp. 5–28.

52. For Catherine's *Rossiiskaia azbuka,* see the citations in *SK,* vol. 1, nos. 2175–2179. For Jankovic's *Rossiiskii bukvar'* see *SK,* vol. 3, nos. 8781–8785. The literature on Jankovic and the School Commission is very extensive. See, for example, Demkov 326–330; and Max J. Okenfuss, "Education and Empire: School Reform in Enlightenment Russia," *Jahrbücher für Geschichte Osteuropas* 27, no. 1 (1979): 50–56. There is almost no discussion of Platon's primer in the secondary literature. The printing figures cited in this paper come from the numerous unpublished reports on the publishing activity of the Moscow Synodal typography in the archive of the Synodal chancellery (TsGIA, f. 796). See op. 58, no. 203; op. 60, no. 238; op. 61, no. 232. For the St. Petersburg editions of Platon's primer, see Gavrilov 316–317.

The Church of the Savior on the Blood

Projection, Rejection, Resurrection

MICHAEL S. FLIER

> The physician can bury his mistakes, but the architect can only advise his client
> to plant vines.
>
> Frank Lloyd Wright[1]

Someone happening upon the Church of the Savior on the Blood—*Spas na krovi*—in St. Petersburg for the first time might be tempted to treat this late nineteenth-century edifice as a mistake, a designer's folly, or as Sidney Monas has put it, "a kind of Disneyland old-Russian exoticism,"[2] so much does it impose itself by style and placement onto the otherwise harmonious Petersburg landscape of baroque and neoclassical design arrayed along a peaceful canal [pl. 1]. This church was surely meant for Moscow, not uniform St. Petersburg, Petersburg of the straight vista and the soaring spire, Petersburg of the Rossi ensemble. Yet our visitor can be assured that this revivalist *mélange moscovite* is no mistake; it is the intentional product of architect and patron.

The Savior on the Blood, officially the Church of the Resurrection of Christ, was begun in 1883 and finished in 1907. It marks the site of an event unprecedented in Russian history: the public assassination of a tsar. On 1 March 1881, Tsar Alexander II was mortally wounded by a bomb thrown by a member of the revolutionary group Will of the People.[3] Bleeding profusely, his legs shattered by the blast, the tsar was placed on a sledge and driven immediately to the Winter Palace, there to die. A makeshift chapel was immediately erected on the site, later replaced by the Savior on the Blood.

It is striking that a work of architecture with such important cultural and political associations has never received a thorough iconographical analysis. The present study is intended as an initial attempt to rectify this oversight. I will confine my remarks here to an analysis of the Church of the Savior on the Blood as a cultural artifact, a cultural message-event as it were, en-

Plate 1: Alfred Parland, *Church of the Resurrection* [Savior on the Blood]. Catherine Canal (now Griboyedov Canal). St. Petersburg. 1883–1907. View looking north. From William Craft Brumfield, *Gold in Azure: One Thousand Years of Russian Architecture* (Boston: David R. Godine, Publisher, Inc., 1983), 320. Reprinted by permission.

coded by architect and patron, and decoded by the public. In the area of authorial intention, I will consider two issues: 1. the official dedication of the church to the Resurrection of Christ, and 2. the contextually inappropriate Russian revival style. As for public reception, I will suggest a possible source for the popular name of the church, Savior on the Blood.

Background

The civic authorities of St. Petersburg decided to build a chapel at the site of the explosion, but when donations for a permanent memorial began pouring in, it became apparent that something more grandiose would have to be constructed, not simply a chapel but a church.[4] The placement of the church was determined by theological prescription: in Orthodox practice the altar must always face east. Therefore the front of the church—the western facade—would have to face the canal, which runs north-south. The ultimate design of the commemorative church was not achieved immediately. An architectural commission was established and a design competition was announced in April 1881.[5] By early 1882, the committee had narrowed down the over thirty proposals to eight and from them had selected four prize-winners.[6]

The entries of all but one of the finalists were done in the Byzantine style prescribed by Konstantin Ton in the 1840s; the lone exception was baroque. Like the other winners, the first-prize entry, "To the Father from the Fatherland," had the assassination site on axis with the altar [pl. 2]. Access to the site was through the main door of the belltower on the western end.

The eight final projects were shown to Tsar Alexander III in March 1882, but he rejected all of them, stating that it would be most desirable to have the church constructed in pure Russian style, a remark noted in the journal supplement *Nedelia Stroitelia* with the comment: "XVII-го столетия, образцы коего встречаются, например, в Ярославле."[7] The committee set a five-week deadline for submitting the new Russianized entries. The tsar reviewed thirty-one new proposals in May, but only in October 1882 apparently did he approve a project by Ignatii Malyshev, archimandrite of the Trinity-Sergius Monastery near St. Petersburg.[8] By 1883, the Academy professor Alfred Parland, himself an architect and specialist in Greek and Roman architecture, entered the project and changed Archimandrite Ignatii's design.[9] The cornerstone was laid in October 1883, at which time the church was named in honor of the Resurrection of Christ. The final plans were not approved by Alexander until May 1887, nearly four years later. Parland noted the tsar's close involvement in the planning of the church.[10]

Plate 2: A. I. Tomishko. "To the Father from the Fatherland," 1882. First-prize winner in the competition for a church to mark the spot where Alexander II fell mortally wounded. From *Zodchii,* 1882, pl. 30.

Alexander III's abiding interest is suggestive of imperial intention beyond the simple memorialization of his father's death. This seems especially likely, given the strained relationship that had existed for years between critical father and obedient son.[11] Alexander III had not originally been the heir apparent and was trained for the military. When his older brother Nicholas died from tuberculosis in 1865, Alexander was reluctantly thrust into the position of crown prince and immediately put into the custody of tutors, who might provide him with at least the rudiments of the education a future tsar would need. The most influential of his tutors were the Russian historian, Sergei Solov'ev, and the reactionary courtier, Konstantin Pobedonostsev. Solov'ev stimulated in the tsar-to-be a messianic view of Russian history and convinced him of the organic nature of continuous historical development.[12] Pobedonostsev, the *éminence grise* of Alexander's reign, played a considerable role in the new tsar's rejection of further reforms and the institution of a repressive reign. The future tsar sided with his mother against his father's blatant affair with Yekaterina Dolgorukaya. The strain between them was exacerbated when the empress died in 1880 and Tsar Alexander II married Yekaterina only forty days after his late wife's demise. Viewed against this sketch of history, Alexander III's determined involvement in the planning of the Church of the Savior on the Blood betrays an interest in symbolism far beyond mere filial devotion. The very choice of the revivalist Russian style is telling, a nostalgic mode favored by the Slavophiles but inappropriate for a memorial to the most un-Slavophile of tsars, the Great Reformer, Alexander II.

These two conscious choices—Resurrection theme and Russian revival mode—illuminate a complex network of cultural relationships when viewed against the background of the tsar in late nineteenth-century Petersburg. The capital was inhospitable to the emperor; revolutionaries were a constant threat on the royal person; government officials continued to clamor for more reforms and a functional constitution.[13] After the assassination some suggested that the capital be moved from European Petersburg back to Moscow.[14] Other voices called for burying the slain tsar in Moscow's Cathedral of the Redeemer near the Kremlin, thus returning the honor of final resting place of the tsars to the first capital.[15] Barring such radical moves, the new tsar could nonetheless take a symbolic stand. At the site of his father's murder, down the Catherine Canal from the Kazan' Cathedral—the staging area for many revolutionary demonstrations—he would build a monument not simply to his father, but to the person of the tsar himself. The style was calculated to resonate with the eschatological model of the Muscovite culture of Ivan the Terrible, that is, Moscow/Third Rome in timebound history, and Moscow/New Jerusalem in the end times at the cessation of human history. If Alexander III could not change Petersburg/Babylon into Moscow/New Jerusalem, he could bring *that* vision of Moscow to Petersburg, a deliberate intrusion of the "real" Russia onto the Petersburg scene, a flamboyant reminder of the identity of Tsar and State and the divine purpose of both. It is thus no mistake of the architect that the church is incompatible with its surroundings. The Savior on the Blood is Old Muscovy plunged into the heart of European Petersburg.

Tsar as Christ

The choice of Resurrection thematics in the Savior on the Blood was in part stimulated by the public response to the assassination, as reported in the press and expressed in personal reminiscences, diaries and letters. The assassination was commonly characterized in biblical-mythological terms. Alexander II was immediately identified as a martyr.[16] The earlier religious-political label of Tsar-Liberator (*Tsar'-Osvoboditel'*) that he had earned after emancipating the serfs in 1861 was supplemented with new ones: he was now Tsar-Martyr, Tsar-Sufferer (*Tsar'-Muchenik, Tsar'-Stradalets*). The newspaper *Molva* referred to him as Sufferer-Born to the Purple (*Porfironosnyi Stradalets*).[17] His murder was not simply *ubiistvo* but *ubienie*. *Russkii Vestnik* refers to his sacred life (*sviashchennaia zhizn'*).[18] In a letter of 22 March 1881 to Alexander III, Pobedonostsev notes a sentiment on the part of the people to establish 1 March as an annual fast day.[19] The historian Tatishchev writes: "Во истину Александр II был для России тот 'добрый пастырь', который, по слову Христа, 'душу свою полагается за овцы'."[20] A commentator for *Moskovskie Vedomosti* juxtaposes the roles of liberator and martyr by presenting Alexander II in the light of Moses, Old Testament precursor, and Christ, New Testament redeemer:

> Всегда тягостно бремя верховной власти, но в Бозе почивший Государь был призван обновить жизнь предводимого Им народа и извести его из египетского плена.... История скажет то чтò и теперь для чуткого ума ясно,—она скажет что все скорби Его жизни и самая смерть Его были искупительною жертвой за Русский народ, за Россию, за ее величие, за ее призвание. Он пал сраженный коварством врагов своей страны.[21]

The newspaper notes the streams of people from all walks of life paying their respects at the temporary chapel erected at the site of the assassination:

На месте *крови* обыденно устроена часовня из зелени, беспрерывно наполняемая приносимыми цветами и венками; в часовне—икона Богоматери. В толпе пред часовней слышатся слова, молитвы и рыдания. А в это самое время, поодаль, войны либерализма *об одежде его мечут жребий....*[22]

This allusion to the Roman soldiers casting lots at Golgotha is by no means an isolated reference to the Crucifixion. The theme is taken up by poets from the folk and the literati as well. *Russkaia Starina* published a poem ascribed to a sect of Bespopovtsy near the Don in which we find the lines: "Государя жизнь скончали/ Второй раз Христа распяли."[23] In *Russkii Vestnik* Apollon Maikov writes: "И вдруг, враги внутри, и адский ков за ковом,/ И царский стал венец Ему венцом терновым!"[24] Afanasii Fet advances similar imagery in his "March 1, 1881":

День искупительного чуда,
Час освящения креста:
Голгофе передал Иуда
Окровавленного Христа.

Но Сердцеведец безмятежный
Давно, смиряясь, постиг,
Что не простит любви безбрежной
Ему коварный ученик.

Перед безмолвной жертвой злобы,
Завидя праведную кровь,
Померкло солнце, вскрылись гробы,
Но разгорелася любовь.

Она сияет правдой новой:
Благословив ее зарю,
Он крест и Свой венец терновый
Земному передал царю.

Бессильны козни фарисейства:
Что было кровь, то стало храм,
И место страшного злодейства—
Святыней вековечной нам![25]

In describing the scene at the assassination site, an English journalist for the *London Standard* provides dramatic evidence that in the popular mind the slaying of the tsar was immediately elevated to the level of a second Crucifixion:

Nearly every face bore the expression, in varying degree, of horror and grief, though a few seemed strangely indifferent. Many were on their knees, both men and women, weeping and praying; others were searching for relics and rubbing their handkerchiefs in the blood-stained snow. There was little noise—a sob, a groan, now and then a passionate exclamation, but for the most part people conversed in undertones or kept silent, overmastered by the horror of the deed.[26]

Such literary and journalistic accounts underscore the biblical, especially Christian, mythology invoked to comprehend the assassination of the tsar. This was the rich text to which a memorial church could allude. A historical murder had been transformed into a timeless sacrifice for Rus': an earthly emperor sent by God in Heaven to deliver Russia had been martyred, Christ had been crucified a second time. It remained only for patron and architect to render these symbolic associations in brick and mortar.

Theme of Resurrection

It was apparently over two years after the assassination that a name was finally given to the church to be erected on the site. The dedication to the Resurrection must have suggested itself as the martyrial interpretation of the tsar's death found official favor. Certain details of Alexander II's biography lead in fact to the Resurrection and its celebration on Easter Sunday. The murdered tsar had been born during Easter Week in 1818. He was assassinated on the Sunday of Orthodoxy, the first in Lent. According to Orthodox belief the soul of the departed is transported to various places on earth, Heaven, and Hell before finally rising to Heaven on the fortieth day to pay tribute to God, who assigns it a place in anticipation of the Last Judgment. Requiems must be said for every one of the forty days, the so-called Sorokoust. As fate would have it, the Sorokoust of Alexander II coincided with the most concentrated period of mourning in the Eastern church, from the first Sunday of the Great Fast to Great (Maundy) Thursday, on the very eve of the church's celebration of Christ's death on the Cross and his Resurrection on Easter Sunday. The fortieth requiem was performed for Alexander II in an elaborate ceremony on Thursday, 9 April, in SS. Peter and Paul Cathedral with the royal family in attendance.[27]

The dedication of the church to the Resurrection of Christ cemented the associative bond between the tsar and Christ, not only through their sacrifice but through the locale of their passion. The site of the assassination would become a piece of Jerusalem itself.

Ever since the capture of Constantinople by the Turks in 1453, the place of honor in Russia among Orthodox churches had shifted from Hagia Sophia to the Church of the Holy Sepulchre in Jerusalem, an edifice that simultaneously houses the site of Golgotha, where Christ was crucified, and the Holy Sepulchre, where he was interred and whence he resurrected after three days. The Russian name for this holiest of Christian shrines is *Tserkov' Voskreseniia Khristova,* the Church of the Resurrection of Christ. The Holy Sepulchre has been well known to Russians since Abbot Daniil described it with great excitement in the early twelfth-century account of his pilgrimage to the Holy Land. In 1464 Metropolitan Theodosius asked for donations from Novgorod and Pskov to help rebuild the Church of the Holy Sepulchre, pillaged by the heathens, and referred to the significance of the church to Orthodoxy: "и о съзиданіи святаго храма, еже есть Сіонъ, всѣмъ церквамъ глава и мати сущи всему православію."[28] We see further concrete evidence of the importance of the Church of the Holy Sepulchre in late sixteenth- and early seventeenth-century descriptions by contemporaries of Boris Godunov, who note his grandiose plan to build a replica of the Jerusalem temple in the center of the Kremlin to replace the Dormition as the main church of Moscow.[29] Some architectural historians believe that the building of the upper stories of the Great John belfry during his reign was part of this plan, interrupted only by political and social upheaval.[30] It was Archimandrite Nikon, later patriarch, who sent Arsenii Sukhanov, a monk of the Trinity Monastery, to Jerusalem in 1649 to take measurements of the Church of the Holy Sepulchre and provide a detailed description of the church.[31] Later Nikon decided to build his own replica of that holy Christian shrine in the New Jerusalem Monastery in Istra northwest of Moscow. For medieval Muscovy the Church of the Holy Sepulchre in Jerusalem carried connotations of religious authority and dynastic power.

The basic design of the Jerusalem Resurrection is striking in its bipolarity [pl. 3]. The altar, located by tradition in the eastern part of the church and representative of Heaven, is placed in tension with the Holy Sepulchre in the western part, representative of Hell. Externally these foci of the east-west axis are surmounted by domes. In a chapel to the south of this axis we find Golgotha, the site of the Crucifixion. An adjacent belfry marks Golgotha externally.

Inside, the Holy Tomb of Christ is covered by a large aedicula or shrine, surmounted itself by a baldacchin or canopy, symbolic of the Crucifixion and burial at Golgotha. From the Early Christian era the baldacchin became a standard feature of an altar, the canopy over the holiest place in a church where the Eucharist is celebrated. By medieval times, the canopy was used to mark the seat of an important personage. The Petersburg Church of the Resurrection built on the "sacred" site of Alexander's demise became a symbolic counterpart of its namesake in the Holy Land. The sacrifice of a modern-day Russian Christ would be recalled by a church whose bipolar

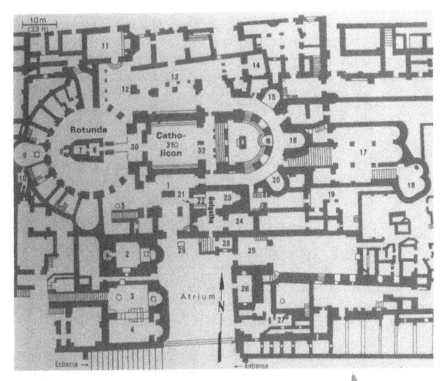

Plate 3: Plan of the Holy Sepulchre. Jerusalem. Late 11th–12th century. Built on site of earlier churches from 4th, 7th, 11th centuries. From *Baedeker's Israel* (New York: Prentice-Hall, n.d.) 148. No. 7 marks the Holy Tomb. Reprinted by permission.

composition paralleled that of the Holy Sepulchre in Jerusalem and its medieval Muscovite instantiations. A new station of the Cross was demarcated over the blood-stained pavement of the Russian capital.

In the plan of the Petersburg Church of the Resurrection [pl. 4], the altar at the eastern pole is opposed to the site of the tsar's martyrdom at the western pole. Since by tradition the tsar had to be buried in the fortress cathedral across the Neva, the symbolically separate sites of sacrifice and burial in Jerusalem—Golgotha and Holy Sepulchre—are merged in Petersburg at the western pole of the Resurrection. The sacred site of Alexander II's martyrdom acquires in this merger the symbolic value of the Passion, the Crucifixion, the Anastasis, and the Resurrection all in one. Like Golgotha, it is surmounted by a belfry [pl. 5]. The tension between the two poles of the church is expressed externally by the decoration of cupolas. Only the cupolas

Plate 4: Plan. From A. A. Parland, *Khram Voskreseniia Khristova sooruzhennyi na meste smertel'nogo poraneniia v Boze pochivshego Imperatora Aleksandra II na Ekaterinskom kanale v S-Peterburge.* (St. Petersburg, 1907), pl. 2. Reprinted by permission, Slavic and Baltic Division, New York Public Library.

of the apses on the east side and the belfry on the west side are in gold. The remaining cupolas are polychrome.

The iconography of internal decoration leaves no doubt as to the attempt to associate the fate of the tsar with the final days of Christ at the western end of the longitudinal axis. Like the Holy Sepulchre itself, the sacred site of Alexander II's assassination is surmounted by a baldacchin [pl. 6]. Four jasper columns support a tent-shaped canopy of semiprecious stones topped with a topaz cross, the design clearly inspired by the tsar's throne, the first and most famous of which is the Throne of Monomakh, built by Ivan the Terrible in 1551 [pl. 7].

The relics of 1 March 1881 were reconstructed by Parland on the site: the Catherine Canal embankment railing, the roadway scarred by the bomb blast, the pavement still stained with the tsar's blood, all surrounded by an elaborate grating between the columns. The baldacchin correlates the sacred site with Ivan IV's Monomakh Throne, symbol of autocratic power in Muscovite Rus', and the Tomb of Christ in Jerusalem, symbol of victory over death. It is of no small consequence that Alexander III himself donated three of the four columns of grey-violet jasper to support it. Jasper has eschatological connotations, being the material from which the walls of the New Jerusalem are constructed (Revelation 21:18–19).

The major icons of the interior underscore the significance of the sacred site. All are done in elaborate mosaics and focus on the biography of Christ, while references to Mary are minimal by contrast. The major images of the nave begin with the Annunciation and end with the Entry into Jerusalem. The eastern part of the church is concerned with the events after the Resurrection. The Descent of the Holy Spirit and the Ascension are reproduced in the conches of the side apses, while Christ in Glory dominates the conch of the main apse, a remarkable substitute for the traditional Mother of God Oranta. The images in the western part of the church are devoted to the Passion, the Crucifixion, the Entombment, and the Resurrection. Over the arch near the window on the western wall is the traditional Second Coming of Christ, but directly linked to the site of Alexander's martyrdom. A guardian angel is depicted on one side of Christ and Saint Alexander Nevsky, the tsar's patron saint, on the other.

The same thematic focus is expressed through the mosaics on the outside of the church. The large northern pediment depicts Christ in Glory; the large southern pediment, the Resurrection. Surmounting the entrances on either side of the belfry are mosaic images of the Bearing of the Cross, the Crucifixion, the Deposition, and the Descent into Hell.

Plate 5: Southwest elevation. Photograph from *Niva,* 1907, no. 36, p. 594. Reprinted by permission, Hoover Institution on War, Revolution, and Peace, Stanford University.

Plate 6: Design of the baldacchin over the site of Alexander II's mortal wounding. From Parland, *op. cit.*, pl. 3. Reprinted by permission, Slavic and Baltic Division, New York Public Library.

Plate 7: *Throne of Monomakh,* Cathedral of the Dormition, Moscow. 1551.

Plate 8: Western elevation. From Parland, *op. cit.,* pl. 5. Reprinted by permission, Slavic and Baltic Division, New York Public Library.

Plate 9: Detail of belfry with coats of arms. Photograph by Russell Valentino. Reproduced by permission.

A chapel on the outer wall of the western axis serves as the external expression of the holy site within. Located where the main entrance of an Orthodox church would normally be, the chapel contains a large mosaic of the Crucifixion [pl. 8], symbolic of the martyrdom of Christ and the late tsar. The striking lack of a western entrance presents one more compositional feature of the Church of the Holy Sepulchre in Jerusalem.

The inscription under the belfry cupola plays on the ambiguous reference of the word *Tsar'*, to the Russian ruler and God, the Emperor of Heaven: "Сам бессмертный Царю, приими моления наша . . . и остави нам прегрешения, яже делом и словом и мыслию, ведением или неведением согрешенная нами."[32]

Parland placed the coats of arms of all the Russian provinces and districts on the three easily visible sides of the belfry built over the sacred spot [pl. 9]. With this gesture the Petersburg Resurrection provides what is perhaps the most powerful individual expression in all Russia of the medieval duality of the Russian tsar as ordained head of Church and State. We see here the embodiment of the sixteenth-century image of *Bogovenchannyi Tsar'*, Christ's representative on the throne of Rus'. The emblems of all the peoples of all the Russias, together with the double-headed eagles over the entrance towers

Храмъ Воскресенія Христова въ С.-Петербургѣ, освященный 19 августа с. г. Въ фот. К. Булла.

Plate 10: *The Royal Family at the 1907 Dedication.* Photograph from *Niva,* 1907, no. 36, p. 593. Reprinted by permission, Hoover Institution on War, Revolution, and Peace, Stanford University.

demonstrate the indissoluble union of venerated ruler and devoted subjects in a sanctified space.

A photograph of the procession with Tsar Nicholas and Alexandra at the dedication ceremony [pl. 10] reveals another external feature used to associate the late tsar with Christ. Twenty inscribed granite plaques are placed around the base of the church on the north, south, and west. Each plaque is devoted to a major event or pronouncement in the life of Alexander II— birth, baptism, marriage, emancipation of the serfs, and so forth—a verbal analogue of the festival tier on an Orthodox iconostasis that provides the milestones of the biographies of Christ and the Mother of God. The cyclical aspect of these Gospel-like events and sayings surrounding the base foundation of the church raises them to eternal significance.

Russian Style

Since Alexander III made such a point of insisting on a pure Russian style for the Petersburg Church of the Resurrection, this component of the church warrants special attention. The central tent tower and proliferation of multi-colored domes immediately brings to mind St. Basil's Cathedral in Red Square. In fact the memorial church combines some of the more striking features of this sixteenth-century monument with the basic composition of the Muscovite seventeenth-century style, which was the chief source of the revival. But the primary allusion to St. Basil's is intentional and thus significant.

St. Basil's was built by Ivan the Terrible to commemorate his tremendous defeat of the Kazan' Tatars in 1552. The western chapel—dedicated to the Entry into Jerusalem—was one of the focal points of the annual Palm Sunday Ritual, a ceremony that emphasized the parallel between Ivan's triumphant return to Moscow and Christ's Entry into Jerusalem. The church and the annual ceremony underscored the claims of Moscow as the New Jerusalem. In fact the church was often simply called "Jerusalem" in the sixteenth and seventeenth centuries. It is the belfry of the Petersburg Resurrection that corresponds compositionally and iconographically to the western, Jerusalem chapel of St. Basil's. And like the Holy Sepulchre in Jerusalem and the Petersburg Resurrection, St. Basil's lacks a western, axial entrance. To evoke the famous Red Square cathedral is thus to recall Moscow of the Apocalypse, the New Jerusalem.

Indirect evidence of Alexander III's interest in Jerusalem in the planning of the memorial church appears in the form of a second commission. In 1883, the year the cornerstone for the Petersburg Resurrection was laid, he commissioned the Church of St. Mary Magdalene to be built in Jerusalem itself in honor of his late mother, Maria Alexandrovna. Although rendered in a subdued seventeenth-century Russian style, this second royal church serves as another manifestation of the ideological Petersburg-Moscow-Jerusalem axis.

Public Reception: The Savior on the Blood

The Church of the Resurrection in St. Petersburg was the result of a conscious attempt on the part of architect Alfred Parland and Tsar Alexander III to erect a monument with a general as well as specific purpose. The church would not only serve as a memorial to the murdered Alexander II, but would allude to the even loftier idea that Russia was destined to lead mankind to salvation with its tsar at the helm, chosen by God. The apocalyptic force of the church was grounded in a correlation of Petersburg and Jerusalem, through the juxtaposition of historical martyrdom located in each city and through the use of the architectural imagery of Moscow/New Jerusalem.

In the last analysis, however, the message of the Jerusalem subtext of the Petersburg Church of the Resurrection was diffused by the time this monument was officially dedicated in 1907, some twenty-six years after the fact.

Alexander III had come and gone, Russia had passed through the Revolution of 1905, and the Duma had been created. The meaning of the church remained particular, bound in time and space to Alexander II. A measure of the personal connection is seen in the appearance of the unofficial, popular designation of the church—Savior on the Blood—that survived in Russian culture.

By portraying Alexander II as an innocent martyr and invoking the ancient principality of Yaroslavl in the external colored enamelwork and mosaics of the commemorative church, Parland and Alexander III invited comparison with another royal martyr from Yaroslavl territory, from the city of Uglich, whose untimely murder signalled disorder, the end of the dynasty and the onset of the Time of Troubles. I have in mind, of course, Prince Dmitri, the infant son of Ivan the Terrible. There are no images of Prince Dmitri anywhere in the Petersburg Resurrection, whereas icons of other martyrs, like the princely saints Boris and Gleb, abound. The reason seems obvious: Prince Dmitri, the symbol of the first dynasty's demise, was the last person the royal court wanted to link to Alexander II.[33]

That there was concern about a connection between the murder of Prince Dmitri and the person of the tsar is stated forcefully in a letter of 3 April 1883, to Pobedonostsev from N. Lebedev, a private citizen, regarding the date of Alexander III's coronation ceremony:

> Сегодня прочел я, что уже регалии царские привезли в Москву. Следовательно, коронация должна быть в мае и даже 15 мая, говорят. Не знаю, может быть, этого требовали высшие государственные соображения, но в мае месяце не женятся и не выходят замуж, чтобы не маяться. Ни одна коронация не была в мае, а главное 15-го мая память убиения Дмитрия царевича. Не суеверия, простите, а присущие русскому человеку убеждения и вера дают мне смелость обратиться к Вам с указанием: удобно ли короноваться государю 15 мая, не заставит ли это многих скорбеть духом и тревожиться за будущее царствование любимого монарха, который примет скипетр и державу под дурным предзнаменованием?[34]

A year before the Savior on the Blood was dedicated, Moscow had celebrated the three-hundredth anniversary of the transference of Prince Dmitri's relics from Uglich to the Moscow Kremlin in 1606, an event heralded in the leading newspapers and magazines of both capitals. There was frequent mention of the building that stood over the site of this arguably most famous of Russian murders: the Church of St. Dmitri on the Blood, *Tserkov' tsarevicha Dmitriia, chto na krovi* [pl.11].[35] The tradition of a church erected "on the blood" is firmly placed in sixteenth-century Muscovite Rus': the victims of Ivan the Terrible's executions on Red Square were recalled as martyrs by the

ЦЕРКОВЬ СВ. ДИМИТРІЯ ЦАРЕВИЧА, ЧТО НА КРОВИ.

Plate 11: *Church of Tsarevich Dmitrii on the Blood.* Uglich. 1692. Built on the site of earlier wooden churches dating from the late 16th century. From *Russkaia Starina* 1 (1848): 68a.

erection of wooden churches built near the Moat "on the blood."[36] For the common people, the assassination of Alexander II was apparently incorporated into this Russian martyrial line.

The connection between Prince Dmitri and Tsar Alexander II, avoided officially, was ultimately more irresistible than the loftier one between the tsar and the apocalyptic image of Moscow-New Jerusalem. The timeless eschatology of the Jerusalem-inspired Church of the Resurrection paled before the contemporary horror and uncertainty of Savior on the Blood, a Muscovite designation redolent of dynastic politics, intrigue, and martyrdom. The popular view turned out to be prescient: in less than a decade the dynasty was overturned and by the mid-1930s the Church of the Savior on the Blood was closed, a potentially dangerous way station of imperial spirit in a transformed proletarian environment.

Notes

I am grateful to the following individuals who assisted me in obtaining research materials used in the preparation of this article: William Brumfield, Daniel Collins, Kristi Grober, Katia Hirvasaho, Simon Karlinsky, Edward Kasinec, Russell Valentino, and Pat Wright. I wish to acknowledge for their assistance the staffs of Doe Library, University of California, Berkeley; the University Research Library, UCLA; Widener Library, Harvard University; the Slavic and East European Library, University of Illinois; the Library of Congress; the Slavic and Baltic Division of the New York Public Library; and the Hoover Institution on War, Revolution, and Peace, Stanford University. I also want to thank Richard Wortman for valuable comments on an earlier version of this article.

1. *New York Times Magazine,* 4 October 1953.

2. Sidney Monas, "St. Petersburg and Moscow as Cultural Symbols," *Art and Culture in Nineteenth-Century Russia,* ed. Theofanis George Stavrou (Bloomington: Indiana University Press, 1983) 29.

3. Dates are given in Old Style: 12 days behind modern reckoning for the nineteenth century, 13 days behind for the twentieth century.

4. "V gorodskoi dume," *Novoe Vremia,* 5 March 1881, 1; "Khronika," *Molva,* 15 March 1881, 2; "Khronika," *Novoe Vremia,* 29 March 1881, 3; "Ezhednevnoe obozrenie," *Novoe Vremia,* 10 April 1881, 1.

5. "Konkurs na proekt khrama 1-go marta," *Novoe Vremia,* 23 April 1881, 1.

6. *Nedelia Stroitelia,* 1882, nos. 1–2, p. 9; no. 7, p. 49; no. 12, p. 89; no. 14, pp. 103–107; no. 15, pp. 115–116; no. 16, pp. 121–122; no. 17, pp. 130–132; no. 18, p. 139.

7. 1882, no. 15, p. 115. The first account of the tsar's rejection appears in *Nedelia Stroitelia,* 1882, no. 12, p. 89, in which he is reported to have expressed regret over the fact that none of the eight finalists was done "во вкусе 'русского церковного зодчества', прекрасными образчиками которого изобилуют великорусские губернии." It is likely that the tsar himself mentioned Yaroslavl', hence the later footnote. Alfred Parland, the architect of the Church of the Savior on the Blood, states that he designed the church at the behest of the sovereign "в стиле времен Московских царей XVII века. Выдающимися образцами этой эпохи являются церковь Василия Блаженного в Москве [an anachronism, since this church actually dates from the mid-sixteenth century—MSF], целая группа храмов в Ярославле, в Ростове и др.," "Khram Voskreseniia Khristova," *Zodchii,* 1907, no. 35, p. 375. I am grateful to William Brumfield for this reference.

8. *Nedelia Stroitelia,* 1882, no. 43, p. 326.

9. See *Éntsiklopedicheskii slovar' "Brokhaus-Efron,"* s.v. Parland.

10. *Zodchii,* 1907, 376.

11. See N. G. O. Pereira, *Alexander II of Russia, 1818–1881,* Russian Biography Series, no. 5 (Newtonville, Mass., 1983) 138–140.

12. See Anatole G. Mazour, *Modern Russian Historiography,* 2d ed. (Princeton, 1958), 100ff.

13. See Richard Wortman, "Moscow and Petersburg: The Problem of Political

Center in Tsarist Russia, 1881–1914," in *Rites of Power: Symbolism, Ritual, and Politics since the Middle Ages,* ed. Sean Wilentz (Philadelphia, 1985), 248ff.

14. Cf. *Moskovskie Vedomosti,* 6 March 1881, reported in *Russkii Vestnik,* no. 152 (March 1881) xxiv–xxv; discussion in "Moskva ili Peterburg?" *Novoe Vremia,* 10 March 1881, 1; "Nabroski i nedomolvki," *Molva,* 15 March 1881, 1, and "Iz gazet i zhurnalov," *op. cit.,* 2; and "Vnutrennee obozrenie," *Vestnik Evropy,* April 1881, 783–784.

15. Letter from Ol'ga Novikova (née Kireeva) to Konstantin Pobedonostsev, 5 March 1881, in *K. P. Pobedonostsev i ego korrespondenty. Pis'ma i zapiski.* Pref. M. N. Pokrovskii (Moscow and Petrograd, 1923), no. 147, p. 180.

16. *Moskovskie Vedomosti,* 14 March 1881, reported in *Russkii Vestnik,* no. 151 (March 1881), xxix.

17. Reported in *Novoe Vremia,* 3 March 1881, 3.

18. March, 1881, no. 152, p. 1.

19. "Pis'ma K. P. Pobedonostseva k Aleksandru III," *Krasnyi Arkhiv* 4 (1923): 325.

20. S. S. Tatishchev, *Imperator Aleksandr II, ego zhizn' i tsarstvovanie* (St. Petersburg, 1903), 1:662.

21. 4 March 1881, reported in *Russkii Vestnik,* no. 152 (March 1881) xv–xvii.

22. *Moskovskie Vedomosti,* 16 March 1881, reported in *Russkii Vestnik,* no. 152 (March 1881) xxxii.

23. "Kak vsplakalas' Rossiia o svoem belom tsare," *Russkaia Starina,* no. 68 (1890) 690, cited in Michael Cherniavsky, *Tsar and People: Studies in Russian Myths* (New Haven and London, 1961) 188, n. 67.

24. "Pervoe Marta," *Russkii Vestnik,* no. 152 (March 1881) xxxiv.

25. "1 Marta 1881 goda," *Polnoe sobranie sochinenii A. A. Feta,* ed. N. N. Strakhov and B. V. Nikol'skii, (St. Petersburg, 1912), 1:397, cited in Cherniavsky, *Tsar and People* 187, n. 66.

26. John F. Baddeley, *Russia in the "Eighties": Sport and Politics* (London, 1921) 105.

27. See "Khronika" and "Segodnia," *Novoe Vremia,* 10 April 1881, 2, 3.

28. *Akty istoricheskie* (St. Petersburg, 1841), 1:128.

29. In medieval Russia the Temple of Solomon and the Church of the Holy Sepulchre were commonly thought to be one and the same edifice, interchangeably called *Tserkov' Voskreseniia Khristova* or *Sviataia sviatym.* See D'iak Ivan Timofeev, *Vremennik,* cols. 341–342, in *Russkaia Istoricheskaia biblioteka,* vol. 13, no. 1 (Leningrad, 1925), and Isaac Massa, *A Short History of the Beginnings and Origins of These Present Wars in Moscow under the Reign of Various Sovereigns down to the Year 1610,* transl. with introd. by G. Edward Orchard (Toronto, 1982) 55. See I. Grabar' and S. Toporov, "Arkhitekturnye sokrovishcha Novogo Ierusalima," *Pamiatniki iskusstva razrushennye nemetskimi zakhvatchikami v SSSR,* ed. Igor' Grabar' (Moscow and Leningrad, 1948) 176, and M. A. Il'in, *Kamennaia letopis' moskovskoi Rusi. Svetskie osnovy kamennogo zodchestva XV–XVII vv.* (Moscow, 1966) 177–178.

30. Il'in, *Kamennaia letopis'* 57–58, and idem, "Proekt perestroiki tsentra moskovskogo Kremlia pri Borise Godunove," *Soobshcheniia Instituta istorii iskusstv,* 1951, no. 1, pp. 79–83.

31. Il'in conjectures that Paisius, the patriarch of Jerusalem who came to Moscow in 1649 to persuade Tsar Aleksei Mikhailovich to liberate Jerusalem, brought with him a wooden model of the Church of the Holy Sepulchre. The existence of this model might then have stimulated Nikon's interest in more details about the church. See *Kamennaia letopis'* 183–185.

32. Alfred Parland, "Khram Voskreseniia Khristova," *Zodchii,* 1907, no. 35, p. 376.

33. Mussorgsky's opera *Boris Godunov* was seldom staged more than once a year in Petersburg. In the late nineteenth century the royal court and high society avoided it, and it was considered the most unpopular opera in the repertory. See Richard Buckle, *Nijinsky* (New York, 1971) 49.

34. *K. P. Pobedonostsev i ego korrespondenty. Pis'ma i zapiski.* Pref. M. N. Pokrovskii (Moscow and Petrograd, 1923), no. 362, p. 361.

35. See *Niva,* 1906, no. 24, pp. 382–384; and 1907, no. 7, pp. 97, 109.

36. M. V. Posokhin et al., *Pamiatniki arkhitektury Moskvy. Kreml'. Kitai-gorod. Tsentral'nye ploshchadi* (Moscow, 1982) 352, 359.

"To the Unaccustomed Eye"

Religion and Irreligion in the Experience
of St. Petersburg Workers in the 1870s

REGINALD E. ZELNIK

> I stopped going to the priest for "confession," no longer attended church, and began to eat "forbidden" food during Lenten fast days. However, for a long time to come I didn't abandon the habit of crossing myself, especially when I returned to the village for holidays.
>
> —Semën Ivanovich Kanatchikov[1]

Anyone who has ever attempted to rouse the Russian people to heroic acts of warfare, labor, or rebellion, be it Minin and Pozharskii, Peter the Great, or Pugachev, has been compelled to work the power of popular religious faith, of Russian Orthodox Christianity or its schismatic offshoots, into his calculus of action. Whether the would-be leader has sought to enlist traditional religious passions to his cause, the most common scenario, or, as in the case of Peter, has sought to reduce the weight of religious tradition, popular religiosity has historically been a major strategic consideration for Russian leaders. In more recent times, however, with the arrival in nineteenth-century Russia of avowedly secular and later even antireligious ideologies, new kinds of political leaders, mostly from the intelligentsia, have felt compelled to seek more complex strategies when facing the challenge of popular religiosity. Starting in the early nineteenth century, we begin to notice some hybrid calls to arms that combine at once religious and irreligious elements that appeal to popular religious sentiment even while summoning the people to cast off the chains of institutional religion.

Perhaps the first attempt by a member of Russia's educated elite to tap, reshape, and redirect the energies and symbols of popular religion was the work of Sergei Murav'ev-Apostol, a leader of the Decembrists' Southern Union. In the fateful December days of 1825, the rebel colonel spun a revolutionary "Orthodox" Catechism from threads pulled out of the Old and New Testaments in a not unsuccessful effort to convince his soldiers that since theirs was the cause of Christ, their oath of allegiance to the tsar was

no longer binding. "In the name of the Father and the Son and the Holy
Ghost" were the Catechism's opening words, and the series of questions and
answers that followed was heavily salted with Biblical quotations and para-
phrases, each interpreted in a manner that turned its religious message into
one of armed rebellion:

Q. Should one obey Tsars when they act against God's will?
A. No. Christ has said you cannot serve Christ and Mammon . . . .
Q. What does our Holy Writ command the Russian people and
    army to do?
A. To repent of their long servility and, rising against tyranny and
    lawlessness, to swear: let there be one Tsar for all, Jesus Christ
    in Heaven and on earth . . . .
Q. In what manner are we to rise with a pure heart?
A. Take up arms and bravely follow those who speak up in the
    name of the Lord, remembering the words of our Saviour:
    "Blessed are they who do hunger and thirst after righteousness,
    for they shall be filled."[2]

If the view of the world that some have described as "naïve monarchism"
could be used to encourage popular rebellion in the name of the tsar,[3] the
premise behind the Catechism's call for rebellion in the name of the Lord—
read aloud to the soldiers by a regimental priest—might by analogy be described as "naïve Orthodoxy." In its simplest terms, according to Murav'ev-
Apostol, the premise was that reading the Bible to the soldiers "could inspire
them with hatred for the government."[4] He might also have added, as the
Catechism shows, that the Bible needed a small interpretive spin, if only in
the form of a simple exegesis in popular language, in order to perform its
revolutionary task.

Between the Decembrist uprising of 1825 and the great revolutionary
cataclysms of 1905 and 1917, many similar cases—each, of course, with a
unique configuration—could be cited, stories of radical *intelligenty* with a
more or less secular worldview who sought a point of contact with potential
followers by striking a religious chord. Sometimes this chord was Orthodox,
but more typically a radical proselytizer would seek out schismatics or sectarians, communities that were persecuted by the state, identified tsar with
Antichrist (in the case of Old Believers), and were thought to be more rebellious than the mainstream Orthodox. Herzen and Ogarev, for example, were
eager to use Old Believers to carry their message of revolt to the peasants.[5]
And the bloody massacre of peasants at Bezdna in early 1861, though Old
Believers may not in fact have been involved, was quickly incorporated into

radical mythology as a clash between oppressive authority and the authentic, democratic Christianity of the *narod*. At a requiem service for the victims, Professor Afanasii Shchapov, who devoted much of his historical research to demonstrating the emancipatory character of the Old Belief, made a bold and moving speech eulogizing the Bezdna martyrs and saluting the "democratic" Christian prophets who had appeared among the peasants since the eighteenth century.[6] In a similar vein Vasilii Kelsiev, comrade of the radical atheist Nikolai Dobroliubov and sometime collaborator with Herzen, was convinced that the religious enthusiasm of sectarians (*skoptsy,* flagellants, etc.) and Old Believers, their "passion for extremes," as he put it, could be tapped by the intelligentsia for its own purposes. Giving traditional Slavophile notions a leftward twist, Kelsiev contrasted the peasants of Russia, especially Old Believers, with those of Western Europe and Catholic Poland. Unlike the others, the Russians thought of "the most important problems that can concern the human soul—truth and untruth, Christ and anti-Christ, eternity, man, salvation . . . . [T]he Russian people searches for truth and then follows what it has found, and does not allow itself to be frightened by floggings . . . ."[7]

In the years that followed, faith in the revolutionary potential of sectarian, schismatic, and to a lesser extent Orthodox peasants continued to animate many radicals, even some participants in the presumably atheistic or at least irreligious Movement to the People of 1874.[8] And indeed, from time to time, though never with consistency, sectarians and schismatics could be seen participating in movements of popular unrest such as the strike at the Demidov ironworks (Perm, 1874), when Old Believers, as part of a militant movement of thousands of workers, denounced the Demidov coat of arms as the "seal of Antichrist."[9] Such occurrences were exceptional, however, and it is fair to say that the radical quest for sectarian or Old Believer followers yielded little fruit and had but a minor impact on the broader course of the revolutionary movement.

In these examples radicals who availed themselves of religious themes in their search for a popular base closely identified religious faith with folk tradition. If Decembrist officers, addressing their men in Christian idiom, conceived of them as representatives of the people, the *narod,* this was even truer of those Populists who invoked religious motifs when addressing villagers later in the century. But what of the first approaches by the radical left to potential followers who were not villagers or soldiers but urban workers? What of the "students" of various radical persuasions who in the 1860s and especially the 1870s began to make contact with the workers of St. Petersburg and other centers of city and factory life? Here, when we first observe self-conscious efforts by *intelligenty* to address and instruct a plebian audience that lived and worked in a cosmopolitan milieu, their mode of operation appears more differentiated and complex, much too varied and contradictory to reduce to one essential pattern. Of course we continue to encounter an awareness of the targeted workers' peasant backgrounds, and by the same token their closeness to the faith of their forebears. But we also begin to notice an important change of direction. Rather than viewing popular religiosity as a useful opening wedge, some "enlighteners" of this period— doggedly rationalist, positivist, materialist, and irreligious, if not militantly atheist, in their formal worldviews—began to assess their "pupils'" faith as an obstacle to their enlightenment. And to overcome this obstacle, they began—with greater or lesser degrees of caution—to look for soft spots, weak links, in the workers' religious views, in the hope that their discovery would facilitate the conversion of the pupil to a secular cosmology, one that, while oriented toward science, would be sweeping enough in its ethical range and powerful enough in its emotional appeal to function as a new religion for the worker whose soul was under siege.[10]

As this process of secular conversion began to develop—even, as often happened, when it was tried and modified or tried and failed, leaving unintended consequences in its wake—government officials and the social elites whose aid they hoped to enlist found themselves looking more and more to religion and education as battlegrounds where the struggle for worker loyalties would be fought. Here, however, the government soon found itself at a disadvantage, one that was grounded, I suggest, in the entire history of church-state relations in the Imperial period.

Gregory Freeze has argued forcefully and convincingly that it is simplistic to view the post-Petrine church as a mere handmaiden of the secular state, or the Holy Synod as a servile bureau of religious affairs.[11] Yet even Freeze is prepared to acknowledge that the church's "political clout" and sphere of authority were declining in the nineteenth century, that an aggressive Chief Procurator (a lay official chosen by the tsar to oversee the Synod's affairs) like Dmitrii Tolstoi (1865–1880) was able to encroach on church prerogatives, and that the government sometimes burdened the church with "worldly tasks."[12] Though the episcopal hierarchy struggled with some success to preserve the church's autonomy and resist the intrusions of the state, including Tolstoi's persistent efforts at church reform, its institutional and cultural ties to the Imperial power (a connection reinforced but by no means begun by the formula "Orthodoxy, autocracy, nationality") forced it to compete from a position of weakness in the urban civic arena that began to emerge in the reign of Alexander II.

For reasons beyond the scope of this paper, the Russian church and its educational institutions had spawned no integrative civic religion, analogous, say, to Lutheran Pietism in Germany, to compete with the more secular modes of thought and feeling that had been challenging the dominant institutions of Europe since the Enlightenment. However much they purported to identify with Orthodoxy, new religious ideologies such as Slavophilism were heterodox and marginal when seen from the vantage point of church or state. The church, in turn, though not without its critics of serfdom, was intimately entangled with the interests and outlook of the autocratic state and its repressive apparatus, sometimes going further than the state itself in its pursuit of conformity, suppression of dissent, and distrust of its parishioners. Given this relationship, the church's sporadic efforts to present itself as a viable alternative to radical proselytizers of the *narod* proved hopelessly compromised and transparent. In short, however unfair the criticism may be in the light of recent research, the church was vulnerable to the charge of servility to secular power; and when it did resist that power, it was more to stem the tide of reform than to claim a leadership role in society.

But the church's civic weakness should not be mistaken for a weakness of the faith itself. Religion, as Moshe Lewin has emphasized, was a major element of the peasant's social and cultural world, where it survived and even flourished quite apart from its formal institutional manifestations. As Lewin says, peasants were neither very clerical nor very dependent on the church as such.[13] Whatever the syncretic mixture of Christian and pagan elements (*dvoeverie*) in the peasant cosmology—always a moot question—the Holy Synod was as distant from the Russian village as the Winter Palace and surely of less symbolic consequence. By contrast, though its forms may have varied, the peasants' attachment to the symbols and rituals of their village and their faith was very real, as those *intelligenty* who contrived to address the villager in a religious idiom correctly understood.

The Russian peasant *away* from the village, however, the peasant decontextualized, severed from his native cultural milieu, was a different matter. Even if only temporarily, the peasant who worked in a factory, shop, or for that matter, a hotel-restaurant in Petersburg or Moscow (Chekhov's "Peasants" comes readily to mind), having ceased to be an integral part of the total social-cultural world from which he came, was soon subjected to a variety of stimulating experiences and seductive influences capable of creating doubts and discomforts about his home environment and its attendant values. The vulnerability of the uprooted peasant's traditional piety was lost neither on the forces of order, secular as well as religious, nor on the exponents of radical change. In the 1860s and 1870s, both sides began to see the soul of the transplanted villager, the new urban poor, as contested terrain for the nation's future.

The full course of this evolving contest has never been charted, and I make no claim to do so in this article. What I offer instead, in what I hope will be a stimulus to further study, is an attempt to bring to light some revealing moments in the first interactions among workers, *intelligenty*, government officials and others, moments that touched on sensitive matters of religious belief and—more elusive—feeling. My focus here is on St. Petersburg, the city that proved to be the most consequential site of these early engagements. The struggle over religion that first took shape there would continue to reverberate on the eve of Russia's twentieth-century revolutions.

A Brief Encounter: The Sunday Schools

The first attempt by *intelligenty*, mainly radical and liberal students in university towns, to reach out to urban workers in a manner that appeared to challenge their faith took place in the context of the Sunday School movement of 1859–1862.[14] We have little information on what went on within the walls of the short-lived Sunday Schools for adults, and we cannot say to what degree the teachers openly and directly engaged in antireligious propaganda. But we may cautiously infer from certain government actions that there was enough in the way of secular scientific instruction to generate a backlash from state and church authorities. Ostensibly an unofficial secular institution devoted to the promotion of literacy, numeracy, and other basic skills, the Sunday School could operate only with government permission, and, like other officially authorized schools, was expected to provide its pupils—mainly artisans, factory workers, and retail clerks—with the rudiments of religious instruction.

In early 1861, however, the two responsible ministries, Education and Internal Affairs, acting under pressure from the ever watchful Third Section, decided to go a step further. A decision was made to appoint an Orthodox cleric to every school, not merely to run its religion program but also to oversee its daily instructional routine. In St. Petersburg, where the schools were most widespread, the posts were filled by Metropolitan Isidor, presiding officer of the Synod, a man deeply troubled by the dangers that secular scientific knowledge posed to the faith. In addition to their teaching duties, the clerics were given the task of safeguarding "the truths of the Orthodox faith," a measure taken in response to reports that had reached the government the previous year: dangerous, secular subjects—science, history, geography, political economy, even modern languages—had been taught at some schools, in violation of their original mandates. To combat this menace, teaching material not previously approved by the Education Ministry was now prohibited, and teachers suspected of questioning the principles of Christian faith and morality were banned from the classroom.[15]

This assault on allegedly antireligious teachings tells us more about the sensitivity of an anxious government—above all, the chronically nervous Third Section—and zealous church than about the actual nature of classroom instruction. To be sure, there is reason to believe that the impetus behind the schools came from men devoted to the secularization, if not the dechristianization of popular education. According to a student deeply involved in these events, the professor who was the force behind the Sunday School experiment had envisaged it as a kind of peaceful revolution, a means for transforming Russia's "semi-Asiatic" society by spreading new kinds of knowledge among the benighted masses.[16] Many teachers shared this vision, and though it did not entail a direct assault on religious faith, a few of them seem to have interpreted it in extreme fashion. In the spring of 1862, the Minister of Internal Affairs reported that pupils from two of the Petersburg schools had told their employers that teachers were propagating antireligious and socialist ideas, in one case even denying the existence of God. As summarized by the minister in a memorandum, the pupils were taught: "Il n'y a pas de Dieu, l'homme n'a point une âme immortelle . . . ."[17]

But such stories were the exception, not the rule. Though they provided ammunition to a government in search of a pretext to close the schools—the same minister spoke with alarm of efforts to shake the foundations of the pupils' faith[18]—they cannot be cited as evidence of a serious or widespread effort to dechristianize the workers. Indeed, if religion was of any serious moment in the schools, it may have had less to do with the content of the teaching than with the mood of the classroom, especially in the first heady days of the movement. When K. D. Ushinskii, editor of the Education Ministry's *Journal* and an avid supporter of the schools, described the atmosphere in a class he visited, he compared the pupils' exalted mood to that of worshipers in a church who felt their attendance to be holy and religious.[19] Later, even revolutionaries would learn that to wean workers from their religious attachments, they would need to pay attention to mood as well as content.

Although another decade would pass before *intelligenty* again dared to raise religious questions in the presence of workers, neither government nor church proved so reticent. Throughout the 1860s and for years thereafter, intensified official efforts to ensure the political loyalty, social passivity, and personal morality of the lower classes would invariably have a religious component. Nowhere was this truer than in the supercharged atmosphere of the capital where, for reasons I have related elsewhere,[20] the late 1860s witnessed a renewed preoccupation, virtually an obsession, among officials with the declining morality (*nravstvennost'*) of the city's poor, whom they perceived as wallowing in depraved and immoral practices—mainly heavy drinking, but sexual excess as well—that could have dire social and political consequences. Among a variety of police-sponsored measures aimed at arresting or reversing this process was a plan to enlist the support of Orthodox clerics —many, no doubt, sincerely devoted to the spiritual welfare of their flock— in a broad effort to oversee the mores of the populace, much as clergy had been asked to safeguard traditional values at the Sunday Schools. At the same time, a parallel program was instituted that assigned policemen to assist the clergy in preserving decorum in the neighborhood of churches, monasteries, and cemeteries, particularly during festive holiday seasons. Police would support the church by providing a show of force when needed; clergy would support police by delivering edifying sermons to counteract "pernicious tendencies."[21] In the same spirit, efforts to enlist religion to the cause of order were made at state plants such as the Cartridge Factory, where confession, fasting, and presence at services were required of all workers, and the Okhta Powder Works, where in 1865 the factory priest was placed on a special committee to assure that a newly created factory school was run with due attention to matters spiritual and moral.[22] By the 1870s the stage was set for Petersburg workers to view the clergy's independence with a cynical eye.

New Experiments: Religion, Science, and the IRTO Schools

If throne and altar entered the 1870s allied in cautious dedication to a usable faith meant to safeguard the worker from the twin evils of moral decay and political subversion, what of the emerging new social actors who hoped to lead the country along a more dynamic path of economic modernization? Did manufacturers and other promoters of economic progress endorse the use of religious indoctrination as a means of social control and political immunization? Or did their own cultural values support a more secular, scientific concept of worker education? And if the latter, how could that concept be brought into harmony with the notion of officially prescribed, state-sponsored religious instruction? Though answers to these questions may not be readily found, the evidence suggests a paradoxical situation: whereas the partisans of progress usually accepted some version of the idea that religious resources should be mobilized to shape the workers' character, the thrust of their practical efforts was to provide the workers with a modern secular education. In general, the latent tension between these two positions was avoided rather than faced.

Most of the men who pondered such questions at the turn of the 1860s were members of IRTO, the Imperial Russian Technical Society, founded in 1866. Because they were the most enlightened, forward-looking, scientifically oriented representatives of the nation's newly emerging industrial-technological élite, we may use them, *a fortiori,* as a way of examining the attitudinal frontiers of that world.[23] In 1870, IRTO was co-organizer in St. Petersburg of an unprecedented "Congress of Manufacturers and People Interested in Native Industry." The first such gathering in Russian history, the Congress and the large Industrial Exhibition that accompanied it were widely seen as emblematic of Russia's entry into a new industrial age. Not surprisingly, religious ceremonial had a prominent role at these events, with two of the church's highest dignitaries, metropolitans Isidor of St. Petersburg and Arsenii of Kiev, leading the prayers at the Exhibition's solemn opening and blessing the site with holy water.[24]

Less predictable was the manner in which religious themes were brought into the Congress's debates, mainly at the sessions conducted under the rubric "The Intellectual and Moral Development of our Working Class" (a combination of words often used in the discussions).[25] To some extent the speeches at these sessions echoed what was now the general government line—worker religiosity must be fostered for the sake of social peace—to which some speakers, crediting religion with the power to improve performance and promote sobriety on the job, added the more practical goal of labor discipline. Occasionally, however, a speaker would hint at possible conflict between customary religious practice and the needs of industry. Here the main issue was the observance of holidays, the complaint being that popular celebration of an exorbitant number of church holy days had a harmful effect on labor discipline and productivity.

This was not the first time such a claim had been made. In the early 1860s, when the government's slowly reviving zeal for industrialization was still rather shaky, an official commission appointed to review Russia's industrial laws concluded that labor productivity suffered from too much holiday celebration, which, "in the interests of industry as well as morality," needed to be restrained. In 1867 the point was repeated at IRTO's first congress, where the prominent industrialist Ludwig Nobel charged that holiday festivities promoted drink and debauchery, which led in turn to low productivity and high labor costs. Now, at the 1870 Congress, one industrialist calculated that Russian workers observed so many holidays that a manufacturer could count on only 265 effective workdays, as compared to 313 in England. Similar claims were made by a German guest at the Exhibition, who, having probably conferred with delegates to the Congress, deplored the persistence of workers' ties to their villages and regretted the labor time lost to holiday festivity, with its inveterate drinking.[26]

Though any attempt to estimate the time and productivity industry actually sacrificed to holiday celebration would be futile, there is little doubt that peasants—the main recruitment pool for factory workers—attached great value to their many work-free church and seasonal feast days, often attended by merrymaking. Cultural taboos on holiday work were strong and were often reinforced by communal punishment of the transgressor.[27] For factory workers in particular, attachment to holidays, even when attenuated by the secular diversions of city life, was readily translated into a gritty defense of their God-given right to time off on a host of different days, including Sundays. This was true even in a setting as urbane as St. Petersburg, where assertion of that right occasionally took the form of organized resistance.[28]

Holiday observance, then, was not a problem that lent itself to easy solutions. To say the least, it would have been an awkward maneuver to press religiosity on workers, asking them to heed the pious fulminations of moralistic sermons, while exhorting them to scale down the ritual celebration of their feast days and suppress their belief that work on certain days was sinful. This was not the kind of plea most workers were likely to entertain with equanimity, for to a believer, as the seventeenth-century schism should remind us, an attack on ritual was virtually an attack on the faith itself. Wisely, then, the 1870 Congress took no aggressive steps to resolve the problem of holiday excess, let alone promote the worker's dechristianization. In the end, those who deplored the pernicious effect of feast days and wished to encourage the creation of a more upright, self-disciplined worker had but one place to turn: support of a broadly conceived program of secular education. At best, though no one made the point explicit, those who chafed at holiday revelry could harbor the hope—though at the risk of planting the seed of religious doubt—that "irrational" customs would one day be eroded by exposure to secular knowledge.

Though placing more emphasis than their predecessors on vocational training and science, the speakers who dwelt on the need for educated workers in 1870 were heirs to the vision of the Sunday Schools. As such, they argued forcefully for a special program of evening and Sunday classes (modeled on a school IRTO had launched the previous year), a proposal eagerly adopted by the Congress plenum. Yet it is noteworthy that in arguing their case for secular knowledge, speakers carefully called attention to IRTO's desire to afford its pupils moral and religious instruction as well as general and technical education. The program approved by the Congress had as its premise that "moral education" was a "necessary basis for the conscientious execution of work," and echoed the standard view that morality must be implanted by the teaching of "religious truths" as well as by good counsel and example. Despite its stress on secular learning, the program required instruction in Christian morality and decorum.[29]

This provision was pointedly consistent with the government's stress on behaviorally oriented religious indoctrination and the Education Ministry's affirmation, as expressed in the 1864 Education Statute, that the goal of elementary education was "to impart religious and moral notions," as well as "useful, basic knowledge," to the people.[30] The authors of the IRTO program, however, eschewed specific reference to Orthodoxy (as distinct from Christian teachings in general) and did not at this stage reveal any plan for the use of Orthodox clergy. Nor was it possible, given their devotion to technology and progress, for IRTO people to indulge in the kind of antiscientific partisanship that characterized the thinking of an Isidor and the more conservative government officials. For the promoters of the new industrialism, religious-moral teaching could supplement and enrich but could not be substituted for a secular educational program. They wished to encourage the growth of a working class that was skilled, enlightened, and developed (*razvityi*), a goal that neither church nor state officials—not even those who had begun to think in terms of the imperatives of industrialization—were ready to embrace wholeheartedly. If members of IRTO, like the police, were willing to deploy religion as a means of preserving social harmony, most of them either viewed it as enlightenment's ally or avoided facing the prospect of conflict. Hence it was possible to support religion while promoting classes in the very subjects—science, history, even political economy—that had frightened the foes of the Sunday Schools just a few years earlier.[31]

In practice, however, the effort to strike a balance between secular and religious education would prove more difficult than anyone was suggesting. There would even be moments, as we shall see, when devotees of enlightenment for workers found themselves in embarrassing if not compromising positions. Though only a detailed study of the IRTO schools from their origins to 1917 could give us an adequate grasp of the range of problems that beset them, a look at some evidence from the 1870s will suggest their general nature.[32]

Notwithstanding the ecumenical tenor of most allusions to religion at the 1870 Congress, in practice the subject of religion (*Zakon Bozhii,* God's or Divine Law) as taught at the schools, required for one or two hours a week, turned out to be the program of the Orthodox church, as it was at all other Russian primary schools. While varying slightly from school to school and year to year, the essential elements of the program were always the same. A typical lesson plan included memorization of the Short Catechism and common prayers, reciting of the Ten Commandments, study of the *Simvol very* (Apostles' Creed), Bible stories, lives of saints, twelve major Orthodox holy days, and icon appreciation. Also covered were the lives of early Christians, the missions of Cyrill and Methodius, and, of course, the baptism of Rus'. All teachers used the same texts, which had to be approved by the Synod. To encourage attendance, religion classes, unlike the others (except for singing, which was partly religious) were free.[33] As in other Russian schools, religion was always taught by a cleric (deacon, priest, or archpriest), though I have seen no evidence that clergymen were asked to play the broad surveillance role assigned them in the Sunday Schools.

Religious instruction was not confined to religion class. Initially taught by a layman, the basic class in Russian—where illiterate and semiliterate workers learned to read and write, and where pupils spent more hours than in any other class—regularly used religious material (including reading in Church Slavonic and translation of Slavonic texts into the vernacular), as did the class in Russian history, the only history taught. Singing class, often an important part of the program, emphasized religious as well as patriotic hymns.

Though few ever graduated from a full three-year program, a couple of thousand Petersburg workers and their children, almost all at least nominally Orthodox, were exposed to instruction at IRTO schools in the 1870s (as were thousands more in the following decades).[34] While many more were unable or unwilling to take advantage of the program, understandably preferring to spend their free time in other ways after 10–15 (usually 12) hours a day, 5½–6 days a week, of hard work, it is safe to say that the IRTO school represented not only the most extensive educational experience of workers in these years, but also, except for those who attended a local church, their primary experience of organized religion.

But it was also their major source of exposure to secular learning—especially math, science and technology—the *raison d'être* for the IRTO program. Beginning with simple arithmetic in the first year and moving on to geometry, technical drawing, and elementary mechanics (all of special interest to machinists and other workers in the growing munitions, machine, and ship-building industries), the schools also offered physics and chemistry to those who made it to the final year. Interest in such courses was particularly intense, as witness a time in 1874 when twenty-five munitions workers requested the introduction of more advanced classes in geometry and physics. Though tuition was always a sore point for IRTO pupils, most of the petitioners were prepared if necessary to pay an additional fee.[35]

Nor did science teachers shy away from the topics that had appeared so dangerous to state and church officials. Thus a typical physics course would include such matters as the character of "natural bodies," the earth's motion, the concept of atoms, the structure of air, water, and light.[36] "Natural history" was often a part of the curriculum, and this at a time when Darwinism, increasingly popular in educated society, was under correspondingly fierce attack from theologians and officials.[37] We do not know the precise ideological angle from which such materials were taught—it surely varied from teacher to teacher—but there can be no doubt that a secular science of sorts was beginning to pass across the intellectual horizon of many workers, and this with the formal permission, though hardly the blessing, of a suspicious government and wary church.

In this secular environment, how successful were the religion teachers in capturing the attention, if not the devotion, of their pupils? The decision to waive tuition already suggests that attendance was a problem. Though our other evidence—which emerges late in the decade—is sparse, it is also revealing. At an 1878 meeting of IRTO's Commission on Technical Education, in a rare public allusion to such problems, the head of the IRTO educational program spoke with sadness of recent trends in the religion classes. At all but one of the schools, Trotskii-Seniutovich reported, the answers (by both adults and children) to questions on religion at the end-of-year exams were so weak that he and his staff felt an urgent need for action. The exception was the Arsenal school, where the religion teacher, Archpriest V. Ia. Mikhailovskii, had engaged his pupils' interest by enlivening his Biblical history lectures with visual aids, including pictures projected on a screen by "magic lantern." At all the other schools, Trotskii-Seniutovich complained, the religion teachers' "monotonous" techniques had yielded disappointing results. Representatives of various schools confirmed this account, revealing their low attendance figures. Alarmed at these reports, the Commission quickly voted to introduce Father Mikhailovskii's visual-pictorial method (*nagliadnye besedy po kartinkam*) at its schools, and invited him to take full charge of its religion program.[38]

Mikhailovskii eagerly accepted the challenge. At the Commission's next meeting he pledged to visit all its schools and hold a monthly demonstration lesson at every religion class. This amounted to a commitment to ten visits and sixteen lesson hours a month, for which, despite the Commission's financial woes, he was paid 500 rubles (plus one and a half rubles an hour for his regular classes at two schools).[39] By the end of the 1878–1879 school year, according to the Commission, Father Mikhailovskii, now invested with the title *rukovoditel'* (or *inspektor*) *urokov*, had turned religion into the schools' most stable, well-taught subject, arresting its decline at all the schools but one.[40]

Only two years later, however, Trotskii-Seniutovich's successor, N. P. Stolpianskii, would paint a much less rosy picture. Acknowledging a wide disparity from school to school in the quality of performance at religion class, he blamed the weak performance of pupils at some schools on the persistence of poor teaching methods.[41] Clearly the miracle expected of Mikhailovskii's magic lantern had not been brought off, certainly not at all the schools. Worse still, with Dmitrii Tolstoi's departure from office in the spring of 1880, the effects of dull teaching were soon multiplied by a recrudescence of ideological pressure on the schools from his two former agencies, the Education Ministry and the Synod. The Synod (now dominated by K. P. Pobedonostsev) insisted on even stricter adherence to a fixed religion curriculum, designed for use in all primary schools, while the Ministry (which, soon after the tsar's assassination in March 1881, took oversight of IRTO schools away from the more moderate Finance Ministry) demanded new measures to improve the pupils' character: more hours devoted to religion (to equal the requirement at village schools); transfer to clergy of those parts of the Russian lessons that used religious texts.[42] At the uneasy start of a new decade, it would seem that the teaching of religious values to worker-pupils was a growing source of anxiety for both the schools and the state.

As to the pupils' response to IRTO's technology and science classes, always among the most popular (though not without their own attendance and performance problems),[43] it is perhaps of some relevance that the successful classroom use of props and visual aids, including the *nagliadnye besedy* that caused such a stir in the crisis over religion classes, had been begun by IRTO science (mainly physics) teachers some years earlier. Such items as globes, drawings, and three-dimensional models had been used in conjunction with modest scientific experiments to "acquaint pupils with nature."[44] Is it fanciful to suppose that it was the excitement generated by this kind of teaching that inspired twenty-five eager munitions workers to seek more instruction in physics? This is not much to go on, and there may well have been workers who derived as much pleasure from religion class— however repetitious or rigidly programmed—as from science. What cannot be denied is the bifurcated nature of the program. Its contradictory offerings did not reflect an exercise of free choice by the instructors and administrators of the schools, even those who may have believed in the full compatibility of science and religion. IRTO instructors (including Trotskii-Seniutovich) and the Commission struggled valiantly and creatively to come up with new texts, appropriate for adult courses in science, language, and especially geometry,[45] but they were repeatedly hemmed in by outside constraints. With so many features of the program having to be set in terms agreeable to external authority, it was hard indeed to move the secular education of workers beyond the constraints of a structure wherein it was assumed that tightly monitored religious instruction must remain in the service of control and subordination.

New Experiments: Religion, Science, and the Workers' Circle

By the end of the 1870s radical students had had an on-again, off-again experience of interacting with Petersburg workers for over seven years. Religious issues played a conspicuous part in this interaction, and, not unike the men who planned and supervised instruction in the IRTO schools, radicals were faced with tough dilemmas as they contemplated the ambiguities of popular religiosity, especially its curious blend of conservative and rebellious components. In the rest of this article, I will follow the tortuous course of student-worker relations in the 1870s insofar as they touched on questions of religion and irreligion. I will map out the landscape of those relations as best I can, attempting to add to our knowledge of the workers' religious (and irreligious) experience, both its general mood and its specific content, in the special context of the workers' circle.

1. Mood: Religion

Let us begin chronologically, with two of the earliest worker-student contacts of the period. The first one began, in a sense, as a resumption in miniature of the Sunday School movement of a decade earlier, the important difference being that this time the teaching of workers was conducted in secret, without official sanction. It took place toward the end of 1871, when a university student, acting not as a revolutionary but rather in the philanthropic-didactic spirit of the typical Sunday School teacher, decided to organize free classes in order to raise the cultural level of workers at his father's chemical plant. The emphasis was to fall on basic education (mainly the three R's), but like his predecessors the student also included such sensitive subjects as history and science. A political moderate, to some extent he was planning to do extralegally what IRTO had just begun to do legally, though without its emphasis on vocational training.

Perhaps in order to guard against the teaching of ticklish subject matter from too political a perspective, the student invited some equally moderate friends, former seminarians from Riazan, to assist him. Eventually, however, as word of the classes spread within the student milieu, people of more radical persuasion were drawn to them, most notably the dedicated young revolutionaries and atheists Sergei Sinegub and Vasilii Stakhovskii. Soon, under their influence, the history and science classes took on a blatantly political character. Sinegub, sensitive to his pupils' peasant origins, and assuming therefore that they had strongly held religious convictions, tried to use the classes to undermine their faith. We do not know exactly how he went about presenting his antireligious teachings or how his pupils reacted, but his efforts quickly brought him into conflict with the former seminary students and led to the closing of the school.[46]

The second contact, which began with an encounter in the Aleksandrovskii Park in the summer of 1872, was to have more lasting consequences.[47] Two young textile workers from Tver, weavers of close peasant background with only a few short years of residence in St. Petersburg, were sitting in the park, struggling to read aloud from a cheap popular picture book, when they were suddenly accosted by a student. After telling them the book they were reading was "trash" (radicals shared the government's concern over popular reading and drinking habits and, in their own way, its belief in the workers' need for moral uplift), the student invited them to his apartment to examine more serious—that is, political—literature. They accepted the invitation, and with this began a series of expanding Saturday- and Sunday-night gatherings of workers and students, soon to be led by none other than Sergei Sinegub. From our vantage point, what is particularly interesting about the meeting in the park is that the weavers, it turned out, had been hoping to run into students of this kind, students who would offer them free lessons; they viewed the encounter in the park as an act of divine intervention. In their own words, uttered before they had been exposed to the antireligious ideas of Sinegub and others, "at last God has sent us a student."[48]

Why were these weavers searching for lessons? There is reason to believe, to draw together some of the threads of our story, that their appetite for learning had been whetted at a recently founded IRTO school. (Only slightly off the mark, one of them remembered it as a "Sunday School.") That school was plagued by organizational muddles, and tuition fees had been causing resentment and enrollment problems, yet certain pupils, the two weavers among them, had found their craving for education aroused there, if not satisfied.[49]

The paradoxical nature of the weavers' new situation becomes apparent when we focus on the image of a believer thanking God for sending him an (unbeknownst to him) *atheistic* teacher. In so doing, the young weaver anticipated the situation of dozens (eventually hundreds) of Petersburg workers, about to embark on similar adventures that exposed them to new experiences that would sometimes—depending on the teacher's approach— put their faith to the test. The range of responses, as we shall see, would be wide, from complete rejection of any antireligious views, to selective acceptance, to outright conversion to one or another form of nonbelief. Yet workers across the spectrum of response were willing to risk their freedom and health by spending precious non-working hours, their "nights,"[50] in the illicit company of these radical missionaries. At the risk of stretching the meaning of the word, I intend to show that part of the seductive power of the students' effort came from their "religious" zeal and from the exalted atmosphere they created at the secret, illegal, politically charged "studies" (*zaniatiia*)—usually on Sunday or holiday evenings and often extending well past midnight—they arranged for their pupils. Like the Sunday School class observed by Ushinskii, but more intense for being forbidden, these lessons took on something of the effervescent character of a heterodox religious experience, providing the workers (in Durkheimian terms) with a new collective sense of the sacred, awakening their sense of moral purpose and enthusiasm, and (in more Weberian terms) exposing them to the magical spells of extraordinary, charismatic figures with esoteric knowledge. By the same token, the books—sometimes handed by teacher to pupil as a gift, with all the gravity of a sacred ritual—could assume the inspirational character of holy scriptures, thereby confirming the charismatic authority of the donor.[51]

The mood of religious fervor that pervaded the lives of student radicals of the 1870s, however agnostic, atheistic, or iconoclastic their ideological postures, has been duly noted by several scholars. Richard Stites, applying to Russia the words of an historian of the French Revolution, suggests that the radicals possessed "religious feelings without religious faith," and cites examples of the way in which their "secular dreams were still couched in a religious apostrophe."[52] The writer Bervi-Flerovskii, who collaborated closely with revolutionary students at this time, frequently compared them with the early Christians and anticipated their becoming the "apostles" of a new religion of equality that would touch the hearts of the Russian people.[53] Nikolai Charushin, a student who was very involved in the political education of workers, recalled that in the winter of 1873–1874 the youth of the capital were fired up by their great expectations and sense of mission. It was "a kind of purely religious ecstasy, wherein rationality and sober thought no longer had any place." Nikolai Chaikovskii was perhaps an extreme case, but as a founder of the famous *chaikovtsy* circle he spoke for others when he wrote of the "mission" he felt summoned to fulfill, a duty to reveal to the people a "truth" known to him and his friends alone, to bring about a social "miracle," "deliver" the people from their sufferings, and take possession of their "soul." When a comrade accused him of trying to create not a political organization but a sect, Chaikovskii seems to have put up no defense.[54]

Similar religious motifs, sometimes dramatized by the fervent use of "religious apostrophe" or gesture, infused the atmosphere of the student-worker meetings of this period, in which Chaikovskii was an avid participant. Lev Tikhomirov, a revolutionary propagandist and then a terrorist before his apostasy from the movement in the 1880s, recalled that when he and his comrades had gained sufficient trust in a worker to take the risk of raising political questions, they would begin with such solemn, ringing declarations as "falsehood and injustice reign in the world."[55] This language struck a responsive chord in pupils such as the deeply religious young textile worker Filipp Zaozerskii, whom Tikhomirov remembered as having "the temperament of a religious martyr" and a great yearning for "truth" (*istina,* with its strong connotation of *sacred* or *God's* truth) and "justice" (*spravedlivost'*). "If he believed in something, he believed in it with all his heart" (*bezzavetno*). Though Zaozerskii's inherited faith would soon be undermined by his teachers, "to a certain extent he still remained a believer." This actually pleased some of the radicals, who read it as a sign of his serious character.[56]

The proselytizing element in the student-worker relationship became particularly apparent when, some months after the encounter in the park, the more ardent teachers began to visit the homes of their pupils and to read aloud to them in their collective living quarters (*arteli*).[57] Since we may surmise, given Sinegub's central role (until 1873), that antireligious ideas were a part, if only a small part, of the group's informal curriculum, what we begin to see at these meetings as the "workers' cause" (*rabochee delo*) spread out to the city's industrial neighborhoods[58] is what soon became a character-istic paradox of the movement: the appearance of antireligious or, more accurately, *ir*religious teaching in an atmosphere that smacked of religious enthusiasm.

At times that atmosphere could produce an effect that was not unlike a religious conversion experience. Lev Shishko, a revolutionary whose Peters-burg apartment (shared with Sofia Perovskaia, the future tsaricide) served as a gathering place for eager pupils in 1873, has told of two such cases among the ten men whom he tutored that summer.[59] The first was Fedor Bolshakov, a textile worker described as a pale, sensitive young man, ner-vous yet phlegmatic in disposition, generally lacking in passion or verve during the lessons. Suddenly one afternoon, to Shishko's surprise, Bolshakov is seized by the excitement of the moment—the stimulating quality of the discussion, the fervor generated by the singing and reciting of revolutionary verse. Overcome by a febrile wave of agitation, Bolshakov turns white, begins to tremble. Asked what is wrong, he cannot explain. Then he quietly pro-nounces his "Hannibal's oath" of devotion to his new cause.

The second was Grigorii, a somewhat older worker, a man of very differ-ent temperament. Pensive, conservative, slow to express himself, Grigorii comes to Shishko with a traditional view of the world, grounded in religious faith. Deeply moved by his Russian history readings, Grigorii undergoes a highly intense emotional-intellectual experience, described by Shishko as a revolution (*perevorot*), and is swiftly transformed into a zealous foe of all injustice. Soon the new Grigorii abandons the city for his native village, determined to move it in a different though unspecified direction. Did he also abandon his Christian convictions or did he retain them while giving them new social content? Shishko provides us with no answer, but in either case the suggestion is there that Grigorii underwent a metamorphosis reli-gious in nature, an experience of revelation and rebirth.

In the year from fall 1872 to late 1873, several groups of workers were meeting clandestinely with dedicated teacher-proselytizers in various parts of the city, each group replicating in its own way the impassioned moral atmosphere of the Shishko-Perovskaia apartment. (In some working-class neighborhoods demand for such teachers began to outstrip supply.[60]) Although we know much less about their individual experiences, if each of these groups had only one or two Bolshakovs or Grigoriis in its midst for every ten pupils, it is reasonable to imagine dozens of similar conversions—

perhaps not all as intense—taking place in the course of that time. It is such transformations that Charushin—who claimed a special interest in the "spiritual [*dukhovnaia*] side of our workers"—may have had in mind when he marveled at how, after only a few months with the students, a weaver could be changed from an "ordinary worker with a narrow worldview" (*oby-vatel'skoe mirovozzrenie*) into someone with "a critical and sometimes even revolutionary orientation."[61] In sum, whatever the importance of their thirst for secular knowledge, a subject to which we now turn, it would be wrong to ignore the spiritual dimension of the workers' attraction to the study circles. Semën Volkov, one of the few workers of the 1870s to leave us a brief autobiographical sketch, wrote that one of the reasons he abandoned the life of a provincial textile worker to study the machinist's trade in Sim-birsk, his way station to the capital, was that he found that life "materially and spiritually impoverished."[62] In a sense, the student apartments that wel-comed the visits of spiritually hungry peasant-workers, most of them far from their native soil, were like little roadside shrines or chapels for the Volkovs, with the teachers, sources of esoteric knowledge, serving them as priests, if not as living icons.

2. The Content: Science

If the mood of the secret "classes" was sometimes that of a highly charged religious gathering and the effect on some pupils that of a religious conver-sion, what can be said of their *content*? Instruction in the sciences (*nauki*) is cited in almost every account of the lessons that went beyond basic training in the three R's, subjects reserved for the less "advanced" workers. *Nauki* included geography and history as well as the natural or physical sciences and math, though most indications point to science in the narrower sense as the major source of intellectual excitement among the pupils. Nikolai Morozov, writing of a Moscow group (modeled on the Petersburg circles) he led in 1874, tells us that the workers wished to learn "about the stars, and about the sun, and about the moon" as well as about life in other lands. In St. Petersburg, Sinegub and others would spend whole days preparing scien-tific experiments—one thinks of the IRTO science classes—in order to demonstrate the laws of chemistry to workers who came by at night.[63]

Workers of all kinds eagerly pursued the sciences with their new teachers, but it was the skilled munitions workers and metalworkers, in part because they already had basic literacy and in part by virtue of the nature of their work, who were particularly avid devourers of physics and geometry, sub-jects they sought out at IRTO schools as well (as in the case of the twenty-five Arsenal workers). At secret meetings devoted to their political and general education metalworkers were instructed in history, geography, and math, but also in sciences such as physiology, a subject used successfully by a medical student to lure workers away from a rival study group and attract new pupils to his class. His pupils were treated to a popular, well-attended series of Bazarov-like anatomy experiments on frogs and mice.[64] Other teachers would strain themselves to prove to the pupils that, appearances to the contrary, the earth was round and revolved around the sun; the pupils, in turn, would busy themselves with globes, maps, and texts, struggling to puzzle out these problems with their mentors.[65] (I know of only one instance of a teacher responding negatively to a pupil's request for science instruction.[66])

Of course the teaching of science, though an implicit challenge to Orthodox dogma, did not amount to antireligious propaganda. The exact extent to which most instructors attempted to deliver a blatantly antireligious message to their charges, advancing openly atheistic themes, is a moot question. Tikhomirov, author of some of the propaganda literature used by the teachers (especially their revamped, polemical folktales), wrote in his opinionated but generally reliable memoirs that, while ashamed of the lengths to which he had gone in those writings, he, at least, had managed to avoid the "filth and blasphemy" (griaz' i bogokhul'stvo) displayed by others.[67] But his own description of the experiments conducted by Sinegub and his comrades, far from being a recital of blatant sacrilege, captures beautifully the almost indefinable discursive confusion of science, "superstition," and religion that accompanied such moments of cultural confrontation. When observing these experiments, Tikhomirov recalled, there were always workers who would question the teachers about the thousands of creatures who, they still believed, populated Russia's fields and forests:

> Does this mean [they would ask] that will-o'-the-wisps [bluzhdaiushchie ogni] are [merely] a manifestation of phosphorescence? Does this mean that the wood goblin [leshii] is nothing more than our shadow, or something like the shadows of a magic lantern [i.e., a projector]?

The instructors would reply with nicely elaborated scientific explanations, while their listeners put down their pencils to engage in debate about miracles and saints. By no means the monopoly of the "advanced" pupils, this curiosity about the "world of science that was opening up before them" extended even to pupils who were illiterate, some of whom, "burning with impatience," would fend off exhaustion to stay up all night learning to read, driven by the desire to gain access to scientific texts.[68]

Except for the passing reference to saints, nothing in Tikhomirov's account suggests an assault on Orthodoxy or on Christianity as such. Indeed, an Orthodox priest or even a high church official might have taken pleasure in signs of declining belief in forest creatures, a "pagan remnant" of pre-Christian animistic "superstitions" that the Synod had wished to extirpate ever since its establishment in 1721.[69] As Brooks has suggested, the secular teacher and the Orthodox priest shared a common interest in combatting such notions.[70]

More problematic, however, is the possibility—implicit in Lewin's essay—that such beliefs were so deeply embedded in the popular cosmology, the *dvoeverie,* that their erosion would perforce destabilize a pupil's entire belief system.[71] The anonymous chronicler of classes held in the Vyborg District has claimed—though without citing examples of individual workers—that no sooner had the pupils grasped such new information as the earth's true age ("millions of years, not 7,000"), the absence of heaven as a physical, tangible place (one is reminded of Gagarin's spaceflight), or man's "descent from the apes," than their religious feelings would begin to dissolve.[72] Still, Tikhomirov's allusion to blasphemy notwithstanding, few of the teachers—Sinegub is the most striking exception—seemed prepared to push very hard or directly against the underpinnings of their pupils' faith. A remark attributed to the student Dmitrii Klements, who told some metalworkers that whereas God could never teach them French, he, Klements, could, was quite exceptional.[73] A more typical attitude is encapsulated in the teachers' sensitive treatment of Filipp Zaozerskii upon realizing that he remained a believer despite the partial erosion of his faith: "[W]hen instructing him in natural history, we endeavored to spare him his freedom of conscience." "We don't believe in God," they said, "you believe in Him. That's your own business; believe, if that's what you like" (*esli tebe eto nravitsia*). They never raised the question with him again.[74] One senses that these teachers trod very lightly and were prepared to accept the notion that, for the moment at least, it was acceptable for their pupils to retain their faith even as they began to absorb a scientific worldview.

Some teachers were even more fastidious than Tikhomirov, and their restraint suggests that for many workers a direct attack on religion would have made continued rapport with the students all but impossible. There is evidence that indicates it was antireligious talk (together with language attacking the tsar) that was most likely to frighten certain pupils, especially the less well educated. The anonymous chronicler cited above, while admitting they did not always succeed, speaks explicitly of the propagandists' efforts "not to touch on religious questions."[75] Prince Petr Kropotkin, for a time an active participant in the workers' circles, was remembered by Tikhomirov (they met in 1873) as a man without "a spark of religious feeling."[76] Later, Kropotkin was accused by the government of attempting to "undermine" his pupils' religious feeling.[77] Yet even Kropotkin felt impelled to urge his comrades to exercise caution when addressing the "less cultured" (*malokul'turnye*) workers (whom he otherwise admired) and resist the urge to say things that might offend their religious sensibilities.[78] Such a person was Nikolai Ivanov, a fourteen-year-old lad fresh from the village who informed police he had abandoned his teacher under pressure from his godfather and cousin, his fellow textile workers. Having heard that the teacher did not pray to God, the godfather had threatened to write to young Nikolai's father if he remained in the class.[79] It may well have been an episode like this that convinced Kropotkin of the need for restraint when tempted to attack a pupil's faith.

Attacking someone's faith, of course, was not the same as attacking priests. Capitalizing on a pre-existing storehouse of popular disrespect for clergy, sometimes bordering on anticlericalism (or "unclericalism"),[80] student radicals showed little reluctance to include the priest and the monk in their litany of stock figures responsible for Russia's ills. Clerics could even be singled out for especially hostile treatment, as when Klements—the man who prided himself in surpassing God as a language teacher—attacked the monks as "parasites" (*darmoedy*).[81] But more often they were simply included along with landlords, capitalists, and government officials (*chinovniki*) in the standard list of the people's oppressors. The medical student Aleksandr Nizovkin, for a while one of the most popular of the radical teachers, was typical in this regard. It was their business, he told a group of Petersburg metalworkers in early 1874,

> to destroy the existing order of things . . . , to destroy the bourgeois, the capitalists, the nobility, the clergy . . . . Tell me gentlemen, don't you find these names strange: capitalist, nobleman, priest? . . . The priest: what kind of [sacred] truth [*istina*] is it that batters and befogs the mind [!]

When asked by one of the workers if he meant that every merchant, noble, and priest should be killed, he replied (to the chagrin of part of his audience): "Of course, that goes without saying."[82] And the anonymous writer who noted the teachers' efforts to avoid religion apparently did not consider it a "religious question," strictly speaking, when teachers provocatively called their pupils' attention to the fact that "landowners, officials and priests" comprised but a small minority of the population.[83]

Somewhere in the intermediary zone between trashing the priests and denying the faith itself lay the demystification of *moshchi*, the saints' relics whose miraculous healing power was commonly invoked by clergymen and whose sanctity was an elemental feature of Russian Orthodoxy. On the one hand, an attack on relics was closer to being an attack on Orthodoxy than was the undermining of pre-Christian animistic beliefs; on the other hand, such attacks could also be seen more narrowly, as part of the negative portrayal of clerics, regularly accused of benefiting financially from popular ignorance. Among the propagandists active in the 1870s, Charushin and Kropotkin were particularly eager to convince their pupils that relics were fraudulent, though we do not know to what extent they framed their case within a fully antireligious argument.[84] Others may have gone quite far, linking the nonexistence of true relics, according to one account, to the nonexistence of God.[85]

It has been my contention that no essential pattern or characterization can be made to capture the nature of the Petersburg workers' early experience of religious, antireligious, and irreligious teaching. Instead, variety and diversity are the traits that marked their experience of this initial phase of what was to become a long and drawn out struggle for ideological hegemony over workers among rival intellectual and political elites: conservative officials for whom religion was a transparent means of social control; pioneers of industrial progress and vocational training, squeezed between their faith in the benefits of science and technology and their own subservience to officialdom; and a radical intelligentsia, secular and rationalist in worldview, populist (until the 1890s) and passionately spiritual in sentiment and style, entangled willy-nilly in the discursive field of its pupils, which it assumed, not without reason, to be in some measure religious.[86]

Workers brought to these encounters an almost irreducible continuum of feelings, values, and ideas, including Christian devotion, anti- or "un"-clerical prejudices, animistic lore, and—the newest element—a craving for secular knowledge, especially the revelations of science. The results of these volatile combinations and interactions were unpredictable, and certainly did not match anyone's expectations.

In their strained efforts to assess the popular culture, officials of the government, especially its police and prosecutory arms, were generally content with some simple equations: religion = order, science = atheism = revolution. Thus officers of the Third Section could summarize the complex experiences we have been examining quite succinctly: radical students were shaking the workers' "faith in God," the "structure of their religious convictions," "their belief in the divine origin of the Tsar's power as God's anointed one."[87] Ironically, there were radical *intelligenty,* rabid atheists such as Sinegub and the somewhat more cautious Kropotkin, who, though their goals were the very opposite of the government's, formulated their own equations in virtually the same terms. And there were indeed some workers to whom these formulas more or less applied: veterans of the circles like the machinist Mark Malinovskii, who, before perishing in prison at the age of twenty six, propagated antireligious views among his comrades, mocking the dogmas and rituals of his former faith.[88] Yet it is useful before concluding to glance at the program of the only purely workers' organization—the most "progressive" radical group of its time, to borrow from another idiom—to emerge from these nocturnal "lessons," the first exclusively workers' political group in Russian history. This was the short-lived Northern Union of Russian Workers (1878–1879), a group still celebrated as the first in Russia to borrow heavily from the repertoire of European social democracy ("our Western brothers") and to combine populist doctrine with a call for civil liberty. In its program, folded into an eclectic language that blended standard populist fare with a more Western stress on the centrality of political freedom, we find a Christian rhetoric—*istina,* "sacred duty," "the great words of Christ"—that recalls both the Decembrist Catechism of 1825 and the mood of religious enthusiasm that we saw in the earlier circles. Fighters for justice, the program vows, shall be recorded in the annals of history:

> We . . . are called upon to be the apostles of a new, but in essence only a misunderstood and forgotten teaching of Christ. They will persecute us as they did the first Christians, they will beat and taunt us, but we will be undaunted . . . . [W]e will renew the world, regenerate the family, establish property as it should be and resurrect Christ's great teaching of brotherhood and equality . . . .[89]

A quarter century later Father Georgii Gapon, whose idiom was not unlike the words just quoted, demonstrated that among Petersburg workers—numbering this time in the many thousands—a volatile mix of politics and religious enthusiasm could still exert great power, as long as the religious component, now embodied in a militant, charismatic priest, could project itself as independent of the state.[90] At a time when the government and many industrialists seemed more committed than ever to bending religion to the purposes of order, and when most Russian Marxists were heaping scorn on anything that smacked of faith, the explosiveness of the *Gaponovshchina* took Russians of all persuasions by surprise.

Recently a historian of the French Revolution has written:

> it was not so simple to divide the traditional religious culture from the new secular political culture of the Revolution in the minds and attitudes of the people . . . . Religion and revolution might mix in unusual ways. To create a secular political culture entirely independent of religion was not so simple as the radical revolutionaries hoped.[91]

The same might be said of Russia, but it should be said as well of *non*-revolutionary Russians, for whom the challenge of combining secular learning, religion, and folk belief in their efforts to educate workers proved just as daunting.

Let us conclude by returning to the IRTO Commission, citing a report to that Commission by a certain Demchinskii, a railroad specialist who visited an IRTO school and spoke with its worker-pupils in 1874.[92] Curious to know how the pupils were progressing in the sciences, Demchinskii decided to engage them in conversation. After one of them related that they had already studied galvanism, magnetism, heat, and electricity, Demchinskii challenged them to describe the origins of thunder and lightning. He was taken aback by the sophistication of the response:

> A young fellow explained thunder to me in the most intelligent way, and his answer was not without a certain eloquence. Unable to conceal my surprise, I burst out laughing involuntarily. Say what you like, but to the unaccustomed eye, isn't it very strange to see before you a metalworker in a greasy blouse, with greasy hands, discussing thunder and lightning? [I felt he was about] . . . to go astray, and say that the prophet Elijah was riding in the sky [causing the thunder]!

Suddenly, as if reading Demchinskii's mind, a worker added:

> [Y]es! we now make fun of ourselves; we used to think that Elijah rides around in the sky, or that it was God's punishment when a person was killed by lightning, but now we understand that he was killed because he wound up in a bad spot, where electricity accumulated.

"Don't you agree, gentlemen," Demchinskii asked rhetorically, after repeating this conversation to his audience, "that hearing such a reasoned argument [*rassuzhdenie*] would astound you?" (Demchinskii was also astounded to encounter pupils with a "splendid grasp" of geometry and technical drawing.)

If there were clergy in attendance, as was often the case at Commission gatherings, they may have been less than happy to hear the speaker praise a worker for replacing Elijah and the wrath of God with naturalistic explanations. But even the most avid partisan of scientific education would have felt some malaise at Demchinskii's hint of possible conflict between the secular and religious values on which the IRTO schools purported to be based. Demchinskii's own response—a nervous mixture of scepticism, amazement, and amusement that a simple soul could shake off his past and learn to talk so scientifically, adopting (albeit awkwardly) the discourse of an educated Russian—bears witness to the anxiety of a tiny group of secular educators floating on a sea of traditional culture. For revolutionary students, progressive educators, and police officials all had this in common: they were warring factions of a single elite that, viewing them with an "unaccustomed eye," endowed the Russian people with a kind of religious purity, and struggled in vain to design a simple way to turn their faith to nonreligious goals.

Notes

An earlier version of this article appeared in *Russian History* 16, nos. 2–4 (1989). It is printed here by permission of *Russian History*.

1. *A Radical Worker in Tsarist Russia: The Autobiography of Semën Ivanovich Kanatchikov,* trans. and ed. by R. E. Zelnik (Stanford, 1986) 34.

2. "Katekhizis," *Vosstanie Dekabristov (Materialy/Dokumenty po istorii vosstaniia Dekabristov),* 4 (Moscow, 1927), 254–255. I follow Marc Raeff's translation, in his *The Decembrist Movement* (Englewood Cliffs, N.J., 1966) 120–123 (quotations from pp. 120–121). See also Raeff's comments on pp. 8, 119, and the "Proclamation" on p. 123. Nechkina attributes coauthorship of the Catechism to Mikhail Bestuzhev-Riumin. M. V. Nechkina, *Dvizhenie Dekabristov,* 2 (Moscow, 1955) 365–366.

3. See Daniel Field, *Rebels in the Name of the Tsar* (Boston, 1976), esp. chap. 1.

4. Quoted in Nechkina, 2:366. (The role of the Chernigov regimental priest is discussed on p. 371.)

5. Franco Venturi, *Roots of Revolution: A History of the Populist and Socialist Movements in Nineteenth-Century Russia,* trans. Francis Haskell (New York, 1960) 114.

6. Field, chap. 2 (includes documents on the Bezdna affair and Shchapov's eulogy); also Terence Emmons, "The Peasant and the Emancipation," in Wayne S. Vucinich, ed., *The Peasant in Nineteenth-Century Russia* (Stanford, 1968) 56–58. On Shchapov, see also Venturi 196–203; Donald W. Treadgold, "The Peasant and Religion," in Vucinich, ed., 76–77.

7. Kelsiev, *Ispoved'* (1859), as quoted in Venturi 115 (see also 114–117); Treadgold 75–76.

8. On the role of religious propaganda in that movement see B. S. Itenberg, "Revoliutsionnye narodniki i voprosy religii (Iz istorii 'khozhdeniia v narod')," *Voprosy istorii religii i ateizma. Sbornik statei,* 11 (Moscow, 1963), and *Dvizhenie*

revoliutsionnogo narodnichestva: Narodnicheskie kruzhki i 'khozhdenie v narod' v 70-kh godakh XIX v. (Moscow, 1965) 345–359; Daniel Field, "Peasants and Propagandists in the Russian Movement to the People of 1874," *Journal of Modern History,* 59, no. 3 (1987). While overstating the case for the *narodniki*'s atheism, Itenberg gives examples of the use of Christian motifs in their propaganda, especially among sectarians. Even a few early Marxists, most notably Vladimir Bonch-Bruevich, explored the sectarians' revolutionary potential. See Glennys Young, "A Parting of Ways: Religion, Sectarian Movements, and Russian Social Democracy" (seminar paper, University of California, Berkeley, 1986).

9. See *Rabochee dvizhenie v Rossii v XIX veke. Sbornik dokumentov i materialov,* ed. A. M. Pankratova, 2, pt. 1 (Moscow, 1950) 496–500. (Hereafter: *Rab. dvizh.* plus volume number.)

10. Émile Durkheim's view of religion as a system of beliefs, symbols, and ritual practices that, whatever its specific content, provides moral bonds and solidarity to a community by drawing a line between the sacred and the profane (*The Elementary Forms of the Religious Life* [New York, 1965]), helps us to imagine the world to which "students" began to expose their "pupils" as an embryonic form of religion. See Anthony Giddens, *Capitalism and Modern Social Theory: An Analysis of the Writings of Marx, Durkheim and Max Weber* (Cambridge, 1971), chap. 8. (I am using the word "student" as it was used by contemporaries, especially workers, to refer to young radical *intelligenty,* whether they were actually in school. "Pupil" always refers here to the worker.)

11. G. L. Freeze, "Handmaiden of the State? The Church in Imperial Russia Reconsidered," *Journal of Ecclesiastical History* 36, no. 1 (1985); for more supporting evidence, see idem, *The Parish Clergy in Nineteenth-Century Russia: Crisis, Reform, Counter-Reform* (Princeton, 1983).

12. Freeze, "Handmaiden" 89–91, and *Parish Clergy* 12–22, and, on Tolstoi's procuracy, chaps. 7–9. On Tolstoi as Education Minister, a post he held almost concurrently, see Patrick L. Alston, *Education and the State in Tsarist Russia* (Stanford, 1969) 77–115; Allen Sinel, *The Classroom and the Chancellery: State Educational Reform in Russia under Count Dmitry Tolstoi* (Cambridge, Mass., 1973).

13. Lewin, "Popular Religion in Twentieth-Century Russia," in *The Making of the Soviet System* (New York, 1985) 58–59. The priest, however, was materially dependent on the good will of his parishioners (Freeze, *Parish Clergy* 54–65, 266–70).

14. See my article "The Sunday School Movement in Russia, 1859–1862," *Journal of Modern History* 27, no. 2 (1965).

15. "Voskresnye shkoly," *Entsiklopedicheskii slovar',* ed. F. A. Brokgaus and I. A. Efron, 7 (St. Petersburg, 1895) 256–257; *Kolokol,* no. 95 (1 April 1861) 800–801. On Isidor's anxiety over threats to Orthodoxy and the rise of atheism among the youth, see Freeze, *Parish Clergy* 216, 234–235.

16. L. F. Panteleev, *Iz vospominanii proshlogo* (Moscow, 1934) 160–161. (The reference is to Prof. Platon Pavlov).

17. *Rab. dvizh.,* 2: 1, 592; for the French quotation, see TsGAOR, f. 109 (Third Section), eksp. 1, d. 263 (1862), l. 10.

18. TsGAOR, f. 109, eksp. 1, d. 263, ll. 19, 70.

19. *Zhurnal Ministerstva Narodnogo Prosveshcheniia* no. 1 (1861), sec. 1, pp. 59,

63. On Ushinskii's views, see Jeffrey Brooks, *When Russia Learned to Read: Literacy and Popular Literature, 1861–1917* (Princeton, 1985) 51–52.

20. *Labor and Society in Tsarist Russia: The Factory Workers of St. Petersburg, 1855–1870* (Stanford, 1971).

21. Annual Report of St. Petersburg Police for 1867, TsGIA, f. 1263 (Committee of Ministers), op. 1, d. 3363, ll. 109–110 (details in Zelnik, *Labor* 255–256).

22. M. Bortnik, "V 70-e i 80-e gody na Trubochnom zavode," *Krasnaia letopis'*, no. 26 (1928): 180; *Trudy . . . 1880–1881* (St. Petersburg, 1882) 282 (report of Okhta factory). References to *Trudy . . .* are explained in note 32, below.

23. On IRTO's early years, see Zelnik, *Labor* 285–297.

24. *Birzhevye vedomosti*, no. 212 (15 May 1870).

25. For protocols of the Congress, see supplements to vol. 5 (1871) of *Zapiski Imperatorskogo Russkogo Tekhnicheskogo Obshchestva* [hereafter *Zapiski*]. The debate on workers is on pp. 45–113 of the supplement to no. 1. (details in Zelnik, *Labor* 310–330).

26. *Trudy kommissii uchrezhdennoi dlia peresmotra ustavov fabrichnogo i remeslennogo* 3 (St. Petersburg, 1864), 105; *Zapiski* 1, no. 3 (1867): 132–133, and supplement to *Zapiski* 5, no. 1 (1871): 77–79; F. Matthäi, *Die Industrie Russlands* (full title in Zelnik, *Labor* 419), 2 (Leipzig, 1873), 463–472.

27. M. M. Gromyko, *Traditsionnye normy povedeniia i formy obshcheniia russkikh krest'ian XIX v.* (Moscow, 1986) 125–129; Mary Matossian, "The Peasant Way of Life," in Vucinich, ed., 31–37. Many of these holidays honored a particular saint (Nicholas, Peter, Philip, George), their relative importance varying by region, even by village.

28. One way to assess the practical import of the holiday issue is to examine the role of conflict over holiday time in fostering labor unrest (a point too sensitive for airing at the Congress). In the Petersburg area the picture is mixed. Of five serious incidents in the early part of Alexander II's reign, two involved disputes over holiday work, and conflict over pay for Easter holidays figured in the big strike at the Nevskaia mill that began while the Congress was in session (Zelnik, *Labor* 163–169, 343–352). For the next eight years holidays had no impact on unrest in the area, but early in 1879 there was a fierce strike at the Novaia cotton mill that originated in the workers' refusal to "sin" by working on St. Michael's Day (8 Nov. 1878). G. Plekhanov, *Russkii rabochii v revoliutsionnom dvizhenii (po lichnym vospominaniiam)* (n.p., 1940, from 2d ed. [Geneva], 1902) 62–63.

29. Supplement to *Zapiski* 5, no. 1 (1871): 48–50.

30. From Art. 1 of the 1864 Statute, as cited in Ben Eklof, *Russian Peasant Schools: Officialdom, Village Culture, and Popular Pedagogy, 1861–1914* (Berkeley, 1986) 53. In 1866, after an attempt on his life, Alexander II went even further, affirming that primary education's goal was to strengthen Orthodoxy and the existing order (ibid., 64).

31. Supplement to *Zapiski* 5, no. 1 (1871) 67–73.

32. What follows is based on annual reports and other works of IRTO's Standing Commission on Technical Education (*Postoiannaia komissiia po tekhnicheskomu obrazovaniiu*), most of them bound with *Zapiski*. The pagination is confusing, and titles of reports are long and inconsistent. For purposes of economy I will refer in my

notes to *Trudy* and the year. When generalizing from material found in several reports, e.g., summaries of the curriculum, I will omit specific references.

33. *Zapiski* 8, no. 4 (1874): 15–17; *Trudy . . . 1878–79* (St. Petersburg, 1880), appendix 1, pp. 16–17.

34. Of the 800 pupils who enrolled in IRTO schools in 1878–79, nineteen were listed as Protestants, fourteen as Catholics, four as Jews and the rest as Orthodox; *Trudy . . . 1878–1879*, p. 89 (also *Trudy . . . 1876–1877* [St. Petersburg, 1878] 163). The word "Orthodox" probably concealed some Old Believers. Since the Commission's terribly erratic data fail to distinguish new from continuing pupils, the total number of pupils exposed to its schools cannot be determined. If we simply add up annual enrollment figures from 1869–1870 to 1878–1879 (*Trudy . . . 1878–1879*, pp. 112–113), the sum exceeds 4,000. From 1869 to 1879, IRTO founded twelve schools (one in 1869, one in 1870, two in 1871, four in 1873, three in 1874, one in 1879), but one was transferred to another jurisdiction. The total enrollment in early 1880 was about 600. *Zapiski* 14, no. 3 (1880): 124 ("Deistviia Obshchestva").

35. *Zapiski* 8, no. 4 (1874): 5. For further evidence of the intensity of pupil demand for instruction in the sciences, see *Otchety shkol dlia rabochikh i ikh detei, uchrezhdennykh Imperatorskim Russkim Tekhnicheskim Obshchestvom . . . za 1873–74 uchebnyi god* (St. Petersburg, 1874) 3.

36. Reports for 1869–1873, pp. 5–8; *Trudy . . . 1878–1879*, appendix 1, pp. 25–27.

37. Alexander Vucinich, *Darwin in Russian Thought* (Berkeley, 1988) 25–31, 45–46, and esp. 103–104 (measures against Darwinism by Education Minister Tolstoi) and 105–107 (attacks on Darwinism in theological journals).

38. Session of 20 Aug. 1878, *Trudy . . . 1878–1879*, p. 1. Active in IRTO schools since 1874, when he first promoted the use of pictorial aids, Mikhailovskii was author of two manuals used in IRTO religion classes and a book of pictures used in his Biblical history course (*Zapiski* 8, no. 4 [1874]: 16; no. 6, p. 139). The crux of his method, unveiled in the school year 1876–1877, was the projection of slides (*tumannye kartiny*) by magic lantern, ancestor of the slide projector. His showings of the life of Christ drew some 200 persons. *Trudy . . . 1876–1877*, pp. 166, 179.

39. Session of 4 Sept. 1878. The Commission approved the plan on 13 Oct. (ibid., 3, 6). On its budgetary problems at the end of the 1870s, see *Zapiski* 14, no. 2 (1880): 37 ("Deistviia Obshchestva"). At least one religion teacher offered to work without pay. *Trudy Kommissii . . . 1875* (St. Petersburg, 1876) 44.

40. *Trudy . . . 1878–1879*, pp. 15, 92–93.

41. *Trudy . . . 1880–1881* (St. Petersburg, 1882) 230–232.

42. *Trudy . . . 1880–1881*, pp. 237–244; . . . *1881–1882* (St. Petersburg, 1883) 10–12, 37; . . . *1883–1884* (St. Petersburg 1884) 16, 18–19. Both Education Ministry and Synod were led by Tolstoi until April 1880. Curiously, though wary of science, partial to religious indoctrination, and conservative on most educational issues, by the 1870s Tolstoi had lost his former faith in the use of priests as teachers and now favored a secular school system. At the end of the decade he resisted efforts by the Third Section and others to clericize education, the policy of his successors, especially Pobedonostsev (P. A. Zaionchkovskii, *Krizis samoderzhaviia na rubezhe 1870–1880-kh godov* [Moscow, 1964] 105–106, 111–112, 117–119; Sinel, *The Classroom,*

chap. 7). Note that the Education Ministry had been able to exert great influence on the IRTO schools even when they were overseen by the Finance Ministry (April 1876–April 1881).

43. Classes in technical drawing and related subjects were particularly well attended; at one school pupils requested an extra hour of instruction, extending each class to three straight hours (*Trudy . . . 1878–1879*, pp. 85–86). The greatest demand, however (not surprising, in view of Russia's high illiteracy rate), was for basic instruction in reading and writing. See *Trudy . . . 1880–1881*, p. 218.

44. See the journal of the Commission's session of 14 Dec. 1873, *Zapiski* 8, no. 4 (1874): 18–20, and *Trudy . . . 1878–1879*, appendix 1, p. 25 (for the quotation). On the use of magic lantern pictures in history classes and their value in holding the attention of tired pupils after long hours of labor, see *Trudy . . . 1876–1877*, pp. 110–111, 146, 166.

45. For examples see *Trudy . . . 1876–1877*, pp. 90, 139–142, 165–166.

46. S. S. Sinegub, "Vospominaniia chaikovtsa," *Byloe* no. 8 (1906): 39–44. On this and the following episodes see my "Populists and Workers: The First Encounter between Populist Students and Industrial Workers in St. Petersburg, 1871–74," *Soviet Studies* 24, no. 2 (1972).

47. My account of this incident is based on Sinegub 50–53 and on the recollections of Nikita Shabunin (one of the two workers initially involved), in N. A. Charushin, *O dalekom proshlom: Iz vospominanii o revoliutsionnom dvizhenii 70-kh godov XIX veka*, 2d ed., rev. (Moscow, 1973), 352n–353n.

48. Sinegub 50–51. Sinegub heard the story of the encounter in the park just a few weeks after it occurred.

49. This was the Samsonievskii school, located in the Vyborg District. Its problems are discussed in *Otchety shkol, 1869–1870 po 1872–1873*, pp. 1–18, and in E. Andreev's introduction to that volume (separate pagination), pp. 1–10. See also *Rab. dvizh.*, 2:1, 566–567.

50. In speaking of their "nights," I loosely follow Jacques Rancière, *La Nuit des prolétaires: Archives du rêve ouvrier* (Paris, 1981) 8:

> Le sujet de ce livre, c'est d'abord l'histoire de ces nuits arrachées à la succession normale du travail et du repos: interruption . . . du cours normal des choses, où se prépare, se rêve, se vit déjà l'impossible: la suspension de l'ancestrale hiérarchie subordonnant ceux qui sont voués à travailler de leurs mains à ceux qui ont reçu le privilège de la pensée. Nuits d'étude, nuits d'ivresse. Journées laborieuses prolongées pour entendre la parole des apôtres ou la leçon des instructeurs du peuple, pour apprendre, rêver, discuter ou écrire. Matinées du dimanche . . . ."

In short, the night represents the worker's struggle to acquire a culture like that of the elites (including radical intelligentsia), one that escapes the limits of the culture of the workplace.

51. For a vivid description of such an evening, see Sinegub 51. See also Shabunin's account in Charushin 352, and Charushin's own account, where he stresses the excitement and passion (*uvlechenie*) with which workers studied and conversed with their teachers (142).

52. Richard Stites, *The Women's Liberation Movement in Russia: Feminism, Nihilism,*

and Bolshevism, 1860–1930 (Princeton, 1978) 150. Stites is referring here to radical *women,* but the point is just as applicable to men; see, for example, James H. Billington, *Mikhailovsky and Russian Populism* (New York, 1958), chap. 8.

53. N. Flerovskii [V. V. Bervi], *Tri politicheskie sistemy: Nikolai I-yi, Aleksandr II-oi i Aleksandr III-ii. Vospominaniia N. Flerovskogo* (Berlin, 1897) 297–298. Flerovskii later abandoned his belief in a popular religion of equality, which he came to view as destructive, conducive to fanaticism and even dictatorship (307–308).

54. Charushin, *O dalekom proshlom* 202; N. V. Chaikovskii, "Cherez polstoletiia," *Golos minuvshego na chuzhoi storone* (Paris), no. 3/16 (1926): 183, 186–187.

55. Lev Tikhomirov, *Zagovorshchiki i politsiia* (Moscow, 1930), trans. of *Les Conspirateurs et policiers, souvenirs d'un proscrit russe* (Paris, 1887) 26.

56. Ibid., 31.

57. Sinegub 52–53; Charushin 141–146.

58. L. Shishko, *Sergei Mikhailovich Kravchinskii i Kruzhok Chaikovtsev. (Iz vospominanii i zametok starogo narodnika)* (St. Petersburg, 1906) 22–23.

59. Shishko, *Sergei* 73–74.

60. L. Chemodanova testimony, TsGAOR, f. 112 (OPPS), d. 211, l. 81; Charushin 192; Shishko, *Sergei* 30; idem, "K kharakteristike dvizheniia nachala 70-kh godov (Iz lichnykh vospominanii)," *Russkoe bogatstvo* (1906) no. 10, p. 79.

61. Charushin, p. 142; his 1874 statement about the workers' spiritual side is in TsGAOR, f. 112, d. 209, l. 154.

62. S. K. Volkov, "[Avtobiografiia . . .]," in *V nachale puti. Vospominaniia peterburgskikh rabochikh, 1872–1897 gg.,* comp. E. A. Korol'chuk (Leningrad, 1975) 141.

63. N. A. Morozov, *Povesti moei zhizni: Memuary* (Moscow, 1962), 1:233 (this section originally published in 1912); Tikhomirov, *Zagovorshchiki* 22 (on Sinegub's experiments).

64. Bortnik 181; *Rab. dvizh.,* 2:1, 454; Archief "Narodnicheskoe dvizhenie" (unpublished manuscript collection, Amsterdam, International Institute of Social History), no. 827/7, "Propaganda u Nizovkina" 5; *Protsess 193-kh,* (Moscow, 1906) 6; Charushin 128.

65. 1874 testimony of the medical student Aleksandr Nizovkin, quoted in Sh. M. Levin, "Kruzhok chaikovtsev i propaganda sredi peterburgskikh rabochikh v nachale 1870-kh g.g.," *Katorga i ssylka* (1929) no. 61, p. 17n.

66. According to the munitions worker Sergei Vinogradov, when he asked Charushin for chemistry lessons in 1872, he was told that chemistry was useless to a worker; political economy and social science would be more helpful. *Rab. dvizh.,* 2:1, 466.

67. L. Tikhomirov, *Vospominaniia* (Moscow, 1927) 75.

68. Tikhomirov, *Zagovorshchiki* 28.

69. See Donald W. Treadgold, "Orthodoxy and Society," in R. L. Nichols and T. G. Stavrou, eds., *Russian Orthodoxy under the Old Regime* (Minneapolis, 1978) 22–23.

70. Brooks, *When Russia* 250–254.

71. For an alternative view, see Pierre Pascal, *The Religion of the Russian People,* trans. Rowan Williams (Crestwood, New York, 1976); first pub. as *La religion du peuple russe* (Lausanne, 1973).

72. Archief "Narodnicheskoe dvizhenie," no. 827/4, "Propaganda na Vyborgskoi storone" B-4.

73. "Obvinitel'nyi akt po delu revoliutsionnoi propagandy" (p. 3), in *Pravitel'-stvennyi Vestnik* (supplement to *Golos,* 1877), Archives of the Hoover Institution, Nikolaevskii Collection, file no. 115: "Iz bumag N. V. Chaikovskogo," item 27; *Protsess 193-kh* (Moscow, 1906) 11.

74. Tikhomirov, *Zagovorshchiki* 31. Soon thereafter, still both a revolutionary and a Christian, Zaozerskii (a.k.a. Petrov) was arrested. According to Tikhomirov, after being visited in prison by a highly placed Petersburg lady who specialized in restoring political prisoners to the faith, Zaozorskii confessed his sins and turned state's evidence. Released, he died at the age of twenty five in his native village in Tver. Ibid., 31–32; *Deiateli revoliutsionnogo dvizheniia v Rossii: Bio-bibliograficheskii slovar',* 2:2 (Moscow, 1930), col. 444.

75. Archief "Narodnicheskoe dvizhenie," no. 827/4, pp. B-3/4.

76. Tikhomirov, *Vospominaniia* 79. On Kropotkin's role in these events see Martin A. Miller, *Kropotkin* (Chicago, 1976), chap. 5. Kropotkin often used the name Borodin at this time.

77. *Protsess 193-kh* 22.

78. Charushin, *O dalekom proshlom* 215. *Malokul'turnye* is Charushin's term, though he may have been quoting Kropotkin without using quotation marks. (Kropotkin also warned against words offensive to the workers' feelings about the tsar.)

79. TsGAOR, f. 112, op. 1, d. 211, l. 72.

80. See the discussion in Pascal 20–22, where the translator uses the term "unclericalist" for the French *peu clérical* (p. 30 of the original). See also Lewin, "Popular Religion" 62, and I. S. Belliustin, *Description of the Clergy in Rural Russia: The Memoir of a Nineteenth-Century Parish Priest,* trans. Gregory L. Freeze (Ithaca, 1985), including Freeze's introduction.

81. "Obvinitel'nyi akt" (Nikolaevskii Collection, file no. 115) 3; *Protsess 193-kh* 11.

82. TsGAOR, f. 112, op. 1, d. 213, ll. 153–54. There is a slightly different version in the archive of the Third Section; *Rab. dvizh.,* 2:1, 448. For an account by an arrested worker who attended this meeting, see ibid., 470.

83. Archief "Narodnicheskoe dvizhenie," no. 827/4, p. B-3.

84. *Protsess 193-kh* 22.

85. Archief "Narodnicheskoe dvizehenie," no. 827/4, p. B-4.

86. Attempts in the 1870s to make social and emotional contact with workers via religion were not limited to those elite groups discussed in my paper. See, for example, Robert Geraci, "The Reformation of the Refined: The Pashkovists and Evangelical Religion in St. Petersburg, 1874–1890" (seminar paper, University of California, Berkeley, 1987).

87. *Rab. dvizh.,* 2:1, 424.

88. TsGAOR, f. 112, op. 1, d. 211, ll. 93–94; *Rab. dvizh.,* 2:1, 424; *Deiateli . . . ,* 2:3 (1931), cols. 865–866.

89. "K russkim rabochim," in E. A. Korol'chuk, *"Severnyi Soiuz Russkikh Rabochikh" i revoliutsionnoe rabochee dvizhenie 70-kh godov XIX v. v Peterburge* (Leningrad, 1946) 247–251 (quotations from p. 250); also in *Rab. dvizh.,* 2:2, 239–242.

90. See Gerald D. Surh, "Petersburg's First Mass Labor Organization: The Assembly of Russian Workers and Father Gapon," *Russian Review* 40, nos. 3–4

(1981): 436–441; Walter Sablinsky, *The Road to Bloody Sunday: Father Gapon and the St. Petersburg Massacre of 1905* (Princeton, 1976).

91. Suzanne Desan, "Redefining Revolutionary Liberty: The Rhetoric of Religious Revival during the French Revolution," *Journal of Modern History* 60, no. 1 (1988): 26–27.

92. The visit is described in *Zapiski* 8, no. 6 (1874): 31–32 ("Deistviia Kommisii"); all quotations are from p. 31.

Colportage and the Distribution of Holy Scripture in Late Imperial Russia

STEPHEN K. BATALDEN

The Holy Synod's publication in 1862 of a complete Russian translation of the New Testament—the first such authorized edition since the era of the Russian Bible Society—opened a new stage in the stormy controversy surrounding nineteenth-century Russian biblical translation. In the half century that followed, an important part of the renewed religious-political debate over Russian biblical translation focused on the issue of who had the right to disseminate Holy Scripture. In its *publication* of the Russian text, the Holy Synod maintained monopoly rights. Here there was a clear contrast with the days of Alexander I when the Russian Bible Society's own independent press, as opposed to that of the Synod, issued numerous printings of Scripture in modern languages of the empire. However, in the matter of *distribution* after 1862, the Holy Synod and its press maintained no such monopoly. Instead, what grew up alongside the Holy Synod's printing establishment was a multi-faceted system for mass dissemination of Scripture—a system known as colportage. This mass peddling of Scripture during the decades prior to World War I—a phenomenon that has been largely overlooked in Western treatments of Russian popular culture[1]—served as a powerful mechanism for the expansion of literacy and popular piety. It is the contention of this article that a well-orchestrated opposition was employed against Bible-peddling colporteurs and reflected fears at the highest levels of the church bureaucracy that popular religious piety was increasingly developing at the fringes of and, indeed, outside of established Orthodox state institutions.

Colportage was very much a part of earlier periods of Russian history and had its own pre-history in the oral transmission of spiritual values through wandering holy men (*stranniki* or *stranstvuiushchie*). The Russian Bible Society had developed its own empire-wide network of sales through branch societies; after closure of the earlier Bible Societies, moral and religious tracts continued to be peddled through Petersburg booksellers like K. I. Meier and G. B. Blister. But the specific use of colportage for Russian biblical distribution began with the founding of the Society for the Dissemination of Holy Scripture in Russia (*Obshchestvo dlia rasprostraneniia sv. pisaniia v Rossii*) in 1863, less than a year after publication of the Holy Synod's New Testament.[2]

The Society for the Dissemination of Holy Scripture in Russia, although it had eight founding members, was primarily the inspiration of Nikolai Astaf'ev, a Petersburg history instructor. Astaf'ev's own apartment became the first meeting place of the Society, and he served as the chronicler of the Society's history until his death in 1906, by which time the Society's activity had been largely subsumed within the St. Petersburg agency of the British and Foreign Bible Society (BFBS).[3] Shortly after its founding, the Society for the Dissemination of Holy Scripture in June 1863 sponsored the first planned journey of one of its members, the long-time Dutch resident of Petersburg, Otton Bogdanovich Forkhgamer (Forschammer?), for the purpose of marketing Holy Scripture at the Nizhnii Novgorod trade fair. In securing copies of the new Russian Scripture for the trade fair, Astaf'ev and the Society turned to an employee and future Petersburg agent of the BFBS, Adalbert Eck.[4] The BFBS had maintained a quiet presence in Petersburg after the closure of the Russian Bible Society in 1826, and it was eager to maintain its role as a provider of Scripture in modern languages within the Russian Empire.

The early alliance of the Society for the Dissemination of Holy Scripture in Russia with the Petersburg agency of the BFBS, despite later strains between the two, was crucial in several respects. The carefully managed and generously supported Petersburg agency of the BFBS was in a position to provide discounted copies of Holy Scripture to the fledgling Society, first at a twelve-and-a-half percent markdown, and ultimately at what came to be the standard twenty percent reduction. BFBS agencies also could provide Scripture in other ancient and modern languages. In the case of the Russian Scriptures, the initial pattern was that the Synodal Press printed and the BFBS Petersburg agency purchased and passed along discounted copies for Astaf'ev's Society. As conflicts later arose over the distribution of free copies by the Society for the Dissemination of Holy Scripture in Russia—a potential threat to the BFBS distribution network—each group, the BFBS agencies and the Society for the Dissemination of Holy Scripture, developed its own sales force of colporteurs. Astaf'ev's Society also came to purchase from the Synod Press directly at the twenty percent discounted price.[5]

By the end of the nineteenth century the efficient BFBS agents directed almost the entire empire-wide colportage operation out of central agencies and sub-depots that dotted the Russian landscape. More cautious than its counterpart Society for the Dissemination of Holy Scripture in dealing with the volatile sectarian issue, the BFBS agencies weathered the political storms of the 1880s and 1890s that so threatened Astaf'ev's Society. Yet, in the 1860s, under the more reform-minded administration of Tsar Alexander II, Astaf'ev's Society for the Distribution of Holy Scripture in Russia, which included well-placed Russian ministerial officials, offered a convenient front for BFBS agents who continued to pressure the Holy Synod for completion of the Russian Old Testament and for ever greater print runs of Russian and Slavonic Scripture. It was also during the reign of Alexander II that the Society for the Dissemination of Scripture managed, with the aid of the pious Russian rail minister, Aleksei Pavlovich Bobrinskoi (head of the *Ministerstvo putei soobshcheniia* from 1871 to 1874), to secure free rail passage for those who were peddling Scripture. In addition, containers of Scripture up to 500 pood (approximately 18,000 lbs.) were permitted to ride the rails without charge. Operating under imperial charter from 1871, Astaf'ev's Society distributed over 1.5 million volumes of Scripture in the first thirty years of its operation.[6]

Meanwhile, as Scripture became available in additional languages of the empire and as publication of Russian Scripture expanded to include the Synod's authorized Old Testament in 1876, the size and scope of BFBS operations, particularly its purchase and distribution at discount to individual colporteurs, greatly increased. In 1880, the first year for which published BFBS colportage statistics were broken down by individual colporteur, thirty-three colporteurs had sold approximately 47,000 volumes of Scripture.[7] Thirty-three years later, on the eve of World War I, the BFBS reported on the individual sales of its hundred and one colporteurs and hawkers—a three-hundred percent increase in the force. That colportage network accounted for sales of over 187,000 volumes of Scripture (whole Bibles or portions), a fourfold increase over 1880 colportage figures. Adding other retail sales to the colportage figures, BFBS agencies reported annual sales by 1913 of over 700,000 volumes of Scripture (in whole or in part).[8] Although comparable sales records are not available for the Holy Synod, its publication records would seem to bear out a total distribution figure, including BFBS agencies and Holy Synod operations, of close to one million copies annually by the twentieth century.[9] The cost of such Scripture varied widely from the ten-kopek copy of the Gospels and the most popular twenty-five-kopek "People's" New Testament, to well-bound Russian/Slavonic diglot editions of the Bible costing several rubles.[10]

Within this larger overall circulation picture, colportage activity can be examined for the period after 1880 by use of published records in the *Annual Reports* of the BFBS,[11] which assumed primary responsibility for Russian colportage in the last three decades before World War I. From 1880 to 1913, over 550 colporteurs and hawkers were employed in the Russian Empire by the BFBS, and were identified by name, region, length of service, and sales record. The terms "colporteur" and "hawker" denoted precise distinctions. Colporteurs (*doverennye knigonoshi*) received no fewer than forty rubles per month as a fixed salary. Hawkers (*vol'nye knigonoshi*) received no more than twenty-five rubles per month. Both colporteurs and hawkers received the same twenty percent commission on sales, but colporteurs alone received free rail ticketing and postage.[12] Colporteurs also could participate in a voluntary deposited savings and retirement plan offered by the BFBS.[13] While colporteurs were thus in a far better material position, they nevertheless were obliged to follow a routing predetermined by the respective BFBS agent or depot superintendent. Hawkers were free to follow their own schedule.

For the period 1880–1913, the BFBS agencies employed 386 colporteurs (roughly seventy percent) and 170 hawkers (thirty percent).[14] While the overwhelming majority involved in colportage were male, there were some notable female *knigonoshi* employed both by the Society for the Dissemination of Holy Scripture in Russia and by BFBS agencies and depots. From 1888 to 1911, the well-known BFBS hawker Mariia Andreevna peddled her Bibles through the streets of Moscow selling almost five thousand volumes a year during her prime in the 1890s.

Most *knigonoshi* worked for much shorter periods of time. Over half the hawkers (92) ended up working for less than one year. Most of the remaining hawkers (62) worked less than five years. Colporteurs tended to be employed for longer periods. Over fifteen percent (57) of the BFBS colporteurs between 1880 and 1913 served for periods in excess of ten years. The largest single group of colporteurs (178) held their posts between one and five years.

Sales varied widely by region. Throughout the thirty-three year period, 1880–1913, the main BFBS agency was in St. Petersburg. But, at differing times, the BFBS also had agencies in Odessa (to 1895), Ekaterinburg (1889–1918), and Tiflis. BFBS depots were located in Moscow and in another half dozen or more cities of the empire. While the greatest number of *knigonoshi* were employed within the St. Petersburg agency, relatively few actually worked in the imperial capital itself—no doubt a reflection of the ready availability of Scripture in local retail outlets. The St. Petersburg agency included colportage in Finland and the Baltic region, Poland, the Muscovite heartland, and, after the closure of the Odessan agency, Ukraine. Sales in the northern Caucasus and Don-Volga River valleys were considerable. The general growth of sales in Siberia after 1896 was also notable, even as far east as Iakutiia. The expansion of colportage into Siberia and the Far East was almost certainly tied to the extension of rail service with the building of the Trans-Siberian Railway. Sales in Siberia, although they amounted to over 70,000 volumes in 1913, were never on the scale of the European agencies.[15]

By language, the Russian texts were clearly the most popular, amounting in 1913 to over a third of the sales in European Russia, over half of sales in Siberia. Sales of Russian and diglot Russian/Slavonic texts taken together constituted over half of all circulation. Sales of Slavonic-only texts trailed well behind with less than ten percent of the total, followed in declining order by Finnish, German, Polish, Hebrew, Latvian, and Chuvash. By 1913, portions of the Bible were sold by BFBS agencies of the Russian Empire in over fifty languages.[16]

The average *knigonosha* tended to reflect the ethnic background of the region where he or she sold. However, there was clearly a disproportionate representation of German names within the colportage lists, especially among those with over ten years' service (e.g., Annwerdt, Bergmann, Garmasch, Lunge, Morgenfeld, Mueller, Pagge, and Streike). This Germanic complexion of the colportage lists reflected also the tendency of colporteurs and hawkers to be drawn more toward awakening evangelical Protestant, sectarian forms of religious piety wherein German settlers had a formative influence.

Such a predisposition toward sectarian piety—Bible reading, prayer meetings, hymn singing, and revivalist preaching—undoubtedly drew participants into the colportage movement. One such early sectarian leader, the grandfather of Pastor Zhidkov of today's Moscow Baptist Church, was identified by BFBS records as having served as a colporteur on the lower Volga for eight years before his proselytizing activity led BFBS officials to discharge him in 1885 under the pressure of mounting official scrutiny of colportage.[17] The official charges, not without foundation, were that colporteurs and hawkers were essentially peddling by day and proselytizing by night. Official fears were that colportage and the Bible reading practices that it encouraged were becoming a front for the conversion of mainstream Orthodox believers into sectarian Protestant groups.

By the 1890s, such official fears led to the organization by Konstantin Pobedonostsev, the Synodal Ober-Procurator, of a series of widely publicized

"Missionary Congresses" at which *knigonoshi* were vilified as dangerous enemies of Orthodoxy.[18] In this climate Astaf'ev's Society for the Dissemination of Holy Scripture in Russia was particularly threatened. The agencies and depots of the British and Foreign Bible Society survived the crisis, but only because of the vigorous efforts of William Nicolson, the BFBS agent in St. Petersburg, to disassociate the British and Foreign Bible Society from any proselytizing. The credibility of the BFBS in that regard, despite the excesses of some of its earlier Odessa agents, was rather high, reflecting the manner in which the BFBS Russian agencies were essentially run as commercial book businesses, much like the parent British agency itself.[19]

Despite the attempt to vilify colportage as an exclusively Protestant outgrowth, the colportage movement in Russia clearly appealed beyond sectarianism, for it was rooted in a popular piety that spread to traditional Orthodox peasants and workers alike. The nature of this popular piety was well represented in the only known memoir of a BFBS hawker, Ivan Ignat'evich Starinenko's "Notes of a Biblical *Knigonosha*," serialized in 1914 in the popular journal *Golos Minuvshago*.[20] BFBS *Annual Reports* document Starinenko's ten-year period as hawker out of the Moscow depot from 1887 to 1896.[21] With the exception of a brief period in 1889/1890 when he was persuaded by BFBS agent Nicolson to become a colporteur in Vladimir, Starinenko confined his activity to hawking in Moscow and its environs. A relatively successful hawker, he sold an average of over 2000 volumes annually, reaching sales of over 2400 volumes in 1892 and 1893. From 1891 to 1895, Starinenko's hawking also involved supplying Scripture in ancient and modern languages to students of the Moscow Theological Academy.[22]

According to Starinenko's "Notes," there were various responses to his attempts to sell biblical materials. Openly hostile were the monastic authorities, whom he portrayed as unwilling on occasion to let him enter to exhibit his books. Even at monasteries where he was permitted to sell, he reported "decidedly no success among the monastic brethren."[23] However, Starinenko noted the sharply contrasting reception he was accorded at women's convents. There he met with a warm welcome and was frequently invited to join the nuns for coffee. Starinenko thought the most hostile reception came from Roman Catholic priests (*ksendzy*). It is curious that he thought the hostility of Catholic clergy to dissemination of Scripture almost matched that of Old Believer priests. He found the Old Believer *bezpopovtsy* to be more open on that score.[24]

Going door to door, Starinenko found that the best purchasers were, predictably, Russian sectarians. He appreciated the respect they showed *knigo-*

noshi, even though he had some reservations about Protestant meetings he had attended—including one at which Dr. Baedeker, the renowned British evangelical, had preached.[25]

Despite the good sales and respect he received from sectarians, Starinenko felt "the warmest and most brotherly welcome" from plant factory workers. Such workers invited him to stay for dinner, gave him a bed for the night, and engaged him in "soul talk" (*pogovorit' po dusham*). Starinenko noted that "the religious question among workers was at the time a large and difficult question. Each of them had some more or less agonizing misapprehension over dogmas or rites."[26] He hesitated to respond to such questions, but advised them to seek counsel in the Scriptures. Invariably upon leaving such a workers' quarter he would be asked by someone to write to the person's family in an outlying village. Starinenko's memoir thus demonstrated, quite unintentionally, how the *knigonosha* was asked by Muscovite workers to serve as a connecting link to the religious and family traditions of a village left behind. The enduring strength of those traditions was to be measured by a popular piety that assured the successful sales of colporteurs and hawkers throughout the empire in the years before World War I.

The result of this interaction between *knigonoshi* and a popular mass audience was undoubtedly the advancement of social processes already well under way. For example, the colportage movement, by its sheer volume of sales, encouraged the growth of literacy in both urban and rural parts of the empire. While diglossia was perpetuated in the sale of Slavonic Scripture—and there were still those whose literacy developed out of contact with Slavonic texts—the mass purchase of the modern Russian Bible, or biblical text in a comparable national language, contributed to literacy, while posing new problems for the Orthodox church nurtured in the Slavonic liturgy.

Among such problems, one of the most nettlesome for church leaders was surely the growth of Protestant sectarianism. Russian sectarians were uniquely positioned to benefit from colportage. The mass distribution of Holy Scripture met an audience caught in the disruptive process of urbanization. For such an audience, the Protestant appeal to the authority of the printed word may well have been heightened in a political culture within which the ability to read was valued and the authority to publish was restricted. Sectarianism also provided a natural outlet for the pervasive anticlericalism of workers and peasants of the Russian Empire. Such anticlericalism was found even among *knigonoshi* themselves, at least judging from the language of Starinenko's memoir published eighteen years after he abandoned the sale of Bibles.

Finally, the anticlerical and sectarian overtones implicit in colportage could not help but draw the movement into the wider political arena. But it was a political arena in which the empire did not speak with one voice. On the one hand, generous subsidies were allowed to colporteurs in the form of free rail ticketing and discounted sales; on the other hand, at least until the edicts of toleration granted in 1905 to Protestants and Old Believers, the Holy Synod's Ober-Procuratorship under Konstantin Pobedonostsev sought to vilify and impede those who would hawk by day and proselytize by night. Facing such pressure and alleged Okhrana secret police oversight, Starinenko abandoned colportage in 1896.[27]

The ambivalence at the top over how to handle colportage and mass distribution of the Bible calls to mind the response a century earlier when Alexander I, envisioning a great Christian empire, welcomed agents of the BFBS in the founding of the Imperial Russian Bible Society. Later he dismantled that society in the face of its unprecedented success and mounting opposition. One key difference, however, at the opening of the twentieth century was that the imperial vision, if it can be called that, was far more secular in its chauvinist appeals to national glory. The colportage network, even though it ironically thrived in that more secular context, nevertheless constituted a curious and powerful witness to an alternative vision of religious awakening and popular piety.

Notes

Research for this article was made possible by grants from the International Research and Exchanges Board and from the Arizona State University College of Liberal Arts and Sciences Summer Research Awards Program.

1. In his excellent treatment of popular literacy in late imperial Russia, Jeffrey Brooks notes the widespread distribution of Scripture at the end of the nineteenth century, but does not treat the system of colportage. See *When Russia Learned to Read: Literacy and Popular Literature, 1861–1917* (Princeton, 1985). Ben Eklof's study, *Russian Peasant Schools: Officialdom, Village Culture, and Popular Pedagogy, 1861–1914* (Berkeley, Los Angeles, and London, 1986), addresses the official church school curriculum, which involved Bible instruction in Slavonic, but he does not consider such "extracurricular" subjects as popular Bible reading and distribution.

2. For the finest account of the Society for the Dissemination of Holy Scripture in Russia, including treatment of earlier Petersburg devotional booksellers, see N. A. Astaf'ev, *Obshchestvo dlia rasprostraneniia sv. pisaniia v Rossii (1863–1893): Ocherk ego proiskhozhdeniia i deiatel'nosti* (St. Petersburg, 1895); idem, *Opyt istorii Biblii v Rossii v sviazi s prosveshcheniem i nravami* (St. Petersburg, 1892). The Society also published its own annual *Otchet*.

3. Astaf'ev was professor of history at the St. Petersburg Historico-Philological Institute. For a brief review of his career and publications, see the entry under "Astaf'ev, Nikolai Aleksandrovich," in the Brokgauz-Efron *Entsiklopedicheskii Slovar'* (St. Petersburg, 1890), 1:333–334.

4. Astaf'ev, *Obshchestvo* 5. Adalbert Eck served as a paid agent of the BFBS in Petersburg from 1860 to 1869. Eck's surviving correspondence is preserved in the BFBS Archive now housed at the Cambridge University Library.

5. Ibid., 256. For an example of the friction that occasionally arose between the Society for the Dissemination of Holy Scripture and BFBS agents in Petersburg, see the BFBS Archive, Cambridge University Library, "BFBS Agents Book No. 125: Russia," letter of William Nicolson to Rev. C. Jackson (St. Petersburg, 20 November 1869 O.S.) 15–16.

6. Astaf'ev, *Obshchestvo* 258. There is a rich secondary literature on the involvement of isolated high-placed tsarist officials with Russian sectarian movements. For a recent account of Bobrinskoi's involvement with Pashkovite and Radstock circles in St. Petersburg, see Hans Brandenburg, *The Meek and the Mighty: The Emergence of the Evangelical Movement in Russia* (New York, 1977) 106–121.

7. In its annual reports from 1881, BFBS published colportage figures for each of its agencies abroad, as well as the names of all colporteurs and hawkers. The figures for 1880 are in *The Seventy-Seventh Report* (London, 1881), Appendix A, 245–246.

8. See BFBS, *The Hundred and Tenth Report* (London, 1914), "Supplementary Tables of Circulation," 11–12.

9. Circulation figures for the Press of the Holy Synod include by the eve of World War I substantial numbers of copies given routinely in connection with graduation from church schools and gymnasia. In principle it is possible to reconstruct Holy Synod Press circulation from the archival records of the press. For 1913, for example, these records demonstrate that while the BFBS was the largest single purchaser of Scripture from the Holy Synod Press, there was substantial circulation outside of the BFBS network. See *Rossiiskii Gosudarstvennyi Istoricheskii Arkhiv* [formerly TsGIAL], *f.* 800, *op.* 1, *d.* 583, "Godovyi otchet za 1913," l. 28.

10. Price figures are noted in the annual reports of the BFBS and are marked in archive copies at the Cambridge University Libary.

11. See note 7 above. Based upon those annual colportage statistics, I have compiled a cumulative sales record by name for each of the colporteurs and hawkers listed between 1881 (circulation year 1880) and 1914 (circulation year 1913).

12. Regarding wages and commissions, see the discussion in I. I. Starinin, "Zapiski bibleiskago knigonoshi [Notes of a Bible Hawker]," *Golos Minuvshago,* 1914, no. 12, p. 182.

13. The BFBS established an "Employees' Savings Fund" in December 1880, the terms of which are set forth in "Appendix A" of the its *Seventy-Seventh Report* (London, 1881) 236–237. The BFBS continued to pay pensions to widows of its former employees well into the Soviet period.

14. The statistics offered here are based upon my tabulation of yearly BFBS colportage statistics. The yearly statistics have been converted to individual files by name. Analysis of the name files allows for information over time regarding, for

example, the total number of colporteurs and hawkers, their average length of service, sales record by name and region, description of the sales force by gender and ethnicity. See also note 11.

15. For Siberian sales in 1913, see BFBS, *The Hundred and Tenth Report,* 11.

16. Ibid., 12.

17. The elder Zhidkov is listed in BFBS published colportage statistics under the name "Schidkoff." For the ongoing controversy surrounding proselytizing and the case of Zhidkov in particular, see the unpublished "Minutes of the Committee" for the 1880s and 1890s, BFBS Archive, Cambridge University Library.

18. For a discussion of these congresses from the point of view of the affected colporteurs, see I. I. Starinin, "Zapiski bibleiskago knigonoshi" 180–181. Starinin recounts an instance of overt hostility directed at himself from the ensuing wave of public vilification.

19. Much of the credit for the management of BFBS Russian operations belongs to William Nicolson, the BFBS Petersburg agent from 1869 to 1897. Nicolson commanded the Russian language and handled both distribution and translation work in Russia for the parent BFBS. There is to date no published biographical treatment of Nicolson, but his letters and reports are heavily represented in the BFBS Archive, Cambridge University Library. See, in particular, "BFBS Agents Books: Russia, 4 vols. (nos. 125, 137, 142, and 149), 1869–74."

20. See note 12. The "Notes" were published under the new name of I. I. Starinin given to Starinenko following his arrest by the Okhrana and a two-year period of surveillance in Moscow following his years as hawker. These circumstances are stated openly in the "Notes," 1914, no. 12, p. 195. The "Notes" were serialized in 1914 in nos. 10, 11, and 12 of *Golos Minuvshago.*

21. The cumulative ten-year record is based upon my tabulation of yearly colportage statistics from BFBS *Reports.* See note 14.

22. Starinin, "Zapiski bibleiskago knigonoshi," no. 12, p. 179.

23. Ibid., 170.

24. Ibid., 171–173.

25. Ibid. For his account of Dr. Baedeker's preaching, see the same article, *Golos Minuvshago,* 1914, no. 10, p. 173.

26. Starinin, "Zapiski bibleiskago knigonoshi," no. 12, p. 175.

27. References to Okhrana involvement and political pressure are noted in ibid., 180, 195.

PART II

Ideological Paradigms and Cultural Mythology

Paradise Now

Heaven-on-Earth and the Russian Orthodox Church

STEPHEN L. BAEHR

In a famous section of the Russian Primary Chronicle, the emissaries of Prince Vladimir reported to him about their experience in the Greek Orthodox church: "We did not know whether we were in heaven or on earth because there is no such sight and no such beauty on earth and we do not know how to tell about it. We only know that God dwells there with men."[1] As I shall argue in the present article, this perceived blur between heaven and earth was not original to Vladimir's representatives or chroniclers but borrowed some basic theological assumptions of Orthodoxy and of Christianity in general. After discussing these assumptions and their reflections in the Russian Primary Chronicle, I will then examine the reappearance of this motif of the church as heaven-on-earth during the debate about secularization at the end of the seventeenth century, when many Byzantine ideas and images reappeared in Russian literature and culture.

Imagery of heaven-on-earth and the earthly paradise was central to the theology of the Orthodox church and frequently symbolized the church itself. More than the Western church, the Eastern church, from the teachings of its fathers to its liturgies, stressed man's abilities to experience there a foretaste of the joys that await the believer in heaven.[2] As Saint Irenaeus wrote, equating the church with the garden of Eden: "The church is planted as a paradise in this world."[3] From Origen's third-century equation of baptism with the entry into paradise[4] to Eusebius's fourth-century *Ecclesiastical History* (where the church is referred to as the earthly likeness of heaven),[5] Saint Ephraem's fourth-century *Hymns on Paradise* (where it is said that "the congregation of the holy [i.e., the church] is similar to paradise"),[6] and Saint Germanus's eighth-century writings (where the church is explicitly called "the heavens on earth, where God, who is higher than the heavens, lives"),[7] the idea is repeated that the church is a terrestrial paradise—an earthly image of the Kingdom of God in heaven.[8] Indeed, imagery of heaven-on-earth was sufficiently widespread among the Eastern church fathers that the monk who wrote the section of the Russian Primary Chronicle quoted at the beginning of this paper needed to have read only a relatively small number of patristic works (or excerpts) in order to have "reinvented" this image; theological sophistication was by no means a prerequisite for such borrowing.

Under the influence of the Eastern church fathers, Orthodox theology stressed that through the church paradise is accessible to the believer not only after death but in *this* life as well.[9] As Saint Germanus wrote in an eighth-century hymn still used today in the Othodox Christmas vespers:

> Come let us rejoice in the Lord and narrate this present mystery. The wall of separation has been dissolved, the flaming sword has turned back and the Cherubim have moved away from the tree of life; and *I partake of the delight of Paradise* from which I had been ejected because of disobedience. . . .
>
> Today the age-old bond of Adam's condemnation has been untied. *Paradise has been opened to us, the serpent has been crushed* . . . . May then all creation dance and exult; for Christ has come to recall it and to save our souls.[10]

It is probable that the influence of the church fathers on the image of heaven-on-earth in the Russian Chronicle came, not only directly but also indirectly, through the intermediary of such prayers in the Orthodox liturgy.[11]

Orthodoxy viewed the church as an image not only of past but also of future perfection. As John Meyendorff has noted, Byzantine theological thought was often characterized by the idea of "realized eschatology"—the assumption that the transfiguration and deification of man is accessible *now*.[12] Indeed, both the Orthodox imagery of heaven-on-earth and the imagery used by Vladimir's representatives to describe their experience of God dwelling in the church with men reflect the clear influence of Revelation 21:2–3, depicting a "new Jerusalem, coming down from God out of heaven" where "the tabernacle of God is with men."[13] The Chronicle image of heaven-on-earth can thus be seen as an anticipation of the ultimate uniting of heaven and earth at the end of time, reflecting the general Christian idea of the church as a "provisional paradise."[14] As Saint John of Damascus wrote in his *Second Treatise in the Defense of Icons,* "The worship which we offer up is an image of things to come, . . . [of] the celestial, immaterial Jerusalem, which is not made by the hand of man."[15] The Damascene's language (using phrases like "an *image* of things to come" and "not made by the hand of man") reflects the essential role of the icon in the Orthodox conception of heaven-on-earth, presenting the church as an earthly image of the heavenly world, which is to reward true believers in the future.[16] Even today in Orthodox prayers, the church is called "the *image* of the house of God" and "the house comparable to [i.e., in the "likeness" of] the heavens."[17]

The symbolism of heaven-on-earth in the Chronicle and in Orthodoxy in general reflects the same theology that underlies the architecture of the Orthodox dome church, projecting the Biblical conception of heaven and earth as a single world.[18] This conception had already been expressed in the architectural symbolism of the earthly Christian church (e.g., at Rome and Ravenna), when the ceiling was referred to as *coelum* ["sky" or "heaven"];[19] the equivalent term—*nebo*—was used for the ceiling decorations of some Russian churches as well.[20] In the dome church (like Constantinople's Hagia Sophia, presumably visited by Vladimir's emissaries), the cupola symbolized the descent of heaven to earth, which it emphasized through mosaic or fresco representations of Christ as ruler of the universe (Pantocrator) or of Christ in judgment. In architecture, as in the Chronicle, such symbolism continued the idea of the descent of the holy spirit to earth, found in both the Old and New Testaments.[21]

During the second half of the seventeenth century, imagery of the church as heaven-on-earth and an earthly paradise reappeared in Russian literature and culture in connection with the renewed Byzantinization of Russian religion advocated by Patriarch Nikon and his espousal of the doctrine of the ninth-century Byzantine patriarch Photius that patriarch and tsar were equals in ruling Orthodox society but that in cases of conflict the patriarch was superior to the tsar.[22] During this period, the church was often referred to as a "spiritual paradise" (*rai myslennyi* or *rai myslei*), as is reflected, for example, in Simeon Polotskii's preface to his *Vertograd mnogotsvetnyi* (*The Garden of Many Flowers,* 1678–1680), where he wrote regarding his authorial aim: "I have tried to add this many-flowered garden of mine to the house of God, *the holy Eastern church, [which is] like a spiritual Eden [edemu myslennomu], a spiritual paradise [raiu dukhovnomu], a heavenly garden,* for the glory of the creator of all things and for the spiritual use of all who are trying to live devoutly."[23]

During the seventeenth century, the image of the spiritual paradise was used by supporters of both patriarch and tsar to propagandize their claims as to who should be the supreme authority in the church. Supporters of Patriarch Nikon, for example, in 1659 published a book entitled *Rai myslennyi* ("The Spiritual Paradise") claiming the ultimate power in the church for the patriarch, who in the typical form of Nikon's reign is compared with Christ, "the great pastor of all."[24]

In opposition to this "Nikonist" vision of the spiritual paradise is Simeon Polotskii's *Privetstvo 10* ("Greeting 10") from his 1678 *Rifmologion*:

> God ordered the cherub to guard the earthly paradise so that no one would dare to enter it, and entrusted a sword to him, this servant of his. The sword was fiery and turned very fast so that the Garden of Eden would remain intact, and the tree of life was entrusted to him so that it would remain untouched. You, o tsar, the true servant of God, are like the cherub, although you are corporeal. To you is entrusted by the living God *our spiritual paradise—the holy church. In it there flowers the tree of life. . . . You are the chosen cherub of this paradise,* and because of this a sword has been given to you by the Lord so that you will be its keeper and protector.[25]

In this poem, written after the victory of the secular "sword" over the sacred, the spiritual paradise (the church) has been entrusted to the tsar for protection from its enemies—the enemies of God—just as the garden of Eden is protected by a cherub.[26]

As a result of the ultimate victory of secular over sacred, there began a widespread appropriation of church concepts, vocabulary, and symbols for redefining the new secular state and its tsar. This general movement of images and ideas from church to state reflects the importance in Russia during the era of secularization of what Ernst Kantorowicz has called "political theology": the transfer of concepts, themes, imagery, stylistic techniques, and terminology from church to state.[27] Among the images transferred from church to state was that of heaven-on-earth, reflecting the fact that after Nikon (in Pierre Pascal's words) "Russia no longer had a church: It had a religion of state." As Pascal has noted, "from there to state religion required but one step."[28]

Some early examples of such wholesale transplantation from sacred to secular and from theology to ideology are reflected in Simon Ushakov's 1668 painting *Nasazhdenie dreva gosudarstva rossiiskogo* (*The Planting of the Tree of the Russian State*). Called an "icon" by Ushakov himself, this painting, which was commissioned by Tsar Aleksei not long after the church council of 1666 had demoted Nikon to a simple monk, depicted Ivan I (the first of the "gatherers of the Russian lands" into the Muscovite state) and Metropolitan Peter (whose shrine made Moscow the spiritual center of Russia) planting together in the Moscow Kremlin a tree with branches extending toward heaven; in the center of the tree is a reproduction of the Vladimir Mother-of-God icon (whose transfer from Vladimir to Moscow symbolized the rise of Muscovite political power), and above the tree is Christ in heaven. The tree grows through the center of the Kremlin's Cathedral of the Assumption (the coronation cathedral of the Russian tsars).

The focus of this painting on the planting of a "tree of *state*" is significant since it recalls the type of imagery used to describe the church the church by Saint Irenaeus and others. Just as God "planted a garden eastward in Eden" (Gen. 2:8), so, as we have seen, was planting sometimes used in the writings of the church fathers to depict the founding of the church, the earthly image or type of the heavenly paradise. Indeed, Ushakov places Christ and the Mother of God in approximately the same positions in his "tree of state" that they would occupy in the typical Orthodox dome church: Christ is at the top center of the painting looking down on earth as He does from the central cupola of the church; the Mother of God is in the middle of the painting, as she would be on a sanctuary wall—a symbolic intercessor between heaven and earth. In effect, the symbolism of the dome church (portraying heaven as descending to earth) is transferred to the new secular state, which, like the church, becomes "a paradise in this world"—an "image" of heaven on earth.

Political theology influenced late seventeenth- and eighteenth-century literary imagery as well—especially literary commonplaces, which, as I have argued elsewhere, often arose not arbitrarily and not simply as borrowings from other literatures but at least partially in response to the cultural concerns of the period.[29] Among the commonplaces that became popular in the panegyric literature of this period was the image of Russia as heaven-on-earth, which was often used to propagandize the new secular state and its tsar. In transferring to the state a central image that had been used for the church, Russian poets continued a tendency begun in Byzantium to depict the state as a "perfected theocracy" in the image and likeness of heaven.[30] Thus, when like other seventeenth-century poets Simeon Polotskii wrote, "I dare to call Russia heaven,"[31] he was reflecting the general tendency of transforming important imagery from sacred to secular; their influence, among others, could still be felt in the mid-eighteenth century when Lomonosov wrote regarding Russia, "I see heaven on earth."[32] By encouraging poets to use such sacred rhetoric to praise the secular state and to depict a new earthly paradise in Russia, the government encouraged the use (and abuse) of religious pattern for the propaganda of its leaders and their goals. The blur perceived by Vladimir's emissaries between heaven and earth, between paradise and the here-and-now, thus became part of Russian *secular* culture. Under the influence of political theology, "realized eschatology"—the doctrine of "last things first"—moved from church to state but remained a central principle in Russian culture.

Notes

Parts of this paper appeared in a different version in my book *The Paradise Myth in Eighteenth-Century Russia: Patterns of Perfection in Early Secular Russian Literature and Culture* (Stanford, 1991). They are printed here by permission of Stanford University Press.

1. *Povest' vremennykh let,* section for 6495 (987 A.D.), in L. A. Dmitrieva and D. S. Likhachev, eds., *Izbornik* (Moscow, 1969) 68.

2. Gerhard Ladner, *The Idea of Reform* (Cambridge, Mass., 1959) 63, 82, and chap. 3 passim.

3. Irenaeus, *Adversus haereses* 5.20.2, quoted in Ladner 70.

4. Origen, *Selecta in Genesim,* quoted in Ladner 70.

5. Eusebius, *Ecclesiastical History,* trans. Roy J. Deferrari (Washington, 1955) 2:267 (chap. 10, sec. 4).

6. Ephraem, "Sixth Hymn on Paradise" 8ff., quoted in Ladner 70n.

7. Quoted in Leonid Ouspensky, *Theology of the Icon* (Crestwood, N.Y., 1978) 28. Ouspensky also mentions Saint Simeon of Thessalonica's description of the consecrated church as "a mysterious heaven."

8. Ouspensky, chap. 1; Ladner, chap. 3; Sévérien Salaville, *An Introduction to the Study of Eastern Liturgies,* ed. John M. T. Barton (London, 1938) 123ff.

9. See Ladner 69.

10. Quoted in Ladner 291. Italics are mine. The attribution of this prayer to Germanus, patriarch of Constantinople, is tentative. Similar images exist in the liturgy for the Easter season. Ladner has observed (p. 292) that this Orthodox emphasis on man's return to paradise is largely absent from the Latin liturgy.

11. The Primary Chronicle was not compiled until at least 125 years after the Christianization of Russia. So Orthodox ideas and imagery had ample time to influence the Chronicle.

12. John Meyendorff, *Byzantine Theology* (New York, 1974) 214–215. As evidence for this point, Meyendorff (p. 219) cites the Eucharistic canon of the liturgy of Saint John Chrysostom, which portrays the Second Coming of Christ as already realized and shows time as transcended.

13. Other probable Biblical influences on the image of heaven-on-earth include Ezekiel 47:1–12 and 2 Corinthians 12:2–4. In Ezekiel, the temple is depicted as being like Eden, with four streams flowing from it in the four directions of the compass. See Joseph Duncan, *Milton's Earthly Paradise* (Minneapolis, 1972) 14. Second Corinthians also depicts a blur between heaven and earth, describing the experiences of a man (presumably Saint Paul himself) who is brought to the "third heaven," which is explicitly identified with the heavenly paradise. Like Vladimir's emissaries, Saint Paul does not know how to describe this experience in human words. Indeed, both Saint Paul's experience in the "third heaven" and the experience of Vladimir's representatives in the church are cloaked in unclarity, emphasizing the epistemological problem of describing a heavenly or a religious experience and stressing the fact that when speaking of the noumenal there can be no true "knowledge" (emphasized in both by the phrase "do not know"). Both the Bible and the Chronicle empha-

size this unclarity in parallel syntax with an "either . . . or" particle: "*ashche v tele, ne vem: ashche li krome tela ne vem*"; "I ne svemy, na nebe *li* esmy byli, *li* na zemli . . . ." On the likely influence of Saint Paul on Orthodox theology, see Sergius Bulgakov, "Le ciel sur la terre" (*Una Sancta* [1927] 42–63), which hints at, but does not explicitly state, a similar connection.

14. On the idea of the church as a "provisional paradise" in Christian theology, see George H. Williams, *Wilderness and Paradise in Christian Thought* (New York, 1962) 27ff. As Leonid Ouspensky has observed, "The new Israel—the church— . . . brings the presence and the promise of the Kingdom of God to the fallen world." See *Theology of the Icon* 22.

15. Saint John of Damascus, *Second Treatise in the Defense of Holy Icons,* chap. 23, quoted in Ouspensky 34.

16. Cf. the idea in Ephesians 1:22–23 of the earthly church as the image of the heavenly church and of the body of Christ, where there occurs a union of "all in all." On the "iconic" structure of paradise in Russian culture of the seventeenth and eighteenth centuries, see my article "Regaining Paradise: The 'Political Icon' in Seventeenth- and Eighteenth-Century Russia," *Russian History* 11 (Summer/Fall 1984): 148–164, and my book *The Paradise Myth in Eighteenth-Century Russia,* chap. 2.

17. Quotation is from Ouspensky 22.

18. On the idea of heaven and earth as a single world, see, for example, Ulrich Simon, *Heaven in the Christian Tradition* (London, 1958) 126; and Bulgakov, "Le ciel sur la terre," passim. Bulgakov argues (on the basis of Hebrews 12:22–24) that in the church "there is neither distance between that which is terrestrial and that which is celestial, nor intervening wall (*mur mitoyen*) between this world and the other, nor separation between the living and the deceased; all are together, all are one, heaven on earth and earth sanctified" (57).

19. See Simon 15.

20. James H. Billington mentions such decorations in seventeenth- and eighteenth-century Russian wooden architecture in his article "Keeping the Faith in the USSR after a Thousand Years," *Smithsonian* 20 (April 1989): 142.

21. In Christianity this descent of God's presence is, of course, most notably represented in the very person of Christ and is celebrated as well in the festival of Pentecost, which marks the descent of the Holy Spirit onto the apostles. Cf. also the Manna of the Old Testament and what Jewish theologians have described as "Shekinah"—the descent of God's presence to dwell among men. (On Shekinah, see, for example, Simon 81.)

22. On the renewed Byzantinization of Russia during the reign of Tsar Aleksei Mikhailovich, see V. M. Zhivov and B. A. Uspenskii, "Tsar' i bog: Semioticheskie aspekty sakralizatsii monarkha v Rossii," in B. A. Uspenskii, ed., *Iazyki kul'tury i problemy perevodimosti* (Moscow, 1987) 93. On the Byzantine influences on Nikon, see George Vernadsky, *A History of Russia* (New York, 1973) 136–137.

23. Simeon Polotskii, *Izbrannye sochineniia,* ed. I. P. Eremin (Moscow and Leningrad: Izdatel'stvo Akademii nauk SSSR, 1953) 206. Cf. the Orthodox liturgy for Good Friday when the church is called a "spiritual paradise." See Ladner (292 and 292n) who relates this image to Saint Irenaeus's lines quoted at the beginning of this article.

24. A. M. Panchenko, *Russkaia stikhotvornaia kul'tura XVII veka* (Leningrad, 1973) 106.

25. Polotskii, *Izbrannye sochineniia* 144. Italics are mine.

26. The "tree of life," which Polotskii in this work depicts as flowering in the *church*, may also have been at the "root" of Ushakov's *Tree of the Russian State*, which was painted some ten years earlier.

27. On political theology, see Ernst Kantorowicz, *The King's Two Bodies* (Princeton, 1957) 15–16, passim. Kantorowicz defines the term "political theology" as the expression of political ideas through a "general framework of liturgical language and theological thought"—a frequent structuring device for political ideas in Western Europe since the Middle Ages (87).

28. Pierre Pascal, *Avvakum et les débuts du Raskol* (Paris, 1938) 574, as quoted in Richard Pipes, *Russia under the Old Regime* (New York, 1974) 239. Cf. Pipes's statement (p. 245) that in destroying the independence of the church during the eighteenth century, the state developed a secular ideology which "sought to realize on this earth the paradise that Christianity had promised to provide in the next," and, as I have been arguing, in this world as well.

29. For a more specific argument, see chapter 2 of my book *The Paradise Myth*.

30. The term "perfected theocracy" comes from T. G. Masaryk, *The Spirit of Russia*, trans. Eden and Cedar Paul (1919; rpt., New York, 1968) 1:41. On this tendency of Russia to see itself as a realized utopia, see also Tibor Szamuely, *The Russian Tradition*, ed., Robert Conquest (New York, 1974) 61. From the time of the Josephites in the late fifteenth and early sixteenth centuries, there appeared, as Serge Bolshakoff has observed, a tendency to describe everything Russian as "sacred and perfect, needing no change or improvement." See Bolshakoff, *Russian Nonconformity* (Philadelphia, 1950) 52. Much Byzantine political thought was premised on the equivalent theocratic assumption that the emperor was the "architect of [this] Kingdom of God on earth." See Sergius Bulgakov, *The Orthodox Church* (New York, 1935) 183.

31. From archival sources quoted in O. Pokotilova, "Predshestvenniki Lomonosova v russkoi poezii XVII-go i nachala XVIII-go stoletiia v Rossii," in V. V. Sipovskii, ed., *Lomonosov: Sbornik statei* (St. Petersburg, 1911) 73.

32. M. V. Lomonosov, *Polnoe sobranie sochinenii*, 10 vols. (Moscow and Leningrad, 1950–1959) 8:758. Pokotilova cites as an example of the seventeenth-century influence on this poem the lines of Polotskii describing the "bright stars of the Russian heaven" (*svetlye zvezdy rossiiskogo neba*).

Tolstoy and Jesus

HUGH McLEAN

A memorable passage in Maksim Gor'kii's reminiscences of Tolstoy contains the following iconoclastic observation:

> О Буддизме и о Христе он говорит всегда сентиментально; о Христе особенно плохо — ни энтузиазма, ни пафоса нет в словах его и не единой искры сердечного огня. Думаю, что он считает Христа наивным, достойным сожаления и хотя иногда любуется им, но — едва ли любит. И как будто опасается: приди Христос в русскую деревню — его девки засмеют![1]

To pious Tolstoyans, and even to many less than pious admirers of Tolstoy the Tolstoyan, such a statement must have seemed shocking, cynical, a vicious calumny. After all, Tolstoy could be said to have devoted to Jesus most of the last thirty years of his life, from the completion of *Anna Karenina* until his death, i.e., to the formulation and propagation of what he considered Jesus's authentic teachings. Tolstoy had proclaimed himself the spokesman of a new, true, liberated "Jesus" Christianity, a Christianity based on what Jesus actually said, not on myths about his life, death, and supposed supernatural deeds. It was to be a myth-free Christianity, cleansed at last from the encrusted errors, falsehoods, and distortions of the ages, beginning with those perpetrated by that arch-deceiver and sell-out, Saint Paul. Surely there must have been passion to sustain such a long and arduous enterprise of demolition, purgation, and reconstruction: the many volumes of treatises and tracts, the vast correspondence, the nurturing and encouragement of disciples from all over the world. Was it all only a facade, a guilt-inspired mask behind which lurked that unreconstructed, primeval pagan sorcerer whom Gor'kii saw sitting by the sea at Gaspra, seeming to command the waves that lapped at his feet and of an age with the rocks that surrounded him? What did Tolstoy really feel about Jesus?

We all remember Dostoevskii's famous statement that if forced to choose between Christ and the truth, he would unhesitatingly choose Christ.[2] Would Tolstoy do the same? It seems unlikely. For it was truth which Tolstoy had melodramatically proclaimed, at the end of "Sevastopol in May" (1855), that he loved with "all the power of his soul" (*vsemi silami dushi*).[3] If Jesus and the truth may be incompatible polarities, as Dostoevskii seems to imply, then Tolstoy's soul would have to opt for the truth, and with all its power. This supposition is confirmed by a more explicit statement, written in 1859 to summarize the results of an earlier religious quest:

> я нашел, что есть бессмертие, что есть любовь и что жить надо для другого для того, чтобы быть счастливым вечно. Эти открытия удивили меня сходством с христианской религией, и вместо того, чтобы открывать сам, стал искать их в Евангелии, но нашел мало. Я не нашел ни Бога, ни Искупителя, ни таинств; а искал всеми, всеми силами души, и плакал, и мучился, и ничего не желал, кроме истины.[4]

However, perhaps in the long run Jesus and the truth would prove not wholly incompatible, and perhaps something salvageable of God and the truth, if not the Redeemer and mysteries, could be found in the Gospels, if sought with sufficient diligence. Some twenty years later Tolstoy would undertake a systematic search for them. His search is called *Soedinenie i perevod chetyrekh Evangelii.*

To translate and harmonize the Gospels, and then to compose a synthetic "Gospel" of one's own, is necessarily to engage oneself with the biography and to some extent, at least, the personality of Jesus. What does Tolstoy's biography of Jesus reveal about his feelings toward his subject? Did Tolstoy's stupendous talent as a writer of realistic fiction enable him, in his life of Jesus, to bring his hero to life in a second *Resurrection,* to make of him a vivid personality worthy to stand immortally alongside such other great seekers of truth as Pierre Bezukhov, Andrei Bolkonskii, Konstantin Levin, and Dmitrii Nekhliudov?

I

The nineteenth century was an age when secular biographies of Jesus were in vogue. David Friedrich Strauss's sensational *Leben Jesu* had first appeared in 1835, and its Gallic twin, the equally sensational and infinitely more readable *Vie de Jésus* by Ernest Renan, had appeared in 1863. The techniques of *Quellenforschung* and comparative philology were being applied to the Scriptures in a less inhibited way than ever before, and it now seemed to many that these sacred texts, far from having been dictated verbatim by the Holy Spirit, were just as much a product of their place and time as other human artifacts. Moreover, they were just as much a series of literary constructs, made by a variety of persons at different times and with various motives, bearing at least as ambiguous a relation to the reality on which they drew as other human literary products—even novels written in the age of realism.

In many respects Tolstoy's *Soedinenie i perevod* would seem to belong to the same tradition, to respond to the same impulses as those that impelled Strauss and Renan. Like them, Tolstoy was a rationalist. He had already denounced at length the dogmatic theology of the Orthodox church, and with a vehemence that might have qualified him for admission, had he lived long enough, to Iaroslavskii's League of the Militant Godless. He too had long sought an earth-bound religion freed from myth and mystery; as early as 1855 he contemplated dedicating himself to the foundation of such a new faith:

> основание новой религии соответствующей развитию человечества, религии Христа, но очищенной от веры и таинственности, религии практической, не обещающей будущее блаженство, но дающей блаженство на земле.[5]

Specifically, Tolstoy did not believe, and at least since childhood had never believed, that Jesus was the Son of God in any sense different from that according to which we are all God's children. He did not believe that Jesus was the Jewish Messiah, and he considered naïve and foolish all attempts to identify episodes from his life as fulfillments of Old Testament Messianic prophecies. Finally, he did not believe in any of the supernatural events recounted in the Gospels, including the resurrection. In all this Tolstoy was quite in tandem with Strauss and Renan. Yet in fact Tolstoy's attitude toward those rationalist exegetes was quite as hostile as his attitude toward the Metropolitan Makarii, author of the Orthodox theology textbook Tolstoy had so savagely reprobated.

Barbs against Renan are scattered profusely through Tolstoy's writings, beginning as early as the drafts for *War and Peace*, where Renan is linked—in the plural—not only with Strauss, but with other liberal thinkers of the nineteenth century who, Tolstoy thought, were unable to reconcile their belief in causal determinism with their need to assert individual moral responsibility.[6] Here Strauss and Renan are included among leading nineteenth-century "positivist" thinkers: Karl Vogt (1817–1895), George Henry Lewes (1817–1878), John Stuart Mill (1806–1873), and Maximilien Paul Emile Littré (1801–1881). In *Anna Karenina* Renan and Strauss, again in the plural ("the Renans and Strausses"), are linked with the Russian painter Aleksandr Ivanov (to whom we shall return) as exponents of an undesirable realistic-historical attitude toward Christ;[7] and in the drafts to the novel Anna herself is said to have lost her faith partly as a result of reading Renan.[8] But in *V chem moia vera* (1883) Tolstoy states more clearly the essence of his objection to Strauss and Renan. In the first place, their attitude toward Jesus is condescending and sentimental. Jesus and his doctrine, say the Strausses and Renans, are an appealing product of the largely oral culture of some primitive inhabitants of Galilee in the first century A.D., but "for us, with our culture, they are only the sweet dream 'du charmant docteur,' as Renan says."[9] But most of all, the Strausses, Renans, and all "freethinking interpreters" as a class have absolutely no interest in putting Jesus's ideas into practice and using them to change *their* world, the world of the supposed lofty culture of nineteenth-century Europe, "with its designs of prisons for solitary confinement, alcazars, factories, magazines, brothels, and parliaments. And since Christ's teachings reject all this life, from Christ's teachings nothing is taken except words."[10]

Despite the seeming parallelism, there is thus a radical difference of mentality between Tolstoy and the "freethinking exegetes." Tolstoy is an activist, a moralist, a social reformer; in the Gospel teachings he finds ideas applicable today, ideas capable of changing the world. If these teachings, at last freed from ecclesiastical doubletalk and made the central focus of religious life, were adopted widely and put into practice, the world would really change, as if miraculously: there would be no armies, no wars, no police, no law courts, no governments, no private property, no rich, no poor, and perhaps even no disorder in sexual relations, as people strove more and more to attain the ideals of chastity articulated in the Afterword to "The Kreutzer Sonata." Tolstoy seems to have really believed—or perhaps only desperately wished to believe—in the attainability of this utopia. At any rate, it was the goal that gave meaning to his life. As he wrote (in somewhat imperfect English) to his English disciple John Coleman Kenworthy, "I choosed [*sic*] this vocation . . . because it is the sole work in this our life, that is worth to work for."[11]

The Strausses and the Renans, however, had no such goal and made no such commitment. They were, Tolstoy asserted, passive in relation to social evil, not interested in social or moral reform. Instead, just for fun, as it were, they set themselves the puzzle of the quest for the historical Jesus, the real man who actually lived and set forth all those teachings Tolstoy admired so much. This historical quest not only did not interest Tolstoy, he considered it evil, since it distracted people from what was really important. Essentially it was only an intellectual game, a pastime, like the chess problems Sergei Koznyshev in *Anna Karenina* works at with as much—or as little—passion as he does at the problems of Russian statecraft he so pompously pretends to solve.

As early as 1857 Tolstoy had noted this tendency of people to distract themselves from the teachings of Jesus by concerning themselves with insignificant details of his biography: "Дали людям учение счастья, а они спорят о том, в каком году, в каком месте и кто дал им это учение."[12] Renan's great discovery, Tolstoy comments ironically, was that there a was a man called Jesus who sweated and attended to other natural functions.[13] But who cares? Even the supposed resurrection is for Tolstoy a biographical detail of little interest: "Какой интерес знать, что Христос ходил на двор? Какое мне дело, что он воскрес? Воскрес — ну и Господь с ним! Для меня важен вопрос, что мне делать, как мне жить."[14]

Furthermore, the liberal historians, according to Tolstoy, do not even understand the basic historical problems they set out to solve. Jesus Christ was remembered and admired and indeed deified not because he was born and lived in a particular place at a particular time, but because he preached ideas, moral ideas, that people recognized as profoundly right. But the historians only concern themselves with trivia:

> Задача, которую им [т.е., либеральным историкам, H. McL.] предстоит решить, состоит в следующем: 1800 лет тому назад явился какой-то нищий и что-то поговорил. Его высекли и повесили, и все про него забыли, как были забыты миллионы таких же случаев, и лет 200 мир ничего не слыхал про него. Но оказывается, что кто-то запомнил то, что говорил, рассказал другому, третьему. Дальше, больше, и вот миллиарды людей умных и глупых, ученых и безграмотных не могут отделаться от мысли, что этот, только этот человек был Бог. Как объяснить это удивительное явление? Церковники говорят, что это произошло оттого, что Иисус точно был Бог. И тогда всё понятно. Но, если он не был Бог, то как объяснить, что именно этот простой человек признан всеми Богом?
>
> И ученые этой школы старательно разыскивают все подробности об условиях жизни этого человека, не замечая того, что, сколько бы ни отыскали подробностей (в действительности же ровно ничего, кроме того, что у Иосифа Флавия и в Евангелиях, не отыскали), если бы они даже восстановили всю жизнь Иисуса до мельчайших подробностей и узнали, когда что ел и где ночевал Иисус, вопрос о том, почему он, именно он имел такое влияние на людей, остался бы все-таки без ответа. Ответ не в том, в какой среде родился Иисус, кто его воспитывал и т. п., и еще менее в том, что делалось в Риме и что народ был склонен к суеверию и т. п., а только в том, что проповедовал этот человек такое особенное, что заставило людей выделить его из всех других и признать его Богом тогда и теперь.[15]

II

Tolstoy's differences from "the Strausses and Renans" thus seem reasonably clear and consistent. The liberal exegetes are sentimental; they are morally inert; and their obsession with unimportant biographical details is distracting. However, as noted above, in *Anna Karenina* Tolstoy links these misguided foreign biographers of Jesus with the Russian painter Aleksandr Ivanov. "It's all the Ivanov-Strauss-Renan attitude toward Christ and religious painting," says Vronskii's friend Golenishchev, whom Vronskii and Anna encounter by chance in Italy. Golenishchev then pronounces certain strictures against the painting *Christ Before Pilate* by the artist Mikhailov, a character in the novel, in which Jesus is represented as ostentatiously Jewish, "with all the realism of that school."

> Я не понимаю, как они могут так грубо ошибаться. Христос уже имеет свое определенное воплощение в искусстве великих стариков. Стало быть, если они хотят изображать не Бога, а революционера или мудреца, то пусть из истории берут Сократа, Франклина, Шарлоту Корде, но только не Христа. Они берут то самое лицо, которое нельзя брать для искусства.[16]

In an argument with Mikhailov, Golenishchev, perhaps to spare his opponent's feelings, attributes these faults to the real Ivanov, not to Mikhailov himself, but the point is not lost on his interlocutor:

> «Он у вас человекобог, а не Богочеловек . . . . Но возьмем хоть Иванова. Я полагаю, что если Христос сведен на степень исторического лица, то лучше было бы Иванову и избрать другую историческую тему, свежую, нетронутую».
>
> «Но если это величайшая тема, которая представляется искусству?»
>
> «Если поискать, то найдутся другие. Но дело в том, что искусство не терпит спора и рассуждений. А при картине Иванова для верующего и для неверующего является вопрос: Бог это или не Бог? и разрушает единство впечатления».[17]

One would hesitate to ascribe Golenishchev's views to Tolstoy, especially since Golenishchev, who has adopted a "lofty, intellectually liberal line" since graduating from the aristocratic Corps of Pages, is clearly presented as rather stuffy and pretentious, incapable of understanding the genuine creativity of Mikhailov, with whom Tolstoy obviously sympathizes. But in fact we can find statements by Tolstoy, speaking *in propria persona* about Aleksandr Ivanov, very similar to those of Golenishchev about both Mikhailov and Ivanov. For instance:

Картина Иванова [the famous «Явление Христа народу»] возбудит
в народе только удивление перед техническим мастерством, но не возбудит никакого ни поэтического, ни религиозного чувства .... [18]

Написать явление Христа народу — искусство, и написать голых де-
вок — тоже искусство.[19]

Одними явление Христа народу считается верхом искусства, другими голые купальщицы считаются верхом искусства .... [20]

And Golenishchev's argument that art should avoid controversial subjects
is repeated almost verbatim in a letter by Tolstoy to Pavel Tretiakov written
in 1890:

Но изображать, как историческое лицо, то лицо, которое признавалось
веками и признается теперь миллионами людей Богом, неудобно: неудобно потому, что такое изображение вызывает спор. А спор нару-
шает художественное впечатление.[21]

When we look at the Ivanov painting, however, surely it is not the "realism" of the Christ figure that strikes us. Jesus appears in the distance,
pointed to with excitement by John the Baptist, alone, majestic, mysterious,
and certainly in no way ostentatiously Jewish. Conceivably one might make
such a statement about two of the neophytes, perhaps a father and son, who
are just emerging from the water; but perhaps what really bothers Tolstoy
about this celebrated painting is the artist's obvious interest in naked flesh
("golye kupal'shchitsy"). At any rate, in his own mind Tolstoy locked
Ivanov irrevocably into an association with Strauss and Renan as a classic
exemplar of a wrong, controversy-arousing treatment of the Jesus subject.[22]
    However, the arguments Tolstoy adduces against Ivanov—excessive real-
ism, controversiality—he does not seem to apply to other Russian painters
of the time, especially those with whom he enjoyed personal relations.
Notable among these are Ivan Kramskoi, with whom Tolstoy made friends
in 1873 while Kramskoi's great portrait of him was being painted, and
Nikolai Ge, who became an ardent disciple and close friend in the 1880s and
1890s. Although depictions of Jesus by both these artists seem markedly and
"realistically" to stress the human qualities of Jesus the man, Tolstoy nevertheless lavishes on them high praise. Kramskoi's *Khristos v pustyne,* a picture
showing a very human, very troubled man in deep meditation, "is the best
Christ I know," Tolstoy wrote to Tretiakov.[23] And with reference to the
paintings of Ge, Tolstoy developed a whole theory of "Jesus art."
    According to Tolstoy, attempts had been made by various painters to

escape the inevitable dilemma in representing Jesus: is he God or a historical person? Some chose one course, some another, still others tried to avoid all dispute by simply taking the subject as one familiar to all and caring only for beauty. But the problem remained unsolved. Next came attempts both to demote Christ the God from heaven and Christ the historical personage from his pedestal by treating him as an ordinary person engaged in the activities of ordinary life, but giving this ordinary life a religious, even a somewhat mystical aura. Such was Ge's painting *Miloserdie*, painted in 1879–1880 and subsequently destroyed by the artist. But then, in *Christ Before Pilate*, a painting on the very same subject used by Mikhailov in *Anna Karenina*, Ge found the solution, and Tolstoy is ecstatic in his praise. Note also how he allows his own novelistic talent to expand upon the figure of Pontius Pilate:

> И вот Ге взял самый простой и теперь понятный, после того как он его взял, мотив: Христос и его учение не на одних словах, а на словах, и на деле в столкновении с учением [*sic* (учеными? H. McL.)] мира, т.е. тот мотив, к[оторый] составлял тогда и теперь составляет главное значение явления Христа, и значение не спорное, а такое, с к[оторым] не могут не быть согласны и церковники, признавшие его Богом, и историки, признающие его важным лицом в истории, и христиане, признавшие главным в нем практическое учение.
>
> На картине изображен с совершенной исторической верностью тот момент, когда Христа водили, мучили, били, таскали из одной кутузки в другую, от одного начальства к другому и привели к губернатору, добрейшему малому, к[оторому] дела нет ни до Хр[иста], ни до евр[еев], но еще менее до какой-то истины, о кот[орой] ему, знакомому со всеми учеными и философами Рима, толкует этот оборванец; ему дело только до высшего начальства, чтоб не ошибиться перед ним. Христос видит, что перед ним заблудший человек, заплывший жиром, но он не решается отвергнуть его по одному виду и потому начинает высказывать ему сущность своего учения. Но губернатору не до этого, он говорит: Какая такая истина? и уходит. И Хр[истос] смотрит с грустью на этого непронизываемого человека.
>
> Таково было положение тогда, таково положение тысячи, миллионы раз повторяется везде, всегда между учением истины и представителями сего мира. И это выражено на картине. И это верно исторически, и верно современно, и потому хватает за сердце всякого, того, у кого есть сердце. — Ну вот, такое-то отношение к христианству и составляет эпоху в искусстве, п[отому] ч[то] такого рода картин может быть бездна. И будет.[24]

Tolstoy also had high praise for Ge's *Povinen smerti* (1892) and *Raspiatie* (1894), the latter certainly as "realistic" as could be imagined, concluding:

"Лет через 100 иностранцы попадут, наконец, на ту простую, ясную и гениальную точку зрения, на которой стоял Ге . . . . и мы все будем восхищаться."[25]

III

The question now arises, to what extent was Tolstoy able to apply these principles to his own representation of Jesus in the *Soedinenie i perevod chetyrekh Evangelii?* Certainly one principle was scuttled from the start: the avoidance of controversy. Art should not arouse *spor i rassuzhdeniia,* but Tolstoy's book on the Gospels is one angry *spor* from beginning to end with virtually all previous translators and interpreters of the Bible, Orthodox, Catholic, Protestant, and secular. Perhaps Tolstoy could except his Gospel book from the "no controversy" rule on the grounds that it is not intended as "art." But certainly the other prescriptions are applied with a vengeance. What is important in the Gospels are the teachings of Jesus. They are all that matters, and the Gospels have therefore been rigorously squeezed and pruned and pressed so as to eliminate from them any biographical details that might lessen the impact of the teachings. Nevertheless, the Gospels are, after all, presented in the form of a narrative biography of Jesus, however sketchy and incomplete, and in his version Tolstoy did not feel justified in abandoning this format altogether, thus making of the Gospels simply a treatise on morals, an extended version, so to speak, of the Sermon on the Mount. Some remnants are therefore left in which Tolstoy had an opportunity to apply his own novelistic talent to the life of Christ.

Literary recreation of Jesus's life and personality was, of course, far from being Tolstoy's primary objective; nor was his modus operandi with the Gospels anything like that of a trained philologist, although he makes a great show of his newly acquired Greek. Tolstoy's mind is anything but open as he approaches his task. He *starts* with what seems to him absolute, incontrovertible knowledge of what Jesus said and even what he meant. Even that formulation perhaps should be restated: not what Jesus actually said or meant, but what he ought to have said and meant. Thus Jesus *per se* is not even very important; what is important are the ideas Tolstoy has extracted and edited from the words attributed to him. (Although Tolstoy does not explicitly make the point, he may also have recognized that the name of Jesus attached to these ideas gave them an impact they might otherwise lack.) In the Gospels this distilled essence, the nucleus of pure, original Christianity, the undefiled teachings of Jesus, has been surrounded by a large mass of extraneous matter—myth, legend, unnecessary biographical detail, all haphazardly put together by those four rather incompetent evangelists. Subsequently, even this already half buried and disfigured nucleus of truth was further distorted and traduced by people who claimed to be Jesus's disciples, especially Saint Paul. So Tolstoy's undertaking with the Gospels is not only to "harmonize" them into one book, but in the process to press out of them everything that does not belong there, i.e., everything that does not enhance and elucidate the core teachings of Jesus. At one point Tolstoy admits that the "personality of Jesus" has no interest for him.[26] Nevertheless, some biographical details do remain, and from these we can perhaps form some idea of Tolstoy's image of Jesus the man.

Like Strauss and Renan, Tolstoy must of course reject or rationalize the birth legends. No manger, no shepherds, no star, no Magi. Of the virgin birth there is left only the germ of what might have beome another adultery novel: "Была девица Мария. Девица эта забеременела неизвестно от кого. Обрученный с нею муж пожалел ее и, скрывая ее срам, принял ее. От нее-то и неизвестного отца родился мальчик. Мальчика назвали Иисус."[27] The whole purpose of the virgin birth story was to cover up the shameful fact of Jesus's illegitimacy.

Tolstoy subsequently uses this interpretation for another purpose, even though it involves him in a psychological implausibility he surely would never had allowed himself as a novelist. Though he had credited Joseph with considerable magnanimity in accepting and marrying a fiancée pregnant by another man, Tolstoy by implication transforms Joseph into a mean and vindictive adoptive father, one who never allowed the boy Jesus to forget the disgrace of his origin. In consequence, Jesus became accustomed to thinking of God as his only father; hence the appellation "Son of God," which has caused so much confusion and error.

This explanation emerges from Tolstoy's treatment of the one episode from Jesus's childhood the Gospels provide, the story of his tarrying in the Temple in Jerusalem at the age of twelve to converse with the "doctors," after his parents had left for home. When they returned, worried and agitated, two days later and found him there, he replied, in what seems a quite typical style of rather obnoxious, pre-adolescent sassiness, "How is it that ye sought me? Wist ye not that I must be about my Father's business?" (Luke 2:49). According to Tolstoy, who makes no real attempt to recapture the emotional dynamics of this scene, Jesus says this because he was keenly aware of the fact that he had no earthly father. In Tolstoy's interpretation, the boy Jesus was "заброшенный ребенок, видевший вокруг детей, у ко-

торых у каждого есть плотский отец и не знавший себе отца плотского
признал отцом своим — начало всего — Бога."[28] According to Tolstoy,
Jesus was doing no more than following Malachi 2:10: "Have we not all one
father? Hath not one God created us?"

Later hints of discord between Jesus and his immediate family (e.g., John
2:4 or Matthew 12:46–50), which Tolstoy the novelist would surely have
exploited, are passed over in silence. But Christ's general admonition (Matthew 10:37) that religious commitment must take precedence over family
attachments is duly incorporated into Tolstoy's own Gospel, perhaps with
some awareness of its relevance in his own case:

> Учение мое как огонь запалит мир . . . сделается раздор в каждом
> доме. Отец с сыном, мать с дочерью, и семейные сделаются ненавист-
> никами того, кто поймет мое учение. И будут убивать их. Потому что
> тот, кто поймет мое учение, для того не будет ничего значить ни отец,
> ни мать, ни жена, ни дети, ни все его имущество. Кому отец или мать
> дороже моего учения, тот не понял учения.[29]

Lacking material from which to construct a *Bildungsroman* of Jesus's
formative years (had he cared to write one), Tolstoy must move directly, as
his sources do, to Christ's ministry. The actual ministry, however, is pre-
ceded by two symbolic events of preparation: the baptism by Saint John and
the temptation in the wilderness. Of the first Tolstoy says almost nothing,
since he disapproves of rituals in general, and the occasion is further spoiled
in his eyes by the supernatural accompaniment, the voice from heaven: "событие неестественное и непонятное. Стихи эти ничего не прибавляют
к учению, но напротив, затемняют его."[30]

During the forty days of fasting in the wilderness, Jesus of course underwent the three temptations of Satan, so powerfully invoked in *Brat'ia Karamazovy*. Tolstoy draws none of Dostoevskii's lofty theological conclusions
(which hardly stand up anyway, since elsewhere in the Gospels Jesus, far
from repudiating them, clearly does invoke "miracle, mystery, and authority"). For Tolstoy this is simply a period of prayerful, spiritual preparation
for a difficult task, especially an effort to make spirit master over flesh. The
figure of Satan is nothing more than a personification of Jesus's own doubts
and hesitations, the voice in him of corporeality. For this Tolstoy adduces
an interesting novelistic argument: if Satan had been a real presence, the
evangelists would naturally have described him, and yet of such description
there is not a word. Therefore, Satan is not a speaking character, only a
personification. Tolstoy also discards the official church interpretation, that
Jesus rejected the temptation to perform unnecessary or unseemly miracles.

In reality, the temptation was only the age-old conflict, which Tolstoy knew so well, between the spirit and the flesh. After such a long bout of fasting, Jesus was at last forced to recognize that although the spirit should rule, the flesh also has its legitimate demands, and these should be accepted, for they too come from God. By eliminating all the supernatural content of the story, Tolstoy also avoids issues that have troubled some ecclesiastical commentators, such as whether it was proper for Jesus to travel in the company of Satan, if that is what he did, to the pinnacle of the temple or the top of the mountain, perhaps magically, rather like Faust with Mephistopheles.

The marriage at Cana can serve as a perfect example of Tolstoy's principles of exclusion. Here is an anecdote, a biographical detail that serves no instructive purpose and is unseemly in addition. Out with it!

> Событие это в Кане Галилейской, описанное так подробно, есть одно из самых поучительных мест в Евангелиях, поучительных по отношению к тому, как вредно принимать всю букву так называемого канонического Евангелия за что-то священное. Событие в Кане Галилейской не представляет ничего ни замечательного, ни в каком бы то ни было отношении значительного. Если чудо, то оно бессмысленно, если фокус, то оно оскорбительно, если же это бытовая картина, то она не нужна.[31]

The episode where Jesus forcibly drives the money-changers from the temple might have caused Tolstoy considerable difficulty, one would have thought, since Jesus's behavior in this instance seems quite violent and disruptive, not at all in accordance with the principles of *neprotivlenie zlu*. Without dealing with the basic implausibility of the episode (the Gospels say nothing of what would surely have been resistance by the tradespeople so abruptly expelled from their stations, nor of the likely intervention by the Temple authorities), Tolstoy gets around the problem by interpreting the "temple" as symbolic of the whole world. Jesus is therefore symbolically attacking all those, specifically the proponents of official Judaism, who concern themselves with technicalities of ritual and worship rather than with matters of the spirit. From this vantage point Tolstoy can then ridicule the ecclesiastical exegetes who assign Jesus the role of fulfilling "police responsibilities with regard to the cleanliness of the temple."[32] In connection with the money-changers episode, however, Tolstoy does evince considerable irritation with Jesus's boast, "Destroy this temple, and in three days I will raise it up" (John 2:19), which the evangelist then proceeds to interpret as a veiled reference to his prospective resurrection in the body. Tolstoy angrily exclaims:

"Хорошо, он воскрес и предсказывал свою смерть. Неужели нельзя было предсказать яснее и, главное, уместнее? . . . Ведь стоит только снять
очки церковные, чтобы видеть, что это не разговор, а бред сумас-
шедших."[33]

Usually, however, when he encounters passages that seem to reflect unfa-
vorably on Jesus, Tolstoy blames the evangelists for misreporting or simply
omits the passage altogether. Tolstoy says not a word, for example, about
the cursing of the fig tree (Matthew 21:18–21), where Jesus, in a spirit of
what seems to be mere petulant annoyance, surely abused his supernatural
powers; and Jesus's upbraiding of whole cities—Chorazin, Bethsaida, and
Capernaum—for failing to respond to his message (Matthew 11:20–24), is
attributed by Tolstoy to a flaw in the Gospel text. Nevertheless, in this
case some of Tolstoy's irritation still seems to spill over onto Jesus himself:
"Стихи эти . . . не имеют не только ничего учительного, но даже никакого смысла. За что он упрекает города? Если они не поверили его
чудесам, то значит незачем было делать чудеса или мало и плохо он их
делал."[34]

Jesus's healing miracles Tolstoy interprets either as purely metaphorical,
as in the case of the blind man whose sight was restored after washing in the
pool of Siloam (John 9:1–41), or as a psychological rather than a physical
event, as in the case of an impotent man healed at the pool of Bethesda
(John 5:1–9). But some details of Jesus's medical practice, such as making
a salve by spitting on the ground and mixing the saliva with clay (John 9:6),
Tolstoy finds repulsive and omits as too realistic—"stupid, useless details."[35]

The greatest of the miracles, the raising of Lazarus, simply irritates
Tolstoy. He makes nothing of the strong emotions attributed to Jesus in this
episode (John 11:33–35), perhaps the strongest anywhere before the passion.
And the miracle itself displeases him:

> Скажем, что воскресение есть проявление могущества Бога. Если так,
> то вместе с могуществом мы невольно думаем и о мудрости его и не
> можем не спросить себя: зачем он воскресил Лазаря, а не Ивана и
> Петра; а зачем он воскресил Лазаря, а не сделал того, чтобы у Лазаря
> выросли крылья или две головы? И мы должны признаться, что в
> этом действии Бога вместе с могуществом не выразилась его му-
> дрость.[36]

In fact the whole story must be rejected:

> Принять эту главу и подобные ей могли только люди церковные, те,
> которые никогда и не понимали учения Христа. Для всех же прочих,

кто ищет учения, не может быть и вопроса о том, что значит рассказ
о воскресении — он ничего не значит, как и все чудеса. Это надо
очистить и отбросить . . . .[37]

But on the whole Tolstoy avoids even implied criticism of Jesus. When the
Jews beg him at last to state clearly and unambiguously whether he is indeed
the Christ, the Messiah (John 10:24), and Jesus again turns the question
aside, Tolstoy at first seems indignant:

Если он был Бог, то как же мог всемогущий, вездесущий, всеблагий
Бог не знать всех тех страданий, которые примут и те евреи, и мы с
миллиардом людей, мучимые сомнениями и лишенные спасения . . . .
И ему стоило только сказать: да, я Бог, и евреи и мы были бы бла-
женны.[38]

And if he was only a man, Tolstoy goes on, even then he could have resolved
people's doubts by a clear answer: "No, I am not the Messiah." Tolstoy
justifies Jesus's "cruelty," however, on the grounds that, deeply believing in
the truth of his teachings, he really did consider himself at one with God
and therefore in some sense "God's anointed." But he knew that he was not
the Messiah-king the Jews expected, and therefore he answered as fully and
truthfully as he could, though metaphorically, with his image of the shep-
herd and the sheepfold.

Unlike Renan, Tolstoy tries to justify Jesus's evasiveness and hair-splitting
disputatiousness in his arguments with the Pharisees and Sadducees. For
example, with the prescription "Render therefore unto Caesar the things
which are Caesar's and unto God the things which are God's" (Matthew
22:21), Jesus successfully avoids the trap, on the one hand, of making an
explicitly seditious statement about Roman rule in Palestine, and, on the
other, of offending orthodox Jewish beliefs by giving civic responsibilities
precedence over religious ones. However, the statement is of no help in
drawing a clear boundary between the two or adjudicating cases where the
two may be in conflict. For his part, Tolstoy acknowledges no civic responsibilities at all. Therefore, despite the clearly parallel structure of the
sentence, implying that both God and "Caesar" have legitimate claims on
us, he interprets the first part as a denial by Jesus of any obligation at all
toward "Caesar." Jesus simply examines the coin proffered him. Is that
Caesar's image on it? Very well, if the coin is his, give it back to him. "Render unto Caesar" in no way means that a believing Christian should pay
taxes: "потому что не из чего будет платить, да и незачем платить чело-
веку, не признающему судов, государств и народностей."[39] However, ear-

lier Tolstoy did admit that it might be permissible to pay taxes in order not to tempt the tax collectors to commit acts of violence, provided one states at the time that taxes cannot be obligatory or necessary for people living according to the will of God.[40]

Tolstoy does ascribe to Jesus some psychological tensions; to follow Christian teachings is not easy, even for their author himself. First, Jesus is beset all his life, according to Tolstoy, by the temptation of cowardice, the "renunciation of the teaching." The cowardice appears in some of his evasive answers to the Pharisees, when he "tries to contradict them as little as possible," and in his withdrawing or hiding when pursued.[41] Jesus's most dramatic—and successful—struggle with cowardice, Tolstoy believes, occurs when he is confronted in the Temple by pagan Greeks who are attracted by his teaching (John 12:20). At that moment he has to decide whether to turn away these Gentiles as uncircumcised and unworthy. He would thus remain, as it were, a critic of Judaism from within the fold. The alternative is to embrace the Greeks and thus alienate himself from Judaism altogether. However, to repudiate Judaism was to place himself in danger:

> Язычники, по понятиям иудеев, — это отверженцы, безбожники, подлежащие избиению, и вдруг он оказывается за одно с язычниками. То он, как будто, исправлял закон иудейский, был пророком иудейским, и вдруг одним сближением с язычниками оказывается явно, что он, по понятиям иудеев — язычник. А если он язычник, то он должен погибнуть и нет ему спасения.[42]

This was the decisive moment. Though Tolstoy points it out only retrospectively, not when discussing the passage itself, he ascribes to Jesus at this point a tremor of fear. To identify with pagan Greeks meant to condemn himself to death at the hands of the Jews. But Jesus summons his resources of courage and resolves to proceed. As the omniscient Tolstoy reads his thoughts:

> И вот это-то сближение с язычниками вызывает в нем решительные слова, выражающие непреклонность его убеждения. Язычник — ну язычник, говорит он себе. Я то, что есмь. И вы, как хотите, понимайте меня. Я погибну, но зерно должно погибнуть, чтобы дать плод.[43]

That moment of truth, according to Tolstoy, was a bold public acknowledgment of what had been implicit all along, that the teachings of Jesus were in no way a fulfillment or reform of Judaism, but a complete break with it.

Tolstoy's treatment of the passion story is reasonably straightforward, though with certain crucial emendations where his beliefs differ sharply from those of the churches. As before, he restrains his novelistic talent and makes no effort to expand the account of Jesus's last days. For instance, he does not elaborate on Christ's relationship with the disciple he particularly loved (John 13:23), nor does he elucidate or make more plausible the motives for Judas's betrayal. A major innovation is Tolstoy's insistence that in saying to Judas, "That thou doest, do quickly," Jesus was not at all referring to the betrayal itself; rather Jesus was warning Judas, by signals comprehensible only to the two of them, to leave in haste lest he be attacked by the other disciples. Jesus has just identified Judas as the future traitor by giving him the sop (John 13:26). If the other disciples had understood the message, they would have killed him:

> Иисусу незачем советовать предать его, но Иисус несколько раз уже намекал ученикам о том, что между ними есть предатель, и он видел, что Иуда тревожится и хочет бежать. Иуде нельзя не бояться. Если бы ученики узнали это, — не говоря про других, Симон Петр наверное бы задушил его. Теперь Иисус указал Иуду и указал Симону Петру. Если бы Иуда не ушел, его бы убили, и потому Иисус говорит ему: беги скорее, но говорит так, чтобы никто, кроме Иуды не мог понять.[44]

In warning Judas, Jesus was simply following his fundamental principle of returning good for evil.

The major psychological drama Tolstoy attributes to Jesus as hero arises from a second temptation, the temptation to use violence in self-defence. In Tolstoy's version, there was a moment during the Last Supper when Jesus, foreseeing the consequences of Judas's betrayal and still surrounded by loyal disciples, seriously considered defending himself by force. First he sends his disciples out to buy swords, but then calls them back when it is discovered that they had two swords on hand (Luke 22:36, 38). As Tolstoy argues:

> Сколько ни бились толкователи над этим местом, нет никакой воз-можности придать ему другого значения, как то, что Иисус собирается защищаться. Перед этим он говорит ученикам о том, что они отрекут-ся от него, т. е. не защитят его, убегут от него. Потом он напоминает им то время, когда не было еще на них уголовного обвинения. Тогда он говорил: не нужно было бороться. Вы тогда были без сумы и ни в чем не нуждались, но теперь пришло время борьбы, надо запасаться пищей и ножами, чтобы защищаться.[45]

This is the most critical moment in Jesus's life, when he is sorely tempted to resist evil by evil. But again he summons his inner resources. He goes out into the Garden of Gethsemane and prays, and he overcomes the temptation. When he prays, "O my Father, if it be possible, let this cup pass from me," he is referring, according to Tolstoy, not at all to the crucifixion, but to the temptation to take up the sword in self-defense:

> Какая же это чаша? По всем церковным толкованиям это — страдания и смерть. Но почему это значит страдания и смерть — не объяснено и не может быть объяснено. Сказано, что Иисус мучился и тревожился, но не сказано о том, что он ожидал смерти. И потом говорится, что он просил Отца о том, чтобы эта чаша отошла от него. Какая же это чаша? Очевидно, чаша *peraismou, искушения*, так как я понимаю это место.[46]

The disciples, however, overcome by sleep during this night of prayer, remain unaware of Jesus's moral struggle and its outcome. When the mob comes to arrest Jesus, therefore, Peter is still imbued with the violent spirit of the night before and cuts off Malchus's ear (John 18:10). Now he receives Jesus's admonition, "Put up again thy sword into his place: for all they that take the sword shall perish with the sword" (Matthew 26:52).

Tolstoy's account of the final tragedy follows closely the Gospel narrative; circumstantial and vivid as it is, it needs no elaboration or commentary. Like Strauss and Renan, Tolstoy ends the essential biography of Jesus with his death on the cross. He appends a brief excursus on the resurrection and Jesus's posthumous appearances, arguing as expected that these legends are unseemly and worthless. Miracle stories do attract some believers, but repel others; and in the long run the underlying truth is contaminated by lies. The first legends give birth to others, and those to still more, until the core truths of Jesus become more and more entangled in falsehood:

> Легенда содействует распространению учения, но легенда есть ложь, а учение — истина. И потому учение передается уже не во всей чистоте истины, но в смешении с ложью. Ложь вызывает ложь для своего подтверждения. Новые ложные легенды о чудесах рассказываются для подтверждения первой лживой легенды. Являются легенды о чудесах последователей Христа и о чудесах, предшествовавших ему: его зачатия, рождения, всей его жизни, и учение все перемешается с ложью. Все изложение его жизни и учения покрывается грубым слоем краски чудесного, затемняющего учение.[47]

Tolstoy's effort has thus been to peel off this encrustation of legend and myth and restore the teachings of Jesus to their supposed original purity. After this process of purification, as we have seen, not much is left of the "hero," the personality of Jesus. As John Coleman Kenworthy puts it, the only hero to be found in the writings of the older Tolstoy is "the Jesus of *The Gospel in Brief*," and "even that Jesus is, with Tolstoy, little more than a body of divinest doctrine."[48] But perhaps enough remains for us to draw some conclusions about Tolstoy's attitude toward his hero. Was Gor'kii right?

Not entirely. To be sure there was undoubtedly something cerebral and forced about Tolstoy's allegiance to Christian doctrine; it did not really come from the heart. Tolstoy was anything but a hero-worshipper or a myth-maker; as Isaiah Berlin has so vividly pointed out, the critical, destructive side of his intellect was infinitely more powerful than the positive, constructive side. Tolstoy could not abide idols on pedestals, and he tried to shoot down some of the loftiest literary ones, including Dante, Shakespeare, and Goethe. But Jesus is an exception. In the Gospels, despite their unsatisfactory literary qualities, there is a nucleus of ideas that struck Tolstoy as startlingly right and as applicable here and now. Though his personality is not important, the man who articulated those ideas must have had admirable qualities, and he did: born with common human weaknesses of flesh and spirit, he struggled with those weaknesses and at the most critical moments overcame them. Even Tolstoy could ask for no more. Whether Tolstoy felt *love* for him is, of course, another matter, and Gor'kii may be right: the emotion conveyed is not love, but rather admiration combined with pity, the two sometimes intersected by feelings of irritation at the contamination with myth and magic for which Jesus himself may have borne some share of responsibility.[49]

Gor'kii's remark about the village girls, however, suggests another dimension to Tolstoy's feelings about Jesus, a suspicion that Jesus was not irreproachably masculine. Tolstoy did in fact level a parallel accusation, as we have seen, against Renan. Did he secretly have the same suspicion about Jesus? Certainly nothing in Tolstoy's "Christian" writings could lead one to this conclusion. However, one could still perhaps argue the point by inference. Non-resistance to evil, *neprotivlenie zlu*, which Tolstoy makes the fundamental principle of Christian morality, is, after all, a principle of passivity, of physical submission, of refusal to defend oneself physically. Freudians would call it masochistic. It runs against the grain of ideals of masculinity found in most cultures. Though Tolstoy officially espoused this ideal and preached it and at least consciously believed it, there may well have been a part of him that never fell in line with it, a part of him that wished Jesus and the disciples *had* defended themselves with the sword. Perhaps this Tolstoy longed for a more forceful, vigorous, red-blooded, *macho* hero than the pale Jesus of the Gospels, even the Gospel according to Saint Leo. It was this Tolstoy who, in his most officially Christian period, used to sneak upstairs to celebrate with his talent a non-Christian hero of a very different kind, Khadzhi Murat.

Notes

1. Cited from *L. N. Tolstoi v vospominaniiakh sovremennikov* 2 (Moscow, 1978) 474.

2. Dostoevskii to N. D. Fon-Vizina, February 1854. F. M. Dostoevskii, *Pis'ma*, ed. A. S. Dolinin (Moscow and Leningrad, 1928) 1:142.

3. L. N. Tolstoi, *Polnoe sobranie sochinenii*, ed. V. G. Chertkov et al. (Moscow and Leningrad 1928–1958) 4:59. Hereafter *PSS*, with volume and page number only.

4. Tolstoy to A. A. Tolstaia, April 1859. *PSS* 60:293.

5. Diary entry for 4 March 1855. *PSS* 47:37.

6. Ibid., 15:243.

7. Ibid., 19:34.

8. Ibid., 20:547.

9. Ibid., 23:330.

10. Ibid. The phrase *vol'nodumnye tolkovateli* is on page 361. I have not been able to find the phrase *charmant docteur* in Renan and am inclined to doubt that it is there at all, since Renan makes a clear distinction between Jesus, a man without any formal education, and the *docteurs*, the learned scribes, lawyers, Pharisees, and Sadducees with whom he disputed. The phrase became fixed in Tolstoy's mind, however: he cites it again in *Tsarstvo Bozhie vnutri vas* (1893), with the same ironic contrast between the "inhabitants of Galilee, who lived 1800 years ago, half-savage Russian peasants . . . and the Russian mystic Tolstoy," on the one hand, and on the other, European culture with its "Krupp guns, smokeless gunpowder, colonization of Africa, subjugation of Ireland, parliaments, journalism, strikes, constitutions and the Eiffel Tower" (*PSS* 28:37).

In Renan's book on Marcus Aurelius the only thing that caught Tolstoy's eye was the characteristically "French" praise of the high art of tailors, hairdressers, and cosmeticians: "La toilette de la femme, avec tous ses raffinements, est du grand art à sa manière" (*PSS* 30:16), a statement Tolstoy considered the height of degenerate absurdity. Likewise, Renan's play *L'Abesse de Jouarre* Tolstoy considered "striking in its lack of talent and especially its coarseness" (*PSS* 30:297). Curiously, the only work by Renan Tolstoy could admire at all was his *L'Avenir de la science; pensées de 1848,* a work of Renan's youth not published until 1890. This work Tolstoy found "все блестит умом и тонкими, глубокими замечаниями о самых важных предметах, о науке, философии, филологии, как он ее понимает, о религии . . . . " Nevertheless, like all scholars of our time, Renan is a "moral eunuch"; he lacks "серьезность сердечная, т.е., ему все, все равно; такой он легченый, с вырезанными нравственными яйцами, как и все ученые нашего времени, но зато светлая голова и замечательно умен." (Tolstoy to N. N. Strakhov, 7 January 1891 [*PSS* 65:216]). Tolstoy never seems to have engaged with Strauss as actively as he did with Renan, but he dismisses him on similar grounds: "Так Страус критикует все учение Христа, потому что жизнь немецкая рассторится, а он к ней привык" (*PSS* 24:406).

11. Tolstoy to John Coleman Kenworthy, 15 May 1894. Quoted in Kenworthy, *Tolstoy: His Life and Works* (London and Newcastle-on-Tyre, 1902) 240; see also *PSS* 67:127.

12. *PSS* 47:205.

13. See Tolstoy to N. N. Strakhov, 17–18 April 1878; *PSS* 62:413.

14. From the memoirs of I. M. Ivakin, a Greek scholar who was tutor to Tolstoy's children; cited in *PSS* 24:980.

15. From "Kratkoe izlozhenie Evangeliia," *PSS* 24:812–813.

16. *PSS* 19:34.

17. Ibid., 19:42–43.

18. "Iasno-polianskaia shkola za noiabr' i dekabr' mesiatsy," *PSS* 8:113.

19. Tolstoy to N. A. Aleksandrov, 1882. *PSS* 30:210.

20. Variant of Aleksandrov letter; ibid, p. 433.

21. Tolstoy to P. M. Tret'iakov, 30 June 1890; *PSS* 65:124.

22. Direct association of Ivanov with Renan, at least with regard to the representation of Jesus, is anachronistic and impossible, since the *Vie de Jésus* appeared only after Ivanov's death. However, Ivanov was indeed influenced by Strauss and in fact made a special journey from Rome to Germany to converse with him. See Mikhail Alpatov, *Aleksandr Ivanov* (Moscow, 1959) 198–199.

23. Tolstoy to P. M. Tret'iakov, 14 July 1894; *PSS* 67:175. Pavel Sigalov wittily suggested to me that a more appropriate title of this picture would be "Zhenit'sia li mne ili net."

24. Tolstoy to P. M. Tret'iakov, 30 June 1890; *PSS* 65:124–125.

25. Tolstoy to P. M. Tret'iakov, 14 July 1894; *PSS* 67:175; Tolstoy to V. V. Stasov, 4 September 1894; *PSS* 67:216.

26. *PSS* 24:537.

27. Ibid., 48.

28. Ibid., 52.

29. Ibid., 356.

30. Ibid., 59.

31. Ibid., 84.

32. Ibid., 124.

33. Ibid.

34. Ibid., 156.

35. Ibid., 468.

36. Ibid., 496.

37. Ibid., 498.

38. Ibid., 486.

39. Ibid., 599.

40. Ibid., 596.

41. Ibid., 704.

42. Ibid., 673.

43. Ibid., 673–674.

44. Ibid., 699.
45. Ibid., 703.
46. Ibid., 706.
47. Ibid., 794.
48. Kenworthy 195.
49. In discussion Richard Gustafson expressed doubt that in any case Tolstoy could have felt "love" for Jesus, who at best is for us nothing more than a tissue of words. I argued, however, that the example of Kutuzov shows that Tolstoy's creative powers were such that he could indeed contrive a "tissue of words" that *can* infect us with love, a love presumably also felt by the author. Could he not have done the same with Jesus had he chosen to do so?

Dostoevsky's Russian Monk
in Extra-Literary Dialogue

Implicit Polemics in *Russkii vestnik,* 1879–1881

WILLIAM MILLS TODD III

Dostoevsky's commitment to Russian Orthodoxy struck his contemporaries as it continues to strike ours—as a deeply felt, complicated phenomenon not easily described in psychological or cultural historical terms. Major books and articles, rarely in accord with each other in either methodology or conclusions, address this commitment, and new publications (such as Geir Kjetsaa's edition of Dostoevsky's New Testament[1]) continue to provide new information and new interpretations of Dostoevsky's Christianity—as a force in his life and fiction.

Because of the variety of this scholarship, it is difficult to summarize. One tendency, however, may be noted, namely that with few exceptions these studies tend to focus upon Dostoevsky's appropriation of particular texts or particular aspects of Christian teaching (such as conversion, sin, guilt, re-demption, or grace). Little attention is paid to the writer's treatment of the church as an institution, its clergy, or its forms of Christian life, such as monasticism. This is hardly inappropriate, since the most spiritual characters in Dostoevsky's writing, until the 1870s, realize their spirituality without benefit of clergy or ritual piety.[2] Sonya Marmeladova and Prince Myshkin spring immediately to mind as examples; in *The Possessed* a *starets* ap-pears, Tikhon, but he is merely an episodic figure, like the *iurodivy* Semen Iakovlevich or the Gospel-seller Sofia Matveevna. With the exception of Leskov and Katkov's stable of space-filling minor novelists for the *Russian Herald,*[3] other mid-century writers practice a similar elision of the church and its clergy in their representations of nineteenth-century Russian culture. In the late 1860s Tolstoy wrote of this exclusion with his usual bluntness: "the lives of officials, merchants, seminarists, and peasants do not interest me and are only half comprehensible to me."[4] Excluding the seminarists locked the parish clergy out of his fictions; ignoring the officials, merchants, and peasantry cut out social groups which provided leading members of the monastic clergy during the nineteenth century, including all of the monks I shall discuss here except the fictional Zosima.

Dostoevsky's last novel, *The Brothers Karamazov*, proved a prominent exception to this policy of exclusion with its crucial monastic scenes, with its lengthy *vita* of the elder Zosima, and with its casting of a novice, Alesha, in a leading role. In placing monasticism as an institution alongside such other contemporary institutions as the legal system, the medical profession, or journalism—all of which figure, with their professional discourses, in this novel—Dostoevsky took cognizance of a development in Russian culture that deserves more mention than it generally receives: the second half of the century witnessed a remarkable growth in the number of Russian Orthodox monasteries and a concomitant increase in the number of Orthodox monks and nuns. By the end of the nineteenth century, fully one third of Russia's active monasteries had been founded during precisely this century, most of them during the reign of Alexander II; Orthodox monks, nuns, and novices of both genders (42,940) comprised nearly one tenth of one percent of the Empire's population;[5] a large group of novices insured that monasticism would have continued to be a vital phenomenon well into the twentieth century.[6]

Despite this availability of monasticism as a cultural phenomenon, Dostoevsky's work on the monastic section of his novel did not go smoothly, and the record of the novel's serialization in the *Russian Herald* shows several large gaps, a practice that Dostoevsky, unlike Tolstoy, had theretofore taken pride in avoiding. This interruption arose in part from the problem of successfully realizing the tremendously difficult and important rhetorical role that the life of Zosima had to play in counteracting Ivan's corrosive "Rebellion" and "Grand Inquisitor." But the delay also involved the necessity of learning something about monasticism, an aspect of Orthodox life which Dostoevsky knew but little before visiting Optina Pustyn' with Vladimir Solov'ev in 1878 and which, as we have seen, was not fixed in the fiction of his time. A glance at the serialization record of *The Brothers Karamazov* (Appendix) shows that the novel appeared but sporadically between May and August 1879, the time that Dostoevsky was preparing the sections on Ivan's rebellion and Alesha's tacit, indirect rebuttal in his life of Zosima. The sources for Zosima's section of the novel, as Victor Terras and others have shown, include a variety of Eastern and Russian fathers, recent Orthodox bishops and elders (Saint Tikhon of Zadonsk, Starets Amvrosii of Optina Pustyn'), and even such Western literary characters as Bishop

Muriel in Victor Hugo's *Les Misérables.*[7] Dostoevsky also needed to study the restoration of the institution of elders and the controversy surrounding it, as well as details of the lives and deaths of Orthodox monks.[8]

The familiarity of the religious sources for Zosima, both specific and generic, might have helped Dostoevsky to create a plausible elder in the eyes of his readers, to say nothing of an elder whose life and teaching might obliquely refute one of the most powerful attacks on Christianity in world literature. However, because Russian culture of the late nineteenth century was not homogeneous, its reading public could not be expected to respond with uniform enthusiasm to the repertoire on which Dostoevsky drew.[9] Nor, as we have seen, was the repertoire uniformly Orthodox, and this paved the way for a remarkable range of critical reviews, which were quick to recognize Dostoevsky's varied sources and the centrality of the novel's religious thematics, but could reach no unanimity in evaluating his use of them.[10] *The Brothers Karamazov* was praised and blamed from all positions on the political spectrum, most vehemently by the left for the mysticism of its hero and, on the right, by the future monk Konstantin Leont'ev, who subsequently reported that the monks at Optina Pustyn' did not consider Dostoevsky's novel a proper Orthodox work.[11]

To address the reviews of the novel is well beyond the scope of this article; by the end of the first of the novel's two years of serialization more than thirty reviews had appeared in the Russian press, secular and eparchal, and many more would appear during the final year and then in response to the first separate edition of the novel (1881). Instead, I would like to analyze three other lives of contemporary monks that the *Russian Herald,* the most conservative of the "thick journals," published either alongside Dostoevsky's novel or else shortly after serialization of the novel had ceased;[12] I will use them as elements in a dialogue to illuminate the choices that Dostoevsky made in developing Father Zosima. This procedure runs a certain risk, from the point of view of modern critical procedures, in isolating this section of the novel from the other sections. As justification for this fragmentation of Dostoevsky's text, I will note that his contemporaries held no such qualms. The novel was reviewed many times before it was completed, contemporary readers discussed it by parts,[13] and Dostoevsky himself consistently mentioned that he wrote it in separate books.[14] Indeed, it can be observed that while themes, characters, and parallel incidents overarch the novel, many of its fourteen books have thematic titles (such as "The Russian Monk") and these parts tend to develop provisional thematic closure.[15] No less an advocate of attention to novelistic "linkages" than Leo Tolstoy attempted to publish "The Russian Monk" section of *The Brothers Karamazov* separately, and only the censorship prevented him from doing so.[16]

The three works that I will consider in relation to "The Russian Monk," Book 6 of *The Brothers Karamazov*, are the following, in order of appearance: 1. "Father Kliment" by Konstantin Leont'ev (two parts, November and December 1879);[17] 2. "Archimandrite Pimen: Prior of the Saint Nicholas Monastery at Ugresha: A Biographical Sketch, 1810–1880" by D. B. (eleven parts, December 1880–August 1883); and 3. "The Posthumous Memoirs of the Ordained Monk of the Skhima [*ieroskhimonakh*] Antonii of the Kievan Crypt Monastery," edited by Countess M. T. (three parts, May, June, November 1881). The introduction to Antonii's autobiography is the only place where one of the texts explicitly mentions Dostoevsky's novel, but Leont'ev's 1880 polemics with Dostoevsky's fiction and Pushkin speech permit us to see Leont'ev's Life of Kliment as at least implicitly critical of Dostoevsky's Zosima, and the appearance of the life of Pimen shortly after *The Brothers Karamazov*, when the *Russian Herald* had published no lives of monks for some years before Zosima's, at least permits us to set this lengthy biography against Book 6 of *The Brothers Karamazov* for purposes of mutual illumination. As I briefly describe each text, I will show some of the ways in which they offer contrasting treatments of several crucial themes: the nature of a monastic calling, paradigms of monastic activity, and the place of learning in a Christian life. It will come as no surprise that the four texts of the 1870s–1880s recapitulate age-old contrasts in Orthodox monasticism—contrasts between ideals of service and contemplation, engagement and retreat, love and fear.[18] It may also come as no surprise, given the traditions of Russian Orthodox argumentation, that these accounts do not depend upon the detailed exposition of Orthodox doctrine, but rather manifest doctrine as a lived phenomenon through the use of narrative form.

Leont'ev's life of Kliment appeared almost immediately after Dostoevsky had buried Zosima, and the contrast between the two monks is the sharpest of the contrasts that the *Russian Herald* offers. Where Zosima's life is presented as the coherent, self-effacing creation of Alesha, in the tradition of the saint's lives, Leont'ev's life of Kliment is the digressive record of encounters between the stubborn Leont'ev and his irascible interlocutor; consequently, where the relationship of Zosima and Alesha is that of loving elder and humble disciple, that of Kliment and Leont'ev is of two disputatious *intelligenty*, as, indeed, the two were. Kliment had studied at Moscow University, had published a master's thesis on Cato the Elder, and had been impelled toward

Christianity in part by his reading of Schelling (K3); he had served as a domestic tutor in the Kireevsky family—a very different background, it hardly needs be said, from that of Dostoevsky's Zosima. Leont'ev multiplies the differences between the two by making his protagonist, the son of a German pastor, a Russian and a devoted Orthodox believer by rational choice, a believer whose thought was always marked by "the clarity and consistency of a philosophically trained mind" (K30). Where Zosima's cultural coordinates are determined by Biblical narrative, the saints' lives, and a feeling for the Russian people, Leont'ev's Kliment defended the Greek clergy, was concerned with the purity of Orthodox religious practice, and longed for a systematization of Orthodoxy. In place of Zosima's intuitive thought and empathy, placed in the service of his spiritual children and visitors to the monastery, Kliment (who refused to serve as a *starets*) offered monastic service as an editor and author of texts: of John Climacus, of articles in religious journals, of an account of his travels, and of biographies of the Optina Pustyn' elders. Zosima's "active love" and sense of paradise on earth, qualities harshly attacked in Leont'ev's critique of Dostoevsky, yield to Kliment's stern overseeing of the younger monks, dogmatic polemics against other faiths, and (in Leont'ev's terms) religious "formalism" (K113). Zosima's broad social concern with the corrupting influences of inequality and modern life find their antithesis in Kliment's lack of concern for social and political questions, both on the international scale and locally, when he refuses positions as spiritual father or administrator. Finally, where Zosima is humble about his vocation, Leont'ev uses Kliment to argue that monasticism is the highest form of Christian life, a matter of strength, ceaseless struggle, and renunciation (K90, K104). When Kliment seems to share a common trait with Zosima, the moment of proximity immediately becomes one of distance. For example, Kliment's love of cocoa recalls Zosima's weakness for sweets, but in Kliment's case the cocoa serves his ascetic vocation as an appetite suppressant (K90).

The second monastic biography to follow Dostoevsky's Zosima, that of the Archimandrite Pimen, took an unpolemical course in response to problems of contemporary monasticism. It aimed instead to provide a dispassionate eyewitness account of the archimandrite, a "photograph" as the author put it, in a concession to the poetics of nineteenth-century realism.[19] Indeed, as one plows through its interminable installments, one wishes that it did have some of Leont'ev's negative animus or some of the narrative flair of the third biography I shall discuss. But the life of Pimen does focus upon important problems in contemporary monastic life that Dostoevsky and

Leont'ev leave out of their accounts, namely everyday problems of administering a monastery in the post-Petrine period: relations with the local hierarchy, with the government and its classification of monasteries, with libelous lay people, and with the occasionally obstreperous and unsober monks themselves. As was the case with Kliment, and in sharp opposition to Zosima, Pimen is not a visionary, not capable of sudden transformation or penetrating insight. At least if he is, the narrative does not reveal this. Instead, it functions, in Leont'ev's contemptuous phrase, as a service record, a *"formuliarnyi spisok"* (K2); it documents Pimen's steady vocation, his movement up the monastic ranks, and his efforts to restore his monastery, which had fallen into grave disrepair after its days of glory in the seventeenth century. This restoration was not only physical and financial, but also spiritual, as Pimen realized his ambition to convert it from a state-supported (*shtatnyi*) monastery, to a properly communal (*obshchezhitel'nyi*) one.[20] In intellectual and literary accomplishments Pimen, the author of articles on monasticism as well as memoirs, does not match Kliment, but it is important to the author to mention this writing activity, which, again, distinguishes him from Dostoevsky's Zosima.

The final monastic narrative, Antonii's, is an autobiography, but it is framed by the preface and afterword of its editor, who, as I have mentioned, relates Antonii directly to Dostoevsky's Zosima. She begins, in fact, by recording a scene similar to that in which Zosima comforts the peasant women (Book 2, Chapter 3), and while her scene cannot match Dostoevsky's in the variety or extremity of its situations, it is based upon a definition of the monastic life close to Zosima's notion of active love: "self-perfection in the spirit of Christian humility for the benefit and service of mankind."[21]

Antonii's death allowed him to finish only enough of his narrative for three installments, which provide an eventful account of his early life as the son of a horsethief father and a mother unjustly condemned to flogging and exile for theft, and as a wanderer between monasteries. With its lively dialogue, feeling for human misery, detailed descriptions, and humorously self-deprecatory narration, the autobiography recalls passages from Avvakum's autobiography or Zosima's early life. More importantly, for our purposes, in contradistinction to the lives of Kliment and Pimen, this narrative—combining as it does social awareness and reverence for God's world with emphasis on works and self-sacrifice rather than formal piety or formal imitation—confirms the ideal of monasticism that Dostoevsky had finished developing the year before Antonii's death.[22]

It would be tempting to say that *The Brothers Karamazov,* drawing upon certain traditions in Russian and Eastern monasticism, had a major impact upon the way that Russian culture came to view this ecclesiastical institution. Without access to Antonii's archive, which might contain some of his 2000 letters, or to the archives of the *Russian Herald* and those of the other writers I have discussed, it is difficult to go beyond speculation. It is clear, from Leont'ev's subsequent treatment of Zosima, or Fedotov's, or that of Antonii's editor that the image of Zosima was one to be reckoned with, that these writers could assume that any reader would be familiar with it.

It is also clear that this image of Zosima could not fully answer the multiple needs and interests of the monastic movement, as the *Russian Herald* chose to present it. None of the subsequent lives makes an issue of the contrast between reason and faith, as does Dostoevsky's novel, and none attempts to represent the miraculous. That each of the other monks was a writer, that one of them was a talented administrator, one an *intelligent,* and that none was a vengeful ascetic like Dostoevsky's Father Ferapont, illuminate and supplement Dostoevsky's depiction of Zosima and Russian monasticism by suggesting that life in the church need not be incompatible with a life of the mind. That none of the other three monks or their monasteries faced challenges so striking as Fedor Karamazov's blasphemy, Ivan's rebellion, or the scandal of Zosima's death implies a belief on the part of the other writers that the real challenges to the monk were to preserve and propagate dogma and to fight the prolonged minor temptations and distractions of everyday life.

In any case, that these debates, implicit and explicit, took place in a prominent "thick" journal, published for a relatively broad public, including the intelligentsia, shows the potential importance to the late nineteenth-century intelligentsia of the debates over monasticism. It shows as well the ability of these thick journals to place imaginative literature in an influential, provocative, indeed central, position in setting the terms of cultural controversies.

Appendix: Serialization of The Brothers Karamazov *and Biographies of* Monks in the Russian Herald, *1879–1881*

Date	Portions of BK	Biographies
January 1879	"From the Author," Books 1, 2	
February	Book 3	
March		
April	Book 4	
May	Book 5, chapters 1–4	
June	Book 6, chapters 5–7	
July		
August	Book 6 ("The Russian Monk")	
September	Book 7	
October	Book 8, chapters 1–4	
November	Book 8, chapters 5–8	Father Kliment
December	[apology for delay]	Father Kliment
January 1880	Book 9	
February		
March		
April	Book 10	
May		
June	[Pushkin speech, *Diary of a Writer*]	
July	Book 11, chapters 1–5	
August	Book 11, chapters 6–10	
September	Book 12, chapters 1–5	
October	Book 12, chapters 6–14	
November	Epilogue	
December		Archimandrite Pimen

December 1880 (dated 1881)—first separate edition

Date	Portions of BK	Biographies
January 1881		
February		
March		
April		
May		Father Antonii
June		Father Antonii
July		
August		
September		
October		Archimandrite Pimen
November		Father Antonii
December		Archimandrite Pimen

Notes

1. Geir Kjetsaa, *Dostoevsky and His New Testament* (Oslo, 1984).

2. Konstantin Leont'ev, in fact, accuses Dostoevsky of never mentioning the church at all in his Pushkin speech and of pretending that Christ could reach people without the church's help, *Nashi novye khristiane, F. M. Dostoevskii i gr. Lev Tolstoi* (Moscow, 1882) 39, 41.

3. Leonid Grossman, "Dostoevskii i pravitel'stvennye krugi 1870-kh godov," *Literaturnoe nasledstvo* 15 (1934): 107. Grossman has in mind here Krestovskii and Kliushnikov, among others.

4. Unpublished preface to the 1805 section of *War and Peace,* L. N. Tolstoi, *Polnoe sobranie sochinenii,* 90 vols. (Moscow, 1928–1958) 13:55.

5. "Monashestvo," Brokhaus-Efron, *Entsiklopedicheskii slovar',* (St. Petersburg, 1896) 38:730.

6. For further information on the little studied resurgence of monasticism, see Brenda Meehan-Waters, "Popular Piety, Local Initiative and the Founding of Women's Religious Communities in Russia, 1764–1907," *St. Vladimir's Theological Quarterly* 30.2 (1986): 117–141.

7. Victor Terras, *A Karamazov Companion: Commentary on the Genesis, Language, and Style of Dostoevsky's Novel* (Madison, 1981) 21–24; Sven Linnér, *Starets Zosima in* The Brothers Karamazov: *A Study in the Mimesis of Virtue* (Stockholm, 1975) chap. 5; John Dunlop, *Staretz Amvrosy: Model for Dostoevsky's Staretz Zossima* (Belmont, 1972); A. V. Chicherin, "Rannie predshestvenniki Dostoevskogo," in V. Ia. Kirpotin, ed., *Dostoevskii i russkie pisateli* (Moscow, 1971) 361–364. G. P. Fedotov draws some important distinctions between Zosima and Tikhon Zadonskii, *A Treasury of Russian Spirituality* (New York, 1965) 185. Konstantin Leont'ev would sardonically list Hugo, Garibaldi, the Socialists, the Quakers, Proudhon, Cabet, Fourier, and Sand as the forebears of Dostoevsky's notions of "peace" and "harmony." See *Nashi novye khristiane, F. M. Dostoevskii i gr. Lev Tolstoi* (Moscow, 1882) 9. For Dostoevsky's own list of his religious sources for the depiction of Zosima, see his letter of 7 August 1879 to N. A. Liubimov, in F. M. Dostoevskii, *Pis'ma* ed. A. S. Dolinin (Moscow, 1959) 4:92.

8. Dostoevsky reported finding a scandalous death like Zosima's in Parfenii's account of Mt. Athos, *Pis'ma* 4:114. Letter of 16 September 1879 to N. A. Liubimov. A letter from K. P. Pobedonostsev to Dostoevsky of 24 February 1879 tells Dostoevsky that the Archimandrite Simeon will give him details on the burial of monks. See Grossman, "Dostoevskii i pravitel'stvennye krugi" 137.

9. My use of the term "repertoire" here is drawn from Wolfgang Iser, *The Act of Reading: A Theory of Aesthetic Response* (Baltimore, 1978) 53–85.

10. For an excellent survey of these reviews, see the commentaries to *The Brothers Karamazov* in F. M. Dostoevskii, *Polnoe sobranie sochinenii v tridtsati tomakh* (Leningrad, 1972–1990) 15:486–513.

11. Dostoevskii, *Polnoe sobranie sochinenii,* 15:498. Leont'ev's statement appears in a posthumously published letter to V. V. Rozanov, *Russkii vestnik,* 1903, 4:650–651.

12. For a survey of the journal's policy and for bibliography, see Catharine Theimer Nepomnyashchy, "Katkov and the Emergence of *The Russian Messenger,*" *Ulbandus Review* 1.1 (Fall 1977).

13. For a selection of contemporary readers' responses to the novel, see L. R. Lanskoi, "Dostoevskii v neizdannoi perepiske sovremennikov (1837–1881)," *Literaturnoe nasledstvo* 86 (1973): 471–521.

14. Letters to N. A. Liubimov of 16 November 1879 and 2 December 1879.

15. On the novel's use of mnemonic devices to give its readers a sense of the whole, see the analysis of its "inherent relationships" and "narrative structure" in Robert L. Belknap, *The Structure of* The Brothers Karamazov (The Hague, 1967), chapters 2 and 4. On the provisional thematic closure of the novel's parts, see my article "*The Brothers Karamazov* and the Poetics of Serial Publication," *Dostoevsky Studies* 7 (1986): 89–91.

16. On this episode see V. K. Lebedev, "Otryvok iz romana 'Brat'ia Karamazovy' pered sudom tsenzury," *Russkaia literatura,* 1970, no. 2.

17. A separate edition of the work appeared as K. Leont'ev, *Otets Kliment Zedergol'm: Ieromonakh Optinoi Pustyni* (Moscow, 1882); it was reprinted by the YMCA Press in Paris in 1978. In this article I shall refer to the Paris edition, using the form (K . . .) for page references.

18. On these and other alternatives in Old Russian and Byzantine Christianity, see G. P. Fedotov, *The Russian Religious Mind* (Cambridge, Mass., 1946 and 1966).

19. D. B., "Arkhimandrit Pimen, nastoiatel' Nikolo-ugreshskogo monastyria. Biograficheskii ocherk (1810–1880)," *Russkii vestnik,* August 1883, p. 754.

20. For an explanation of these terms, see "Monashestvo," *Èntsiklopedicheskii slovar'* 38:731–732.

21. "Posmertnye zapiski Ieroskhimonakha Kievo-pecherskoi lavry Ottsa Antoniia," *Russkii vestnik,* May 1881, pp. 359–361.

22. Ibid., pp. 386–395, 405–411.

The "New Religious Consciousness"

Pavel Florenskii's Path to a Revitalized Orthodoxy

BERNICE GLATZER ROSENTHAL

Pavel Florenskii (1881–1937), the scientist-priest, was called the Russian Leonardo because of the diversity of his achievements. Poet, philosopher, theologian, linguist, mathematician, physicist, he also wrote on art history, archaeology, and anthropology, and was a major contributor to Soviet technology in the 1920s and early 1930s. An intellectual who came to Christianity, he had a religious sense that was existentialist, intuitive, visceral, and was motivated by his search for a coherent worldview that would encompass all areas of human experience. His writings demonstrate that elements within the Orthodox church, of which he was an outstanding example, did attempt to respond creatively to the spiritual crisis of the early twentieth century. They are immensely popular in Russia today, being issued by both secular publishers and the patriarchate.

Florenskii was one of the most vehement critics of the "new religious consciousness"; yet, the movement had a catalytic effect on his thought. His major theological works, *The Pillar and Affirmation of Truth* (1914)[1] and his theological essays of 1918–1922,[2] constitute his response to issues first posed by the "God-seekers" and reflect ideas and attitudes derived from them.[3] This essay argues that the "new religious consciousness" stimulated and channeled Florenskii's rediscovery of Russian Orthodoxy and the ways in which he interpreted it. I will use the terms "new religious consciousness," God-seekers, and Symbolists interchangeably, for many leading Symbolists were also God-seekers; indeed, Symbolism can be considered the aesthetic expression of the "new religious consciousness."

The "new religious consciousness" refers to the cluster of ideas associated with Dmitrii Merezhkovskii and Zinaida Gippius and their fellow "seekers" of new religious truths, Dmitrii Filosofov, Andrei Belyi, Viacheslav Ivanov, Aleksandr Blok, Vasilii Rozanov, Nikolai Minskii (Vilenkin), Sergei Bulgakov, and Nikolai Berdiaev. Merezhkovskii insisted that religion was the most basic of all human needs, attacked intelligentsia Positivism, materialism, and rationalism, and tried to develop a new interpretation of Christianity based on the Second Coming of Christ, which he believed was imminent. In the 1890s, he had popularized French Symbolism and Nietzsche, but in 1900, he turned to Christ. Rather than abandon Symbolism and Nietzsche, however, he maintained that Christianity and paganism (equated with Nietzsche's philosophy) constituted two halves of a yet unknown greater truth to be revealed by Christ Himself in a forthcoming Third Testament. Merezhkovskii disdained "historical Christianity" as obsolete, rejected the asceticism, humility, and otherworldliness preached by the Russian Orthodox church, and tried to found a new Church of the Holy Spirit. In 1901, he, Gippius, and Dmitrii Filosofov founded the Religious Philosophical Society of St. Petersburg to proselytize their views. It featured debates between clergymen and lay intellectuals on issues such as free speech, Tolstoy's excommunication, Gogol' 's Orthodoxy, and Christian attitudes to worldly pleasures, especially sex. The Society was shut down by Pobedonostsev, the Ober-Procurator of the Holy Synod, in 1903, but reopened after the Revolution of 1905; branches were founded in Moscow, Kiev, and other cities as well. The meetings attracted large audiences, and the Society became the nucleus of a religious renaissance. In 1902, Merezhkovskii and Gippius had founded a review, *Novyi Put'* (*New Path*), to showcase the new trends in art and thought, especially Symbolism.[4]

Russian Symbolism was not simply an artistic schoool, but a worldview based on a mystical epistemology, which held that this world is but a reflection of a higher reality, and that art, imagination, and intuition, rather than reason and science, are the means to new psychological and metaphysical truths. Indeed, in some respects, Russian Symbolism served as a religion of art, whose central values were beauty, aesthetic creativity, and emotional liberation. Emphasizing the "inner man," the soul, and the psyche, the Symbolists rejected the Populist tenet that art must serve the people and were resolutely apolitical and asocial until the Revolution of 1905, which they interpreted as the coming of the Apocalypse. They expected the Revolution to culminate in a new society, characterized by freedom, beauty, and love, in which people would enjoy unlimited individual freedom and total integration into a loving community.

The exact date that Florenskii learned about the "new religious consciousness" cannot be determined, but we know that he studied philosophy with S. N. Trubetskoi, a disciple of Solov'ev (whose thought influenced the Symbolists), and that he attended the meetings of the St. Petersburg Religious Philosophical Society and was a founding member of the Moscow branch.[5]

His very first articles appeared in *Novyi Put'*; he belonged to some of the same private religious study circles and was very friendly, at different times, with Belyi, Rozanov, Bulgakov, and Ivanov. From 1903 to 1906, he was particularly close to Belyi; they considered founding a journal that would approach religion from a philosophical, mystical, scientific, and historical perspective. They even agreed to enter a monastery together, but their request was refused.[6] During the Revolution of 1905, Florenskii joined other Society members in movements for church reform and spiritual renewal, was a founding member of both the Brotherhood of Zealots for Church Renewal and the Christian Brotherhood of Struggle, and wrote for the religious periodicals that sprouted up at the time: *Vek, Zhivaia Zhizn', Khristianin,* and *Voprosy Religii*. The latter published "On Spiritual Truth," an early version of *The Pillar and Affirmation of Truth*. Although he entered the Moscow Theological Academy in 1904, began studies for the priesthood in 1906, was elected Professor of Philosophy at the Academy in 1908, and was ordained in 1911, he continued to follow developments in art and literature, especially Symbolism, and was especially close to Rozanov and Bulgakov until Rozanov's death (1919) and Bulgakov's emigration (1923). His writings are studded with excerpts from poems by Belyi, Blok, and Ivanov, and assume familiarity with Ivanov's views on Dionysus, myth, cults, and cultic theater. He believed that Symbolism invalidated Positivism and that humanity was on the threshold of a new nonpositivist science. In 1910 he wrote to Belyi congratulating him on the publication of *Symbolism* and expressed his admiration for the high level of thought and the "scientific aspects" of the book, by which he meant Belyi's experiments with rhythm in prose. Like Solov'ev's *Three Conversations* (*Tri razgovora*), *Pillar* is couched in dialogue form—twelve letters that invite a response—and pose questions rather than dictate answers.[7]

The "new religious consciousness" had a crucial impact on Florenskii's thought, for it introduced an impressionable and searching young man to a whole new set of ideas and attitudes, thereby providing a channel and direction for his own spiritual quest. Reared in a secular household (his parents were typical nineteenth-century Russian intellectuals), he knew almost nothing about his own Orthodox heritage; he had, however, been somewhat of a mystic since childhood.[8] As a university student, he had first looked to mathematics rather than religion as the basis for a new cosmological worldview. Attracted to the God-seekers, who shared his spiritual yearnings, he formulated questions that Merezhkovskii and Gippius could not answer. He found their philosophical ideas insufficiently rigorous and scientific, objected to their emphasis on the faults of the historical church, and explicitly opposed their plans to build a new church.[9] Still, the new religious consciousness had set him on the path which ultimately led him back to Orthodoxy, but an Orthodoxy informed by a modern sensibility and permeated with ideas taken from Symbolism, Nietzsche, and new findings in mathematics, science, anthropology, archaeology, and linguistics.

Having made his decision to return to the church, he insisted that such was the only correct path[10] and lambasted Merezhkovskii and Gippius as "people of false consciousness" with "no real soil under their feet," who spoke in empty words that they themselves were beginning to believe. Linking them to a long chain of heretics that stretched back to the first century, he stated that throughout history, the "new" consciousness had always turned out to be "not higher than the Church, as it sees itself, but against the Church and against Christ." While he endorsed their emphasis on the Holy Spirit,[11] he accused them of trying to call it to life prematurely, all by themselves, seeking to perceive it without holiness or purity (never defining what he meant by these), ignoring time and dates, and vulgarizing Christianity. He also claimed that they failed to offer firm ground for spiritual speculation or for the affirmation of a truly new human consciousness. Instead of finding eternity, such people inevitably fall into heresy and replace true spirituality with subjective creations and demonic novelties. He concluded that subjective, unguided mysticism was dangerous,[12] that spiritual quests must be pursued within the confines of the Russian Orthodox church, not apart from it or against it as Merezhkovskii and Gippius were doing. Very likely he had become disgusted with Merezhkovskii's attacks, during and after the Revolution of 1905, on the Russian Orthodox church as an aspect of the Antichrist. *Salt of the Earth* contains the narrative of a sophisticated theology professor "satanically hardened with Church problems, fed up with politics, bishops, Merezhkovskii, the Theological Academy and all its professors,"[13] who visited the simple Elder Isidore and found spiritual solace. After 1908, he totally lost interest in politics, did not participate in the debates on church reform that were burning issues of the day, nor was he involved in the Renovationist controversy of the 1920s.

Incidentally, Florenskii associated Tolstoy with the God-seekers, despite Tolstoy's own antipathy toward them, because Tolstoy's rejection of the church as an institution struck him as similar to Merezhkovskii's rejection of "historical Christianity" and the "historical church" and because both writers interpreted the Gospels their own way. Still, his own theology virtually ignored the legal-juridical aspects of the institutional church, emphasized feelings rather than dogma, aesthetics rather than ethics, and focused on early Byzantine and medieval Russian spirituality, in essence by-passing the theologians of the Petrine church. Indifferent to the legal-juridical structure of the church, he was in a sense returning to its origins, before the full hierarchy had developed. He too rejected, but never explicitly, aspects of church history and doctrine that he found uncongenial.

Florenskii's theology bears the imprint of the "new religious consciousness." His insistence that religion must be grounded in concrete forms, tangible symbols, clearly visible images, and direct religious experience (participation) stems from his attempt to overcome what he regarded as its defects— diffuseness, amorphousness, openendedness, eclecticism, incoherence, reliance on abstract ideals, myths, or allegories. He retained the Symbolists' mysticism, aestheticism, and psychologism (emphasis on feelings and passions), and attempted to refute certain God-seekers' critique of Christianity, Nietzsche-influenced, especially on the subject of asceticism.[14] Yet, he assimilated aspects of Nietzsche's views into his own theology. After the Bolshevik Revolution, he described Christianity in cultic terms taken from Ivanov, Nietzsche, and Wagner. Although Florenskii's mysticism, aestheticism, and psychologism were intricately connected, they can be analyzed separately so long as we recognize their place in the whole of his thought.

Florenskii's mysticism predated his association with the Symbolists, but his discussions with them fortified and validated it. He opposed rationalism in all its forms, but was especially critical of rationalism in religion, which he associated with diabolic pride. "A reasonable faith," he maintained, "is an infamy and a stench before God."[15] He claimed that it stemmed from a desire not to accept God in oneself but to set oneself against God; indeed, he considered reason itself diabolic. Like Kierkegaard, whom he does not appear to have read, Florenskii spoke in terms of "either/or," "a Gehenna of doubt or a *podvig* of faith." Like Pascal, whom he quoted, Florenskii was skeptical about the claims of science and detested the idea of a mechanical universe. He accused Tolstoy of religious nihilism and especially resented the arrogance he found implicit in Tolstoy's rather free interpretation of the Gospels, which omitted the miraculous and reduced Jesus to a teacher of ethics.

His most fervent attacks, however, were directed against Kant, probably as a reaction to the "back to Kant" movement initiated by Berdiaev and Bulgakov and the neo-Kantianism that pervaded the universities and theological academies and influenced Belyi and Ivanov as well. "No system," Florenskii wrote, "is more evasively dangerous, more 'hypocritical' and more 'crafty' than the philosophy of Kant . . . . Not one word of his philosophy has a pure tone . . . . He is the great deceiver."[16] According to Florenskii, Kant depersonalized Christianity, diminished it to an abstract conception, "a model to be copied," a "pedestrian moral rule," instead of positing the image of Jesus Christ, who was a person, as the principle of a new life and as the link between the visible and invisible worlds.[17]

Objecting to Kant's morality of duty, Florenskii maintained that moralism is outside divine love,[18] that the holy is above every "No," and that morality and juridical structures are alien to the church. Quoting Saint Paul on the spiritual danger of making laws, he argued that unlike Kant, Christianity does not demand moral perfection outside the self, but moral development.[19] He feared that a religion of ethics focusing on external actions ignores or undermines spiritual life. Thus, he advocated a personal religion, a religion based on a real person rather than on an abstract idea, a religion that stressed the feelings, inner life, and true spirituality, and that encompassed the energies of both good and evil will.[20] Florenskii's assertion that love constitutes a "Yes"[21] recalls Ivanov's and Merezhkovskii's attempt to refute Nietzsche's charge that Christianity is life-denying, as well as Ivanov's rejection of the negativism of the Ten Commandments ("Thou shalt not") and consequent search for a new morality "beyond 'Yes' and 'No'."[22] Florenskii's contrast of positive prayer with negative prohibition and his general indifference to law recall Merezhkovskii's emphasis on Jesus's statement, "Think not that I have come to destroy the law or the prophets: I am come not to destroy but to fulfill" (Matthew 5:17). Orthodoxy is not as legalistic as Roman Catholicism, and it places less emphasis on Judgment Day, but it does reject mysticism that seeks to dispense with moral rules and cannot be understood as sanctioning amorality. The subtext of Florenskii's hostility to ethics was Nietzsche, especially his concept of "beyond good and evil."

Florenskii did not deny the existence of ultimate truth, as Nietzsche did, but regarded truth as a living essence rather than a static or a formal concept. He eschewed logical proofs and rational argumentation, believing that truth can be expressed in old and in new forms and that it is potential rather than given. In this respect, Florenskii's theology is a version of progressive revelation,[23] as is Merezhkovskii's. Merezhkovskii, however, expected an imminent "Third Testament," whereas Florenskii envisioned a slower process, similar in many ways to the process theology of Teilhard de Chardin. Rejecting consistent and logical systems, Florenskii maintained that truth is an antinomy and must be all inclusive. This stance enabled him to incorporate unresolved contradictions and doubts into his theology, shift its focus from moral to psychological and existential issues, and emphasize new perceptions and experiences of the spiritual world, the psychologism alluded to above, rather than objective truth or external law.

Florenskii shared the Symbolist belief that other worlds exist and that art is a path to them, but for him the crucial division was not near and far but visible and invisible (the spiritual world); the latter is all around us and is made visible by art. He believed that eternal truths are revealed through sight and sound and are expressed in concrete images and forms and that the holy is another existence that transcends this world. For him, the symbol was not a sign, nor an indication of something else, nor a path "from the real to the more real,"[24] but is itself fully real. Like the Symbolists (and Nietzsche), he believed that new truths require new forms and that symbols cannot be invented, but emerge from the depths of reality; they are perceived psychologically and intuitively:

> The symbol is not a conditional entity that we construct capriciously or whimsically. Symbols are constructed by the spirit according to definite laws and by an inner necessity—and this happens every time that certain aspects of the spirit begin to function in an especially vivid manner. That which is symbolizing and that which is being symbolized are not connected to each other by chance. Historically one can prove the parallelism of the symbolic systems of various peoples and various times.[25]

His description of formless content and contentless form as a Scylla and Charybdis is a formulation typical of Merezhkovskii and echoes a similar passage in Merezhkovskii's famous essay, "On the Causes of the Decline of Russian Literature" (1893), often considered the manifesto of Russian Symbolism.[26]

Aestheticism is perhaps the most single striking aspect of Florenskii's theology. Indeed, Georges Florovsky considered *Pillar* an "esthetic seduction."[27] Florenskii regarded beauty, truth, love, and spirituality as intertwined aspects of one absolute essence, which he described as absolute, infinite, eternal, and all-incorporating. Although he alluded to a "metaphysical triad" of truth, love, and beauty,[28] in the last analysis his concepts of truth, love, and spirituality are related, directly or indirectly, to beauty. Many examples of his aesthetic perception of spirituality can be given: "my spiritual life, my life in the spirit . . . is beauty, that special beauty of the first created creature";[29] "there is no one . . . more beautiful than Christ";[30] *tserkovnost'* is the beauty of a new life in Absolute Beauty—in the Holy Spirit.[31] He believed that a special spiritual beauty is a criterion of the correctness of this life, and he linked love for wisdom with love for beauty and beauty with love: "The phenomenon of truth is love, realized love is beauty." He considered beauty the form of love, assigned a special role to the artist who gives beauty to the world, and stated that the Holy Spirit reveals itself in the ability to see the beauty of the creature.[32] He associated Sophia with beauty as well, inner beauty especially.[33] The prominent role of Sophia in his theology stems from Solov'ev and the Symbolists, but requires a separate essay because it is too complex to be discussed here. Beauty even superceded morality in his eyes; he maintained that ascetic practices create a beautiful rather than a good man, for "goodness" exists among carnal people as well. Even if they are great sinners, ascetics have a spiritual beauty, "the blinding radiant beauty of the light-bearing person . . . that is unattainable to the plump and carnal."[34] In essence substituting aesthetics for ethics, he defined evil as "spiritual crookedness." The expression recalls the Russian word for "deformed," *bezobraznyi;* sin is that which leads to "spiritual crookedness."[35] Unlike Nietzsche, however, he associated evil with self-centeredness, striving for self-deification, the desire to be as God, and with fragmentation, the destruction of the whole.[36] According to Florenskii, the opposite of evil is not good, but love, which restores the lost wholeness. As he used the term, wholeness is an aesthetic, a psychological, and a sociocultural concept. Indeed, his entire approach recalls Nietzsche's statement that "culture is, above all, unity of style in all the expressions of the life of a people."[37]

By way of Symbolist aesthetics, Florenskii returned to some of the central tenets of Orthodoxy: the emphasis on light, beauty, transfiguration, and the Holy Spirit. Orthodoxy holds that on the day of the resurrection the body will be outwardly transfigured by divine light, as Christ's body was transfigured on Mount Tabor. Kievan envoys, reporting on the Orthodox services they witnessed in Constantinople stated: "We knew not whether we were in earth or in heaven . . . . we cannot forget this beauty." At the miracle of Pentecost, the Holy Spirit descended on the Apostles in tongues of fire: "And they were all filled with the Holy Spirit (Acts 2:3–4). That it touched them individually, in separate tongues of flame, is part of the mystery of *sobornost'*. If the Symbolists secularized, somewhat, aspects of their Orthodox heritage (about which they actually knew relatively little), Florenskii went back to the original, so to speak, but viewed it through the prism of Symbolism.

Aestheticism is also obvious in his apotheosis of the icon, which is indeed a symbol in the way that the Symbolists used the term. Orthodoxy regards the icon as a window between the celestial and the earthly worlds. Veneration (not worship, for only God is worshipped) of the image on the icon constitutes an integral part of Orthodox liturgy and dogma. After 1904, when new techniques made possible the restoration of the brilliant colors of the icon, artists and intellectuals wishing to create a new Russian culture became very interested in it as a specifically Russian form of art. Avant-garde painters such as Kandinskii adapted iconic forms to abstract art. Florenskii's appreciation of the icon was not only aesthetic, but philosophical and religious. He argued that icons sanctify reality in Christian terms and show that the spiritual (invisible) world is real. He regarded the icon as a fact of divine reality, which expresses the ontological reality of another world.[38] The icon has no perspective, because it is not intended to be realistic in the mundane sense of the word. Rather it is a vision of the spiritual world, divine truth made visible, a new revelation of an eternal reality, whose truth is immediately obvious. "There is the Trinity of Rublev, therefore there is God."[39] Note the contrast to Descartes's statement, "I think, therefore I am."

Florenskii did extensive research on the icon, tracing its history back to the death masks of ancient Egypt. These, he wrote, were not so much physical likenesses of the deceased as idealized visions of his essence, based on the belief that the deceased lived on in another world. From the Egyptian Christians, who considered icons holy, the idea passed to Greece and was absorbed into Byzantine Christianity. According to Florenskii, the masks of the Dionysian rites stem from ancient Egypt as well. The occult doctrines of theosophy and anthroposophy, popular at the time, idealized Egypt as the fount of all religion. Whether or not Florenskii shared this view, he wanted to break the hold of secular culture, epitomized to him by pagan Athens and the Renaissance, on the minds of his contemporaries. He described the iconostasis, the wall of icons that separates the sanctuary from the nave, as a metaphysics of existence, for it expresses the organic wholeness and completeness of church culture, as distinct from the "eclectic" and "contradictory" culture of the Renaissance.[40] He contrasted the integral nature of the iconostasis, the absence of anything abstract or accidental in it, with the "sinful fragmentation of the creature" and the opposition of man and nature in the new art[41] (Cubism or Futurism, according to the context). He also described the iconostasis as a "crystal in time of imaginary space," an example of his incorporation of scientific and mathematical concepts into his theology.[42] The crystal possesses electromagnetic properties and is related to Florenskii's metaphysics of light, which is in turn related to his concept of God. Light is very important in Orthodox theology.

Florenskii adapted the psychologism of the Symbolists to his own theology. The Symbolists constantly alluded to "inner experience" and considered "mutual inner experience" and "shared religious experience" the "social cement" of the new organic society they hoped would result from the Revolution of 1905. Florenskii spoke of the "living religious experience" or "direct experience" that is related to something tangible or visible. He considered such experience the only way to "survey and evaluate the spiritual treasures of the church"[43] and to reach a true understanding of church dogma.[44] He advocated a new life in the spirit, neither abstract, nor rational, nor juridical, nor archaeological, but biological, aesthetic, and supralogical. He also emphasized feelings and passions in church life.

Tserkovnost', literally churchliness or ecclesiasticism, is the theme of *Pillar*. As Florenskii used the term, *tserkovnost'* has several layers of meaning related in one way or another to the Holy Spirit and the invisible church— the living continuity of church traditions and doctrines, and the feeling of being part of a church, an organic union of believers joined to one another and to Christ. In this sense, *tserkovnost'* is a return to the original meaning of *sobornost'*, an ecclesiastical concept connoting the unity of all believers in the mystical body of Christ. Florenskii described *tserkovnost'* as the spiritual beauty that manifests itself when one is united with all creation by way of love for its creator, and he believed that loving union constitutes and is made possible by life in the church and that existence is meaningless without love.

He also placed great emphasis on friendship between men. His concept of the friend as another I, a mirror,[45] echoes Nietzsche's "On the Friend" in *Zarathustra* (Part 1). Alluding to Goethe's famous statement that no man is a hero to his lackey, Florenskii maintained that this is because one is a hero and the other is a lackey;[46] the lackey cannot recognize heroes. Though the allusion is to Goethe, the spirit is Nietzschean—the true friend encourages and recognizes greatness in the other. Citing the examples of David and Jonathan, Peter and Jesus, he interpreted friendship in Christian, terms a spiritual *podvig*, carrying another's cross, though it also brings joy. He also noted that in medieval times friends often entered monasteries together.

The Symbolists stressed the elemental passions of the Dionysian rites as the integrating force of the cultic community. Florenskii, somewhat surprisingly, praised the passion of jealousy (*revnost'*), quoting approvingly Nietzsche's statement that the Greeks were the most jealous people.[47] He believed that *agape* alone is an insufficient basis for *tserkovnost'*, that passion is required as well. He regarded jealousy as a positive and necessary force and asserted that alongside the unifying force of love, there must be a separating force that creates the boundaries of diffusion and impersonality, a sense of exclusiveness, of being special or different, though not necessarily better. "This force is jealousy." Without it:

there is no definite Church life, with its definite structure, but it would be protestant, anarchic, communistic, Tolstoian, and so forth—a mixture of everything with everything—complete formlessness and chaos. The force of jealousy is alive in friendship, in marriage, in the *obshchina*-parish, in the monastery-community, in the bishopric-eparchy, in the local Church— everywhere. Everywhere definiteness of ties and constancy of unions are demanded.[48]

His view that the church should be local (*uezdnyi*)[49] may imply a series of cults based on an elder and underscores his emphasis on personal ties and direct religious experience.

At the Religious-Philosophical Society meetings Merezhkovskii talked about "holy flesh"; Rozanov advocated a kind of biological mysticism, based in part on the Old Testament; and Ivanov idealized the loss of self in the mystical/erotic ecstasy of the Dionysian rites.[50] All of them assumed that historical Christianity prescribes asceticism and denigrates the body. To refute them, Florenskii studied early Orthodox teaching on sexuality and the body.[51] He concluded that the God-seekers misunderstood Christianity, especially the doctrine of metaphysical dualism, for rather than denigrate the body, Christian doctrine holds, and has always held, that the body will be resurrected along with the soul. When filled with the Holy Spirit, the flesh is transfigured and becomes holy. The intelligentsia's condescending attitude to the body, their ignorance of its "mysterious depths, its mysterious roots," stems, he said, not from Orthodoxy, but from Gnosticism specifically, from the Gnostic heresy that the material world is evil, which in turn stems from Lucifer rather than Christ. He also maintained that asceticism did not originate in Christianity, but in charismaticism, and that as a historical phenomenon, asceticism was a spontaneous continuation of charismaticism.[52] Here again, Florenskii was taking a somewhat secularized Symbolist doctrine, "holy flesh," and restoring it to its original meaning, the Orthodox doctrine of the transfiguration of the flesh.

He accused the advocates of the "new religious consciousness" of failing to distinguish marriage from lewdness[53] and claimed that Tolstoy's "Kreutzer Sonata," which he considered blasphemous, typified their view of marriage as well. "So-called 'love' outside God," he said, "is not love but only a natural cosmic phenomenon . . . like a physiological function of the stomach."[54] He also rejected Vladimir Solov'ev's view, in "The Meaning of Love" (1892–1894), which sanctioned sexual love as a means to transcend egoism and isolation, asserting that it is best to leave the self through spiritual communion—friendship. According to Florenskii, marriage is two in one flesh; friendship is two in one soul. He did not expect a wife to be a friend; these are two separate and distinct relationships. He wrote much about friendship but hardly anything about marriage and had a very traditional view of woman's role. He also asserted that true love is an objective metaphysical phenomenon, a transfer from the empirical plane of existence to a new reality, a new supra-empirical overcoming of the naked self identity of I=I and that both Solov'ev's and the God-seekers' views on sex were too psychological and subjective. His philological analysis of the exact meaning of love in Greek thought and in the Old and New Testaments was an attempt to introduce philosophical rigor into the discussion and is strikingly reminiscent of Nietzsche's philological argument in *The Genealogy of Morals*. Distinguishing among the Greek concepts of *eros, agape, philia,* and *storge,* Florenskii argued that *agape* and *philia* constitute the truly Christian understanding of love, and he downgraded *eros*.[55]

He regarded God and the world, spirit and flesh, virginity and marriage, as antinomies, which, in the higher religious consciousness, become internally one, internally whole, thereby attaining inner beauty, and spiritual wholeness.[56] "Only pure marriage, only blessed marital consciousness allows us to understand the significance of virginity: only the married man understands that monasticism is not an 'institution' of the Church-juridical structure, but is established by God Himself and that it is qualitatively different from bachelorhood."[57] He told his friend Aleksandr El'chaninov (24 September 1909):

> I could have killed in myself everything connected with sex, but then my scientific creativity would have died within me first of all. You say that this is necessary—that all the ascetics had to go through such a death. I know that, but they will not allow me to go to a monastery—they order me to give lectures. Why is it that from many writings—textbooks and so on, especially the seminary texts—there is a smell of death? . . . It is because they were written by "eunuchs." I could write that way but who needs such books?[58]

The "smell of death" suggests the influence of Nietzsche or Rozanov or both. He was then going through a personal as well as a religious crisis, drinking heavily, and even considering leaving the church. He told El'chaninov, "I want real love. I understand life only as together [*vmeste*]; without this 'together' I do not even want salvation. I am not rebelling, not protesting. I simply do not have a taste for life, nor for the salvation of my soul as long as I am alone."[59] The statement may allude not only to loneliness but to a struggle with his own sexuality, for the crisis was, apparently, resolved by his decision to marry; he married the sister of his roommate in the summer of 1910.

Florenskii's device of the diary of a monk to support his own views on sex is a typical example of his finding precedents within church history to bolster his own argument. The monk had written that sexual abstinence, unharmful if there is no sexual arousal, even seems to develop new occult and mystical abilities. But abstinence that is connected with arousal is definitely harmful; the soul becomes dirty and decays, just as the body perishes. The chief harm, the monk concluded, is, perhaps, from constant dissatisfaction.[60]

Florenskii's Christian "rehabilitation of the flesh" connected certain parts of the body with mysticism. He posited three kinds of mysticism, each connected to different religions: that of the breast (church mysticism), that of the head (Hinduism and theosophy), and that of the stomach (organistic cults and Catholicism).[61] He considered mysticism of the breast or heart "normal mysticism," the mysticism of Russian Orthodoxy, and warned that mysticism of the head leads to demonic pride, to life without a center.[62] The Macarian homilies of the early fifth century emphasize the heart and signify the whole man, not only intellect but also will, emotions, and even body.[63] Florenskii's view went beyond this concept, for it also reflects certain occult doctrines that posit a symmetry between the upper and lower parts of the body, whose point of focus is the middle part of man, the breast or the heart. Mysticism of the stomach would seem to include the reproductive organs, but Florenskii's religious writings ignore the phallic mysticism of the religions of the ancient Near East, which Rozanov praised, as well as Rozanov's belief that a pregnant woman is sacred. Florenskii did discuss male/female fertility symbols in his archaeological writings, on the stone babas, for example,[64] but without Rozanov's sense of mystical exaltation. Later he went even further and connected the seven sacraments to bodily processes.[65]

Florenskii's "justification of the faith" entailed coming to grips with Nietzsche, the Antichrist himself, and a major influence on the God-seekers. Nietzsche's views must have been a great temptation to Florenskii, for he had identified with the rebellious Prometheus as a child and was still trying, one suspects, to overcome his own theomachy: "I early understood the cult of humanity as human self-deification, early heard in Beethoven's music this infinite element of titanism which I found congenial . . . I momentarily rose against God, not wishing to deny Him, not wishing to subjugate myself. I well knew the pantheistic meaning of rebellion." Similarly, "I do not deny God; but I, a man, am also God, I want to be God to myself."[66] Note the similarity to Nietzsche's statement, "If God exists how could I endure not to be a God?" Significantly, perhaps viewing it as too great a temptation, he did not quote Athanasius's statement that God became man so that man might become God, though he must have known about it.[67] To Florenskii "titanism" implied theomachy or rebelliousness (Prometheus was a Titan), refusal to accept limits, a stance associated with the cosmic elements of Goethe's Faust, Ivan Karamazov's refusal to accept the world God has created, Ivanov's theomachy (*bogoborchestvo*), and Nietzsche's Dionysian principle. He described "titanism" variously as pure power, the potential in every activity, as the "primordial and unlimited truth of the earth,"[68] and as beyond good and evil. The truth of the earth is Merezhkovskii's phrase. Florenskii used "titanic" rather than Dionysian, he explained, because Dionysus was a person, whereas the Titans were creatures of the impersonal earth; they represent an impersonal force—pure power. Titanic activity blindly rejects limits, whereas Apollonian activity operates creatively within them.[69] He specifically stated, however, that "titanism" was not a sin, but a good, the power of life, existence itself, though it can lead to sin—the sin of self-affirmation,[70] which Nietzsche celebrated and Orthodoxy condemned. Florenskii's statement, "I even at times feel sorry for God, that he created such a bad creature,"[71] may allude to his own "titanism." He confessed to the sins of pride, malice, and drunkenness, and he admitted that when he read about Dionysus he got as excited as if he had himself participated in the orgies.[72] His emphasis on humility, personified in Elder Isidore, indirectly reflects his attempt to overcome the sin of pride, for Florenskii's powerful intellect made him a kind of superman. In Isidore's simple cell, he stated, "was unlimited power."[73] But Isidore was also "fearless and independent" (traits that a Nietzschean would esteem); he even dared to defy the Archimandrite, by looking him straight in the eye and saying, "I am not afraid of you."[74]

Although Florenskii denigrated Nietzsche's "tragic optimism" as the "smile of a slave who fears to tell his master he is afraid of him,"[75] his own view of the origins of religion follows Nietzsche's *The Birth of Tragedy* to a certain extent (people create illusions to deliver them from the terror of a universe devoid of meaning). Florenskii argued that all non-Christian religions have frightening spirits (he ignored the obvious exception of Judaism), emphasized that in Buddhism the very gods were demons, and claimed that fear of this "many-sided demonic essence" led man to create black magic (note the reference to the occult) and "tragic optimism." But Nietzsche's phenomena are devoid of authentic reality; they are "skin" or "covering," beautiful forms, and that is all. No real self is expressed in them, and chaos reigns above them.[76] Florenskii's conclusion—" 'Better not to look' was the slogan of ancient culture"[77]—is an allusion, not only to Lot's wife, but to Nietzsche's views in *The Birth of Tragedy* on facing reality without becoming rigid with fear. His debt to Nietzsche is also evident in the following statement:

> The world is tragically beautiful in its fragmentation. Its harmony is in its disharmony, its unity in its enmity. Such is the paradoxical teaching of Heraclitus, followed by the paradoxical development of Friedrich Nietzsche's theory of "tragic optimism." Even the basic tone of his mood, its sap and its color . . . consists, all in all, in one word . . . contradiction.[78]

Florenskii even developed his own theory of tragedy—the collision of essence and hypostasis. His essays on art employ Nietzschean terminology, for example, the "Dionysian dispersion of the bonds of the visible," the "Apollonian vision of the spiritual world."[79]

Florenskii's concept of the Person combines Christian and Nietzschean concepts. The term "Person," as he as well as Ivanov used it, implies body and soul, spirit and flesh, as distinct from and opposed to the *individuum,* a purely secular concept. They emphasized the Personhood of Jesus and contrasted His face (*litso*) to the faceless All of Buddhism. The word *litso* originally referred to the persons in the Holy Trinity, but Florenskii and Ivanov applied it to human beings as well, for the Bible states that man is made in the image and likeness of God. The Russian word for "image," *obraz,* also means "form." The human face, Florenskii asserted, is the clearest revelation of the divine form in this world.[80] Nietzsche associated the Apollonian impulse with individuation, as distinct from the dissolution of the self in the Dionysian orgies, and with reintegration, the transition from chaos to cosmos. Florenskii described the Person as an Apollonian principle, a hypostasis of thought, reason, and intellect, and as a living unity,[81] Christianity's answer to the impersonal "titanic principle" and to the unbridled passions of Dionysianism:

> Man is not only dark desire but also holy form, not only elemental pressure [passions, instincts] but is also a face, shining through in its reality, clearly taking its place among the saints artistically depicted in the icon . . . Man is not only existence, but also *truth* [*pravda*], not only life but *philosophic truth* [*istina*], not only power, but also intellect (νοῦς), not only flesh but also spirit.[82]

Florenskii's writings contain many other references to Nietzsche, direct and indirect; examples include his reference to "self-affirmation against God,"[83] his warnings against mixing God and the demon,[84] and his insistence that love does not mean altruism. His statement, "We like the look of slaves,"[85] is a clear challenge to Nietzsche's charge that Christianity is a religion of slaves; his contention that Jesus preferred the company of real harlots to that of the Pharisees because He found their company more pleasant, and that Jesus loved sinners for their simplicity and humbleness, is an implicit reply to Nietzsche's description in *The Antichrist* (chapter 31) of Jesus as a decadent. Nietzschean formulations, such as the "will to never forget"[86] and Nietzschean images, like stormy summits, mountains and valleys, ascent and descent[87] (the latter as interpreted by Ivanov, especially), appear frequently in his writings. He even asserted that epistemology originated in the ritual emergence from self and subsequent identity of subject and object in the "cult of annual intoxicating plants," presumably the grape and the rites of Dionysus or Bacchus, the Roman god of wine.[88] As indicated above, Florenskii's distaste for moralism, his rejection of the categories of "yes or no" and "good or bad," and his preference for beauty over goodness have a distinct Nietzschean flavor.

Another striking example of Florenskii's adaptation of Nietzsche (and Wagner), directly and through Ivanov,[89] is his cultic interpretation of Christianity. Between 1904 and 1908, Ivanov had advocated the re-creation of the Dionysian theater, as a locus of "new religious experience" and "mythcreation." In this theater, which would replace the church as the *axis mundi* of popular life, a "new religious synthesis" would emerge and engender a new Russian culture and a new society. Ivanov's ideas influenced the experimental theater and mass festivals of the early Soviet period, when Florenskii's essays on temple and cults were written.[90] They constitute his implicit reply to Ivanov, Nietzsche, Wagner, and the early Soviet use of their ideas. They may also signal his attempt to find new ways of keeping Christianity alive in a society where the institutional church was under attack.

Florenskii agreed with the Symbolist view, based on Nietzsche, that art, poetry, and culture originated in religion (the myth),[91] but vehemently objected to transforming a purely religious view into semitheatrical mystery. Years before, Belyi had asked what kind of mystery would be celebrated in Ivanov's cultic theater and who or what would be worshipped—Christ, Buddha, Mohammed, or Satan?[92] In the same spirit, Florenskii attacked onedimensional secular culture:

> There is Voltaire, and Bossuet, and the Madonna, and the Pope, and Alfred de Musset, and Filaret. How can one lump them together in place of God? What then is culture? It is everything, absolutely everything that is produced by humanity. There is the Hague Peace Conference, but there is also poison

gas, there is the Red Cross, but there are also people burning each other with hot liquids. There is the Creed, but there is also Haeckel with his World Riddles. . . . There is the Gospel of John, but there is also the Luciferian gospel of Pike. There is Notre Dame, but there is also Moulin Rouge. How in the flatness of culture can one distinguish the church from the tavern or an American gadget for breaking locks from the commandment "Thou Shalt Not Steal"—also an item of culture? How in this flatness can one distinguish the great canon of repentance of Saint Andrew of Crete from the works of the Marquis de Sade? All of this is equal in culture and within the limits of this culture, there are no criteria for choice.[93]

In other words, only a higher ideal incarnated in a living Person (*Litso*) enables people to orient themselves and establish priorities and values. There are no self-contained essences, no culture without God. "In the area of culture, if we are not with Christ, we are against Him." The relationship to God cannot be neutral; Christians cannot be passive in relation to the world, but must actively work to transform it.[94] Christianity must permeate all areas of life—art, philosophy, science, politics, and economics.

Florenskii wanted to restore the emotional intensity of the cult experience to Christianity. We know the world only as a cult, he insisted; it is the incarnation of a higher world in ours through concrete and living symbols.[95] He regarded the cult as a living organism that descends from above to earth (from the invisible to the visible world), rather than vice versa, and it focuses on a real person, not an abstraction or an interpretation. His writings on cults exemplify "regressive-progressive thinking," using the past to discredit the present and provide "new" models for the future.[96] Using the findings of archaeology and anthropology, he noted that in the ancient world, the cult was the very center of life. In ancient Greece, for example, some cults centered on the real body and real blood of Dionysus; the Hebrew command "Remember!" originated in a cult of the ancestors, and the Russian Orthodox memorial service connotes a religion of the family. A cult of believers needs a concrete, tangible center, a centripetal force, to prevent its dissolution into formlessness. Christian philosophy, therefore, must focus on Jesus Christ, on His body and His blood[97] (the Eucharist). Florenskii also stressed other real and concrete elements in the Christian cult (his term), such as the cross, light,[98] and liturgy, the way the cult organizes the world and defines its conceptions of time and space. All cults have rituals, he explained; they are composed of symbols, including words, which are in themselves symbols.

Liturgy, of course, is a form of ritual and is particularly important in Russian Orthodoxy. Literally, *Pravoslavie* means both "right worship" (or "glorification") and "right belief"; the two are intertwined. Obliquely,

Florenskii resisted any attempt to tamper with the liturgy, by theological liberals or the government, or both. Indeed, it was the liberals within the church who dismissed him as editor of *Bogoslovskii Vestnik* in 1917.[99] He had a sense of the mysterious force of every word, of every name; he believed that words have invocative power, for example, the "Black Hundred" effect of the word *zhid*[100] that he had witnessed as a child. Symbolist doctrine, especially as expressed in Belyi's famous essay "The Magic of Words," Kabbalist discussions on the Name of God, and Florenskii's own readings in black magic, reinforced these childhood impressions. Ivanov attacked the orthographic reform for similar reasons; he believed that it severed the vital link of the earthly and the divine Word.

Florenskii described the temple, the space where ritual worship occurs, as a phenomenon of the cult and regarded it as the embodiment and expression of beauty and holiness and an instrument of cultural activity as well. All the elements in the Temple are concrete and converge in "all-unity" (Solov'ev's term). He called the Trinity-Sergius monastery "a Russian Athens," "a new Hellas," a product of "all-Russian national creativity," "a living museum of Russian life"; and he regarded the icons, architecture, music, and folk art of the monastery as a creative deed (*podvig*) of the Russian people (*narod*). These arts, he emphasized, were enjoyed by all the people, not just by monks or an elite. He lauded the monastery as a kind of "experimental station and laboratory for the study of contemporary aesthetics" and as a rich store of ethnographic and anthropological materials. Indeed, he asserted, the "synthesis of the arts" that Wagner and his followers, including the Symbolists, strove to achieve, had long since been realized in the great monasteries of the Russian Orthodox church. Written to persuade the Commission for the Preservation of Monuments of Art and Antiquity of the new Bolshevik regime not to demolish famous churches and monasteries, these essays[101] asserted the "democratic" and "popular" nature of Christian art and used secular terminology. Nevertheless, Florenskii's conviction of the importance of Orthodox art and church culture was sincere. He truly believed that Russian culture need not imitate foreign models such as pagan Greece because it was at least equal to them, if not superior, and that Orthodoxy and *tserkovnost'* represented the summit of Russian culture and the living source of continued creativity. He refused to leave Russia after the Bolshevik Revolution, desiring to protect and study the icons in Sergeev Posad (renamed Zagorsk in 1930), where he was living.[102]

The "new religious consciousness" was the point of entry of Florenskii's path to Orthodoxy, but was this "Orthodoxy" as the term is generally understood? A simple "yes" or "no" answer cannot be given, for Russian Orthodoxy has never made a clear distinction between theology and mysticism. It regards both as necessary and offers far more latitude to mystical speculation than the systematized rational theology of the Roman Catholic church. There is a great deal of intellectual pluralism in Orthodoxy. Florenskii was never excommunciated or even deposed; he was only criticized by some peers, but is now being republished by the supposedly very conservative church establishment.

He did accept church canons, viewing them not as irksome constraints but as channels which direct spiritual energy to new attainments and creative flights, sometimes defending them on extra-ecclesiastical grounds. Inspired by the God-seekers' emphasis on beauty, mysticism, psychologism, and epistemology, and challenged by their Nietzsche-inspired critique of Christianity, he found theological sources for his own views in the early and medieval Orthodox church and revitalized them by using concepts and terms that derived from Symbolism, Nietzsche, and modern science and scholarship. He wished to develop an all-encompassing Orthodox worldview as the cosmological basis for a specifically Christian society and culture. Detesting the fragmented modern world, he rejected rationalism and emphasized the emotional aspects of religion and direct personal experience, thereby introducing existentialist themes into Russian Orthodoxy.

It was this in particular that Florovsky criticized, arguing that Florenskii placed full weight on personal subjective experience, selected only what appealed to him from Orthodoxy, lacked a sense of history, and was incapable of objectivity. Florovsky objected to the absence of Christology in Florenskii's writings and claimed that Sophia, not Christ, was the real object of his devotion.[103] By contrast, Vladimir Lossky, who appreciates mysticism and emphasizes the apophatic nature of Russian theology (what one cannot know about God), refers to Florenskii simply as a "modern Russian theologian" and does not condemn him at all.[104] Lossky is actually more illustrative of the common and accepted view of Florenskii—that of a highly respected and influential thinker within the Orthodox church. Neither Florovsky nor Lossky discusses Florenskii's objections to ethical rules and moral norms, surely a difference in degree if not in kind, from traditional Russian Orthodox teachings. After 1922, he claimed to have outgrown *Pillar*. An examination of this claim is beyond the scope of this paper, but let us simply note that he died in the Gulag, a martyr to his faith. His commitment to Orthodoxy, however defined, cannot be doubted. His case demonstrates that the Orthodox church was not as monolithic as its detractors assert and that a great deal of creative intercourse took place between persons teaching in church academies such as Florenskii and the people of the "new religious consciousness."

Notes

I would like to thank George L. Kline and the late Fr. John Meyendorff for their helpful comments.

1. P. A. Florenskii, *Stolp i utverzhdenie istiny* (Moscow, 1914). Henceforth cited as *Stolp*.

2. "Sviashchennik Pavel Florenskii: Iz bogoslovskogo naslediia," *Bogoslovskie Trudy* 17 (1977), henceforth cited as *BT*.

3. V. V. Zenkovsky, *A History of Russian Philosophy,* trans. George L. Kline (New York, 1953), 2:878–880, 896. Zenkovsky states that Florenskii was connected to the God-seekers by "invisible bonds" and that his theology included many "extra-ecclesiastical ideas," but does not specify which these were, nor does he identify the "new wine in old bottles" to which he alludes. Georges Florovsky maintains that Florenskii's most famous book, *The Pillar and the Affirmation of Truth* (1914), "demonstrates in the clearest possible way every ambiguity and failing in the religious-philosophical movement." *Ways of Russian Theology* (Vaduz, 1987) 1:276.

4. For details on Merezhkovskii, see B. G. Rosenthal, *D. S. Merezhkovsky and the Silver Age* (The Hague, 1975); C. H. Bedford, *The Seeker* (Lawrence, 1975); Jutta Scherrer, *Die Petersburger Religiös-Philosophischen Vereinigungen* (Wiesbaden, 1973).

5. George Putnam, *Russian Alternatives to Marxism* (Knoxville, 1977) 58, Scherrer, pp. 206–207; Michael Hagemeister, ed., *Mnimosti v geometrii* (Moscow, 1922; rpt. Munich, 1985), especially "P. A. Florenskij und seine Schrift *Mnimosti v geometrii*" 6–8.

6. See "Pis'ma P. A. Florenskogo k B. N. Bugaevu, in *Vestnik,* no. 114 (1974): 149–168, and "Zhiznennyi put' Florenskogo," *Sobranie sochinenii* (Paris, 1985) 1:23; henceforth cited as *SS*.

7. *Stolp* 24.

8. In "Vospominaniia detstva," *Vestnik,* no. 100 (1971): 253–254. Florenskii recalled his vivid sense of an invisible world, of a mysterious unity in which everything that lives is connected to everything else and makes up the fabric of universal correspondences. See also *Vestnik,* no. 106 (1972): 188, 194.

9. "I do not believe in the possibility of 'constructing' a Church," he wrote to Belyi. The Church is ours . . . . Either it is entirely absurd or it must grow from a holy seed." He feared that their apocalypticism might be premature, fretted over whether he and Belyi were Christians in the usual sense of the word and if the Christ of the first Christians was the same as the Christ of the Second Coming. "Pis'ma," *Vestnik,* no. 114 (1974): 161. See pp. 153–155, for Florenskii's graph of the degrees of ignorance of Christ over time and his assumption that the maximum stage of ignorance had been passed. Also note his use of the fish ideogram for Christ and of mathematical terminology, $X°$, for Christ.

10. *Stolp* 5, 125–134.

11. Ibid., 129.

12. Like those of many God-seekers, including Belyi, Florenskii's spiritual search included interest in the occult, but he soon came to the conclusion that the occult is demonic. Significantly, his very first articles were on the temptation of the occult: see "O sueverii," *Novyi Put'*, no. 8 (1903): 91–121; "Spiritizm kak antikhristianstvo," *Novyi Put'*, no. 3 (1904): 149–167. The extensive footnotes on occult literature in *Pillar* show that he read virtually everything that was available to him on the subject; *Pillar* 622–624, 694–695, 718, 730–731, 752.

13. Paul Florensky, *Salt of the Earth: A Narrative of the Life of the Elder of Gethsemane Skete Hieromonk Abba Isidore*, trans. Richard Betts, Saint Herman of Alaska Brotherhood (Piatina, California, 1987) 96. I am indebted to Robert Nichols for calling this book to my attention. On the title page, Florenskii referred to himself as Isidore's "unworthy spiritual son." Florenskii was then experiencing deep depression— the "learned professor" may speak, at least in part, for himself.

14. On this, see Bernice Glatzer Rosenthal, ed., *Nietzsche in Russia* (Princeton, 1986) and Edith W. Clowes, *The Revolution of Moral Consciousness: Nietzsche in Russian Literature* (DeKalb, 1988), chapter 5, "The Mystical Symbolists," pp. 115–176.

15. *Stolp* 64.

16. "Kul't i filosofiia," *BT* 122.

17. *Stolp* 232. The Council of Chalcedon, 451, ruled that Jesus was both divine and human; in Florenskii's eyes, rationalism constituted a revival of earlier heresies that denied either His human or His divine nature.

18. Ibid., 91.

19. "Ikonostas," *SS* 1:309.

20. *Stolp* 225.

21. Ibid., 92; see, for example, Viacheslav Ivanov, *Po zvezdam* (St. Petersburg, 1909) 108.

22. *Po zvezdam* 120–122.

23. The idea seems to have originated with the Franciscan monk, Joachim of Fiore, who preached that God reveals Himself in stages: the Old Testament is the revelation of God the Father; the New Testament of God the Son, and there will be a Third Testament of God the Holy Spirit.

24. The phrase was used by Ivanov after 1908 in the context of discussions on Symbolism which Florenskii followed.

25. Letter to Belyi, 18 June 1904, *Vestnik*, no. 114 (1974): 158.

26. D. S. Merezhkovskii, "O prichinakh upadka i o novykh techeniiakh sovremennoi russkoi literatury," *Polnoe sobranie sochinenii* (St. Petersburg, 1914) 18:175–275; see especially pp. 215–218.

27. Florovsky, 2:281.

28. *Stolp* 75.

29. Ibid., 84.

30. Ibid., 99.

31. Ibid., 321.

32. Ibid., 310.

33. Ibid., 390. He also associated Sophia with divine contemplation, joy in common unity, and the mystical unity of the Universal Church.

34. Ibid., 99.

35. Ibid., 263.

36. Ibid., pp. 171–173.

37. Friedrich Nietzsche, *Untimely Meditations,* trans. R. J. Hollingdale (Cambridge, 1989) 5. Nietzsche continues: "the opposite of culture [is] barbarism . . . lack of style or a chaotic jumble of all styles" (6).

38. "Ikonostas," *SS* 1:230, 311.

39. Ibid., 225.

40. Ibid., 299.

41. Ibid., 289.

42. Ibid., 205.

43. *Stolp* 3.

44. Ibid., 3.

45. Ibid., 411, in the twelfth letter, "Friendship."

46. Ibid., 437.

47. Ibid., 470. See p. 473 for his discussion of the selective/exclusive nature of love, the element of free choice.

48. Ibid., 462.

49. S. N. Savel'ev, *Ideinoe bankrotstvo bogoiskatel'stva v Rossii* (Leningrad, 1987) 174.

50. On this, see Bernice Glatzer Rosenthal, "The Transmutation of Russian Symbolism," *Slavic Review* 36 (December 1977): 608–627.

51. In one of his letters to Belyi, Florenskii claimed that Rozanov cannot understand the "third animal element; he cannot see the aspect of Bethlehem sufficiently clearly and *purely,*" and cannot tell the difference between Bethlehem and Golgotha; *Vestnik,* no. 114 (1974): 153–154.

52. *Stolp* 297. Jaroslav Pelikan, *The Spirit of Eastern Christendom* (Chicago, 1977) 224–225, notes the Orthodox struggle against extreme asceticism and its view of the material world as potential, not evil.

53. *Stolp* 292.

54. Ibid., 90.

55. Ibid., 396–397.

56. Ibid., 299.

57. Ibid., 300.

58. "Iz vstrech s P. A. Florenskim (1909–1910)," *Vestnik,* no. 142 (1984): 72. El'chaninov and Florenskii attended the same gymnasium in Tiflis and remained close friends.

59. Ibid., 73.

60. *Stolp* 455.

61. Ibid., 266–273.

62. Ibid., 273.

63. Timothy Ware, *The Russian Orthodox Church* (Baltimore, 1963) 74.

64. I am indebted to Nicoletta Misler for this information.

65. "Deduktsiia semi tainstv," *BT* 146.

66. "Vospominaniia detstva," *Vestnik,* no. 99 (1971): 78–80.

67. Ware 236; Vladimir Lossky, *The Mystical Theology of the Eastern Church* (Crestwood, N.Y., 1976) 9–10.

68. *BT* 141.

69. "Tainstva i obriady," *BT* 139–140.

70. Ibid., 139–141, 146.

71. El'chaninov, *Vestnik,* no. 142 (1984): 75.

72. Ibid., 72.

73. Florenskii, *Salt of the Earth* 98.

74. Ibid., 81, 89. Isidore follows no rules at all—a combination of Jesus fulfilling the spirit rather than the letter of the law and Nietzsche's insistence on obeying one's own law.

75. *Stolp* 277.

76. Ibid., 276.

77. Ibid., 277.

78. Ibid., 155.

79. "Ikonostas," *SS* 1:205.

80. Ibid., 109.

81. *Stolp* 80.

82. "Tainstva i obriady," *BT* 141.

83. *Stolp* 242.

84. Ibid., 276.

85. El'chaninov, *Vestnik,* no. 142 (1984): 74. The editors of *Salt of the Earth* consider the statement an allusion to Tuitchev's untitled poem which ends: "In slavish image Heaven's King/Has walked across you, blessing you" (p. 16, note 7).

86. *Stolp* 19.

87. See, for example, "Ikonostas," *SS* 1:204.

88. El'chaninov 70.

89. On this see Bernice Glatzer Rosenthal, "Theater as Church: The Vision of the Mystical Anarchists," *Russian History,* 4, pt. 2 (1977): 122–141; "Wagner and Wagnerian Ideas in Russia," *Wagnerism in European Politics and Culture,* ed. David Large and William Weber (Ithaca, 1984) 198–245 ; Lars Kleberg "'People's Theater' and the Revolution," in Nils Nilsson, ed., *Art, Society, Revolution: Russia 1917–1921* (Stockholm, 1979) 179–197; George Kalbouss, "From Mystery to Fantasy: An Attempt to Categorize the Plays of the Russian Symbolists," *Canadian-American Slavic Studies,* 8 (Winter 1974): 489–494.

90. "Khramovoe deistvo kak sintez iskusstv," *SS* 1:41–55, "Troitse Sergeeva Lavra i Rossiia," *SS* 1:63–84, "Kul't, religia i kul'tura, *BT* 101–119, "Filosofiia kul'ta, *BT* 195–248, "Tainstva i obriady," *BT* 135–142, "Kul't i filosofiia," *BT* 119–135.

91. "Ikonostas," *SS* 1:253.

92. Andrei Belyi, "Teatr i sovremennaia drama," in *Teatr. Kniga o novom teatre,* ed. Georgii Chulkov (St. Petersburg, 1908) 270–276.

93. "Kul't i filosofiia," *BT* 127; internal quotation marks removed.

94. "Khristianstvo i kul'tura," *Zhurnal Moskovskoi patriarkhii,* no. 4 (1983) 53–54; first published in England, *The Pilgrim* 4.4 (1924): 421–437. The essay reflects his conviction that Christians must fight Soviet atheism.

95. "Kul't i filosofiia," *BT* 126.

96. Ophelia Schutte uses the term to describe Nietzsche's thought. *Nietzsche Without Masks* (Chicago, 1984) 8. The same pattern can be seen in other areas;

Florenskii tried to develop a new cosmology based on the writings of Ptolemy and Dante.

97. According to Gippius, Florenskii's emphasis on blood led him to believe that Mendel Beilis was guilty of ritual murder in the famous trial; she also implies that Florenskii influenced Rozanov's notorious writings on the subject. Florenskii's insistence on the real body and real blood of Dionysus and Jesus may imply a fascination with rituals of sacrifice, which he may have projected onto the Jews. Saveliev (pp. 174–175), citing archival sources, states that Merezhkovskii, Belyi, and Solov'ev accused Florenskii of "black hundredism," but does not explain why. Zinaida Gippius, *Zhivye litsa* (Prague, 1921), pt. 2, pp. 75–76. In *Salt of the Earth,* (pp. 66–67) Florenskii emphasizes Isidore's kindness to Jews, but they are Jewish converts to Christianity, i.e. no longer Jews.

98. "Kul't i filosofiia," *BT* 131 .

99. I am indebted to Paul Valliere for this information.

100. "Vospominaniia detstva," *Vestnik,* no. 99 (1971): 82–83.

101. "Troitse-Sergeeva Lavra i Rossiia," *SS* 1:83–84; "Khramovoe deistvo kak sintez iskusstv" 42–46.

102. I am indebted to John Lindsay Opie for this information.

103. Florovsky 2:276–281.

104. Lossky 65, 106.

The Merezhkovskys' Third Testament
and the Russian Utopian Tradition

OLGA MATICH

Although representative of the *fin de siècle,* the Merezhkovsky Religion of the Third Testament belongs to the Russian utopian tradition, religious and revolutionary. In keeping with the Symbolist spirit of the time, the neo-Christian utopia proposed by Zinaida Gippius and Dmitrii Merezhkovsky was characterized by self-conscious religious and cultural eclecticism, fusing Christian, pagan, and nineteenth-century radical beliefs and rituals into one. Like many of their contemporaries, they applied the esoteric principle of correspondences to religion, thus creating a symbolic system of equivalencies, not religious hierarchies. In the complex system of double exposures that typify the Merezhkovsky utopian enterprise, religion was superimposed on Nietzschean self-deification and the quest for sexual identity; politics, in turn, was superimposed on religion; and the whole process was expected to result in a grand synthesis.

Uniting eros, religion, and sociality, the neo-Christian ideology of Gippius and Merezhkovsky reflects what from their philosophical perspective are key concerns of Russian culture. Love, religion, and social action commonly form a triad in the Russian utopian tradition, resembling the innumerable dialectical triads of philosophical idealism. In the nihilist and anti-nihilist ideology that developed in the 1860s, erotic love and religion assumed the form of militant asceticism and militant atheism, but functionally their roles in the triad remained the same. Although the fusion of the three elements always remains incomplete, the desire to reconcile them characterized Russian thought of the second half of the nineteenth and early twentieth centuries. I am referring to the ideologies of such seminal figures as Nikolai Chernyshevsky, Fedor Dostoevsky, Nikolai Fedorov, Vladimir Solov'ev, Gippius, and Merezhkovsky.

Examining the second half of the nineteenth century through the prism of Gippius's and Merezhkovsky's metaphysics, one is struck by the eschatological impulse toward redemption or resurrection at the expense of procreation. Intertwined with the utopian desire to reconcile the spirit and flesh[1] in the

New Jerusalem was the polarization between procreative and redemptive love. The radical and later Symbolist vision of the future resurrection of mankind conflicted with the procreative ideal associated with the immediate future, not some distant time. It may be claimed that the Aksakov family idyll and Tolstoy's *War and Peace* (*Voina i mir*) represented the high points of the Russian procreative vision. In the words of Merezhkovsky, Tolstoy's heroines respond to the men's "philosophizing" by retorting "with a silent and irrefutable argument, the bringing into the world of a fresh child."[2] Perhaps, in fact, this is the last unequivocal affirmation of the traditional procreative ideal in Russian literature.

In the course of the nineteenth century, the traditional family ideal was gradually replaced by the ideal of the "new man" as developed by Chernyshevsky, Dostoevsky, Nietzsche, Fedorov, and Solov'ev, for whom eros was the agent of rebirth or resurrection, not procreation: the "new man" gives birth to himself and to the "new word," or "new gospel," that will transform life. Some of the attacks on Chernyshevsky's utopia in *What Is to Be Done?* (*Chto delat'?*) focused on the question of children: "Predpolagaiutsia li deti?" (Are children intended?) was one of the polemical questions underlying the sharply negative response to the novel by such authors as Vasily Botkin and Afanasy Fet.[3] Dostoevsky's treatment of the family was also ambiguous— certainly it is not represented as an ideal in his novels. Even the prophet of procreation, Tolstoy, rejected it at the end of his life. Despite the loud voice of procreation raised once again at the turn of the twentieth century by Vasily Rozanov, it was countered successfully by the powerful will to resurrection on the part of the Symbolists.

The emphasis on resurrection in Russian culture is, of course, rooted in Orthodoxy, in which Easter is more important than the celebration of Christ's birth. "What Gogol once said is true—that nowhere, even in the Orthodox East, is this holiday celebrated as it is in Russia."[4] In contrast to the Western church, there is a strong element of concreteness in the Orthodox treatment of redemption and resurrection. Instead of the abstract "Joyeuses Pâques," "Happy Easter," or "Fröhliche Ostern," the common holiday greeting in Catholic and Protestant countries, the Eastern Orthodox Easter greeting emphasizes the concrete act of Christ's resurrection: the exclamation "Christ has risen!" is reinforced by the obligatory response "Indeed He has risen!" The same concreteness characterizes the Orthodox Easter icon ("Descent into Hell") in which Christ is pulling the sinners out of Hell in a reenactment of the actual redemption.[5]

Dostoevsky's writing reflects both the utopian triad and the will to resurrection subsuming the procreative ideal. Raskolnikov and Sonia can be seen as examples of the attempt to bring about the desired synthesis of love, religion, and social action. But instead of the "new man" Raskolnikov, who invokes the image of the apocalyptic New Jerusalem, it is the Christian Sonia who enacts the triadic union. As a saintly prostitute, she unites sex and religion, and in the end creates a sense of brotherhood in which Raskolnikov can be redeemed and resurrected. Prefiguring Solov'ev's and the Merezhkovskys' image of Sophia as Virginal Mother and Holy Spirit, Sonia seems to possess some of their salient characteristics. Not only is her name Sof'ia, but she is also the icon-like Virgin Mother despite her profession, and like the Symbolists' Holy Spirit she mediates and resolves the dialectical conflict in Raskolnikov's soul.

In describing his theory of the extraordinary man to Porfiry Petrovich, Raskolnikov explicitly subordinates procreation to his generation's redemptive "new word": "Men are *in general* divided by a law of nature into two categories: an inferior one (ordinary), that is to say, the material whose only purpose is to reproduce its kind, and the people proper, that is to say, those who possess the gift or talent to say *a new word* in their particular environment."[6] Raskolnikov's anti-procreative stance is reinforced by his apparently asexual relations with women.[7] At the other end of the religious and political spectrum, the saintly Prince Myshkin, apparently afflicted by impotence, embodies the transfigurative ideal of resurrection instead of procreation. Shatov's Slavophile reverence for all new life and its sublime mystery[8] is repudiated by the Christ-like atheist Kirillov, whose objective is the transformation of man in *this* world. In an example of Dostoevskian dialogicity, his censure of procreation is delivered as Marie Shatov is giving birth next door: "I think man must stop reproducing himself. What's the point of having children? Why strive for progress when the goal has already been achieved? It says in the Gospel that in the resurrection they shall not have children, but be as the angels of God."[9] Although the explicit reference to children is Kirillov's own, which is significant for my argument, the statement is a paraphrase of Jesus's response to the Sadducees who question him about men who die childless: "in the resurrection they neither marry nor are given in marriage, but are like angels in heaven" (Matt. 22:30; Mark 12:25). Furthermore, instead of propagating, one "must be either physically transformed or die," Kirillov suggests to Shatov.[10] In discussing *The Possessed* (*Besy*), Merezhkovsky places special emphasis on Kirillov's utopian views, which anticipate the future "gradual but literal 'physical transformation of man.'"[11] Kirillov himself associates man's transfiguration on earth with those moments of "eternal harmony" that he experiences with increasing frequency.[12]

The most explicit and eccentric treatment of the opposition between resurrection and procreation in relation to the nineteenth-century triad was Fedorov's utopian project of resurrecting the dead. It prescribed collective abstinence and propounded the replacement of "the will to procreation" by the "will to resurrection." Opposing sexual and filial love, Fedorov declared that the former is atavistic[13] and mortal; the latter results in the universal resurrection of parents and personal immortality on earth. By his definition, mankind's "common cause" was the actual physical resurrection of ancestors, associated with rebellion against the fundamental evil "of nature itself, of the unconscious . . . of procreation itself, and of death that is inextricably linked to birth."[14] To establish the kingdom of God on earth, men and women must abandon the desire to propagate and become only sons and daughters, limiting familial feeling to love of parents.[15] Although unpublished and little known in his time, Fedorov had a profound influence on some of his contemporaries, especially Dostoevsky, Tolstoy, and Solov'ev, all of whom grappled in their own way with similar questions. Fedorov's call for universal resurrection must have contributed to the further demotion of procreative love in the Symbolist era.[16]

The preference for resurrection or transformation over procreation continued into the Soviet period. In Fedor Gladkov's *Cement,* Dasha Chumalova's daughter Niurka is sacrificed to the socialist utopia; instead of mother and wife, Dasha becomes a "new woman" who possesses the "new word." Much has been made by Roman Jakobson of Vladimir Mayakovsky's rejection of children and his infatuation with the utopian future, which

> is linked . . . with a pronounced dislike of children, a fact which would seem at first sight to be hardly consonant with his fanatical belief in tomorrow. But . . . in Mayakovsky's spiritual world an abstract faith in the coming transformation of the world is joined quite properly with hatred for the evil continuum of specific tomorrows that only prolong today . . . and undying hostility to that "broody-hen" love that serves only to reproduce the present way of life.[17]

Mayakovsky's anti-procreative stance is also reflected in Boris Pasternak's description of his contemporary's view of eros, which can be read against the background of Raskolnikov's statement about the extraordinary man:

> For no one knew as well as [Mayakovsky] all the vulgarity of the natural fire when it has not been gradually enraged by cold water. Nor did they know as he did that the passion that suffices for the continuation of the

race is not adequate for creativity, which needs a passion sufficient for the continuation of the race's image, that is, a passion that inwardly resembles Christ's Passion, and whose newness inwardly resembles the Divine Promise.[18]

In keeping with its preference for eclecticism and the union of opposites or the principle of double exposure, the Russian intellectual elite at the turn of the twentieth century interpreted the opposition procreation/resurrection in Dostoevskian, Nietzschean, Fedorovian, and general Apocalyptic terms. Kirillov kills himself with the goal of vanquishing death. Nietzsche's superman overcomes the spectre of death by giving birth to himself in an act of self-deification. Fedorov proposes what can be described as a Tantric inversion of desire, conquering death by physically resurrecting the fathers. Equally preoccupied with death, the anti-Nietzcheans, many of whom adopted Dostoevsky's and Solov'ev's Godman as their ethical model, sought to conquer death by a higher form of love. For them, the ideal was represented by the Christ-like Prince Myshkin and Alesha Karamazov.

Formulated in *The Meaning of Love* (*Smysl liubvi*, 1892–1894), Solov'ev's theory of eros became the seminal text on love for the Symbolist mystics, ranging from the Merezhkovskys to Bely and Blok. According to Solov'ev, the only divine form of love is erotic, but its object is not propagation of the species, since child-bearing results in the continuing cycle of birth and death. The ordinary union of two lovers cannot conquer death; this can only be accomplished by the restoration of man's androgynous unity lost at the time of the Fall:

> In empirical reality there is no man *as such*—he exists only in a one-sided and limited form as a masculine or a feminine individual. . . . The true human being . . . cannot be merely a man or merely a woman, but must be the higher unity of the two. To realize this unity or to create the true human being as the free unity of the masculine and the feminine elements, which preserve their formal separateness but overcome their essential disparity and disruption, is the direct *task* of love.[19]

In Plato's *Symposium,* which influenced Solov'ev's philosophy of love, the primal androgyne lost that higher unity when it rebelled against the gods. While preaching abstinence, Solov'ev extolled the divine transformational power of erotic love. Therein lies the paradox of *The Meaning of Love* that captivated the sexually-troubled imagination of the Symbolist generation.

The affinity between the Merezhkovskys and the utopian thinkers—who, on the one hand, hoped to integrate eros, religion, and sociality, and, on the other, sought to change nature by depreciating procreation and promoting man's transfiguration—is obvious. Particularly striking are the similarities between Solov'ev's and the Merezhkovskys' views on the sacredness of erotic love accompanied by aversion to its physical consummation. Their philosophical circle—which in the beginning (1900) included Rozanov, Dmitrii Filosofov, Aleksandr Benois, Leon Bakst, Petr Pertsov, and Valentin Nuvel'—was especially concerned with the "unsolved mystery of sex" and its relationship to God. "Many desired God as a justification for sex," according to Gippius.[20] And since they sought to eliminate procreation, they also considered tampering with the sex act, inventing a new form of erotic union which would be based on the equality of both partners.[21] In contrast to Merezhkovsky and Filosofov, Gippius preferred its abolition: "there is much more reason to believe . . . that there will be no sex act, not that it will be preserved. . . . Conversely we must . . . assert the phenomenal transfiguration of the flesh."[22] Her concern can be compared to Kirillov's notion of ecstasy which if prologed will lead to the physical restructuring of man. Gippius describes her divine love for Filosofov in 1905 as having actually elevated her to the status of the utopian "new man" (*budushchii dalekii chelovek*).[23] And despite the absence of an apparent link between her circle's interest in the physical transformation of the human body and Fedorov's project, there exists a clear typological connection.

Like some of their utopian predecessors and contemporaries, Merezhkovsky and Gippius were preoccupied with the esoteric significance of numbers, especially the mystery of the androgynous "two in one" and the Trinitarian "three in one." In an effort to provide their Religion of the Third Testament with an inner developmental logic and expand it into the social realm at the time of the 1905 Revolution, Gippius formulated her theory of the "tripartite structure of the world." According to her mystical, yet dialectical numerology, "one" refers to the uniqueness and indivisibility of the individual; "two" to divine erotic love (or the "two in one") all the while preserving individual uniqueness; and "three" to community, or sociality, which becomes the "three in one," without destroying the erotic "two." This deceptively simple scheme offered a comprehensive program for the future organization of society; following the nineteenth-century utopian triad, it ensured the perfect harmony of the personal, religious, and social needs of the individual and the collective.

Typifying the occult principle of correspondences, these mystical numbers and numerical formulae had multiple esoteric meanings for the Merezhkovskys, which they artfully intertwined in their triadic philosophy of resurrection. Like Solov'ev, they extended the Chalcedonian formula regarding

Christ's divine and human nature to the reunification of the two aspects of man, spiritual and physical. In a post-Nietzschean *imitatio Christi,* the "two in one" of the Third Testament came to symbolize the non-procreative union of the spirit and flesh, which would result in the "new man." Also known as "consecrated flesh," it was designed to transcend the asceticism of historical Christianity but without the consummation of love. The "two in one" became the emblem of immortal love or fusion of heavenly and earthly Aphrodite; procreative love, by contrast, always results in death.[24] At the most sublime level of their religious hierarchy, it represented the androgyne and androgynous love, which would bring to an end the procreative process. According to Gippius, *agape,* or Christian spiritual love, resurrects the androgyne as one of the manifestations of the "two in one." Quoting Clement of Rome, a church father of the first century, Merezhkovsky described the coming Third Testament as a time "when two shall be one, that which is without [shall be] as that which is within, and the male and the female, neither male nor female."[25]

In keeping with his well-known predilection for dialectics and "historiosophy," Merezhkovsky developed the Apocalyptic Teaching of the Third Testament, predicated on the Trinitarian "three in one." Traditionally, this mystical phrase invoked the Holy Trinity, but in his discourse, it also signified the future religion. Originally presented by Joachim of Fiore (Floris), an Italian mystic of the twelfth century, the Covenant of the Third Testament formulated a prophetic theology of history, according to which history was divided into three ages: God the Father, God the Son, and God the Holy Ghost. In the third and last age, mankind would be ruled by an *intelligentia spiritualis,* resembling the Symbolists' chiliastic kingdom. Although the actual evidence of Joachim's direct influence on modern European thought is problematic,[26] many contemporary historians associate nineteenth-century utopian radicalism with his Trinitarian theology. According to the authors of *Utopian Thought in the Western World,* "when translated into secular terminology, the 'three states' of Joachimism became, in the nineteenth century, the dominant philosophy of history ending in a utopia."[27]

Joachim's teachings may have entered Russian utopian thought in the middle of the nineteenth century through George Sand, who transformed the mystic's ideas into a theory of radical social revolution. Solov'ev's Trinitarian view of history and Nikolai Berdyaev's religious philosophy have been linked directly to Joachim's ideas and to Johannine Christianity.[28] Besides synthesizing the Old and New Testaments in accordance with Joachim's teachings,[29] Merezhkovsky was obsessed with the reconciliation of all opposites, including

Dionysus and Apollo, paganism and Christianity, and, of course, man and woman in an all-encompassing, eclectic union.[30]

Although there seems to be no evidence of the direct influence of Fedorov on the Merezhkovskys,[31] some of their favorite concerns resemble his ideas on resurrection and the Holy Trinity.[32] Based on the concept of tri-unity (*triedinstvo*), the Trinity, according to Fedorov, is the church of immortals, and the Trinitarian deity is the God of resurrection and the future: "The cause of death is absent in the Trinity, which contains all the conditions for immortality" and is the source of resurrective love uniting man with God.[33] In Fedorov's philosophy, the Trinity, revealing the path of the future, provides the model for an ideal society in which all mankind will be saved.[34] Merezhkovsky's Religion of the Third Testament also emphasized the seminal role of the Trinitarian ideal and its inextricable link to the transcendence of death and the creation of the "new man."

One of the results of the androgynous ideal and Trinitarian thought at the turn of the century was the devaluation of woman's traditional role in everyday life. Eros, motherhood, and social mediation as practiced by women were transferred from the social realm to the mystical. The female image was deified by Solov'ev and his followers, and a whole set of correspondences, in the Symbolist sense, was established. The Eternal Feminine was associated with Sophia and the Virgin Mother, who were in turn identified with the Holy Spirit mediating the Christian "three in one." Finding a place in this courtly male culture, which rejected woman's biological function, became one of Gippius's central concerns. In an effort to become the "new man" of the Third Testament, Gippius chose to enact both numerical formulae.

Laying bare her own sexual ambiguity, she described her person as an emodiment of the "two in one": "I do not desire exclusive femininity, just as I do not desire exclusive masculinity. Each time someone is insulted and dissatisfied within me; with women, my femininity is active, with men—my masculinity! In my thoughts, my desires, in my spirit—I am more a man; in my body—I am more a woman," wrote Gippius in her private diary "Contes d'amour."[35] The Merezhkovsky marriage can also be viewed as an androgynous union, in which she played the male role, and he the female.[36] In the public domain, her androgynous stance was revealed in her male poetic persona and use of male pseudonyms.[37] Gippius's provocative, playful reenactment of Cleopatra and the Pushkinian dandy in her social behavior had a similar function.[38]

The Trinitarian "three in one" was revealed in the Merezhkovsky *ménage à trois,* carefully orchestrated by Gippius. Predictably, she was the pivotal

figure in the *ménage,* which included Merezhkovsky and Filosofov.[39] Like
Fedorov, Gippius was interested not only in the sublime, but also in the
practical, everyday connotations of the Holy Trinity, reenacting it in her
personal life. Thus, her interpretation of the Merezhkovsky triple union can
be compared to Fedorov's description of the "indivisible Trinity" as a close-
knit friendship or personal association of three people.[40] Reifying the neo-
Christian Holy Trinity, the Merezhkovsky triple union was mediated by
Gippius, who played the role of Sophia-Virgin Mother-Holy Spirit; all three
were mutually interchangeable in her eclectic mystical teachings.[41] For example, in the poem "The Eternal Feminine" ("Vechnozhenstvennoe," *Siianiia*),
based on a series of mystical correspondences, the androgynous persona
clearly identifies with the Eternal Feminine and her other equivalents. In
"Blagaia Vest'" ("Annunciation," 1904), one of Gippius's very few poems
written from the perspective of a female persona, the lyrical "I" is that of the
Virgin Mary; reenacting the Annunciation, the poem ends with the lines:
"Khochet On—khochu i ia./ Pust' voidet Liubov' Gospodniaia."

Besides representing androgynous love and the Holy Trinity respectively,
the Merezhkovsky marriage and their *ménage à trois* were also designed as
agents of social action in the nineteenth-century radical sense. Viacheslav
Ivanov actually accused Merezhkovsky of practicing the heresy of utilitarianism: "the heresy of social utilitarianism . . . is still alive, finding its last
champion in Russia ["na Rusi"] in the person of D. S. Merezhkovsky."[42]
Although Gippius dismissed *What Is to Be Done?* as crude materialism, she
described Chernyshevsky in heroic and saintly terms.[43] As I have written
elsewhere, one of the models for the Merezhkovsky marriage and subsequent
triple union was the chaste radical marriage[44] and triangular love depicted in
this novel[45] To Gippius's Vera Pavlovna, Dmitry Sergeevich Merezhkovsky
played the role of Dmitry Sergeevich Lopukhov; Filosofov later assumed the
part of Kirsanov, the third member of the Chernyshevskian triple union. By
no means a courtly or romantic triangle, the Merezhkovsky *ménage* was a
society of ideological collaborators; it reflected Gippius's theory of the
"tripartite structure of the world" and served as a model of the new order.
Anti-procreative by definition, the *ménage* was seen as a form of the new
marriage, which was reflected in the liturgy that they performed to celebrate
their first coming together. Emphasizing the resurrective nature of love and
the marital status of the triple union, the liturgy combined the Russian
Orthodox marriage and Easter services.

In political terms, the triple union, intended as the secret nucleus of their
New Church, was, at first, the guiding force behind the Religious Philo-

sophical Meetings of 1901–1903. Conceived by Gippius as a gathering of the educated clergy and the religious members of the intelligentsia, these meetings had a hidden agenda of creating the Church of the Third Testament, which would reunite the established Russian Orthodox church and the secular intelligentsia in a final synthesis of "new sociality." In keeping with the utopian ideal of the Merezhkovskys and their collaborators, many of the meetings focused on the meaning of love, sex, and marriage.

Like many of their Symbolist contemporaries, the Merezhkovskys were politicized by the Revolution of 1905, about the time they began to broaden their religious ideas to include social concerns and Socialist Revolutionary political ideology. The personal impulse was their new friendship with Il'ia Fondaminsky-Bunakov and Boris Savinkov, whom they tried to convert to their religion.[46] As a result of this meeting, Gippius wrote that she "understood the soul of the old Russian revolution and came to love it. Its truth and *falsity*. Internally I felt its *dark* bond with Christ. The possibility of enlightenment and then of strength."[47] She became particularly close to Savinkov, the controversial leader of the Socialist Revolutionary Fighting Organization.

From the perspective of revolutionary tactics, the triple union resembled the function and structure of an underground cell as described by Nechaev, with the exception that his secret group was to consist of five people, not three. Like Nechaev and subsequent Russian revolutionaries (cf. Lenin's pamphlet *What Is to Be Done* [*Chto delat'?*]), the Merezhkovskys tried to organize other triple unions modeled on their own to promote the Religion of the Third Testament. The Merezhkovskys and Filosofov even went to Europe in 1906 in search of ideological collaborators who would form triple unions, functioning as the "yet invisible [inner] Church."[48] The only other known anti-procreative triangle of this kind that lasted for any significant length of time was that of Anton Kartashev[49] and Gippius's two sisters, Tat'iana and Natal'ia. It fell apart, however, because Kartashev wanted an exclusive personal love, which included sexual relations, family, and children.

The Merezhkovskys' neo-Christianity was shockingly provocative for its day and eclectic in its reliance on the Christian theology, the occult, numerology, and the esoteric principle of "as above so below." Moreover, many components of the model had an underside. And in keeping with the Symbolist principle of *zhiznetvorchestvo* (life-creation), the Merezhkovskys attempted to embody their favorite abstractions into life practices. Perhaps the most surprising hidden facet, or underside, of the Merezhkovsky mystical program was its nihilist (Chernyshevskian) substratum. Although their anti-procreative, androgynous, and triadic religion was rooted in Christian mysticism and Nietzschean values, it can be viewed as a part of the Russian utopian tradition, ranging from Chernyshevsky and Dostoevsky to Fedorov and Solov'ev.

Notes

1. The Merezhkovskys' preoccupation with the union of spirit and flesh (*sviataia plot'*) may be traced to Solov'ev's ideas about transforming and spiritualizing matter, associated with the function of art: "So long as the spirit is incapable of giving direct external expression to its inner content and of incarnating itself in material phenomena, and, on the other hand, so long as matter is incapable of receiving the ideal action of the spirit and of being penetrated by or transmuted into spirit, there is no true unity between these two main realms of being . . . . Neither abstract spirit incapable of creative incarnation nor soulless matter incapable of spiritualization corresponds to ideal or worthy being." See "The Meaning of Art," in *A Solovyov Anthology*, ed. S. L. Frank, trans. Natalie Duddington (Westport, 1950) 144.

2. Dmitri Merejkowski, *Tolstoi as Man and Artist, With an Essay on Dostoievski*, trans. John Cournos (New York, 1931) 213.

3. For a discussion of this issue, see P. S. Reifman, "Predpolagaiutsia li deti?" *Trudy po russkoi i slavianskoi filologii* 14 [= *Uchenye zapiski Tartuskogo Gosudarstvennogo Universiteta* 245] (Tartu, 1970) 357–363. According to Reifman, Saltykov-Shchedrin, despite his radical sympathies, may have also raised the question of children in his response to *Chto delat'?*

4. V. V. Zenkovsky, *A History of Russian Philosophy*, trans. George L. Kline, vol. 1 (New York, 1953) 25–26.

5. Bridging the Old and New Testaments, the "Descent into Hell" (also known as the "Harrowing of Hell") pictures Christ suspended over an abyss, literally pulling out Adam and Eve, the Old Prophets Abraham and Isaac, Moses, King David, other key figures of the Old Testament, and John the Baptist. Since the Orthodox Easter icon focuses on the redemption of Christianity's Old Testament precursors, it can also be seen in terms of Fedorov's resurrection of ancestors.

6. *Crime and Punishment*, trans. David Magarshack (New York, 1966) 277.

7. His first fiancée was a sickly cripple who dies before the beginning of the novel; Sonia is asexual even though she is a prostitute.

8. The exchange between Shatov and Mme Virginskaia regarding Marie's infant boy reflects their opposing ideological positions. Shatov tells Mme Virginskaia that "the mystery of the arrival of this new creature is a great and ungraspable one, . . . and it's very sad that you don't appreciate it . . . . There were two and now suddenly there's a third—a new human being, a new spirit, entire, complete, such as no human hands could fashion; a new thought, a new love. It's frightening. There's nothing greater than this in the world!" In response to Shatov's effusive enthusiasm, Mme Virginskaia refers to the newborn as a "superfluous man . . . who should never have been brought into this world." She tells Shatov to "first change the world so that they [the newborn] can be useful and then breed them." *The Possessed*, trans. Andrew R. MacAndrew (New York, 1962) 612.

9. Ibid., 610. The translation has been emended to correspond to the original (O. M.).

10. Ibid., 609.

11. Merejkowski 265.

12. Although Kirillov's utopian ideal seems to resonate more forcefully than Shatov's celebration of a new child, Dostoevsky's own position was predictably dialogic. In agreement with Shatov, he made the following strong "pro-life" statement: "Nothing smarter than giving birth to children has yet been invented . . . . To have children and give birth to them is the most important and most serious job in the world." See *Dnevnik pisatelia za 1876 god* in *Polnoe sobranie sochinenii v tridtsati tomakh*, vol. 23 (Leningrad, 1981) 92. But as A. K. Gornostaev points out, these words are spoken by a "paradoxalist," and the author of the diary warns the reader that "he is not always in agreement with his views." See *Rai na zemle: k ideologii tvorchestva F. M. Dostoevskogo. F. M. Dostoevskii i N. F. Fedorov* (Kharbin, 1929) 36. After making an ostensibly serious commitment to the procreative ideal, he proceeds to subvert it by having the paradoxalist describe the ideal dutiful life of women in absurd terms: they must marry and "give birth to as many children as possible, not two, not three, but six, ten, to the point of exhaustion and infirmity." *Dnevnik pisatelia za 1876 god* 92.

13. According to Fedorov, "the process of giving birth is uncharacteristic of beings that have [gone from a horizontal to a] vertical position." N. Fedorov, *Sochineniia*, ed. S. G. Semenova (Moscow, 1982) 516n.

14. *Filosofiia obshchego dela*, vol. 1 (Vernyi, 1906) 401. See also Fedorov, *Sochineniia* 486–487.

15. Fedorov, *Sochineniia* 148.

16. In 1904, Briusov, who was interested in Fedorov, published an excerpt from his writings in *Vesy*. Written shortly after he emigrated, Merezhkovsky's *Taina trekh: Egipet i Vavilon* (1925), especially the section on the cult of Osiris, has a great deal in common with Fedorov's utopia.

17. "On a Generation That Squandered Its Poets," *Major Soviet Writers: Essays in Criticism*, ed. Edward J. Brown (New York, 1973) 20–21.

18. "A Safe Conduct," *Collected Short Prose*, ed. Christopher Barnes (New York, 1977) 78.

19. "The Meaning of Love," *A Solovyov Anthology* 164.

20. "About the Cause," *Between Paris and St. Petersburg: Selected Diaries of Zinaida Hippius*, trans. and ed. Temira Pachmuss (Urbana, 1975) 54.

21. Temira Pachmuss, *Intellect and Ideas in Action: Selected Correspondence of Zinaida Hippius* (Munich, 1972) 64.

22. Ibid., 67.

23. Ibid., 71–72.

24. Dmitrii Merezhkovskii, *Taina trekh: Egipet i Vavilon*, (Prague, 1925) 182.

25. *Secret of the West*, trans. John Cournos (New York, 1931) 336. According to Clement, these were among Christ's most profound words, not recorded in the New Testament, but appearing in the Coptic Gospel (p. 336).

26. Marjorie Reeves and Warwick Gould, *Joachim of Fiore and the Myth of the Eternal Evangel in the Nineteenth Century* (Oxford, 1987) 1–5, passim.

27. F. E. Manuel and F. P. Manuel, *Utopian Thought in the Western World* (Oxford, 1979) 33–34.

28. E. Benz, *Evolution and Christian Hope: Man's Concept of the Future from the Early Fathers to Teilhard de Chardin,* trans. H. Frank (London, 1967) 46.

29. Although Reeves and Gould claim that there is no evidence of Merezhkovsky's familiarity with Joachim of Fiore, despite the similarity of their religious views (pp. 306–308), Merezhkovsky and Gippius knew about the Calabrian abbot and even planned to visit his monastery in 1937 (*Ideas in Action: Selected Correspondence of Zinaida Hippius* 291).

30. For a thorough discussion of Merezhkovsky's reconciliation of historical opposites, see Bernice Glatzer Rosenthal, *Dmitri Sergeevich Merezhkovsky and the Silver Age: The Development of a Revolutionary Mentality* (The Hague, 1975).

31. For that matter, in a 1937 letter to her friend Viktor Mamchenko, Gippius spoke very negatively of Fedorov, claiming that he did not understand the nature of personality (*lichnost'*); moreover, she referred with some disgust to the idea of resurrecting one's ancestors, but, like Fedorov, she asserted that the function of real love is to save "the other" by affirming his existence at a significant moment. *Intellect and Ideas in Action* 452.

32. See note 16. Gippius's confidant and suitor in the second half of the 1890s, Akim Volynsky, was a critic and editor of *Severnyi vestnik,* which published the Merezhkovskys. He was at least indirectly familiar with Fedorov's ideas, as reflected in Volynsky's book on Dostoevsky, *Tsarstvo Karamazovykh* (1901). Gornostaev suggests that Volynsky learned about Fedorov from Fedorov's own anonymous article in *Don,* no. 80 (1897), published in conjunction with selected passages from Dostoevsky's letter about Fedorov's ideas (pp. 77–78). (Dostoevsky does not refer to Fedorov by name in his letter.) Following Gornostaev's conjectures, I propose that Volynsky could have told Gippius about these new utopian ideas, which she and Merezhkovsky absorbed, incorporating them into their own ideology.

33. Fedorov, *Sochineniia* 132.

34. Ibid., 141–142.

35. "Contes d'amour," *Between Paris and St. Petersburg: Selected Diaries of Zinaida Hippius* 77.

36. According to Vladimir Zlobin, the Merezhkovskys' secretary of many years, "the guiding male role belonged not to him, but to her. She was very feminine and he masculine, but on the creative and metaphysical plane their roles were reversed. She fertilized, while he gestated and gave birth. She was the seed, and he the soil, the most fertile of all black earths." *A Difficult Soul: Zinaida Gippius,* ed. Simon Karlinsky (Berkeley, 1980) 42–43.

37. Her best known pseudonyms were Anton Krainii and Tovarishch German, under which she wrote her literary criticism.

38. For a discussion of Gippius as Cleopatra and Pushkinian dandy, see Olga Matich, "Dialectics of Cultural Return: Zinaida Gippius' Personal Myth," in *Cultural Mythologies of Russian Modernism: From the Golden Age to the Silver Age,* ed. Boris Gasparov, Robert P. Hughes, and Irina Paperno (Berkeley, 1992) 52–72.

39. The son of the well-known feminist and social activist Anna Filosofova, Dmitrii Filosofov was the cousin of Sergei Diagilev and a journalist and critic, at

first associated with *Mir iskusstva,* later with *Novyi put'* and other Merezhkovsky publications.

40. Fedorov, *Sochineniia* 129.

41. Ibid., 140–141. According to Fedorov, the Holy Spirit is the prototype of the ideal woman, who is a daughter, not a wife, mother, or lover.

42. "Ekskurs: O sekte i dogmate," *Borozdy i mezhi. Opyty esteticheskie i kriticheskie* (Moscow, 1910) 11–12.

43. *Zhivye litsa* (Prague, 1925) 158–159.

44. See Gippius's description of their courtship, wedding, honeymoon, and first apartment in Petersburg in *Dmitrii Merezhkovskii* (1959), a biography published posthumously.

45. See Matich, "Dialectics of Cultural Return." For a discussion of radical marriage and the chaste triple union in the culture of the 1860s, see Irina Paperno, *Chernyshevsky and the Age of Realism: A Study in the Semiotics of Behavior* (Stanford, 1988) 89–158.

46. A proponent of terrorism like Savinkov, Fondaminsky-Bunakov was a member of the extreme left wing of the Socialist Revolutionary Party. Perhaps under the influence of the Merezhkovskys, he moderated his political views and became intensely religious. From 1920 to 1940 he was one of the editors of *Sovremennye zapiski* in Paris.

47. "About the Cause," *Between Paris and St. Petersburg* 145.

48. Ibid., 133.

49. A theologian, Anton Kartashev was the president of the Petersburg branch of the Religious Philosophical Society, the last Procurator of the Holy Synod, Minister of Religion in the Provisional Government, and Professor of the Theological Academy in Paris.

The Old Belief and Sectarianism
as Cultural Models in the Silver Age

RONALD VROON

Меня пытали в старой вере.
—Aleksandr Blok

The secular examination of Russian religious dissent dates back roughly to
the bicentennial of the church council that initiated the Great Schism in the
Orthodox church.[1] As an event the anniversary was of far less consequence
than the millennium of Christianity in Russia recently celebrated, but it
marked an important change in attitude toward the Old Belief and sectarianism. Up to this point they had been treated for the most part as dangerous
religious movements; most of the literature dealing with them was pejorative
and designed to counter their pernicious spread. From the 1860s on, however, the Russian intelligentsia grew more and more interested in the economic, social, cultural, and political life of the religious dissidents. The
pioneering studies of Mel'nikov, Shchapov, Prugavin, Andreev, Mel'gunov,
and others appeared in the latter half of the century. These were followed
by detailed scholarly reexaminations of the ritual and liturgical bases of the
schismatic conflict, often in favor of the Old Belief.[2] Tsar Nicholas's Edict
of Toleration—the Ukase of 17 April 1905—occasioned a second wave of
publications on sectarianism and the Old Belief, this time by the religious
dissenters themselves. Scores of new journals, newspapers, and occasional
publications took up not only religious matters, but also social and political
issues associated with the growth of religious dissent.

Given this high visibility, it is not surprising that almost all the major
writers of the Silver Age felt the need to address the phenomenon in some
way. What is surprising, however, is the depth and scope of their reaction.
It did not merely enter their articles, speeches, and poems. They felt the need
for living encounters with communities that clung to old and, for many,
arcane systems of belief. They sought out local sectarians for discussion and
debate and made pilgrimages to centers of dissidence. Dmitrii Merezhkovskii,
in his early populist days, spent a summer wandering along the banks of the

Volga and the Kama, talking to villagers, and trying to grasp the "spirit of the folk."[3] In preparation for his detailed treatment of the Old Belief and sectarianism in *Peter and Aleksei,* he made a field trip "across the Volga to Kerzhenets, to the town of Semenov and Svetloe Ozero where, according to tradition, the invisible city of Kitezh lies." Here, he says, "I spent the night of Ivan Kupala on the shores of the lake, talking to pilgrims and teachers of various faiths who gather here from all over Russia on this night."[4] Zinaida Gippius accompanied her husband on this occasion and produced an extensive description of her encounters with religious dissenters in an "ethnographic" diary.[5] A few years later a young Mikhail Prishvin made a similar pilgrimage to the legendary Svetloe Ozero and described his experiences in a series of sketches entitled *By the Walls of the Invisible City* (*U sten grada nevidimogo*).

Vasilii Rozanov is one of several prominent intellectuals who welcomed contact with sectarians in the Petersburg area and described at some length his encounters with their communities. Another is Nikolai Berdiaev. In his autobiographical *Self-knowledge* (*Samopoznanie*), he recounts his energetic disputes with sectarians whom he sought out in Moscow and Liubotina, a town near Khar'kov, in 1909 and 1910. He found these encounters so engaging that he invited Andrei Belyi to join him, knowing that the latter was at work on a novel dealing with a mystical-anarchist sect.[6] Belyi refused, but not from lack of interest. Years after the appearance of his "sectarian" novel, *The Silver Dove* (*Serebrianyi golub'*), he admitted that he had been engaged in his own form of preparation, spending times in the Moscow teahouses, Petersburg diners, and peasant cottages, talking to the people about political, moral, and religious issues.[7]

The most extreme expression of interest in religious dissenters was the actual adoption of sectarian ways. Aleksandr Dobroliubov's founding of a mystical sect is the best known example. The lure of the religious periphery drew others as well, among them the poet Leonid Semenov, a Tolstoyan, and Archimandrite Mikhail (Semenov), whose conversion to the Old Belief scandalized the established church. Andrei Belyi described his own retreat into anthroposophism as a "withdrawal" [*ukhod*] similar to that of Dobroliubov.[8] Even Aleksandr Blok at one time contemplated abandoning his family and estate and joining an unspecified sectarian community.[9]

What accounts for such extraordinary fascination with unorthodoxy? Aside from the growing visibility of the dissenters themselves following the 17 April Ukase, one must turn to the broader sociopolitical context to understand this phenomenon. Cultural historians generally acknowledge that the turn of the century was marked by a sense of impending crisis. On the political front it expressed itself in the increasingly active, and increasingly radical, opposition to the czarist regime. On the cultural and spiritual fronts the battle lines were drawn between what Merezhkovskii termed the exigencies of idealism and materialism.[10] Looking back on the period, Berdiaev writes that "toward the end of the nineteenth century there arose in Russia a pessimistic mood associated with the sense that the world was coming to an end and that the Antichrist would appear. What was expected was not a new Christian era and the coming of the Kingdom of God so much as the coming of the Kingdom of the Antichrist."[11]

This particular zeitgeist brings to mind the binary cultural models identified by Iurii Lotman and Boris Uspenskii as typical of the eighteenth century and earlier, when the conflict between new and old was viewed, not in terms of progress or evolution, but in terms of "total eschatological change."[12] The eschatological fever of the fin de siècle was not unlike that which gripped Aleksei Mikhailovich's Russia in the late seventeenth century, except that now there were many competing eschatologies, with a range extending from the Marxist to the millennialist. Among the models of opposition and radical change were several of purely native provenance—the ones proffered by the Old Believers and the sectarians. Two features made these particular models unique. First, they were promulgated by living institutions. Despite the repressive measures enacted against them, the major Old Believer denominations, as well as the sectarians, experienced considerable growth in the second half of the nineteenth century and into the twentieth.[13] The second feature was a paradoxical admixture of the religious and political. On the one hand, the religious dissenters as an aggregate constituted the largest and potentially most powerful anti-establishment force in the country. On the other hand, they championed, for the most part, a religious and cultural order that was historically regressive.

The immediate intellectual forebears of the Symbolists found it difficult to deal with this paradox. Their solution was to make one-dimensional models of opposition that suited their own well-defined ideologies. The established church insisted that the Old Believers were exclusively religious dissidents, and that suppressive measures were justified by virtue of the harm that could be done to the church and to the faithful. One of the textbooks on the schism used in Orthodox seminaries at the close of the century states forthrightly that "in the spirit of their own beliefs [the schismatics] are not only incapable of being political activists, but even an instrument of such activists."[14] Needless to say, this view was belied by the civic activism of the

Old Believers at the turn of the century. In response to the increasingly repressive measures adopted by Konstantin Pobedonostsev, they continued a strenuous course of passive resistance, collected petitions, distributed illegal literature, and attempted to shift public opinion in their favor at various open forums.[15]

The liberal and radical intelligentsia created an equally naïve political model of the Old Believers. They took their cue from the studies of A. P. Shchapov, who determined that Russia's schismatics were not religious dissenters trapped in a time warp, but among the most progressive members of society, dedicated to opposing the established church and state in the cause of freedom and democracy. Herzen and Ogarev, among others, played on these supposed sentiments, attempting to draw the dissenters into their camp in the interests of what they assumed was their common cause. Needless to say, they were rebuffed, as were the Populists who subsequently attempted to exploit the political disaffection of the Old Believers. Addressing his flock in 1863, Metropolitan Kirill said, "Do not heed the baying of these dogs from hell . . . ."[16] Faced with a choice between God-fearing adversaries and godless friends, the Old Believers generally opted for the former.

Such, in the most general terms, were the polar models—one religious and the other political—that prevailed in the latter years of the century. The elaboration of new models, somewhat more complex though perhaps no less self-serving, can be found in the writings of two major thinkers whose works bridge the period between the age of Realism and the Silver Age. Vasilii Rozanov and Vladimir Solov'ev both dealt at some length with the issues surrounding religious dissidence.[17] They did so for the most part from the explicit vantage point of traditional Orthodoxy, and as a consequence their views tended in certain areas to reflect those of earlier apologists of the state church. Both, for example, shared the view that the Old Believers were excessively concerned with the external expressions of piety and an inappropriate valorization of local tradition.

Vladimir Solov'ev was the more conservative of the two philosophers; his remarks on the schism reveal little sympathy with the Old Believer position, and do not constitute a major break with the position of official Orthodoxy. Nonetheless, the model he fashioned involved a reevaluation of the schism. His original position, as V. P. Riabushinskii notes, was marked by a typically Western legalism, but he eventually came to see the Old Belief as a confession based less on an obscurantist devotion to old ritual forms than on a different conception of the church itself.[18] This view stemmed from his analysis of the schism as a struggle between clericalism and populism, between those who saw the hierarchy as the ultimate locus of authority in matters of faith and practice (the Nikonian camp) and those who saw that locus in the people who constitute the body of the church. Both positions, wrote Solov'ev, were partially right, but equally wrong in their claim to universality; that is, both sides were making claims about faith and authority that could properly be made only in a truly ecumenical forum.[19] A recognition of the provincialism of their own positions would have permitted the parties to achieve a compromise in the interests of church unity.

The views Rozanov expressed in the 1890s concerning the Old Belief and sectarianism are more controversial and represent a substantial break with the preceding tradition. In his "Psychology of the Russian Schism," he associated the Old Believers' insistence on pre-Nikonian ritual, not so much with a particular canonical stance as with the "ancient typicon of the life of righteousness,"[20] a rule based on the spirit that informed Kievan Christianity. This spirit, he insisted, devolves from a uniquely holistic approach to faith: instead of reducing the means of salvation to a set of rules, the Old Believer follows, in all its particulars, a behavior that has been canonized by virtue of the sanctity of its practitioners. In essence, Rozanov argued, this approach is fundamentally aesthetic: just as a sculptor might legitimately destroy a statue because of a perceived flaw, so too the Old Believer rejects even the smallest ritual or liturgical modification as a potentially mortal defect in the artifice of faith. This extreme devotion to the whole *in all its particulars* lends the Old Belief that extraordinarily strong ethical cast, that affective force in everyday life, which constitutes its inner spirit and poetry. These are precisely the areas where traditional Orthodoxy, in Rozanov's view, is impoverished, and where it might do well to adopt the "ancient spirit" of the Old Belief with its uncompromising devotion to a way of life as well as a system of dogmas.

In analyzing the sectarians (the Khlysty, Dukhobory, and Skoptsy, whom he deals with more or less generically under the Khlyst rubric "Spiritual Christians" [*dukhovnye khristiane*]), Rozanov expressed even more forcefully his approbation of the living spirit that informs their ways of life and belief. Standing at the opposite side of the canonical spectrum in attitudes toward religious form and ritual, they reflect the "irrational ethical and aesthetic idea," the creative initiative, that should characterize real faith. The sectarians live constantly in a state of spiritual "intoxication," the "instinctive delight on account of which man says, 'I live and I *want* to live.'"[21] Both the Old Belief and sectarianism, said Rozanov, are branches extending in opposite directions from the body of the church itself; it must acknowledge them as extensions of its own body and draw them back to their common source.

Rozanov and Solov'ev, for all their differences, assumed a similar attitude toward religious dissidence in one major respect: both ascribed the Old Believers' defense of a particular ritual and liturgical order to considerations other than those of a dogmatic or canonical nature; that is, both sidestepped the issue that lay at the heart of the schism: the legitimacy or illegitimacy of the Nikonian reforms. Solov'ev's reductionist approach to the schism was essentially anachronistic. The Nikonian camp did not claim that the hierarchy had a total monopoly on the truth, nor did the Old Believers assert that the believing laity and white clergy were *by definition* the ultimate repository of the true faith. Both appealed to church tradition, each side claiming that its own rituals and liturgical formulae were of greater antiquity, and therefore of greater legitimacy, than the other's.[22] Rozanov's position was equally untenable. He defended the Old Believers' wish to imitate past forms, not because they are more canonical, but because they reflect a "method" of thinking that is irrational, aesthetically grounded, and holistic. This justification may be appropriate, but it has little or nothing to do with the Old Believers per se, who, Rozanov's protestations to the contrary, were quite prepared to defend their views in precisely the same canonical and dogmatic terms as the official church, and with equal if not greater cogency.

It is clear, in short, that Solov'ev's and Rozanov's models of the Old Belief and sectarianism have little to do with the historical or theological realities of these phenomena. To understand their peculiar shape, one must turn to the cultural agenda each thinker was promoting. Solov'ev's had to do primarily with his interest in religious and political ecumenicism. His models of the Old Belief as a manifestation of conservative religious democracy, and of Nikonianism as a form of clerical absolutism, were designed first and foremost to enhance his defense of Russia's Western orientation during the reign of Peter the Great. Imputing an excessive parochialism and a particular ecclesiastical polity to both sides in the schism served to highlight Peter's cosmopolitanism and his enlightened authoritarianism.[23] What made Solov'ev's model subversive was not the attribution of false features to the two sides—good cases could be made for Old Believer parochialism or Nikonian absolutism, for example—but his misrepresentation of these features as possessing the force of canon law. This tactic, on the one hand, allowed him to reject them on *canonical* grounds; on the other hand, it opened the way for a purely heuristic defense of Peter's *Spiritual Regulation,* his abolition of the patriarchate, and the establishment of the Holy Synod, an ecclesiastical body without precedent in the Orthodox tradition and manifestly Protestant in origin.

Rozanov's cultural agenda in the 1890s was almost as transparent as
Solov'ev's. In the opening to his article on the psychology of the Russian
schism he presented a picture of two Russias: the Russia of appearances, the
empire with its artifice of laws, regulations, codices, and formal order, as
opposed to the Russia of essences, with its organic formlessness, its indistinct
beginnings and endings, its life and blood and faith. Religious dissidence in
all its forms belonged to the latter category.[24] Over and over Rozanov returned to the critical contrast between the life-force of the Old Believers and
mystic sectarians, on the one hand, and the dearth of life and creativity in
all the enterprises of empire, including the established church, on the other.
It even extended to the area of church rhetoric. In one of his aphoristic
"embryos" he declared that "the most dangerous aspect of Christianity in
the nineteenth century is that it is beginning to be rhetorical," that is, it
reduced faith to the level of style; he contrasted this tendency to the Old
Believers' insistence on the pre-Nikonian spelling of Jesus's name (*Isus*),
reflecting the tendency to raise even the smallest, most insignificant "jot" to
the level of faith.[25] In contrast to Solov'ev, who used the antinomy between
the Old Believers and Peter to enhance the latter's stature, Rozanov declared
that the only truly Petrine institution comparable in life and spirit to the
"essential" Russia was his army and that his heirs had, in effect, castrated
their fatherland.[26]

Familiarity with Rozanov's subsequent interest in a holistic "natural religion," one capable of responding affirmatively to the material and biological
aspects of human existence as well as the spiritual, allows us to discern its
outline in his model of the religious dissidents. But the model was little more
than a forensic tool. Its status as such, independent of historical realities, is
borne out by its use in polemics after 1905. The more Rozanov became
enamored of "natural" religion, the more he came to see Christianity as
thanatophilic cult. Where he had once insisted that "Christianity is joy, and
only joy, and always joy,"[27] he now saw it as a religion centered on a weeping Face.[28] Accompanying this change in attitude was an almost complete
reversal in his attitude toward the Old Belief and sectarians. In his collection
of essays, *The Dark Face,* a casebook of religious pathology designed to illustrate the fanatical pessimism of the Orthodox Christian world outlook,
Rozanov selected most of his examples from the lives of priestless Old Believers and sectarians. Their fanaticism, reflected in such acts as self-immolation
or self-immuration, was in his view nothing more than a logical, inescapable
expression of fervent Orthodoxy.[29] In short, he fashioned a new model of religious dissent wholly antithetical to the one previously employed.

Rozanov and Solov'ev set the stage for subsequent treatments of the Old Belief and sectarianism, which in various ways subverted the historical model in the interests of new cultural agendas. When we turn to the leading voices of the Silver Age, we can distinguish three different approaches to the Old Belief and sectarianism, each with its own special bias. The first belongs to those writers who approach religious dissidence as a cultural venue for verbal elaborations of the national ethos. Chief among them are Bal'mont (*Zelenyi vertograd*), Gorodetskii (*Iar', Perun, Dikaia volia*), and Remizov (*Posolon', Otrechennye povesti, Rossiia v pis'menakh*, etc.). These are the imitators of folk ways who appropriated the style of "dissident" texts to produce works with an explicitly Russian bias.[30] Their fundamental indifference to the belief systems, political views, or social organization of these groups places them on the margins of this study, but one must acknowledge the role they played in bringing the ethos of the Old Belief and sectarianism to the attention of the reading public.

The two other approaches are more closely linked to those that were current in the mid- to late nineteenth century, as well as to those of Rozanov and Solov'ev. Some of the Symbolists chose to define religious dissent primarily in metaphysical terms, whereas others began to look at it in political terms, following the example of the liberal intelligentsia. Like Rozanov the Symbolists did not do so from rigorous, pre-defined ideological positions. Rather, they sought out dissenters, questioned them on various religious and political issues, and were in turn confronted by issues that the dissenters raised. In other words, where the majority of their predecessors, including Solov'ev, had placed themselves in a subject-object relationship to the dissenters, the Symbolists entered a dialogue with them. The results of that dialogue, as we shall see, were to play an important role in the way the Symbolists viewed themselves.

Those who, following Rozanov's lead, viewed the Old Belief and sectarianism primarily in religious terms are best represented by Dmitrii Merezhkovskii, Zinaida Gippius, and Maksimilian Voloshin. Merezhkovskii dealt with the question of religious dissent in two works of historical fiction and several essays. The most important for our purposes is the narrative poem "Avvakum" (1887), a loose, first-person rendering of the archpriest's autobiography.[31] There is no question that Merezhkovskii draws a very positive portrait, but it has little to do with either the historical Avvakum or the Avvakum of the autobiography. The archpriest, in the words of one contemporary reviewer, is transformed from "a fanatic, wild schismatic" into "a Protestant of modern times, a creature of humility, patience and love."[32]

Gone are all the disputes about the sign of the cross, the proper number of alleluias in the liturgy, and the "Latin heresy." Avvakum is made to oppose the established church for enforcing its views with the whip and knout in contrast to Christ's rule of love. In the closing lines of the poem he says:

> Потрудился я за правду, не берег последних сил:
> Тридцать лет, никониане, я жестоко вас бранил.
>
> Если чем-нибудь обидел, — вы простите дураку.
> Ведь и мне пришлось не мало натерпеться, старику.
>
> Вы простите, не сердитесь, — все мы братья о Христе,
> И за всех нас, злых и добрых, умирал он на кресте.
>
> Так возлюбим же друг друга — вот последний мой завет.
> Все в любви — закон и вера...выше заповеди нет.

(I labored for the truth, I did not spare my last ounce of strength: for thirty years, O Nikonians, I cruelly berated you. If I have offended you in any way, forgive this fool— after all, I, an old man, also had to put up with a lot. Forgive me, do not be angry, we are all brothers in Christ, and on the cross He died for all of us, the good and the bad. So let us love one another—that is my final testament. Everything is contained in love— the law and faith—there can be no higher law.)

In short, Avvakum is wholly emasculated, shorn of his distinctive Old Believer cast.[33]

The second of Merezhkovskii's works to deal with religious dissent is his novel, *Peter and Alexei,* the third part of the trilogy, *Christ and Antichrist.* While Merezhkovskii seems to be very much in sympathy with the Old Believers because of the torments they suffer at Peter's hands, it is clear that the fundamental religious positions of both the Old Belief and of "Khlystovshchina" are unpalatable to him. The true hero of the novel, the wanderer Tikhon, finds the theological disputes of the schismatics incomprehensible and reprehensible.[34] After he survives the catastrophe of self-immolation by the Old Believers to whom he is attached, he decides that "the old church is no better than the new" and resolves to "go back into the world and search for the true Church,"[35] which is ultimately identified as the "Church of the Third Testament." His involvement with a group of Moscow sectarians of the Khlyst sect ends with an equally unequivocal rejection of their claims to the truth.

Zinaida Gippius is similarly straightforward in her dismissal of those she had ostensibly come to interview on the shores of Svetloe Ozero. While she was impressed by her interlocutors' preoccupation with the Apocalypse of Saint John and various eschatological problems, she yielded nothing of her own convictions, and in a brief but crucial exchange with a defender of the

Old Belief, she insisted that the established church was closer to the truth than the schismatics because it admitted the efficacy of both its own rituals and those of the Old Believers, whereas the Old Believers insisted on the exclusive validity of theirs and theirs alone.[36] She closed her diary, however, with an acknowledgment of the one thing that united her with the religious dissidents: their constant search for the Truth, beyond all the givens of established churches and cults.

Voloshin's contribution to the remodeling of religious dissent is contained in two narrative poems, "Archpriest Avvakum" and "Tale of the Monk Epifanii."[37] The latter, based on the anonymous "Life of Epifanii," is a more or less accurate paraphrase with no obvious ideological overtones to complement or distort those of the original. The former, like Merezhkovskii's poem, is a first-person retelling of Avvakum's *Autobiography*. It presents Avvakum's life story in greater detail, however, and also with greater attention to the historical realities of the schism. Unlike Merezhkovskii, Voloshin does not hesitate to set forth the specific points of dispute between the Old Believers and the Nikonians—the correction of the liturgical texts, the proper execution of the sign of the cross, the spelling of Jesus's name, and so on. The historical substance of the poem, in short, accurately reflects the schism. What distorts the model is the narrative frame. The poem opens with Avvakum in heaven, observing the creation of man, and receiving God's instructions to descend like a flame and set the world on fire. The poem closes with his return to the Heavenly Jerusalem on the wings of the flames that consumed him.

The purpose of this frame is twofold. The first is that it places Avvakum and his Old Belief within a gnostic, anthroposophist framework. Avvakum's pre-existence at the moment when God creates man suggests that he is an "angel of the tenth order" (in Rudolf Steiner's cosmology) who takes on human flesh and then returns to his original, fiery state. The peculiarly anthroposophist cast of this doctrine is born out in Avvakum's reminiscences during his sojourn on earth. According to Steiner, the recollection of one's existence before birth is particularly important in establishing the continuity of consciousness from past to present and future.[38] Thus it is, for example, that Voloshin's Avvakum, after his famous vision of the three ships, acknowledges to himself:

> Аз есмь огонь, одетый пеплом плоти,
> И тело наше без души есть кал и прах.

(I am fire, dressed in the ash of flesh, And without a soul, our bodies are excrement and dust.)

A recollection of his previous angelic state comes later, when Tsar Aleksei Mikhailovich allows him to return from exile:

> А на Москву приехал —
> Государь, бояра — все мне рады:
> Как ангела приветствуют.

(And I came to Moscow—The sovereign, the boyars—all were happy to see me. They greeted me like an angel.)

At the end of the poem Avvakum acknowledges with joy that his execution at the stake will return him to his original angelic state:

> Святая троице! Христос мой миленький!
> Обратно к Вам в Ерусалим небесный!
> Родясь — погас,
> Да снова разгорелся!

(Holy Trinity! My beloved Christ! I return to you, to the Heavenly Jerusalem! When I was born I was extinguished; Now once more I have caught fire!)

The second purpose of the narrative frame is to assign Avvakum a place within the historical continuum of anarchists and incendiaries, both religious and political, who for Voloshin formed the backbone of Russian history. In a sense Avvakum is merely a reincarnation of the same Insurrectionist who has appeared time and again—in the form of the False Dmitrii, Sten'ka Razin, Pugachev, and Bakunin. Here Voloshin began to cross over to a political model of the Old Belief, placing it anachronistically within the context of "Christian anarchism."[39] This aspect of the model, however, is apparent only from the cycle of poems in which "Archpriest Avvakum" appears, and from Voloshin's own commentary on the poem in his personal correspondence.

In the writings of Merezhkovskii, Gippius, and Voloshin, we see what happens when the confrontation with religious dissidence takes place, not from the perspective of an Orthodox or neo-Orthodox ideology, but from a position that is itself sectarian, or at the very least agnostic. When they approach the Old Belief and sectarianism on historically valid terms—that is, on terms that are actually or hypothetically dictated by adherents of these groups—they tend to reject them outright as either an atavism or as a false system of belief. Yet there is something sufficiently attractive about them to draw their attention, and it leads them to fashion new models that they can appropriate and use for their own purposes: a kind of neo-Protestant universalism in Merezhkovskii's case, a militant agnosticism in Gippius's case, and an explicitly Steinerian gnosticism in Voloshin's.

Such a repudiation and/or subversion of dissident views constitutes an obvious affirmation and assumption of the model, particularly that of the mystical sectarians, for it reflects a search for truth based on idiosyncratic interpretations of Divine Revelation and a concurrent rejection of ecclesiastical authority. As Voloshin says of his Avvakum, "The religious value of the struggle lies not in its causes or slogans, but in how a man believes . . . ."[40] Avvakum is useful to Merezhkovskii as a Luther, not as an Athanasius, because he himself plays the role of a radical reformer rather than a defender of the faith. We know, of course, that this was more than just a literary attitude. Merezhkovskii and Gippius did, in fact, attempt to establish a new religious order with its own liturgy and redefined hierarchy. It is not surprising, therefore, that he appears as a schismatic to Aleksandr Blok,[41] and that he served as one of the models for Kudeiarov, the leader of a mystical sect in Andrei Belyi's *The Silver Dove*.[42]

A second approach to sectarianism and the Old Belief was to treat it as a primarily political model, as had the Populists. The seeds of this approach can be seen in Solov'ev, who, as we have observed, identified the ideology of the Old Believers as a form of religious democratism. The further politicization of the model is particularly striking in the case of Blok and Belyi. Both of them developed an interest in the issue of religious dissent following the 1905 Revolution. It grew particularly strong for Blok after he entered into correspondence with Nikolai Kliuev, whose association with both the Old Believers and mystical sectarians played a pivotal role in their relations.

The earliest mention of religious dissent in Blok's work occurs in his essay "The Literary Scene in 1907" ("Literaturnye itogi 1907"), part of which was subsequently reprinted under the title "Religious Strivings and the People" ("Religioznye iskaniia i narod").[43] Here he sets the tone for all future discussions of the topic, placing it within the general framework of a fundamentally secular opposition between "the people" and "the intelligentsia." Citing the reproaches contained in a recent letter from Kliuev, Blok excoriates a nobility that "hates to work, is bored by listlessness" and spends hours in fruitless discussion of metaphysical issues while in the real world of Russia an "enormous and terrifying phenomenon" called sectarianism looms on the horizon. Their religious interests and strivings, he goes on to say, are beyond the ken of the intelligentsia precisely because of the cultural divide between the two groups. He quotes Kliuev to the effect that the dissenters' withdrawal to wilderness monasteries and sketes is an expression of their desire to "get away from the gentry."

In a later essay, "The Elemental and Culture" ("Stikhiia i kul'tura"), Blok

establishes even more forcefully his identification of "the people" with religious dissenters. The peasants, he says, can be divided into two groups:
the "Orthodox folk, lulled by the liquor outlet, with vodka in its church
basements and with drunken priests," and the sectarians, who are a vol-
cano waiting to erupt. He quotes from a letter written by a sectarian to
Merezhkovskii in which the author declares, "We are mystics of a particular
type, after the Russian mold. We really are men of the earth, for we believe
that the Millennium will not be beyond the grave, not in heaven, but on
earth. . . . I believe our sectarians to be revolutionary, the only difference
being that their program was dictated by an Unknown Power."[44]

In his poetry, as well, Blok treats the Old Believers in basically political
rather than metaphysical terms. In one of the most memorable pieces of the
cycle, "Homeland" ("Rodina"), the poet evokes the image of those ancient
stalwarts who in ages past "felled timber and sang of their Christ." They
now carry the news of a "burning Christ," the Christ of insurrection, to a
terrified Russia.[45] The same association is drawn in the closing lines of "The
Twelve." The Christ who suddenly appears in front of the Red Army ma-
rauders is not the "Iisus" of establishment Orthodoxy. Blok chooses, rather
to spell His name "Isus," marking Him as the Christ of the Old Belief.

The politicization of the dissident religious model is also present in the
image of Faina, the heroine of Blok's play "The Song of Fate" ("Pesnia
sud'by") and one of many incarnations of Blok's Beautiful Lady.[46] An Old
Believer, she emerges out of the flames of self-immolation to search for, and
be sought by, her unknown beloved, the nobleman German. Thus "the people" and "the intelligentsia" are made to confront each other once again in
the persons of a religious dissident and a member of the gentry. Faina is
described by one of her admirers as one who "has brought us part of the
soul of the people . . . . We writers live an intellectual life, while Russia,
unchanging in its essence, laughs in our faces. These millions are enveloped
in night, but they despise and hate us . . . . In my heart an abyss opens up
when I hear Faina singing. Her songs are like fires burning the intellectual's
desolate, flaccid soul."[47]

The plot of "Song of Fate" is echoed in *The Silver Dove*, Andrei Belyi's
early novel on religious dissidence in provincial Russia. Here a mystical sect,
rather than the Old Belief, is the focus of attention. Belyi claimed that the
religious group he was describing was an essentially fictional construct, but
the name he assigned it (the Doves), as well as its central images, make it
clear that he has the Khlysts in mind.[48] Indeed, in a postscriptive remark on
the novel he casually refers to the leader of the sect as a Khlyst.[49] His major

subversion of the sectarian model is, as with Blok, its politicization, a fact he underscores in describing the novel's central conflict as a battle between East and West: it is not so much the metaphysics of the sectarians that makes them worthy of attention or depiction, but rather the threat they represent as an anarchic force destined to set Russia aflame.[50] Underscoring the political implications of the novel some time after its composition, Belyi noted that its purpose was to "illustrate the decay of the dark peasant masses of the countryside . . . i.e., the destruction of Czarist Russia." In the figure of the sect's leader, Kudeiarov, he claimed to have prophetically outlined the character and role of Rasputin in Russian society, and only the novel's aesthetic prematurity led to an error in setting—the dusty provincial towns of Likhov and Tselebeevo rather than St. Petersburg.[51]

In order to make this sort of portrayal convincing, Belyi further subverted the historical model of the Khlyst sect. Their telos, as he conceived it, is the generation of a child in their midst who will be capable of performing certain sacraments, which will in turn allow members of the brotherhood to do battle against "the enemy of the human race in those days when internecine strife would break out all over Russia."[52] The novel's plot centers on the seduction of a young nobleman (representing the cultural and spiritual forces of the West) by the sect leader's wife (representing the anarchic forces of the East). The product of this union is to be the Messiah-child. The sexual metaphor Belyi has chosen for the ominous encounter of East and West may have some basis in the popular mythology surrounding the Khlysts, who were reputed to conclude their secret gatherings with orgies, but it is very much out of place against the background of the Khlysts' utter aversion to the idea of procreation.

The modeling of sectarianism and the Old Belief would not be complete without a brief account of those poets who were themselves products of a sectarian or Old Believer milieu, chief among them Nikolai Kliuev.[53] The picture he projects of religious dissent differs from that of all those whom we have described in that it is holistic, encompassing the cultural and political and religious spheres. This is to be expected because he is both a product and an integral part of the ethos born of the schism, and therefore every aspect of his poetry is bound to be colored in some way by the cultural and religious system out of which he emerged. Even a cursory reading of his verse makes it abundantly clear, for example, that the lyrical subject approaches and evaluates not only other belief systems, but the world as a whole, from the standpoint of a mystical sectarian with a strong Old Believer bias.[54]

The holism of the model is best observed in those relatively rare instances
where Kliuev turns explicitly to his own ideological position. Speaking for
all those who share a pre-Nikonian worldview in a post-Petrine world, he
declares in an autobiographical note: "My life follows the path of the Milky
Way. It stretches from the Solovets Islands to the blue mountains of China,
a path marked by many tears and mysteries. The roots of my genealogical
tree twist down into the times of Tsar Alexei; its branches curl among the
wondrous Stroganov icons, the gold-leafed flames of the Three Youths in
the Fiery Furnace, of play towers. My tree extends from the siege of the
Solovets Monastery to the self-immolators of the Paleostrov Monastery to
the Vyg Monastery's unbending pillars of folk beauty."[55] The commingling
of the political, religious, and aesthetic is typical here. It is equally apparent
in Kliuev's characterization of Avvakum as "champion of ancient Orthodoxy and the folk beauty of the church [*narodno-tserkovnaia krasota*]."[56]

Kliuev's comparisons of his own camp and that of the "unbelieving
world" provide additional evidence of his almost medieval holism. His relations with the Symbolists in general, and with Blok, in particular, are very
telling in this regard. When he attacks them, he does so from the vantage
point of one who judges all things in terms of their relation to his own all-
encompassing eschatology. As was the case with those whom he calls his
forebears, neither art nor any other manifestation of culture can exist within
a neutral axiological sphere. In a letter to Blok, Kliuev writes: "The works
of the decadent writers have unquestionably done greater harm than good.
The worst thing about them is their absolutely indiscriminate attitude
toward real life, their distortion of life's truth on arbitrary grounds, only for
the sake of introducing ideas (about God, about love, about the World Soul)
that are false and which the authors themselves don't understand . . . .
Writers will not grasp Eternal Beauty until they breathe and spit on Satan,
renounce the world and that false art with which they gratify themselves and
the Prince of the Air. But since they have signed an oath of allegiance to the
Beast in their own blood, they cannot believe in the unspoken, they cannot
be creators of the invisible and must bear the shame for their foolish
babbling about such things as God, the World Soul, Beauty and Love."[57]

Given this attitude, it is not at all surprising that Kliuev's contemporaries
reacted to him in much the same way that they reacted to the Old Belief and
sectarianism in general. Merezhkovskii, for example, who at one time welcomed the appearance of a poetic voice "from the people," eventually came
to regard Kliuev as promoting a kind of dangerous atavism. According to
Blok's testimony, Merezhkovskii characterized Kliuev's Christianity as "noc-

turnal," "reactionary," and "seductive," recalling Tikhon's rejection of the Old Believers and sectarians in *Peter and Alexei*.[58] Blok himself received and welcomed Kliuev as a representative of the people and the peasantry, but at the same time resisted his attempts to conscript the poet for his religious and revolutionary cause. Significantly, his counterarguments were formulated in the same secular spirit as his principal model of the Old Belief: he counted himself a member of the intelligentsia and was unwilling to give up the intellectual and cultural trappings—in particular, those of Western European provenance—that constituted his birthright and his heritage.

Given their ambivalent attitude toward the Old Belief and sectarianism, it is curious that the writers we have examined were nonetheless obsessed with their image and felt compelled to remodel the ideology of these dissident movements in both fictional and nonfictional works. The impetus for doing so appears to lie in the very same attitude toward historical change that dominated in the pre-Petrine period, but raised to a fully conscious level. Lotman and Uspenskii point out that in the medieval period the "new" was traditionally perceived, not as an evolutionary development, but as an inversion of the old, and that "repeated transformations [could] lead to the *regeneration* of archaic forms."[59] The poets and writers discussed in this article viewed the times in apocalyptic terms; that is to say, they perceived the coming changes as an inversion of the existing order. An apocalyptic worldview dictated that such a transformation be perceived, at least in certain respects, as a *reversion* to a pre-Petrine cultural system.

The crucial point, however, is that this system had not been entirely displaced, but continued to exist on a subcultural level in contemporary society. Its representatives could make two claims that set it apart from every other cultural system: a direct link to the pre-Petrine past and a centuries-long tradition of resistance to the ecclesiastical and political establishment. Such a *modus vivendi* called attention to itself and ultimately assumed greater significance than the actual belief systems that generated this resistance.

If the actual content of a dissident religious ideology or metaphysics did not coincide with a given author's ideas of what it should be, it would simply be discarded or redrawn so that it might better serve as a metonym for apocalyptic change. The perception of cultural synonymy between the pre-Petrine past and the future is strikingly illustrated in Andrei Belyi's memoirs, where he idealizes a retreat from the world in the spirit of those who fled the world of the Antichrist two centuries earlier. "I dreamt of a quiet, upright life," he writes, "all of us together somewhere in the forest, or on the shores of Lake Svetloiar, awaiting the rising of Kitezh (or of the Holy Grail) . . . .

It is not surprising that at the dawn of 'symbolism,' the dawn of our cultural
life, it seemed to us that we could all withdraw from the old world pure and
simple, because the New World would come to meet us."[60] That New World
found its reflection, not only in the city of Kitezh, but also in the communities of Old Believers and sectarians that flourished at the turn of the
twentieth century.

Notes

1. The critical tradition is reviewed succinctly in Sergei Zenkovskii, *Russkoe staroobriadchestvo* (*Forum Slavicum,* 21) (Munich, 1970) 14–23. See also V. F. Milovidov,
Staroobriadchestvo v proshlom i nastoiashchem (Moscow, 1969) 3–7.

2. Zenkovskii cites, in particular, the pioneering work of N. F. Kapterev, A. K.
Borozdin, and E. E. Golubinskii.

3. D. S. Merezhkovskii, "Avtobiograficheskaia zametka," in *Russkaia literatura
XX veka (1890–1910),* ed. S. A. Vengerov (Moscow, 1914) 1:292.

4. Ibid., 293.

5. Z. N. Gippius, "Svetloe ozero (dnevnik)," *Alyi mech* (St. Petersburg, 1906) 349–
419.

6. Nikolai Berdiaev, *Sobranie sochinenii,* vol. 1: *Samopoznanie,* 2d ed. (Paris, 1983)
227–234.

7. Andrei Belyi, [untitled], in *Kak my pishem* (Leningrad, 1930) 11–12.

8. See K. Azadovskii, "Pis'ma N. A. Kliueva k A. Bloku," in *Literaturnoe nasledstvo,* 92, Book 4 (Moscow, 1987) 435, 458.

9. In his diary entry for 17 February 1909 he writes, "Poekhat' mozhno v Tsaritsyn
na Volge—k Ione Brikhnichevu. V Olenetskuiu guberniiu—k Kliuevu. S Prishvinym
povalandat'sia? K sektantam—v Rossiiu:" Aleksandr Blok, *Zapisnye knizhki* (Moscow, 1965) 131.

10. See Dmitrii Merezhkovskii, *O prichinakh upadka i o novykh techeniiakh sovremennoi russkoi literatury* (St. Petersburg, 1983).

11. Nikolai Berdiaev, *Russkaia ideia (Osnovnye problemy russkoi mysli XIX veka
i nachala XX veka* (Paris, 1946) 206.

12. Iurii M. Lotman and Boris A. Uspenskii, "Binary Models in the Dynamics of
Russian Culture (to the End of the Eighteenth Century)," in *The Semiotics of Russian Cultural History,* ed. A. D. and A. S. Nakhimovsky (Ithaca, 1985) 32.

13. See V. F. Milovidov, *Staroobriadchestvo v proshlom i nastoiashchem* 57.

14. P. S. Smirnov, *Istoriia russkogo raskola staroobriadchestva* (St. Petersburg,
1895) 6.

15. V. F. Milovidov, *Staroobriadchestvo v proshlom i nastoiashchem* 64.

16. Ibid., 58.

17. The major statements of the two philosophers are found in the following
sources: Vladimir Solov'ev, "O raskole v russkom narode i obshchestve," in *Sobranie
sochinenii* (St. Petersburg, n.d.) 3: 245–280; "Neskol'ko slov v zashchitu Petra Velikogo," in ibid., 5: 161–180; V. V. Rozanov, "Psikhologiia russkogo raskola," *Religiia*

i kul'tura (St. Petersburg, 1899) 23–54; *Apokaliptsicheskaia sekta (khlysty i skoptsy)* (St. Petersburg, 1914).

18. V. P. Riabushinskii, *Staroobriadchestvo i russkoe religioznoe chuvstvo* (Joinville le Pont, 1936) 80–82.

19. V. Solov'ev, "Neskol'ko slov" 171.

20. V. Rozanov, "Psikhologiia russkogo raskola" 48.

21. Ibid., 50.

22. Cf. in this connection Lotman's and Uspenskii's remarks: "The desire of Nikon and his followers to "correct" ecclesiastical texts was founded on the conception of a primary and correct (Greek) order ("Binary Models in the Dynamics of Russian Culture" 48).

23. V. Solov'ev, "Neskol'ko slov" 172.

24. V. Rozanov, "Psikhologiia russkogo raskola" 23.

25. V. Rozanov, "Émbriony," in *Religiia i kul'tura* 246.

26. V. Rozanov, "Psikhologiia russkogo raskola" 49–50.

27. V. Rozanov, "Émbriony" 244.

28. V. Rozanov, *Temnyi lik. Metafizika khristianstva* (St. Petersburg, 1911) ix.

29. Ibid., 111.

30. Cf. in this connection George Ivask's comment on Bal'mont's *Zelenyi vertograd* in "Russian Modernist Poets and the Mystic Sectarians," *Russian Modernism: Culture and the Avant-garde, 1900–1930,* ed. George Gibian and H. W. Thalsma (Ithaca, 1976) 90–91.

31. D. S. Merezhkovskii, *Polnoe sobranie sochinenii* (Moscow, 1914) 22:99–107.

32. K. Govorov, "Stikhotvoreniia D. Merezhkovskogo (prodolzhenie)," *Ezhenedel'noe obozrenie* 8, no. 214 (21 February 1888), col. 2694.

33. As A. I. Mazunin notes in his review of the poem, "the archpriest dreamt of getting even with the Nikonians, of 'flattening' all of them together with Nikon himself when the opportunity arose. Avvakum and the Old Believers preached undying hatred toward their worst enemies, the Nikonians, not love and forgiveness" ("Tri stikhotvornykh perelozheniia 'Zhitiia' Avvakuma," *Trudy Otdela drevnerusskoi literatury,* 16 [Leningrad, 1958] 409).

34. D. S. Merezhkovskii, *Petr i Aleksei,* in *Polnoe sobranie sochinenii,* 5:168.

35. Ibid., 196.

36. Z. N. Gippius, "Svetloe ozero (dnevnik)" 406–407.

37. Maksimilian Voloshin, *Stikhotvoreniia i poèmy v dvukh tomakh,* ed. B. Filippov, G. Struve, and N. Struve (Paris, 1982–1984) 1:261–289.

38. See Emmanuel Rais, "Maksimilian Voloshin i ego vremia," in M. Voloshin, *Stikhotvoreniia i poèmy* 1: LXXIX–LXXX.

39. See Voloshin's letter to A. Petrova, 9 January 1919, cited in I. T. Kuprianov, *Sud'ba poèta* (Kiev, 1978) 192.

40. Cited by Al. Gorovskii, "Voloshin i Tiutchev," in *Voloshinskie chteniia,* ed. T. M. Makagonova (Moscow, 1978) 69.

41. Aleksandr Blok, "Merezhkovskii," in *Sobranie sochinenii v vos'mi tomakh,* ed. V. Orlov et al. (Moscow and Leningrad, 1960–1963) 5:365.

42. See Maria Carlson, "The Silver Dove," in *Andrei Belyi: Spirit of Symbolism,* ed. John Malmstad (Ithaca, 1987) 65.

43. Aleksandr Blok, *Sobranie sochinenii* 5:210–216.

44. Ibid., 358.

45. "Zadebrennye lesom kruchi . . . ," in ibid., 3:248.

46. Ibid., 4:103–167.

47. Ibid., 134. The correlation between the words spoken by Faina's admirer and Blok's response to Nikolai Kliuev's letters on the relation of the people to the intelligentsia is discussed at length by M. Niqueux in his article, "Blok et l'appel de Kljuev," *Revue des études slaves* 54, no. 4 (1982); see also K. Azadovskii, "Pis'ma N. A. Kliueva k A. Bloku" 467.

48. Maria Carlson, "The Silver Dove" 67, n. 25.

49. Andrei Belyi, *Kak my pishem* 18.

50. The irony of Belyi's politicization of the Khlyst sect is that the novel itself can be read as a kind of theurgic act, and its chief protagonist follows a path of spiritual evolution set forth in a wide variety of gnostic and theosophist texts. See Maria Carlson's fine study of the novel in John Malmstad, ed., *Andrej Belyj.*

51. Andrei Belyi, *Kak my pishem* 12.

52. Andrei Belyi, *Serebrianyi golub'*, in *Izbrannaia proza* (Moscow, 1988) 42.

53. Most of the poets associated with the "New Peasant School" had ties with the Old Belief or mystical sectarians, among them Sergei Klychkov, Petr Oreshin, Pimen Karpov, and Sergei Esenin.

54. On the peculiar admixture of the Old Believer and Khlyst doctrine in Kliuev, see Emmanuel Rais, "Nikolai Kliuev," in Nikolai Kliuev, *Sochineniia,* ed. G. P. Struve and B. A. Filippov (1969) 2:70–71.

55. Nikolai Kliuev, *Sochineniia* 1:211.

56. Ibid., 2:352.

57. K. Azadovskii, "Pis'ma N. A. Kliueva k A. Bloku" 500, 502.

58. Aleksandr Blok, *Sobranie sochinenii* 7:105.

59. Lotman and Uspenskii, "Binary Models in the Dynamics of Russian Culture (to the End of the Eighteenth Century)" 33.

60. Cited by K. Azadovskii in "Pis'ma N. A. Kliueva k A. Bloku" 458, n. 39.

Сектантство и литература

(«Серебряный голубь» Андрея Белого)

JOHANNA RENATE DÖRING-SMIRNOV

...следует <...> отказаться от личного творчества жизни...
(Андрей Белый, «Серебряный голубь»)

1. Не пытаясь дать сколько-нибудь ответственное определение «сектантству», я буду вести речь о том его проявлении, которое к началу нашего столетия привлекло к себе особое внимание «религиозных искателей из интеллигенции» (Андрей Белый)[1]: о хлыстах.

В предисловии к роману «Серебряный голубь», не вошедшем в переиздания, Белый писал о том, что изображенная им секта «голубей» символизирует религиозные шатания как таковые, но тем не менее признавался, что он взял за основу для показа сектантства именно хлыстов:

> Многие приняли секту голубей за хлыстов; согласен, что есть в этой секте признаки, роднящие ее с хлыстовством. Но хлыстовство, как один из ферментов религиозного брожения, не адекватно существующим кристаллизованным формам у хлыстов; оно — в процессе развития; и в этом смысле *голубей,* изображенных мною, как секты не существует; но они — возможны со всеми своими безумными уклонами; в этом смысле голуби мои вполне реальны.[2]

2. Называя описанных в романе сектантов «голубями», Белый концептуализирует хлыстов прежде всего как общину, для которой на первом месте стоит идея «Духа Святого», т.е. пневматика.[3] Эта идея была положена в основу хлыстовской христологии: Христос рождается в мир с этой точки зрения не однажды, он может являться многократно как воплощение Святого Духа. Точно так же воспроизводима роль Богородицы, поскольку Святой Дух и теперь нисходит на женщин.

Сакральная история, таким образом, повторяется. Хлысты были убеждены в том, что Божественное Откровение — это не только чудо, которое было даровано Апостолам на Троицу, но вновь и вновь разыгрывающееся событие. Хлысты ссылались на Третью (апокрифическую) Книгу Ездры, в которой Саваоф пророчествует о своем новом земном воплощении (что предполагает новое Творение). Свои экстатические танцы (радения) они толковали в регенерационном смысле (как смерть Адама и воскресение Христа).[4]

Итак, хлыстовство по природе своей имитационно, что сказалось и на отношении этой секты к православной церкви. Хлысты посещали церковные богослужения по воскресеньям, отправляя свои радения по субботам, ночами; т.е. не столько отрывались от церкви, сколько удваивали ее. Хлысты не отказывались от христианской традиции; скорее, они пытались воссоздать ее в иной форме: они придерживались вместо десяти Заповедей двенадцати; причащались не вином, но водой; почитали пот, натруженный во время радений, как воду, которой крестят.

Повторяемость сакральной истории хлысты проецировали на историю социальную. России предстоит второе рождение:

> Весьма чудес много будет,
> Второй Христос страшен суд засудит.
> Какой пойдет по новой России звон,
> Илья-Пророк многих выгонит
> Из старой России вон,
> Которых отдаст в полон.
> Илья-Пророк новой и второй
> Так будет греметь громко...[5]

Перейдем к теории искусства, которую развил Белый. В сборнике статей «Арабески» он писал:

> Искусство в мире бытия начинает новые ряды творений. Этим искусство отторгнуто от быта <...> Художник — Бог своего мира. Вот почему искра Божества, запавшая из мира бытия в произведение художника, окрашивает художественное произведение демоническим блеском.[6]

Если в этом высказывании Белый осознает искусство как демоническое подражание сакральному акту творения, то в брошюре «Кризис жизни» он замечает, что Люцифер соблазнил Россию в хлыстовство.[7] И то, и другое демонично. Подражательность есть, по Белому, бесовское наваждение. В подражательстве сектантство и искусство сходятся.

3. Примитивный глава сектантов, столяр Кудеяров, и поэт-декадент Дарьяльский потому и тянутся друг к другу, что один намеревается снова начать священную историю, а второй мечтает о воскрешении умершего прошлого. В то время как Кудеяров надеется на то, что будет рожден новый Христос («голубиное дитятко»), Дарьяльский занят поисками древней Греции, сохранившейся, в его восприятии, в России:

Новый он видел свет, свет еще и в свершении в жизни обрядов греко-российской церкви. В православии, и в отсталых именно понятьях православного (т.е. по его мнению, язычествующего) мужичка видел он новый светоч в Мире грядущего Грека[8] (I, 174–175).

Оба усматривают друг в друге творческий потенциал, которым каждый из них не обладает. Кудеяров, слишком старый, чтобы произвести на свет ребенка, уступает место отца Дарьяльскому (тем самым позиция отца удваивается: духовный отец существует наряду с телесным); поэт, чье дарование иссякает, пытается почерпнуть вдохновение у «голубей».

Сходство Кудеярова и Дарьяльского подчеркивается тем, что последний в конце концов увлекается плотницким трудом, подобно первому: «Отчего же <...> и мне не столярничать?» (II, 92).

Однако попытка взаимного сближения Кудеярова и Дарьяльского терпит крах. Божественный ребенок не рождается. Сектанты убивают поэта. Перед нами не состоявшаяся, разрушенная аналогия. Сектантам не удается имитация акта творения. Художник находит в настоящем не прошлое, но свою смерть.

4. Принципом разрушенной аналогии, положенным в основу романа, Белый руководствовался и в своем подходе к источникам текста.

Об этом свидетельствуют уже имена двух главных протагонистов «Серебряного голубя», Кудеярова и Дарьяльского.

Фамилия столяра-сектанта восходит к имени разбойничьего атамана в балладе Некрасова «О двух великих грешниках» из его поэмы «Кому на Руси жить хорошо»:

> Было двенадцать разбойников,
> Был Кудеяр — атаман,
> Много разбойники пролили
> Крови честных христиан.[9]

И в стихотворении Некрасова, и в романе равным образом упоминаются Соловки и старый дуб, что делает интертекстуальную связь Кудеяр-Кудеяров несомненной. Но у Некрасова великий грешник добивается прощения за преступления, убивая еще одного грешника, пана Глуховского. Между тем убийство Дарьяльского, скорее, ассоциировано с расправой «бесов» над Шатовым: это не спасительное убийство, но вероломное злодейство.

Фамилия «Дарьяльский» отсылает нас к поэзии Лермонтова. Любовь Дарьяльского к Матрене являет собой контакт двух несовместимых миров и в этом смысле как будто аналогична влечению Духа Зла к земной красавице в лермонтовской поэме «Демон» (имя «Матрена» почти анаграммирует имя «Тамара»). Но если Лермонтов изображает попытку избавиться от демонического начала, то Белый, напротив, рисует любовь Дарьяльского к Матрене как падение, как демонизацию:

> Падает глыба гранита в грозное дно ущелий; если дно это еще и поверхность вод, падает еще ниже глыба гранита <...> и <...> предела нет у души человеческой, потому что может быть вечным паденье, и оно восторгает, как над пропастью мира пролетающих звезд след <...> И для Дарьяльского полетом стало его паденье: он уже без оглядки бежал туда, где мелькал сарафан Матрены Семеновны (I, 275–276).

Точно так же квази-аналогичен текст Белого по отношению к стихотворению Лермонтова «Тамара», где, как и в «Серебряном голубе», фигурирует Дарьяльское ущелье. В обоих случаях любовь оказывается ловушкой, попав в которую мужчина погибает. Но лермонтовская Тамара прекрасна; в «Серебряном голубе» же речь идет о любви к безобразному:

> ...все те черты не красу выражали, не девичье сбереженное целомудрие; в колыханьи же грудей курносой столярихи, и в толстых с белыми икрами и грязными пятками ногах, и в большом ее животе, и в лбе, покатом и хищном, — запечатлелась откровенная срамота <...> тут ты увидишь, что эти все осветляющие глаза — косые глаза; один глядит мимо тебя, другой — на тебя; и ты вспомнишь, как коварна, обманна осень (I, 280–282; ср.: «Прекрасна, как ангел небесный, Как демон, коварна и зла»[10]).

Интертекстуальная аналогия допускается в «Серебряном голубе» там, где имитация предстает в сниженном, профанированном виде. Роль низкого имитатора отводится в романе генералу Чижикову. Он разыгрывает себе разные роли, будучи, в действительности, правительственным шпионом. В интертекстуальном плане его имя сопоставимо с «Чичиков».[11] К тому же и гоголевский герой, и доносчик из «Серебряного голубя» выдают кажимость за реальность: первый скупает мертвые души, второй собирает ложные сведения. В то же самое время одно из имен генерала, Гуд-Гудай-Затрубинский, делает этого персонажа подобным вождю сектантов — ср. «Кудеяров» и «Гуд-Гудай-Затрубинский» (обратим внимание на присутствие редупликации в этом имени генерала). Корневая морфема 'труб' может быть понята при таком сравнении в связи с мотивом возвещения Страшного суда, распространенным в песнопениях хлыстов и скопческом ответвлении этой секты:

> Во всех местах
> И во пречистых устах —
> Будет трубушка трубить.[12]
> Да где трубушка трубит,
> Где сам Бог говорит:
> Ой Бог![13]

5. Как известно, Белый пользовался, работая над романом, материалами по истории хлыстовства, собранными А. С. Пругавиным и В. Д. Бонч-Бруевичем («я их [хлыстов] изучал и по материалам (Пругавина, Бонч-Бруевича и других)»).[14]

По мысли В. Д. Бонч-Бруевича, корень хлыстовства — в том, что оно принадлежит

> к очень старым восточным сектам, до сих пор в своих воззрениях сохранившим следы принципов древнего гностицизма.[15]

Не обсуждая того, прав или не прав В. Д. Бонч-Бруевич, можно, однако, заметить, что его понимание хлыстовства делает ясным, почему Дарьяльский в своих поисках архаики в настоящем обращается именно к «голубям».

Как явствует из этого примера, Белый не отклонялся от научных источников в том, что касается концептуализации хлыстовства. Но тогда, когда он находил в научной литературе о русском сектантстве некоторый сюжет, он обращался с такой историей так же, как и с содержанием литературных претекстов.

Мотив покушения сектантов на жизнь отступника Белый заимствовал, по-видимому, из исследования священника К. Кутепова «Секты хлыстов и скопцов», где рассказывается о случае некоего Матусова, которого скопцы вначале хотели отравить, а затем зверски избили.[16] Белый делает жертвами отравления и избиения разных персонажей. Дарьяльского, как и Матусова, избивают четверо мужчин, но поэт погибает, тогда как его прототип выжил. Эта неполная аналогия сочетается в романе с другой аналогией, носителем которой выступает второстепенный персонаж, купец Еропегин. Сектанты подносят ему отраву, причем, как и у Кутепова, это делает женщина. Читатель «Серебряного голубя» остается в неведении насчет того, каков конец Еропегина. Возможно, он погибнет. Как бы то ни было, отрава, подействовав на него, позднее отчасти теряет свою силу:

> ...только крепко душа Луки Силыча, знать, была привязана к телу; из недели в неделю тянулось это Богу души отдаванье; и даже странно

сказать: доктора ждали смерти со дня на день, а вот уже более недели к Луке Силычу слабое вернулось и руками обладание и ногами... (II, 234).

6.0. В художественной литературе XIX в. хлыстовство описывалось П. И. Мельниковым (Андреем Печерским) в романе «На горах» и Л. фон Захер-Мазохом в повести «Die Gottesmutter» (на оба произведения указывает, кстати, в своей работе К. Кутепов).[17] Мы не располагаем сведениями о том, был ли Белый знаком с этими текстами. Мы знаем, впрочем, что он встречался с сыном Мельникова-Печерского.[18] Книга Захер-Мазоха была переведена на русский язык в 1880 г. под названием «Пророчица» и напечатана в «Ниве».[19]

6.1. Хотя у нас и нет данных о том, читал ли автор «Серебряного голубя» «На горах», сопоставительный анализ этих двух произведений позволяет с большой долей вероятности предположить, что роман Мельникова-Печерского послужил Белому одним из важнейших источников его текста.

Значительную часть романа Мельникова-Печерского[20] составляет история богатого купца-старообрядца, Марка Смолокурова, и его любимой дочери Авдотьи, которая постепенно отстает от старообрядчества и становится тайной хлыстовкой. Члены хлыстовской секты зарятся на обильное приданое девушки. В «Серебряном голубе» то же намерение вынашивает Кудеяров, рассчитывающий завладеть приданым невесты Дарьяльского, Катерины, с тем, чтобы построить новые хлыстовские «корабли» (I, 85).

Чем ближе Авдотья знакомится с хлыстами, тем более отталкивающим кажется ей хлыстовское смешение спиритуального с сексуальным. В решающий момент, когда она встречается с «араратским пророком», Егором Сергеевичем Денисовым, чтобы узнать от него «тайну духовного супружества», тот пытается изнасиловать Авдотью, но ей удается убежать из помещения через окно, замаскированное священным изображением (картиной, на которой написан медиоланский священник Амвросий).[21]

Попавший в ловушку в доме Еропегина Дарьяльский, как и Авдотья из романа «На горах», хочет спастись бегством через окно, но видит за стеклом «какую-то харю, нагло глядевшую на него в упор» (II, 242). Вместо спасения — гибель, вместо помощного сакрального изображения — живое профанированное лицо убийцы, — так расходятся сюжетные линии Авдотьи и Дарьяльского, развертывавшиеся по началу параллельно (мотивы увлечения обоих персонажей сектантством, меркантильного интереса хлыстов к обоим, запертой комнаты-ловушки).

В противоположность Дарьяльскому, негативному аналогу Авдотьи, Еропегин вполне подобен ее отцу (как подобен он и Матусову). После того как купец Смолокуров открывает, что его дочь вела двойное существование, его хватает удар. Он лишается речи и способности к передвижению.[22] Теми же симптомами характеризуется болезнь Еропегина, последовавшая за отравлением. И тот и другой теряют те свойства, которые составляют необходимое условие для сакральных действий хлыстов — для их песнопений и танцев. Смолокуров и Еропегин парны и в том отношении, что первый — отец хлыстовки, а второй — муж таковой.

6.2. Похоже, что Белому была известна и повесть Захер-Мазоха, в центре которой стоит конфликт между молодым крестьянином-католиком Sabadil'ом (в русском переводе: «Венцеслав») и красавицей, которую зовут Mardona (в русском переводе: «Марьяна» — ср. имя героини «Серебряного голубя» «Матрена», которое, судя по всему, восходит не только к «Тамаре» Лермонтова, но и к сложению: «Mardona» + «Марьяна» = «Матрена»). Mardona — богородица сектантов, которых Захер-Мазох называет «духоборцами» (sic!).[23] Русские читатели этого текста, однако, считали, что Захер-Мазох ведет речь о хлыстах. К. Кутепов пишет:

> Автор «Пророчицы» заимствует свой сюжет из быта тарговицких хлыстов и сообщает прекрасные сведения о том важном значении, какое имели пророчицы и богородицы в хлыстовских кораблях.[24]

Sabadil (Венцеслав) влюбляется в сектантскую богородицу, но затем изменяет ей с двумя другими сектантками, после чего Mardona (Марьяна) распинает его на кресте.

Sabadil принимает муку как радость, получает, как всегда у Захер-Мазоха, наслаждение от страдания (т.е. альголагнию):

> «Schmerzt es?» fragte Mardona mit einem liebevollen Lacheln.
> «Ich leide gern, da Du es willst», erwiderte er, sein Blick ruhte mit fanatischer Hingebung, fast trunken auf dem schonen Weibe (198). «Ich sterbe gern, wenn Du es willst, und der Tod wird suß sein, wenn Du es bist, die ihn mir gibt» (202).

Оба мотива — распятие и альголагния — оставили след в романе «Серебряный голубь» — там, где рассказывается о предчувствии Дарьяльского:

> Обреченный на боль и на крестное распятие, которого уже нельзя никак избежать, силится ведь это распятие еще и благословить (II, 179).

Ср. также «блаженство», которое Дарьяльский ощущает, когда его и впрямь убивают:

> ...и только после того уже он блаженно вернулся, блаженно глаза полуоткрыл и блаженно он видел... (II, 244).

Главное, в чем сближаются оба произведения, — это трагический конец мужчины, соблазнившегося женщиной из секты. При всем тематическом сходстве повести Захер-Мазоха и романа Белого очевидно, что в «Gottesmutter» герой становится вторым Христом, а в «Серебряном голубе» повествуется о нерожденном новом Христе, о не появившемся на свет «голубином дитятке».

Примечания

1. Андрей Белый, *Между двух революций* (Ленинград, 1934), стр. 354.

2. Андрей Белый, *Серебряный голубь* (Москва, 1910), ненумер., курсив автора.

3. Ср.: K. K. Grass, *Die russischen Sekten I. Die Gottesleute oder Chlüsten nebst Skakunen, Maljowanzü, Panijaschkowzü u.a.* (Leipzig 1907), стр. 643 f.

4. К вопросу о хлыстовском учении о *«таинственной смерти и таинственном воскресении»* (подчеркнуто автором) см.: П. И. Мельников (Андрей Печерский), *Белые голуби*. В: *Собрание сочинений в восьми томах*. т. 8 (Москва, 1976), стр. 146–157.

5. Н. В. Реутский, *Люди божьи и скопцы. Историческое исследование (из достоверных источников и подлинных бумаг)* (Москва, 1872), стр. 152.

6. Андрей Белый, *Арабески. Книга статей* (Москва, 1911), стр. 152.

7. Андрей Белый, *На перевале. Кризис жизни* (Берлин, Петербург, Москва, 1923), стр. 139.

8. Цит. по: А. Белый, *Серебряный голубь* (Ann Arbor, Michigan [без года]). В скобках после цитат названные римские цифры обозначают части романа, латинские же цифры — страницы издания.

9. Н. А. Некрасов, *Сочинения в трех томах*. т. 3 (Москва, 1953), стр. 212. Б. М. Гаспаров обращает внимание на тот же текст Некрасова, послуживший источником поэмы Блока «Двенадцать». Ср.: Б. М. Гаспаров, «Поэма Блока 'Двенадцать' и некоторые проблемы карнавализации в искусстве начала XX века». В: *Slavica Hierosolymitana*, I (Jerusalem, 1977), стр. 120 f.

10. М. Ю. Лермонтов, *Собрание сочинений в четырех томах*. т. 1 (Москва 1957), стр. 73.

11. Ср. подробнее: В. М. Паперный, «Андрей Белый и Гоголь. Статья вторая», *Ученые записки Тартуского университета*, т. 620 (Тарту, 1983), стр. 90–91.

12. Реутский, стр. 198 и след.

13. Мельников (Печерский), стр. 179.

14. Андрей Белый, *Между двух революций,* стр. 354.

15. В. Д. Бонч-Бруевич, «Раскол и сектанство в России. Доклад В. Д. Бонч-Бруевича Второму очередному съезду Российской социал-демократической рабочей партии». Опубл. в: *Рассвет,* 1904, 6–7, стр. 161–174. Здесь цит. по: Б. Б. Бонч-Бруевича, *Избранные сочинения в трех томах* (Москва, 1959), стр. 183.

16. К. Кутепов, *Секты хлыстов и скопцов,* изд. 2-е (Ставрополь-Губернский, 1900), стр. 219–221.

17. Там же, стр. 14.

18. Ср.: Андрей Белый, *Начало века* (Москва-Ленинград, 1933), стр. 307.

19. В книжках 3–10 без имени переводчика.

20. Мельников (Печерский), т. 5–7. Впервые роман был опубликован в: *Русский вестник,* 1875–1881.

21. Мельников (Печерский), т. 6, стр. 473–474.

22. Там же, т. 7, стр. 36 и след.

23. L. von Sacher-Masoch, *Die Gottesmutter.* Neue Ausgabe (Leipzig-Reudnitz, без года), стр. 26. После цитат в скобках названные цифры указывают на страницы этого издания.

24. Кутепов, стр. 14.

Johanna Renate Döring-Smirnov/Summary: Sectarianism and Literature (Andrei Belyi's Silver Dove*)*

On the eve of the twentieth century the Russian intelligentsia was extremely interested in historiosophic problems, religions other than their own, and sectarianism. Andrei Belyi considered sectarianism to be homologous with art: they both imitate the act of holy creation and are demonic. This tendency he found especially prominent in the sects of *khlysty*. Belyi took their theological conceptions as a thematic impulse for his novel *The Silver Dove*. He developed this subject to show the final crash of all artificial imitations of the holy creation (the birth of a new Christ).

Belyi studied literary and historic writings about Russian sects, especially *khlysty*. However, he transformed his sources in such a manner that analogies were sometimes obliterated. Two literary texts were of central importance to Belyi: P. I. Mel'nikov's (Andrei Pecherskii) *Na gorakh* (*On the Hills*) and Leopold von Sacher-Masoch's *Die Gottesmutter,* a novel translated into Russian already in 1880. The article comments on Belyi's creative use of the theological conceptions of *khlysty* and these literary texts dealing with the sect.

Religious Holiday Literature and Russian Modernism

A Preliminary Approach

HENRYK BARAN

The two great holidays in the Christian calendar, Christmas and Easter, prompted the development of a special literary practice in nineteenth- and twentieth-century Russian culture: writing and publishing works connected to these holidays. Few readers and critics, usually familiar with some better known examples of this practice by Dostoevskii, Chekhov, and Gor'kii, are aware of the narrative tradition from which such texts arose. This paper, part of a larger study of this tradition, focuses on one stage in its history: the period during which modernism, broadly understood as covering Symbolism and related trends, played a dominant role in Russian literature, approximately 1905–1917.[1]

Background

During the nineteenth century, a tradition developed in Russia of publishing literary works, mostly short stories, linked to the Christmas season. The general term used for such tales was *sviatochnye rasskazy,* though the more narrow *rozhdestvenskie rasskazy* was also sometimes employed. Subsequently, there developed a custom of publishing literary texts connected to Holy Week, and the general term *paskhal'nye rasskazy* came into use.[2]

Very often, such genre designations would be present in the subtitle of a text, though this was by no means obligatory. Also, since an author could always remove the subtitle in a later publication, relying on its presence to identify a holiday text can be misleading. The key factors that determine whether a work belongs to the category of holiday literature are date of publication and contents.

Yuletide or Christmas tales spring from two sources—a native tradition and foreign models. The former, analyzed in detail by E. Dushechkina in a series of studies,[3] originates in the folk practice of telling anecdotes during Yuletide, anecdotes usually involving encounters with the supernatural (*by-*

lichki), as well as literary adaptations of this pattern.[4] The foreign model was provided by Dickens's "Christmas Books," translations of which started appearing in the mid-1840s with *A Christmas Carol* (1843), *The Chimes* (1845), and *The Cricket on the Hearth* (1846) receiving a particularly warm reception: Dickens's tales were lauded, among others, by such critics as Belinskii, Apollon Grigor'ev, and P. A. Pletnev.[5] In the following decades, new translations of Dickens reinforced the interest in the Christmas story genre.

Only a few years after the Christmas Books were read and discussed in Russia, D. V. Grigorovich created what was perhaps the first Russian Christmas tale of the Dickensian type, "Zimnii vecher. Povest' na Novyi God."[6] It depicts in detail the poverty of the family of a professional actor and their salvation through the intervention of a kind-hearted physician. Igor' Katarskii notes that this text anticipates most of the devices and weaknesses of the subsequent mass-production of holiday tales in Russia, which began in the last third of the nineteenth century and continued into the twentieth.[7]

The Dickensian contribution to the Christmas stories helped shape their rather constricted narrative structure and thematics. Leskov defines the genre in one of his own Christmas works, "Zhemchuzhnoe ozherel'e," in the following terms:

> Это такой род литературы, в котором писатель чувствует себя невольником слишком тесной и правильно ограниченной формы. От святочного рассказа непременно требуется, чтобы он был приурочен к событиям святочного вечера—от Рождества до Крещенья, чтобы он был сколько-нибудь фантастичен, имел какую-нибудь мораль, хотя в роде опровержения вредного предрассудка, и наконец—чтобы он оканчивался непременно весело. В жизни таких событий бывает немного, и потому автор неволит себя выдумывать и сочинять фабулу, подходящую к программе. А через это в святочных рассказах и замечается большая деланность и однообразие.[8]

Leskov's list includes the *maximal* expectations for a Christmas text: some degree of the fantastic, a didactic component, a "happy end," and a link to the holiday season. Fitting all these in a single work was difficult and could indeed lead to artificiality and monotony. Although there were attempts to create tales that met all the requirements of the genre—like *A Christmas Carol* itself—in most cases holiday works fell into two basic, usually separate *types*, both called *sviatochnyi rasskaz:* those with a sentimental-didactic orientation, be it directed at social or individual phenomena, and those where the fantastic played a primary role.[9] The former type was usually linked with Christmas Eve or Christmas Day (*rozhdestvenskii rasskaz*), since the story of the Nativity provided a powerful counterpoint to illuminations of contemporary evils, and the didacticism normally would be prompted by a sentimental plot situation like that of Bob Cratchit and his family. The latter type was associated with Christmastide as a whole (i.e., the period between Christmas Day and Epiphany), with New Year celebrations, and with the attendant folkloric traditions—mummery, village games, the loosening of the supernatural, fortune-telling (particularly by young girls).[10]

Initially, like most literary works in mid-nineteenth century, Christmas texts were published in the "thick" journals, and continued to appear there into the twentieth century. Occasionally, there were separate publications in the form of inexpensive booklets by one or more authors.[11] By the mid-1870s, a new type of publishing vehicle—periodicals aimed at a broader, family audience ("thin" journals)—turned the occasional Yuletide tale into a full-blown journalistic celebration of the holiday. The case of A. F. Marks's weekly *Niva,* which was started in 1870 and which adhered to a platform of publishing intellectually and morally uplifting materials, shows how this process developed. For a few years, issues which appeared on or around Christmas carried only individual texts devoted to the holiday, alongside other materials.[12] By 1876, however, the last issue in December was mainly devoted to Christmas, as reflected in both verbal texts and illustrations.[13] Subsequent years furthered the practice of publishing full-blown Christmas issues, where both verbal and visual art reinforced a single theme.

During the same period, with Suvorin's *Novoe vremia* leading the way, Yuletide tales as well as occasional poems came onto the pages of the increasingly numerous Russian newspapers. While in the 1880s only some major newspapers dailies featured full-blown Christmas issues, by the early 1890s the practice was widespread in the provinces as well as Petersburg and Moscow.

There were good reasons for the increasing role of newspapers in the publication of holiday literature. Not only could they pay authors quickly, but also, particularly in the provinces, they were less clannish and less inclined to discriminate on the basis of ideology than the major journals. Both these factors were important for many writers. Newspapers were also an ideal outlet for delivering Christmas stories to a mass audience as close to the holiday itself as possible, something the monthly periodicals, and even the weeklies, were ill-suited to provide. By the 1890s most Christmas texts were appearing in special Christmas Day issues of newspapers, although one can also find such publications in other issues during the holiday period.[14]

The Easter story becomes established quite a bit later, in general imitation

of the Christmas tale.[15] During the 1870s and 1880s, special Easter issues are
rare. In *Niva,* for example, the celebration of Easter was usually marked by
the appearance of a couple of drawings of scenes from Passion Week.[16] By
the end of the 1890s the so-called *paskhal'nyi numer* comes into being, em-
braced with differing speed by various periodicals.[17] In some, it is ushered in
by articles and essays on the meaning of the holiday and on customs associated with its celebrations, whereas in others the focus is on fictional texts.[18]

Unlike Christmas, Easter was not surrounded by ambivalent, carnivalesque
elements, a fact reflected in the development of a class of texts with unambiguous thematics. Easter tales generally focus on the sense of the miraculous, on the believer's reaction to the reenactment of the Passion during the
events of Holy Week, on recollections of childhood celebrations of Easter
and of a happier, purer state than adulthood. This is often linked with a
didactic component, since the story of Jesus's triumph over sin and death is
used as a counterpoint to human suffering here and now. The supernatural
and the fantastic play only minor roles in such works.

Two works by minor writers are typical of Easter fiction. The protagonist
of "V sviatuiu noch'. Nabrosok" is Sergei, a convict in a Siberian jail. On
Easter night, he recollects his past, particularly the reason for his imprison-
ment, his killing his unfaithful wife. As the sounds of church bells and songs
reach him, Sergei breaks out of his cell, but is confronted by a prison guard
with a gun. The convict asks for mercy, and a miracle occurs:

> —Пощади!... тихо-тихо проговорил Сергей. И растаяло сердце стро-
> гого воина; думал-ли он, что Сергею далеко не уйти, или вспомнились
> ему слова Спасителя: "И ненавидящим нас простим!"—Ступай с Бо-
> гом!—сказал он; отвернулся и вытерев серым рукавом шинели глаза—
> отправился к противоположному концу стены . . . ."[19]

The other Easter work involves a conversation between a dying actress and
her friend, the "entrepreneur" (troupe manager) Amplii Egorovich Katava-
sov. The actress, who had been complaining about the difficult life faced by
a woman in the world of the theatre, suddenly recollects her childhood love
of Easter, and her face lights up: "Мне слышатся нежные голоса, поющие
'Христос Воскресе,' за спиной у меня вырастают крылья, и мне становится легко . . . совсем легко. . . ."[20]

Christmas and Easter issues had to be filled with thematically appropriate
materials. In part, this need was met by translations, especially in provincial
publications. In both the nineteenth and early twentieth century, we find
calendar works by a variety of foreign authors, particularly the French: Jean
Aicard, François Coppée, Anatole France, Jules Lemaitre, Jean Lorrain,

Pierre Loti, and Émile Zola. There are also translations of Bret Harte, Maria Konopnicka, Selma Lagerlöf, Andrzej Niemojewski, Max Nordau, Bolesław Prus, Georges Rodenbach, August Strindberg, Mark Twain, and Clara Viebig. At the same time, native writers of very diverse orientations and talents were drawn to calendar fiction.[21] Creating such works became a set activity for authors, including prominent ones, who belonged to the "stable" of a particular periodical or newspaper.[22]

Major authors who contributed to calendar fiction include Dostoevskii, whose "Mal'chik u Khrista na elke" (1876) stands out against a background of similar works by lesser writers. Leskov started with "Zapechatlennyi angel" (1873) and "Rozhdestvenskii vecher u ipokhondrika" (1879), and followed with a whole series of pieces, ending with "Pustopliasy" (1893).[23] An entire volume of his tales appeared in 1886.[24] Among these, we find such classics of the genre as "Zver'" and "Prividenie v Inzhenernom zamke," as well as texts that strain at the boundaries of the tradition, such as the anti-Semitic "Zhidovskaia kuvyrkollegiia" and "Puteshestvie s nigilistom."[25]

Among creators of holiday stories, Chekhov occupies a special place: his writings offer a spectrum of the various narrative strategies an author could pursue with regard to this form. These include, among others, "Krivoe zerkalo" (1883), "Vosklitsatel'nyi znak" (1885), and "Noch' na kladbishche" (1885), all of which parody the fantastic variant of the Christmas story. The year 1886 brings not only three Christmas stories—"Na puti," "Van'ka," and "To byla ona!"—but also a marvelous Easter story, "Sviatoiu noch'iu." Some years later, the lapidary "Na sviatkakh" (1900) uses the occasion of Christmas to offer a moving glimpse into the spiritual sufferings of an old couple separated from their married daughter.[26]

Other major writers who produce holiday literature during the late nineteenth century include Korolenko, with the memorable peasant hero of his "Son Makara" (1883), and Kuprin, whose early fiction includes such works as "Zhizn'. Rozhdestvenskaia skazka" (1895), "Bonza" (1896), "Nedorazumenie" (1896, later title "Putanitsa"), and "Taper" (1900). There is the marinist K. M. Staniukovich, whose holiday tales include "Elka" (1880), "Rozhdestvenskaia noch'" (1892), "Svetlyi prazdnik" (1893), "V rode sviatochnogo rasskaza," and "Zagadochnyi passazhir" (1901). One can also point to Mamin-Sibiriak's volume of Christmas stories, mostly devoted to the life of the Old Believers.[27]

Gor'kii, too, sometimes works within the parameters of holiday literature, as in "Na plotakh" (1895), an Easter tale, and "Izvozchik" (1895). More often, however, he treats the conventions of the tradition ironically. In the

story "O mal'chike i devochke, kotorye ne zamerzli" (1894), he undercuts
one of the standard Christmas plots, as indicated by the title. In another
work, "V sochel'nik" (1899), Gor'kii presents two petty thieves who listen
to a drunken confession of a tax bureau official: the man pours out to them
his disgust with his own well-ordered existence. A sudden realization of
social barriers sends him scurrying back, without his wallet, to the home he
had previously criticized. The sentimental expectations of the Christmas
story are partially met, but the reality of class divisions proves even stronger
than fiction.

In spite of the constraints of the form, several features in the calendar
stories made them appealing to serious writers. For one, they could be used
by a realist, yet contained elements that lightened the constraints of realist
poetics. Christmas and Easter stories could be used, in the manner of Dickens,
to depict in detail social conditions and inequities. Poverty, injustice, and
human suffering could be presented in a telling way, and an appropriate dose
of didacticism could be injected into the text. A holiday story could be used
to explore religious feelings and reinforce Christian values. Similarly, progressive and radical authors, whose opportunities for direct expression of
their views were often constrained, could use the mechanism of an innocent
holiday narrative to offer a pointed social and political commentary, and
could buttress their arguments by reference to Christian ideals.[28] At the same
time, holiday traditions, which called on men to pause in their everyday life
and to direct their thoughts inward, offered possibilities for plot resolutions
that could diverge from those dictated by the logic of economic conditions
and the protagonists' individual psychology. A holiday-based narrative reversal—a happy end—was a possibility, should an author wish to exercise it.
This, combined with the Christmas tradition of the fantastic, gave writers of
the late nineteenth century opportunities for flights of fancy not found since
the Romantic period.

By the late 1890s, in sum, holiday literature was being produced in increasing quantity and was reaching readers through several publishing
vehicles. However, as shown by some of Gor'kii's and Chekhov's works, this
literary tradition had already developed a tendency for self-parody, often at
the hands of its prominent practitioners. Such self-parody was prompted by
several factors. The origins of holiday literature were too recent, too easily
identifiable to everyone. At a time when the very notion of generic taxon-
omy was unpopular, the author of a Christmas or Easter tale (or the occasional poem) felt constrained by his readers' clear expectations of what such
a work should contain. Repeatedly, writers indicated that the narrative pos-

sibilities of the genre had become exhausted, that its reliance on the fantastic was unconvincing, that its lexicon was cliched, and that its sentimentality too often descended into bathos. Such concerns led to the appearance of comic pseudotexts—frequently in the holiday issues themselves.

Parodic and satirical treatments of holiday works offer insights into both the contents of works produced in this tradition and the publishing mechanisms that produced them. For example, the practices of writers in newspapers are laid bare in the introduction to a 1905 text:

> Ведь так уже спокон веков повелось: во все остальные дни года мы, журналисты, говорим с вами об этике и эстетике, о политике, о городских делах, передаем вам все события мчащейся и ползущей—смотря по эпохе—жизни, а на Рождество и на Светлый праздник рассказываем вам сказки.
>
> На Светлый праздник рассказывается что-нибудь розовенькое, сентиментальное, если кто умеет, так даже стихами, а для Рождества принято приготовить что-нибудь пострашнее. На Рождество газету редко кто читает в обычное время, за утренним чаем. Утро уходит на праздничные заботы и приемы, а в газету заглядывают вечером. В праздное вечернее время так приятно легкое щекотанье нервов, и вот тут-то и прочитываются рассказы о привидениях, о замерзающих в рождественскую ночь детях и женщинах, о чудесных елках, о покойниках, обо всем, отчего у невзыскательного читателя начинают слегка лазить мурашки по спине.[29]

The narrative commonplaces of the great mass of calendar texts are exposed in the following opening of a piece by the satirist O. L. D'Or:

> Всякий человек, имеющий руки, двугривенный на бумагу, перо и чернила и не имеющий таланта, может написать рождественский рассказ. Нужно только придерживаться известной системы и твердо помнить следующие правила:
>
> 1. Без поросенка, гуся, елки и хорошего человека рождественский рассказ не действителен.
> 2. Слова «ясли», «звезда» и «любовь» должны повториться не менее десяти, но и не более двух-трех тысяч раз.
> 3. Колокольный звон, умиление и раскаяние должны находиться в конце рассказа, а не в начале его.
>
> Все остальное неважно.[30]

Thus, by the early twentieth century, holiday literature was in an unsettled state. Though writers of talent had enriched it with a number of artistically significant works, much of what was being written was of questionable merit. Holiday fiction seemed destined to be relegated to the periphery of literature,

when it was affected by new developments, both within and beyond literature. The former involved the rise of modernism, which came into its own
during the 1900s; the latter—the political situation in Russia during and
after 1905. The impact of the 1905 Revolution on holiday literature will be
considered first.

Holiday Literature and Politics

Traditionally, calendar issues of newspapers contained editorials expounding
on the meaning of the celebration. The editorial in the Christmas 1900 issue
of *Novosti i birzhevaia gazeta,* a typical example of such a text, asks where,
at the start of the new century, one can find "peace and goodwill." The answer offered: nowhere, since "civilized" peoples strive to surpass each other
in cruelty, and men continue to injure each other. Under the circumstances,
one can only wait for the righteous judge who is sure to come.[31] Such a message is essentially timeless and could easily have been published any other
year, as could any of the fictional offerings in the same issue.[32]

The pre-1905 Russian press, bound by strict censorship, for the most part
did not comment on domestic developments in the holiday issues. Sometimes
it responded to foreign events like the Boer War. In 1899, holiday editorials
in some newspapers did focus on the famine gripping a number of provinces.
However, these were essentially appeals for humanitarian assistance, without
any political conclusions being drawn.[33]

With the Russo-Japanese War, a degree of responsiveness to current developments entered holiday issues. Initially, there were some expressions of
support for the conflict, including comments on the "yellow peril" and the
"pagan enemy."[34] As the human cost of the war increased, antiwar sentiments appeared in some holiday texts. A new publication, L. Khodskii's
radical-leaning newspaper *Nasha zhizn',* offered a foretaste of what was soon
to come. Some of the works in its Christmas 1904 issue used the holiday
setting to condemn the war and social conditions in Russia: particularly
effective was a story about a peasant girl, left helpless with her mother after
her father is drafted into the army, who dies of starvation during Christmas.[35] Other works, only marginally connected to the holiday, either depicted scenes of brutality in Russian life or voiced hope about coming
changes; among their number was a story by Gusev-Orenburgskii about the
abuse of authority in a village and the local priest's compromise with this
evil, and one of Sologub's "political fairy-tales."[36] By Easter 1905, still before
the battle of Tsushima but after the disasters on land in Manchuria, the antiwar theme is even stronger in some holiday issues.[37]

The Imperial Manifesto of 17 October, the formation of political parties, and the relaxation of censorship, brought drastic changes. Large numbers of new newspapers, generally linked to newly created political parties, were established. The press as a whole, given freer rein, used the holiday tradition as a vehicle to comment on developments inside the country and to engage in open political debate. Generalized themes of Christian love, charity, and faith in resurrection were no longer sufficient; newspapers employed the narrative conventions of holiday literature to express their specific views on the events of the day. Typically, the tone would be set by the editorial, which interpreted the meaning of the holiday, relating it to current conditions. Several (sometimes all) of the holiday stories and poems in the issue would offer vignettes of Russian life through the prism of the holiday or related situations.

Extensive use of holiday literature in the service of politics started with Christmas 1905. The workers' revolt in Moscow had been suppressed only a few days before; actions by the rebels and government troops had resulted in heavy loss of life. The publications reflected the ferocity of the civil conflict, greater even than the bloody events in the days following the October Manifesto, though assessments of blame differed greatly, in line with the newspapers' and their authors' political views.

The response from the right was generally straightforward: it featured claims of a conspiracy by the radicals and the Jews, whose incitement of the people, it was charged, had caused the tragedy.[38] In the reactionary *Moskovskie vedomosti* a minor poet, L. Kologrivova, uses the characteristic lexicon and imagery of Christmastide verse to declare the radicals guilty of bringing the country to its present bloody state:

> И ныне над нашей Державой
> Царит непроглядная мгла
> Крамола с враждою лукавой
> На гибель ей сети сплела.[39]

The same issue also features a prose tale. "Kroshka Bobik" takes a stock plot situation—a family on Christmas Eve, a sick child, and a father trying to get home in time—and adds a political twist. The child has developed an inflammation of the lungs because of a chill caught during the recent "disturbances": "Толпа взбунтовавшихся проходила мимо нашей квартиры и один из них камнем вышиб стекла в окне . . . Холодом охватило малютку—и вот. . . ." The boy's father is kept away from home by a railroad strike, which has halted all travel within Russia. The narrator editorializes on this and other events:

Наступила Рождественская ночь. Людская злоба у колыбели Христа
не утихала. Бунты и забастовки продолжались и давили народ, как
страшный кошмар, порождая тысячи несчастий и горя. Прикрываясь
маской любви к пролетариату, преследуя свои кровожадные хищные
цели, *народолюбцы* душили этот пролетариат и народ на глазах у
растерявшегося Правительства.[40]

Literary offerings in this issue of *Moskovskie vedomosti* were quite limited.
Novoe vremia, the leading conservative organ, featured many more holiday
texts where the antiradical, antiliberal message was propounded in various
ways, with extensive use of satire. One work, "Rozhdestvenskie koshmary,"
presents the nightmare of an army general who finds himself called into the
service of the revolution. Another, "Milioner-pokoinik. Moskovskaia legenda XX stoletiia," is a contemporary variation of the Christmas ghost story.
Its millionaire protagonist becomes involved with Social Democracy, wastes
a fortune on revolutionary propaganda, and ultimately saves himself from
further demands by staging his own funeral and fleeing to Western Europe.
In a more serious vein, "Kosti sukhie" offered a vision of Saint Mercurius
of Smolensk as protector of Russia against the Tatars, the Poles, and the
French—the analogy to Russia's condition at the time is unmistakable.
Finally, yet another tale, "Rozhdestvenskii poezd," uses a cross-section of
passengers on a train to present the passions and political absurdities of
contemporary society—vicious yet capable of being stilled by the natural
beauty of a Christmas Eve night.[41]

The liberals reacted to December's events with horror and dismay. A
column in *Birzhevye vedomosti* compared the current period to the Tatar
invasion and the Time of Troubles, enumerated details of the fratricidal
struggle, and exclaimed: "Что наши неудачи на морях и на манчжурских
полях в сравнении с тем, что теперь творится на Руси в эти незабвенные
и трижды проклятые декабрьские дни."[42] Those papers that were allowed
to publish carried a similar message.[43] The holiday issue of *Sibirskaia zhizn'*
[Tomsk], which openly discussed the educational role of the liberal,
democratic press at a time of transition to a constitutional monarchy,[44]
included, among others, such works as a poem on the birth of Jesus, where
an analogy is suggested between Herod and Nicholas II; and a prose tale
about a fir, cut down and turned into a Christmas tree, in which the
overturning of a frequent motif in holiday tales carries a message in praise
of freedom.[45]

A few months later, in 1906, in the middle of the elections to the First
Duma, Easter issues were fully caught up in the political fray. In the liberal

press, feelings of optimism led to explicit parallels between the Passion and Resurrection of Christ and the fate of Russia. The Cadet Party was winning a majority in the Duma, and its newly formed newspaper, *Rech'*, made full use of this analogy: "В перезвоне пасхальных колоколов—разве вы не слышите немолчного трепета жизни, звонких и радостных, перекрикающихся голосов: 'Да здравствует свободная Россия, да зравствует свободный народ!'"[46] An even stronger message was carried by another newly created newspaper, *Dvadtsatyi vek,* where the editorial celebrated the survival of hope:

> И оказалось, она все-таки жива! Оскорбленная, забитая—она поплыла по реке народной свободы, как плыли некогда христианские мученицы с нетленным венцом над головой . . . .
>
> В мрачной тьме—просвет. В небе среди свинцовых туч—луч рассвета . . . .
>
> Это первая Пасха мужественной надежды.
>
> Христос воскресе!
>
> Дума приближается![47]

In sharp contrast to this, the editor-publisher of a Black Hundred newspaper from Kishinev, Pavel Krushevan,[48] trumpeted his unhappiness with a society that, in his eyes, for a year and a half had tolerated tragedy and criminal anarchy. He symbolically proclaimed his refusal to print a traditional Easter message:

> Общество, среди которого такие утратившие душу человеческую выродки могут быть терпимы—не имеет права называться христианским обществом!
>
> Вот почему я не могу сегодня обратиться к вам с обычным христианским приветом, не могу сказать вам «Христос воскресе!»[49]

In the liberal press, calendar texts generally mirrored the optimistic political mood in early 1906. A tale by T. Shchepkina-Kupernik deals with a young girl waiting for news from her fiancé, who had become involved in the "liberation movement" while in the army, and had to flee abroad to escape arrest and execution. The work portrays the girl's feelings of helplessness: "часто с немой тоской глядела на огромную карту России, висевшую в детской классной, и вся эта Россия представлялась ей одной гигантской мышеловкой, западней которая захлопнется за ним и не выпустит его на свободу." However, at the end, a telegram from London, with the message "Christ Has Risen," signals her beloved's safety, and, by extension, joyful news about Russia as a whole.[50]

A more explicit message of optimism about coming political changes is found in Vladimir Botsianovskii's "Sud Pilata. Dramaticheskaia kartina v odnom deistvii," which follows one of the narrative models in holiday literature—creating a story around some episode in the New Testament. The text closes with the suicide of Judas and this comment by Pilate:

> Вот казнь первая. Погиб предатель. Теперь черед за судьями, за нами. Я чувствую, что это не пройдет нам даром, что отзовется это и на Риме. Да что на Риме—всюду. Пожар начался в Галилее; ничтожной, дикой Галилее. Но искры от него летят уже повсюду. Вспыхнет скоро Иудея, а там и Греция, и Рим . . . и мир весь вспыхнет. Пожар начался . . . Охватит он всю землю, испепелит весь старый мир, все чем до сих пор мы жили . . . Я это чувствую, почти что вижу. Каким из пепла встанет новый мир, что придет на смену—сказать я не могу, но старому конец.[51]

Besides such overt anticipations of the future, numerous stories from 1906 offered glimpses into life at a time of revolution. In general, there was an attempt to link them to the holiday. One work, "Kum," is an anecdote about the arrest of the son of a wealthy miller at his father's Easter table; the order is issued by his godfather, who is then, appropriately, termed a Judas. Another text, "Uchitel' i uchenik," takes a common science-fiction motif—a molecule as a self-contained microworld similar to ours—and develops it by having a teacher and student observe through a microscope scenes of conflict and horror reminiscent of humanity and culminating in the equivalent of an Easter procession.[52]

A different situation is portrayed in "Ozhidanie," a story about the aristocracy's fears concerning the Revolution. An old woman's Easter is poisoned by thoughts of what may be taking place on her estate and by imagined confrontations with peasants. For her, the sound of church bells, traditionally linked with joy during Easter, carries a message of fear: "Но княгине чудились в ночной темноте звуки набата, жуткие, страшные и призывные. Не дивнозвучная хвала, а злобный гул несся к ней со всех сторон, упрямо подступал, терзал душу и обжигал пламенем, языки которого, казалось ей, прыгали в темноте."[53]

Conservative newspapers countered liberal fiction with their own tendentious works. The protagonist of one of these, "Kak v detstve," is a young man whose two years at the university in Petersburg have left him in mental torment caused by disenchantment with radicalism: "Когда . . . он слышит теперь эти великие когда-то для него слова: *свобода, правда, справедливость, равенство,* то чувствует, будто его чем-то грязным, отвратительным бьют по щекам. И он готов вцепиться в оскорбителя и нанести ему удары . . . ." He joins his mother and sister in their country home, feels alienated from their goodness and religious faith, but is saved by the sounds and feelings of the Easter procession. At the end, the student tells his mother: "я больше не поеду туда, в город . . . к ним . . . к этим . . . не могу . . . Я останусь с вами . . . здесь, на земле . . . Нигде больше нет правды, и нет больше свободы, как здесь, на земле . . . вместе с народом . . . с его верой . . . ."[54]

The editorials and the artistic texts published in connection with Christmas 1905 and Easter 1906 contain the key elements that shape holiday literature, in varying degree, over the next couple of years. For polemicists, the two holidays offered ready-made symbolic complexes that could be easily used to deliver a powerful political message. For the liberals, Easter was especially appropriate: the story of the Passion, of torment and triumph, was a natural analogy to what had been endured by the Russian people and to what was hoped for in the future. Like Jesus, Russia was to be resurrected, preferably in a constitutional monarchy. The symbolic possibilities of Christmas in the political arena were more limited, basically operating through contrast. The infant Jesus, and the themes associated with the story of his birth—love, innocence, and goodness—could be used *in opposition* to life in Russia: to show the disparity between the ideals celebrated during the holiday and everyday Russian reality. The liberal press made full use of this device.

The right-wing press, which strongly opposed any political concessions by the government, could not use the symbolism of the holidays in the same way. For the most part, it applied the rhetorical dichotomy "ideals of the holiday—Russian life" to both Easter and Christmas. The religious themes of the holidays, together with evocations of national traditions in celebrating them, were commonly employed to underscore the message that the current situation in Russia was a violation of everything the nation had held sacred.

By December 1906, the government was in the midst of a political coun-teroffensive. The First Duma had passed into history, and rules governing elections for the Second were more restricted. Field courts-martial had started handing down death sentences to arrested activists, and the mood in the country had turned more somber. The Christmas editorial in *Birzhevye vedomosti* contrasts fictional horrors expected from holiday tales with the reality of Russian life:

> Но в этой сфере творчества, что могла бы создать наиболее богатая фантазия, что могло бы придумать наиболее талантливое перо после тех ужасов, которые нагромождены действительностью, самою жиз-нью?

> Разве в наших городах, селах и деревнях, в течение всего истекаю-
> щего года каждый день, каждый час земля не обагрялась кровью
> братьев, избиваемых братьями, воздух не оглашался стонами мучи-
> мых, преследуемых, голодных? Разве не стали обычными спутниками
> нашей жизни зрелища эшафотов и казней, грабежей и всякого рода
> насилий, чинимых над людьми, располагающими властью и над людь-
> ми, всякой власти лишенными?[55]

The editorial is especially pointed about the retributions being exacted by the government. At a time when newspapers regularly published "body counts"—so many executed, so many sentenced to die, so many murders—this appeal, as well as others, had special urgency.[56]

Increasingly, politically oriented calendar works featured scenes of suffering and expressions of horror at a life so much at odds with the holiday spirit. To take one example, N. Rakhmanov's "Krug vechnosti" is filled with visions of suffering workers, of pogroms, of insane asylums, and ends with this un-Christmas like passage: "Перекликались голодным воем фабрики и заводы. И труд пробуждался от кошмарного сна и торопился отдать свои соки. В предрассветном тумане колыхались миражи домов и кре-постной церкви. Шел взвод солдат . . . Где-то пировала смерть."[57] Another case is Kazimir Barantsevich's "Slava Bogu," where an aged couple on Christmas Eve fantasize about the son they never had, but recoil from their creation when the inner logic of their vision leads their imaginary offspring to the gallows, and they are horrified to realize that somewhere there are mothers whose sons have indeed ended up beneath a shroud.[58]

Over the next two years, as the government succeeded in regaining its control over society, holiday literature, too, reflected the ebbing of politics in Russian life. While holiday editorials continued to deliver political messages, fewer literary works published for Easter and Christmas involved (or could be read as involving) clear-cut political thematics.[59] By Easter 1908, the positions of the left and the right were quite different from what they had been two years earlier. An editorial in *Rech'* essentially admitted defeat—national resurrection was still in the future, while Russian life was gripped by apathy and disunity: "Никто ни во что не верит, никто ни на что не надеется, но никто ничего и не боится . . . К звукам пасхальных колоко-лов прислушиваются без тревоги и волнения; и в противность единому чувству, еще недавно владевшему всеми, каждый слышит в них то, что хочет."[60] *Rus'* was even more explicit: "В наши очередные дни, дни суро-вой ликвидации одного из периодов освободительного движения, привет 'Христос воскресе' раздается в широких народных массах как страстная и непоколебимая вера в лучшее будущее, как всеисцеляющее лекарство от тягостей и печалей очередной, современной русской действительности . . . ."[61] By comparison, on the same day the right-wing *Rossiia* (linked to the Ministry of Internal Affairs) was able to proclaim that "С каждым новым днем нашей государственной жизни губительные силы духовной и нравственной смерти слабеют и уступают место воскресению народного духа."[62]

The literary section of the Easter 1908 issue of *Rech'* also shows considerable changes. While political motifs are present in some holiday works, such as Kuprin's satirical "Moi pasport" and Vladimir Azov's "Zhizn' russkogo cheloveka" (a political parody based on Andreev's well-known work), these are set alongside texts where the universal themes of Easter are clearly dominant (e.g., Amfiteatrov's "Paskhal'nye pamiatki," a set of reminiscences and musings on the celebration).

A Christmas 1908 article by Aleksandr Benois, who uses the holiday to discuss problems of Russian children's literature, further demonstrates the shift in sentiments. To the extent that it exists, Benois asserts, it is spoiled by "noble humanitarianism," "noble weepiness." Children need joy, enthusiasm, optimism—as does Russian society as a whole:

О, как важно было бы для всей русской культуры, если бы мы повеселели и научились у детей веселью. Русской жизни нужна бодрость и смелость, ей нужна яркость и красота, ей нужно веселье. Довольно нытья: слезами горю не поможешь, а, пожалуй, смехом и поможешь. Перестанем учить наших детей жалости и слезам. Заразимся от них их светлым весельем, их сильной беспечностью, их внутренней страстностью, всем их антиутилитарным бытьем . . .[63]

Thus, by the end of 1908, the role of domestic political concerns as a major factor shaping holiday literature largely comes to a close, to reemerge only in the spring of 1917.[64] Political topics arise only occasionally in holiday issues of newspapers. For example, an editorial in *Rech'* on Christmas 1911 addressed the notorious "blood accusation" against Mendel Beilis, whose case had recently begun to agitate the Russian public.[65] On the same page, the cause of tolerance was taken up in a poem by Bal'mont, "Golos ottuda," which emphasized the Jewishness of Jesus.[66] Similarly, on Easter 1912 *Rech'* raised the issue of major famine in parts of Russia.[67]

However, one issue—that of executions for political crimes—outlasted the decline of broad political concerns in holiday literature. As already noted,

executions of revolutionary activists were a principal theme in holiday issues
in 1906, and they were discussed for several years afterwards. Waves of judi-
cial killings by hanging and by firing squad continued to sweep the country
and led to Lev Tolstoi's "Ne mogu molchat'" (1908) and other public protests. In line with these, from holiday to holiday, editorials in the liberal
press highlighted the glaring contrast between the religious ideals officially
espoused by the government and the cruelty of its policy. Thus, on Easter
1909 *Rech'* proclaimed:

> И если кто-либо из тех несчастных, кого завтра поведут на казнь, стоя
> под виселицей и считая последние секунды своей жизни, обратится к
> палачу и скажет «Христос Воскрес», то и отверженнейший из людей,
> навеки заклейменный печатью Каина, надевая петлю и готовясь вы-
> бить скамейку из под-ног своей жертвы, должен откликнуться: «Воис-
> тину воскрес» .... В воскресении Христа залог победы Его над ми-
> ром. Но мир еще не побежден, пока имя Христа, славимое устами, не
> расцветает в сердцах. В самой возможности такого внешнего испове-
> дания, уничтожаемого внутренним отрицанием,—величайшая победа
> лжи и отца лжи.
>
> И эта победа всего решительнее и безпощаднее там, где внешнее
> призвание учения и подвига Христа всего теснее сплетается с повсе-
> дневным течением языческой жизни. Там, где одновременно подписы-
> вается исполнение «христианского долга»—исповеди и причащения, и
> утверждаются смертные приговоры, имя Христово поругано и униже-
> но. ....[68]

These expressions of outrage were echoed in artistic works, such as, for
example, Sologub's "political fairy-tale" "Angel-Stepanida Kurnosaia."[69]
Similarly, following the editorial in *Rech'* cited above, executions were the
focus of an article by Merezhkovskii ("Kogda voskresnet") and of a short
poem by P. Solov'eva (Allegro) ("Mertvyi led").[70]

To complete this part of the discussion, we must mention that from time
to time the politicization of holiday literature brought forth parodic responses. O. L. D'Or, already cited in the previous section, devotes one of his
pieces to holiday editorials: "За несколько дней до Рождества передовики
столичных газет удалились в пустыню, чтобы вдали от людей и соблаз-
нов обдумать и написать свои 'праздничные' статьи." He follows with
samples of imaginary editorials from various newspapers, including *Novoe
vremia, Russkoe slovo,* and the Black Hundred *Russkoe znamia,* using motifs
characteristic of each of these publications. Thus, the chauvinistic appeals
of *Novoe vremia,* temporarily "suspended" for the holiday, are parodied in
this passage:

Братья! Сегодня в Вифлееме родилась Любовь . . . Сегодня мы растроганы. Сегодня хочется плакать и молиться. Сегодня хочется любить, любить. . . .

Братья! Инородцы тоже люди! . . .

Финны—тоже христиане! Конечно, их не мешало бы перевешать. Но не сегодня, братья! Не сегодня!

Сегодня мы должны протянуть им руку и сказать с искренней любовью:

—Придите в наши объятия, чухонцы проклятые! Примите скорее наши лобзанья, ибо послезавтра мы снова начнем ковать для вас цепи и кандалы, которые так любит наша газета.[71]

Not only the editorials, but holiday fiction itself also was parodied. In his "Kak pisat' sviatochnye rasskazy," A. Izmailov presents a "Rasskaz istinno-russkii" and a "Rasskaz liberal'nyi." The comic plot of the former involves a certain Sila Trifonych ("человек добрых старых устоев, высокий патриот и член союза русского народа"), who finds an abandoned baby on Christmas Eve and decides to bring him up. During the baptism, the midwife discovers that the baby had been circumcised. Amidst the general horror, Sila Trifonych demonstrates his strength of character: "Тяжелое испытание послал мне Бог. Но побеждаю искушение! Усыновляю его, хотя он и жид. Пусть весь мир видит красоту истинно-русской души! . . . Певчие прослезились. Акушерка плакала навзрыд. Щенок подвывал в соседней комнате. За окном тихо гудели рождественские колокола."[72] For its part, the "Liberal Story" presents a village devastated by famine: "Опустошенная 9 казаками, разграбленная урядниками, изнуренная тифом деревня валялась в болотистой низине, забытая Богом и (его превосходительством) *), губернатоором."[73] In this setting, a pair of young people, dying of typhus, intermingle talk of Lassalle and Skabichevskii with the admission that they love each other. A police official who hurries to arrest them, dreaming of a promotion, is sorely disappointed: "Он вошел в комнату фельдшерицы и остолбенел. Его мечты разлетелись. И он, и она лежали мертвыми. В углу притаился страшный призрак тифа с опущенными и сморщенными черными крыльями . . . Бум!—грянуло с колокольни. И призыв к рождественской службе прозвучал как набат. . . ."[74]

Izmailov's piece contains one other parody, "Rasskaz stilia-modern," in which references to Blok and Osip Dymov mingle with allusions to Bunin and Gusev-Orenburgskii. The existence of a parody is a sign of a literary phenomenon—in this case, of the growing influence of modernism on holiday literature, which developed during the 1905–1907 period, but which came into its own afterwards. The impact of modernism on Christmas and Easter fiction will be examined below.

The Impact of Modernism

Earlier, I noted the opportunities holiday fiction presented to late nineteenth-century authors. It is now necessary to consider some of the problems these authors, mostly realists, encountered while working in this tradition.

Basically, Christmas and Easter literature required a sense of the miraculous: in theory, a writer should be able to suffuse a holiday text with religious feeling in a way that would render credible an epiphany, a plot reversal, or a fundamental personality change. With few exceptions, however, realism, grounded in a materialist, scientific worldview, did not handle either religion or miracles very well. Ideology carried over into poetics: by and large, realist narratives would try to explain a miracle in nonsupernatural terms, reducing it to alcohol, trickery, psychology (a miracle is a subjective phenomenon, occurring in the minds of those who believe in it), or simply leaving out an explanation. This put constraints on what realists could do in holiday fiction. Whatever the private religious feelings of a realist writer, the fundamentals of his artistic method came into conflict with the tradition's requirements.[75]

By contrast, modernist authors were unhampered by such constraints and were in a good position to invigorate holiday literature. The very nature of the Symbolist model of the world, with its differentiation of lower and higher levels, was conducive to the creation of texts in which the fantastic and the miraculous play decisive roles. Even someone like Briusov, whose aesthetics did not involve religion, was in a position to go beyond realist plots, thanks to his exploration of borderline psychology, of twilight states of the human soul. Others, like Merezhkovskii, Gippius, Blok, and Ivanov, for whom religion played a central role, and who explored theological matters and mystical visions in their art, could address particularly well the issue of the gap in religious sensibility.

Two works by Aleksandr Amfiteatrov confirm both the tension within holiday literature and the activities of the modernists within it. In the essay cited previously, Amfiteatrov briefly considers the problem of depicting Easter:

> Лучшие литературные отражения русской Пасхи—впрочем, только деревенской, Пасхи на снегу, талой Пасхи—весны—дали Левитов и Л. Н. Толстой в «Воскресеньи». Писать Пасху трудно. Надо верить, т.е. чувствовать воскресшего Христа, как трепещущий символ единения восторженного человека с пробужденною природою. А где в литературе взять таких верующих людей? За исключением названных, все русские изобразители Пасхи—либо более или менее искусные деклама-

торы и притворщики под веру, им чуждую, либо Пасха для них—лишь далекий и красивый фон, на котором возникают и проходят интересующие их прекрасные поэтические фигуры.[76]

His comments could easily be extended to cover literature celebrating the Nativity.

In the other text, a Christmas tale, Amfiteatrov exposes to humorous scrutiny the process by which holiday tales are created. His protagonist, a writer, argues with his Conscience about various plot situations he might use. All are seen as dated or implausible (particularly those with political motifs). Frustrated, the writer reminisces:

> —Как все было проще в старину!—вздохнул писатель.—Подумать только, что двадцать лет назад я самым спокойным образом писал «Елку у волков», и—ничего, на глазах слеза дрожала . . . ты молчала . . . публике нравилось . . . критика одобряла, что я хорошо понял звериную психологию. . . .[77]

A different time—a different sensibility. The writer's predicament points to a crisis in calendar literature, where narrative commonplaces are no longer adequate to the drama of real-world existence.

At one point, the writer considers a ghost story ("С привидениями, что, махнуть что-нибудь?"). The response offered by his Conscience mixes current politics and literary trends:

> Да и какие теперь привидения? О революционных привидениях «фантастическую правду» напишешь—рассказ конфискуют, издателя оштрафуют, а тебя под суд отдадут. А остальные привидения—ну, их!—по декадентскому департаменту.
> —Беса побеспокоить?
> —Предоставь это господину Ремизову. «Бесовские действа»—его монополия и специальность. К чертям, брат, так сразу, без подготовки, нельзя. До чертей дойти надо! Это, своего рода, ученая степень.[78]

Such humorous references indicate the growing role of Russian modernism in Christmas and Easter literature.

This role antedates 1905. In particular, Sologub's and Briusov's early holiday texts offer two major models of potential solutions to the dilemmas facing the tradition: either convincingly *strengthen the religious component* or *revive the level of narrative,* creating plots that would rejuvenate the old holiday formulas.

The former model is followed by Sologub in several poems. In "Skuchnaia lampa moia zazhzhena" the lyrical "I" addresses himself to God, asking for a miracle to overcome the constraints of his daily existence:

Дай мне в одну только ночь
Слабость мою превозмочь
И в совершенном созданьи одном
Чистым навеки зажечься огнем.[79]

Another poem, "Angel blagogo molchaniia," has the lyrical "I" eulogize the image of an angel who has protected him from others and from himself:

В тяжкие дни утомленья,
В ночи бессильных тревог
Ты отклонил помышленья
От недоступных дорог.[80]

In both cases, there is an almost complete absence of signs of the holiday, but, thanks to the lyrical form, there is an expression of faith and love that is integral to any religious celebration. Also—and this is characteristic of later works as well—the two poems are only tangential to Sologub's central vision: his pessimism and rejection of life are shown as yielding to religious feelings.

Briusov, author of an article on the subject of Christmas stories,[81] takes a different tack in dealing with holiday literature. Apparently seeing this tradition as a challenge for himself as a writer, he debuts with a couple of stories at about the same time as the article, to be followed by a couple more a year later. One of these works, "V zerkale,"[82] is a fine example of what Briusov, in his introduction to *Zemnaia os'*, called "rasskazy polozhenii": "все внимание автора устремлено на исключительность (хотя бы тоже 'типичность') события. Действующие лица здесь важны не сами по себе, но лишь в той мере, поскольку они захвачены основным 'действием.'"[83] The text represents the first-person account of a woman's fascination with mirrors, a passion that leads her to a fateful encounter with her own reflected image, which, she imagines, is alive and influences her will. Sometime in December, before the holidays, the woman and her reflection change places, and she is trapped in the reflected world. Subsequently, yet another switch takes place, as she in turn psychologically dominates her rival. At the end, the woman is left wondering whether or not she is real, and expresses her continued attraction for mirrors.

Like other examples of Briusov's prose, the story explores the boundaries of sanity and madness. At the same time, it both operates with and diverges from the conventions of holiday literature. This is indeed a tale of the fantastic, suitable for certain type of Christmastide story-telling. Yet the apparatus of supernatural terrors does not come into play: the horror originates within the heroine's psyche. In this way, Briusov presents one device through which the Christmas tale could be made interesting.[84]

At this time, the Symbolists were still generally outside the mainstream periodical press. Their access to the major journals and newspapers eased during the 1905 Revolution. The Symbolists were caught up in the political and social turmoil; in their works, some of which were published in holiday issues, they reacted to contemporary events. For example, Sologub, particularly active politically, was featured in the left-leaning *Narodnoe khoziaistvo* and *Nasha zhizn'* with the poems "Velikogo smiateniia pokhoronili . . ." (a kind of marching song, with almost nothing religious in it) and "V svetlyi den' poxoronili . . . ," published in time for Easter 1906, and centered on the analogy between Christ's and Russia's resurrections.[85] By Christmas 1906, he appears in the Cadet *Rech'* with the story "Strana, gde votsarilsia zver'." The plot of this work revolves around a ruler whose exercise of power changes him into a beast, at first figuratively, and then, in response to the Christ-like submission of his main victim, quite literally. This is an obvious allegory to the bloodletting in Russia.[86]

By 1907, the old traditions of *napravlenstvo*—of a periodical publishing works by writers of a well-defined ideological and aesthetic orientation—had collapsed, as major publications sought out writers and poets able to address their readers' troubled mood: "Газеты и журналы ('Русь,' 'Новь,' 'Товарищ' и др.) открыли двери декадентам, и М. Волошин, Г. Чулков, Чуковский и др.) могут излагать свои мнения (*horribile dictu*) на страницах какой-нибудь 'Нивы' или 'Русской мысли.'"[87] Innovative writers, philosophers, critics, and artists were given the opportunity to speak directly to a mass audience, and, as part of this process, had a powerful impact on holiday issues.

Nearly every modernist author of note, as well as a number of lesser-known writers, contributed to holiday literature. Blok, Sologub, Ivanov, Kuzmin, and Remizov wrote particularly frequently. Thus, between 1907 and 1916, Blok publishes in holiday issues almost every year, and, on a number of occasions, is featured during the same holiday with several texts in different papers. The same is true of others, especially Sologub.[88]

The modernists responded to the challenge in different ways. Generally speaking, they expanded the boundaries of holiday literature by enlarging the role of poetry, by basing their works on sources that previously had been left largely untapped, and by creating narratives that departed from the conventions of the tradition. The nature of this expansion, which falls naturally into several categories of texts, is reviewed below.[89]

1. *Increase in the number and diversity of poetic texts.* The occasional poems found in nineteenth-century calendar issues were, for the most part, the products of an essentially unpoetic, imitative age. The majority of these efforts were by minor authors[90] and generally either depicted some aspect of the original sacred event (Nativity or Passion) and drew conclusions for humanity at large, or concentrated on the lyrical "I"'s response to the holiday. Like much of holiday prose, such works mixed sentimentality with didacticism (both elements accentuated in a lyrical text), and invariably operated with a small number of "accessories," motifs: for Christmas—the star, shepherds, etc., and for Easter—the Cross, church bells, etc.[91] There were also occasional poetic feuilletons, which used the conventions of the genre to reflect on current trends in politics and culture.[92]

Although prose still constitutes the bulk of calendar publications in the Silver Age, there is a marked increase in poetic contributions. Texts by Bal'mont, Sologub, Blok, and Ivanov appear frequently. Other groups are also represented, by such disparate figures as Kuzmin, Gorodetskii, Bunin, and Khodasevich.

Modernist poems for Christmas and Easter interact with the holiday tradition in complex ways. Many attempt to follow its requirements (choice of religious subject, presence of certain motifs), yet the private world model of the individual poet, as well as the central myth of that world, is often highly visible, even dominant. Such a poem may embody the central concerns of the poet to a far greater extent than those of the holiday it is supposed to honor. Going further, in a number of instances the poems are unconnected to the holiday: their themes are secular, clearly nonreligious, and their publication in a calendar issue says much about changes taking place within the tradition.

A look at some of Blok's texts shows what occurred when an integral poetic model of the world overlapped with the universe of holiday literature. A number of the works he published in Christmas and Easter issues were *not* created for the occasion; they mirror his broader thematic concerns and operate with motifs characteristic of particular collections and periods of his development. For example, in the poem "Starushka i cherteniata," written in July 1895 and originally published on Easter 1906, Blok depicts, with both irony and tenderness, some of the denizens of the lower orders of Russian folklore, as he does in other texts in the "Puzyri zemli" section of *Nechaiannaia radost'*. The poem's "plot"—the response of the little devils to the sight of an old woman pilgrim—is not linked to Easter, and falls outside the parameters of canonical practice:

> Ты прости нас, старушка ты божия,
> Не бери нас в Святые Места!
> Мы и здесь лобызаем подножия
> Своего, полевого Христа.[93]

However, the basic theme—faith in the Savior to come, as expressed in the poem's final stanza ("Но за майскими тонкими чарами/ Затлевает и нам Купина . . ."), renders it appropriate for a holiday publication.

In another poem, "V glukhuiu noch'" ("Stoiu na tsarstvennom puti . . ."), the lyrical hero depicts himself surrounded by darkness, with a glimmer of light signaling a promised land, but aware that the path to it is difficult. The scene contains elements of magic:

> Ступлю вперед—навстречу мрак,
> Ступлю назад—слепая мгла.
> А там—одна черта светла,
> И на черте условный знак.

These can also be interpreted, through the prism of the conventions of holiday literature (in particular, the star), as linked to Christmas.

This is not the case with two other texts, "Noch'—kak noch', i ulitsa pustynna" and "Ia tol'ko rytsar' i poėt," both published in 1909. The situation depicted in the former involves the lyrical "I" and a woman, to whom the poem is addressed. The central themes of the poem are rebellion, death, and the hopelessness of eternal recurrence:

> И который раз, смеясь и плача,
> Вновь живут!
> День—как день; ведь решена задача:
> *Все умрут.*[94]

The latter work, originally entitled "Dame s parokhoda" (also "Vstrechnoi") and published on Christmas Day, is equally detached from the traditional meanings of the holiday. It is addressed to a woman, and combines contemptuous remarks about her husband with an overt erotic challenge:

> Я только рыцарь и поэт,
> Потомок северного скальда.
> А муж твой носит томик Уайльда,
> Шотландский плэд, цветной жилет . . .
> Твой муж—презрительный эстет.
>
> . . . .
> И неужели после бала

Ты не смежала томный взгляд,
Когда воздушный свой наряд
Ты с плеч покатых опускала,
Изведав танца легкий яд?[95]

The publication of these poems in a holiday issue is indicative of how much looser the criteria for the genre had become during this period.

Some of Blok's works consciously use the holiday framework for other themes. Thus, the poem "Rossiia" (subsequently "Novaia Amerika"), written in mid-December 1913 and published two weeks later in *Russkoe slovo,* uses the setting of Christmas ("Праздник радостный, праздник великий,/ Да звезда из-за туч не видна . . .") to present a vision of a new Russia, resurrected through its growing mines and factories. The poem concludes with a unique blending of two sets of motifs—the industrial and the religious:

Черный уголь—подземный мессия,
Черный уголь—здесь царь и жених,
Но не страшен, невеста, Россия,
Голос каменных песен твоих!

Уголь стонет, и соль забелелась,
И железная воет руда . . .
То над степью пустой загорелась
Мне Америки новой звезда![96]

Among poets contributing to holiday issues, Blok is the most faithful to his own mythology, and the most reluctant to abandon it for the occasion. However, others sometimes appear in print with texts that could be viewed as antithetical or at best unrelated to the literary-religious context in which they appear. Briusov's "Na pliazhe," which describes the double suicide of a pair of lovers, and Khodasevich's "Dosada" ("Chto serdtse. Lan' . . ."), addressed to a woman, are typical of this tendency.[97]

At the same time, modernist holiday poetry includes numerous texts where religious themes are uppermost. Sometimes, as in the case of Ivanov's "Bogopoznanie," a theological question serves as the point of departure for a blending of intellectual analysis and religious feeling:

Мужи богомудрые согласно
Мудрствуют, что Бог непостижим.
Отчего же сердцу дивно ясно,
     Что оно всечасно
     Дышит Им,
И его дыханию сопричастно,
     И всему живому с Ним?[98]

At other times, the religious message may be rendered from an unusual point of view, which, in turn, sharpens the sentiments conveyed. An example of this is Sergei Gorodetskii's "Stebel' svidetel'," which offers an earthworm's indirect account of Jesus's resurrection. This unusual lyrical "I" describes how, on the way to see Christ, he saw a stalk of mint broken from its own efforts of trying to reach the Savior, and was struck by the mint's happy death. The exoticism of this scene is heightened by the conflation of Christian thematics with non-Christian beliefs, since the earthworm's tale concludes with references to metempsychosis:

> Я в долгом веке был и птицей,
> Змеей и зоркой древеницей,
> Я человеком дважды был.
> Но никогда б я не забыл,
> Какому б телу не отдался,—
> Как мертвый стебель улыбался.[99]

World War I brings a marked change in the poetry published for Christmas and Easter. While some focus on private myths still remains, poets generally respond with texts much closer to the holiday norm, in which traditional motifs blend with responses to events in the war and to Russia's situation. Thus, on Easter Day 1915, several poets writing in *Russkoe slovo* link the celebration of Christ's Resurrection with the triumph of the Russian army in taking the fortress of Peremyshl' and with expected victories over Turkey. Sologub's "Paskha novaia" is a typical example of such works:

> И гром победы, и голос славы,
> И возвращение твое, весна!
> Пути пред нами, я верю, правы,
> И даль пред нами ясна, ясна!
>
> Пускай мы были так нерадивы,
> Тая под спудом так много сил,
> Но гром, упавший на наши нивы,
> Тебя ль, Россия, не разбудил!
>
> Христос воскресший, за Русью нашей
> Ты не попомнишь безумств и зла.
> Она склонилась пред страстной чашей
> И, как невеста, Тебя ждала.
>
> Христос воскресший, иди к невесте,
> Веди невесту из зыбкой тьмы,
> И с нею вместе, с Россией вместе,
> Я верю, верю, воскреснем мы![100]

2. *Introduction of works based on medieval Russian culture.* Prior to the rise
of modernism, there had been few attempts to model holiday texts on medieval works.[101] The key figure in changing this was Remizov, whose bibliography between 1907 and 1918 includes upwards of forty works first published
in connection with either Christmas or Easter.[102] Most of these involve
reworkings of ancient textual materials drawn from Graeco-Slavic apocrypha,
from other traditions in Russian religious folklore, and from other categories
of Russian and Slavic folk texts (particularly fairytales).[103]

Remizov's apocrypha and folktales, reworked on the basis of ancient texts
and scholarly studies, are an important factor on the holiday pages of newspapers and journals. For one, they restore a genuinely Russian (Slavonic)
religious element, a connection with a tradition of medieval-folkloric culture
that was notably absent in the various biblical and pseudobiblical legends,
translated from West European authors, or made up by Russian writers,
that were a staple of holiday issues in the late nineteenth century. Derived
from pre-modern sources, and part of Remizov's larger practice of publishing apocryphal material, independently of Christmas or Easter, they often
depart from the narrative and stylistic conventions of holiday tales. Thus,
neither in "Khristov krestnik" (later "Iov i Magdalina") (1908) nor in "Stra-
sti Presviatoi Bogoroditsy" (1910) do we find the sentimental reconciliation
of all creatures, tied to the sound of the church bells, which is called for by
the genre. In his wanderings, Job meets groups of sinners who ask him to
intercede, but though he does so, only one of them—a pike, not a human
being!—is offered release from punishment. The apocrypha reiterate the message of Christian humility and love of fellow men, but they link it to a much
harder, often terrifying vision of divine justice and punishment.[104]

Other writers join Remizov in his use of medieval and folkloric religious
traditions. Gorodetskii's primitivist scene in verse, "Chudo rozhdestva Khristova," is modeled on a *vertep* performance and contains exchanges by both
human beings and inanimate objects (a chorus of stars, the star of Bethlehem).[105] In a different vein, Nikolai Roerich's "Son" begins with prophetic
dreams before the start of the World War, all involving a dragon. This is
followed by an account of a Christmas Eve dream, involving Saint Procopius
of Ustiug and Saint Nicholas (instead of the Magi), which ends with appeals
to Saint Nicholas:

> Злые силы на нас ополчены. Защити, владыко, пречистый град!
> Пречистый град—врагам озлобление!
>   Прими, владыко, прекрасный град! Подвигнь, отче, священный меч!
> Подвигнь, отче, все воинство!

Чудотворец! Яви грозный лик! Укрой грады святым мечом! Ты можешь! Тебе сила дана!

Мы стоим без страха и трепета.[106]

3. *Introduction of folklore-based works.* As indicated previously, the fairytale element originally present in Christmas tales had, over several decades, become a narrative commonplace, with little of the sense of wonder present in the best of Dickens. Modernist authors repeatedly turn to folklore as a way of restoring to holiday literature a touch of the marvelous. Their treatment of folkloric sources ranges from the serious to the playful.

Once again, Remizov is an important figure in this approach. He contributes reworked nonreligious (or, at least, superficially nonreligious) folktales to a number of holiday issues. In 1909, for example, he published two such works on Easter Day: "Krasnaia sosenka" and "Chudesnye bashmachki."[107] The former is a variation on the Cinderella story; the latter incorporates a classic chase by a wizard from Russian folklore. Both end happily, in line with the joyous conclusion of Passion Week, though neither contains overtly religious elements.[108]

Some of Sologub's stories also fall into this category. In "Snegurochka" (1908), a fairytale creature comes to life, brings joy to children, but is ultimately destroyed by well-meaning, though wrong-headed adults.[109] "Ocharovanie pechali" uses the familiar fairytale plot of a stepmother jealous of her stepdaughter, but modifies it by the imposition of a mythology that inverts the usual values attached to life and death. In a curious parody of the Resurrection, Queen Mariana casts her stepdaughter Ariana into a deep sleep by taking upon herself the girl's "enchantment of sadness," sorrows for the world's griefs. After Ariana is awakened by magical means, the stepmother kills herself in order to yield to her this load of sorrows. At the end, the souls of the two are united, as Ariana assumes a special burden: "По воле созидающего и разрушающего души вернулась она в мир,—нести ему очарование печали."[110] In spite of this reference to the Creator, the story ranges far from traditional Christian beliefs.

4. *Introduction of works based on historical materials.* Most of these involve Russian subjects and are basically anecdotes or contributions to a fictionalized *petite histoire.* Their connection to the holiday varies. Sergei Auslender's "Sviatki v starom Peterburge" consists of a series of stories, in part dramatic and in part humorous, about Christmas celebrations at the courts of Peter I, Elizabeth, and Paul.[111] Boris Sadovskoi's "Izmailovskii chasovoi,"

an anecdote about Alexander I and his brothers, takes place during the holiday season, but its focus is on the personalities of Alexander, Nicholas, and Count Arakcheev, on details of court life, and on political undercurrents during the early period of Alexander's reign (including the murder of Paul I three years earlier).[112]

Non-Russian materials are used in Briusov's "Poslednii imperator Trapezunda," which describes the death of Emperor David I of Trapezond at the hands of Sultan Mehmet the Conqueror. A weak man, ready for political compromise, the defeated monarch remains faithful to Christianity and is martyred along with his sons.[113] The episode is not specifically linked to Easter, but is certainly appropriate for a holiday publication.

5. *Introduction of works based on non-Christian religious and cultural materials.* This small category of texts is a reflection of Symbolism's and, more broadly, modernism's transcultural interests, of a search for common patterns of myth and religious belief. In some works, such as Voloshin's lyric "Serdtse mira, solntse Alkiana . . . ," non-Christian mythological motifs (in this case, Greek), serve as background for a reference to Christianity.[114] There are also larger texts, such as Bal'mont's essay "Egipetskaia gorlitsa," in which he celebrates Egyptian ideas concerning carnal and spiritual love, drawing parallels to attitudes in other cultures. Published on a day celebrating the birth of Christ, the essay's depiction of a polytheistic, exotic world is only tangentially, if at all, connected to the Nativity.[115]

Occasional scholarly articles dealing with other religions contribute to the widening of cultural and spiritual boundaries within the holiday tradition. Articles such as "Prazdnik sveta i spaseniia" by the noted philologist Tadeusz Zieliński, in which he traces the roots of Christmas in Greek and Roman religious practices, are a far cry from the many publications on Muscovite customs that are frequently encountered in late nineteenth- and early twentieth-century periodicals.[116.]

6. *Creation of texts where the fantastic, derived from the human psyche, is the dominant factor.* Briusov's previously cited story "V zerkale" is an early attempt to refresh the fantastic component of the holiday tale. His approach —to produce a tightly knit narrative where the tension is intimately linked with the protagonist's psyche—is followed by other authors. Holiday issues during the period under review contain a number of works where the focus of attention is on the consequences of erotic love and other passions.

Briusov himself, who wrote almost nothing for holiday issues of newspapers during the period 1903–1909, is represented later by two stories that fall into this category. "Za sebia ili za druguiu?" (1910) and "Ee reshenie" (1911) both deal with psychological dilemmas.[117] In the former, a man encounters a woman who closely resembles someone he had once loved and is tormented by uncertainty as to her identity. The woman's role playing and the lack of resolution of the mystery render the story appropriate for a Christmas issue. This is not the case with "Ee reshenie" (published on Easter Day), where an older woman must decide whether she will take a younger, innocent man as her lover, or whether she will disillusion him by revealing her many previous affairs. Either course of action could lead to his death, and, in fact, that is what occurs, but the reader is left uncertain as to how the woman finally acted.

Fantastic reversals resulting from passion are also at the center of Sergei Auslender's Christmas story "Roza podo l'dom," which is concerned with two brothers, one of whom, shot in a duel over a dancer, obtains a promise from the other that he will avenge him. When the younger brother, Nikolai, meets the woman, she declares herself ready to submit to whatever punishment he wishes to inflict. However, a kiss from her overwhelms the young man and leads him into her arms, vengeance forgotten.[118]

Erotic attraction is explored in one of Nina Petrovskaia's tales, "Mademoiselle 'bez chetverti desiat' .'"[119] Set in a European resort, the story involves a young woman, who, though in love with an Italian violinist, ultimately gives herself to an elderly French gentleman. Her decision flows out of her basic indifference to herself and a willingness to die. The message is hopelessness, very far from the themes of Easter Day, when the work was actually published.

Eroticism, woven with the theme of vampirism, is the subject of works by two different authors. One is Sologub's "Krasnogubaia gost'ia" (1909), where the vampire who visits the protagonist, Vargol'skii, is a woman named Lidiia Rotshtein. She calls herself Lilith,[120] is a principal figure in Sologub's private mythology, and is closely linked with death. Usually, the poet makes her a positive figure in his model of the world. In this text however, in clear deference to its date and place of publication (a Christmas issue), traditional, life-affirming values prevail, and Lilith is banished thanks to the intervention of a heavenly messenger.[121] The other story is Georgii Chulkov's "Ubiistvo panny Marii."[122] In this case, there is no supernatural; rather, vampirism is an obsession of a man who learned about it from his reading and was led to murder a young girl. The story is essentially a detective puzzle, with a

strong shock element, where the mystery of a corpse in a "locked room" is
solved only at the end.

7. *Creation of texts in which the author consciously plays with elements of the
holiday tradition.* Remizov is the most notable contributor to this category
of texts, in which the norms of Christmas and Easter fiction are subverted
in various ways. One example of this is the Christmas tale "Po vole," later
renamed "Sviatoi vecher," which was written in 1905, but not published
until 1908. The hero, Skorokhodov, is taking a train out of Petersburg to
the country in order to celebrate Christmas Eve properly. A major element
in his expectations for the holiday is to do something impossible in the city:
invite a folkloric creature, Grandfather Korochun (*Ded Korochun*), who rules
over winter and is said to have invited the Christ child into his stable, to
share in the traditional *kut'ia*. This serious treatment of a peasant custom
is innovative in itself. There is also a scene featuring a cross-section of the
politically divided Russian society, reflecting the passions of 1905 in crude
interchanges between various characters. Toward the end, a traditional
Christmas star appears, and the sound of a carol is heard, yet most of the
passengers are not affected by these, thus breaking with the plot conventions
of the genre. Indeed, the song has to compete with echoes of "Na boi krova-
vyi," with cursing, and with conversations in which talk of strikes mixes with
claims of sorcery. In the end, Skorokhodov is able to invite Korochun, but
he does so alone, on the platform of the railroad car, and using bread as a
substitute for *kut'ia*. At best, this is an ambiguous conclusion.[123]
  Two stories from 1911, "Galstuk" and "Glagolica," are quite different.
The former, an Easter tale, features an exotic visitor to Petersburg, an
African student. This naïve hero, nicknamed "Turka" and reflexively noble,
brave, and passionate (all women are his "fiancées"), is sometimes unable to
hold back his exuberant personality, and ends up spending Easter in Kresty
Prison. There he encounters a Jewish teacher from a religious school who
has spent two years imprisoned because of a denunciation. Once freed,
"Turka" meets Roza, a prostitute, who turns out to be the wife of the
melamed from Kresty and who is overwhelmed by shame and grief when she
hears of her missing husband. At the end, the student is arrested for disturb-
ing the peace, while his attempt to help Roza financially is likely doomed to
failure—the final scene has the weeping woman alone with a policeman.[124]
From the choice of protagonists to the pessimistic conclusion, Remizov's
work undermines the conventions of the genre.
  A more complex story, "Glagolitsa," the first of three texts later incorpo-

rated into *Uchitel' muzyki,* features Aleksandr Aleksandrovich Kornetov, a retired railway inspector.[125] There is a narrative frame, a gathering at Kornetov's, for interpolated narratives told by his guests and his old woman-servant. These short works are attempts at Christmas season horror tales; however, only the old woman is able to tell a tale that favorably impresses the majority of the guests, thus fulfilling requirements of the genre's conventions. The story's frame is particularly fascinating and goes far beyond the occasion of Christmas. Kornetov himself is nicknamed "Glagolitsa" because "единственный на всем земном шаре писал письма и всякие дружеские послания глаголицей." He is a collector of trivia, who makes wrapping paper from different stores into knickknacks; he is a collector of names and unusual people; and he takes food items bought in stores, removes their labels, and pretends that they are of his own make. In short, he is a game-playing modernist narrator-*bricoleur*—like Remizov himself. The parallel is strengthened when he tells the assembled company of seeing a devil during Christmas, in a passage that at one point expresses a sense of the demonic ruling over Russia, yet turns comic when Kornetov imitates the sounds the devil supposedly uttered.

The playful treatment of Christmas story conventions in "Glagolitsa" is repeated in the subsequent "Okazion. Rasskaz" (1913).[126] Narrative games are also present, with new variations, in "Na ptich'ikh pravakh," which finds Kornetov and his guests in wartime Petersburg.[127] Here, the humorous situation of telling fantastic stories is moderated when a true story of an encounter in a streetcar illustrates man's inhumanity to man and prompts one guest to exclaim at the fate of Russia: "Родина моя, или уж твой конец пришел, —не от врага, а от твоей же рваной забитой доли?"[128] Even though the ending of "Na ptich'ikh pravakh" is comical and thoroughly discredits Christmastide deviltry, the apostrophe to Russia retains its force.

As has been shown, a tension between the religious and the secular occurs in holiday texts written by modernist authors. In some works, religious or spiritual elements are deepened, providing a fundamental link with Christmas or Easter. Other texts draw away from religious thematics toward the aesthetic, the purely literary. Because of such fictional creations, some holiday issues tend to become above all a platform for new literature.

The pull of the aesthetic was not limited to individual works, but was also displayed in broader ways. First, holiday issues were used to publish significant literary materials, either parts of forthcoming works or variants of texts that had already appeared. Thus, one daily featured chapters from Merezhkovskii's forthcoming novel *Aleksandr I*.[129] Some years later, an Easter issue carries a variant of Tolstoi's "Chem liudi zhivy," "Arkhangel," and a publication by Kornei Chukovskii, "Zabytoe i novoe o Dostoevskom."[130] In 1916, a fragment from Belyi's *Kotik Letaev* was published in a Christmas issue.[131]

Second, there was the rise of "special issues," wholly or in part devoted to a particular topic. One example was the Christmas 1913 issue of *Utro Rossii,* which focused on contemporary women writers. The newspaper featured photographs of and stories by four writers: Z. Gippius, N. Petrovskaia, E. Nagrodskaia, and A. Krandievskaia.[132] Another example was the handling of the centennial of Herzen's birth in 1912. That year, holiday issues took special note of the fact that the celebration coincided with both Easter and the Feast of Annunciation. *Russkoe slovo* devoted the entire literary section in its Easter issue to Herzen and his anniversary, featuring contributions by A. Izmailov, P. Shchegolev, P. Boborykin, D. Filosofov, and others.[133]

This discussion should not suggest that the modernists dominated the holiday tradition. As in literature at large, the post-1905 period in holiday fiction sees a coexistence between the broadly defined camps of realism and modernism, with more than a few links between the two. In holiday issues of periodicals and in special collections, next to Sologub, Ivanov, and Kuzmin, we find such figures as Tolstoi,[134] Kuprin, Gor'kii, Bunin, D. Mamin-Sibiriak.[135] There are also newer names, reflecting the entrance of fresh talent into the literary arena—authors who are basically realists, but are influenced by modernist poetics, or who draw on such traditions as the *skaz* (such as Shmelev, Zaitsev, Prishvin, and Tèffi).

Like the modernists, realist writers also extend the boundaries of what constitutes an Easter or Christmas text. A survey of the press finds numerous works that are highly imaginative in conception but are only tenuously connected with the holidays or only partly meet the narrative expectations of readers.

Thus, Kuprin's "Poprygunia-strekoza" is a brief account of a group of men from the upper classes living in a house in the country. At a holiday recital, one of them, the narrator, is moved by the fable of the Grasshopper and the Ant and interprets it as a threatening allegory of the relationship between the gentry and the people, raising the question of a future settling of historical accounts.[136] The subject of another story, "Puteshestvenniki," is the oppressive life endured by a minor police official whose wife betrays him with his superior. The only joy in the man's life comes from imaginary trips he and his teenage son plan together. Though published on Easter, the story, realist to the core, contains no Easter motifs at all, and even the happiness experienced by father and son is transitory at best.[137]

Bunin's frequent contributions to calendar issues include lyrical accounts of his travels in Palestine, such as "Pustynia d'iavola" and "Gennisaret."[138] Closer to holiday traditions is another text, "Vesna," which explores the connections between Easter and the spring, between spiritual and natural renewal. The tone is optimistic, and the account of a crowd celebrating the holiday, including both nobles and peasants, emphasizes the genuineness of their religious feelings.[139] Bunin's "Sviatochnyi rasskaz," which he himself terms "v starom, dobrom stile," is an ironic, Gogolian account of an old archivist's existence and sudden death during the heady days of the "liberation movement."[140]

Holiday issues offered an excellent vehicle for Ivan Shmelev, whose many stories explored the Russian Orthodox religious sensibility. His "Vesennii shum" tells of a church deacon's son whose expulsion from the seminary throws him and his family into despair. However, springtime and the advent of Easter bring the young man a new, optimistic sense of a life, an understanding of different possibilities in human fate. The message, wholly appropriate to the holiday, is conveyed in an original, unclichéd manner.[141] Feelings of optimism, linked to springtime and love, are also at the center of A. Serafimovich's "Veselyi obman."[142] Here, a woman disappointed in her marriage warns her younger sister against it, while the latter, Elena, affirms that love is valuable even if illusory.

Several holiday works by Mixail Prishvin include "Bab'ia luzha," a charming skaz-based narrative of an alcoholic priest in a provincial parish, who goes mushroom hunting with his dog.[143] A small dose of humorous, whimsical fantasy provides a possible link to Christmas, though clearly the work could have been published just as well on any occasion.

The plot of another story, Aleksei N. Tolstoi's "Samorodok," involves a gold-miner who finds a bit of ore with the help of a young peasant woman, celebrates with her help, and ends up in her bed. She in turn calls in her boyfriend to steal the gold. The miner is chased by the pair, throws away the ore, and is left to die in a swamp.[144] The atmosphere in this account of passion and murder is fatalistic, even anti-Christian. The sole connection to the tradition of the holiday tale is the element of terror.

Finally, there are the many stories of Nadezhda Tèffi, whose narrative gifts are evident in the diversity of her conceptions—again, often far from the norm of the holiday tradition. Thus, one of her works, "Olen'," ends with the suicide of a young boy.[145] Almost as gloomy is "Nezhivoi zver'," a story of a girl whose life falls apart after her parents' divorce, and whose favorite stuffed animal, which she had received during a happier Christmas a year earlier, is thrown onto the rubbish heap and torn apart by rats.[146] On a lighter note, "Kulich," is a pure anecdote where the Easter connection is completely artificial, as the narrator openly indicates: "Все следует делать своевременно. Если человек носит звонкую фамилию 'Кулич', то когда же и поговорить о нем, как не на Пасху?"[147]

Conclusion

Holiday literature, which was in a state of crisis at the turn of the century, flourished again during the post-1905 period, thanks to three developments. First, for a limited time, it was used as a polemical tool by various sides in the political struggle following the Revolution of 1905. Second, modernist authors entering this field experimented with narrative organization, sources, and thematics, resulting both in works embodying deep-seated religious feelings and works where a purely aesthetic element was dominant. Third, leading realist writers worked within similar parameters, helping transform holiday issues of periodicals into striking literary showcases.

Two tasks require further consideration. First, it is necessary to look at the publishing mechanisms from the inside: to investigate how the press itself regarded the phenomenon of holiday literature and how decisions were made regarding choice of material. Second, we need to study the readers' response to various levels of these literary creations. Finally, since the Soviet state essentially ended the holiday tradition in the periodical press, the literature of the Russian emigration must be examined, to map out further developments in Christmas and Easter texts.

Notes

1. For her comments and advice regarding this paper, I wish to thank Elena Dushechkina (St. Petersburg University).

2. In what follows both types of works will sometimes be referred to as "holiday texts" or, following Dushechkina, "calendar texts."

3. See her "Sviatochnyi rasskaz: vozniknovenie i upadok zhanra," in *Prostranstvo i vremia v literature i iskusstve. Metodicheskie materialy po teorii literatury,* ed. F. N. Fedorov et al. (Daugavpils, 1990) 42–44. *Russkaia kalendarnaia proza: Antologiia sviatochnogo rasskaza. Uchebnye materialy k spetskursu,* comp. and intro. by E. V. Dushechkina (Tallin, 1988).

4. Some authors, including Leskov, pointed to Gogol' as an early exemplar of holiday fiction writers. Literary Yuletide tales are found already in the eighteenth century.

5. See the excellent discussion in I. Katarskii, *Dikkens v Rossii. Seredina XIX veka* (Moscow, 1966), 139–150.

6. Published in *Moskvitianin,* nos. 1–2 (1855). Tolstoi's "Sviatochnaia noch'" was written slightly earlier, in 1853, but whether it belongs to this category of texts is an open question. Although the brief plot is set during Christmastide and contrasts memories of the holiday in the country and the reality of the city ("Мир Божий и мир человеческий"), the text lacks other expected elements of the genre—the mixture of the fantastic and the real, the role of the holiday in softening the human psyche, etc.

7. Katarskii 247. Grigorovich also wrote some other Christmas tales, e.g. the slightly earlier "Prokhozhii. Sviatochnyi rasskaz" (1851), which was oriented toward the folklore model of the calendar tale, and "Rozhdestvenskaia noch'. Rasskaz" (1890).

8. N. S. Leskov, *Polnoe sobranie sochinenii,* 3d ed. (St. Petersburg, 1903) 18:7.

9. Leskov himself keeps the fantastic to a minimum and finds a particular motivation for it. In the Preface to his *Sviatochnye rasskazy,* he notes: "Из этих рассказов только немногие имеют элемент *чудесного*—в смысле сверхчувственного и таинственного. В прочих причудливое или загадочное имеет свои основания не в сверхъестественном или сверхчувственном, а истекают из свойств русского духа и тех общественных веяний, в которых для многих, и в том числе для самого автора, написавшего эти рассказы, заключается значительная доля странного и удивительного." See *Polnoe sobranie sochinenii* 18:5.

10. A collection of seven works by F. Nefedov, *Sviatochnye rasskazy* (Moscow, 1895), exemplifies this dichotomy within the genre. Three texts, all linked to celebration of the Nativity, either involve the impact of the occasion on the protagonist or explore some moral issue. The remaining four stories involve peasants and the fantastic—either the result of deception upon the credulous or caused by drunkenness. The basic split within holiday literature is also reflected in a story *about* the creation of a Christmas tale by an aspiring author: "Дело в том, что я никак не мог подобрать для своего рассказа подходящего сюжета. Перебирая в памяти все прочитанные мною в жизни святочные рассказы, я пришел к заключению, что из ста этих рассказов семьдесят были с привидениями, с смертельным ужасом, с холодным потом и судорогами во всем теле, двадцать из них были с благодетельной феей, опускающейся в комнату бедняка, и десять с замерзшим мальчиком на улице." See A. Turkin, "Deistvitel'nost'," *Ural,* no. 564, 25 December 1898, 1–2.

11. For example, the *Rozhdestvenskii al'manakh* (Moscow, 1871).

12. Thus, the 1872 Christmas issue contains a four-part poem, "Elka," by Gustav Nenado, a pseudonym of N. P. Kil'berg. *Niva,* no. 52 (1872): 830. The 1873 issue contains a tale about peasant mummers on Christmas Eve (Parvov, "Khristoslavy-vertepshchiki [s natury]," *Niva,* no. 52 [1873]: 822–826).

13. The issue opened with a brief essay, "Ob obychae prazdnovaniia elki" (872), which referred to the January publication by Dostoevskii of "Mal'chik u Khrista na elke." Next, a story by Ivanov, "Chem pokorila? (Malen'kaia povest' o predmete bol'shoi vazhnosti)," is not labeled a Christmas tale, but its theme of meekness overcoming hostility and anger fits the broad themes of the holiday (872–880). Finally, an unsigned work, "Na volosok ot smerti (Sviatochnyi rasskaz)," belongs to the horror subgenre of the tradition: it deals with railroad machinists in Germany

and the near-fatal accident one of them had had on one New Year's Eve (881–885). There are also commentaries on the artwork, providing readers with a ready-made flight of fancy for each illustration.

14. The New Year brought a smaller, related group of texts, the *novogodnii rasskaz.*

15. An early example is Grigorovich's "Svetloe Khristovo Voskresenie" (1850).

16. For example, in *Niva,* no. 16, 17 April 1872, there is a reproduction of Rubens's painting of the removal of Christ's body from the cross (p. 245).

17. Even *Novoe vremia* did not offer a full-blown Easter issue during the early 1890s. For Easter 1891, for example, it offered readers only a poem by Aleksandr Amfiteatrov, "Svetlyi prazdnik (ispanskaia legenda)." See no. 5440, 21 April [3 May] 1891, 2.

18. The Easter 1897 issue of *Rus',* no. 84, 13 (25) April 1897, contained a column by Vladimir Solov'ev, "Khristos Voskres!" ("Pervaia reshitel'naia pobeda zhizni nad smert'iu! . . ."); an essay by N. Engel'gardt ("Khristovo Voskresen'e"); a story about holiday customs in Odessa (Ia. Abramov, "Razgoven'e"); and a drawing of Saint Isaac's Cathedral during Easter services. With the Greek-Turkish war dominating the news, the paper also included a Bosnian folk legend about the eventual triumph of Russia and Orthodoxy over Turkey; this text, echoing the theme "Moscow—Third Rome," broadly fits in with the holiday. There is no purely literary text. A Petersburg paper, *Novosti i birzhevaia gazeta,* shows the change in its Easter issues at the start of the twentieth century: in 1901, it published a poem and a story about Easter customs. See no. 90, 1 (14) April 1901, 2–3. In 1902, it came out with seven prose tales. See no. 103, 14 (27) April 1902, 3–4. In 1903, six stories and two poems appeared. See no. 95, 6 (19) April 1903, 2–3.

19. N. A. Ivanov, "V sviatuiu noch'. Nabrosok," *Sibirskii vestnik* [Tomsk], no. 41, 12 April 1892, 2–3.

20. A. Gruzinskii, "Na Paskhe. (Siluėty). I. Khristos Voskrese!" *Iuzhnyi krai* [Khar'kov], no. 6284, 18 (30) April 1899, 2–3. A reworked, even more saccharine version of this text (the name of the manager changed to Amplii Egorovich Sheresperov-Ural'skii), appeared on Easter 1917. See A. Ligovskii, "Kryl'ia smerti," *Moskovskie vedomosti,* no. 66, 1 (14) April 1917, 1.

21. In a parody by Diogen, pseudonym of V. V. Bilibin, "Chort (sviatochnyi rasskaz)," the protagonist, a writer, is shown composing stories ordered by a number of publications: "Время близилось к полуночи . . . Но Илларион Николаевич не замечал времени. Он сидел за письменным столом уже 48 часов подряд, торопясь приготовить к сроку все заказанные ему святочные рассказы." In accordance with the tradition of the fantastic in the Christmas genre, he is visited by a devil, who protests against being exploited by writers and demands his share of the honoraria. *Novosti i birzhevaia gazeta,* no. 357, 25 December 1900, 2–3.

22. The process of creating Christmas stories in a provincial setting is the subject of a work by Kazimir Barantsevich, in which an editor gives two reporters, the gloomy Zasidkin and the dandy Tolkunchikov, orders to write one by the 24th. They can be expected to come in with very different works; in the editor's words: "Хотел было Засидкина привлечь, да Бог его знает, размазня он какой-то! Начнет скулить, ныть, гражданскую свою слезу подпустит. Только тоску нагонять! А нуж-

но, знаете, что нибудь повеселее, остроумное что нибудь, с шаржиком, этак, знаете, ковырнуть этак кой-кого! Пробрать." Zasidkin goes to several police stations looking for a possible story about someone freezing. His search is in vain. He then has dinner, drinks heavily, and freezes to death on the street, while thinking about various story plots. See K. Barantsevich, "'Rozhdestvenskii rasskaz,'" *Ural'-skaia zhizn'* (Ekaterinburg), no. 235, 25 December 1899, 2–3.

23. Hugh McLean notes that "Zapechatlennyi angel" (1873) and "Na kraiu sveta" initially bore subtitles which linked them to the holiday genre, but that their length puts them in the category of novella and outside of Leskov's own definition of the genre. See his *Nikolai Leskov: The Man and His Art* (Cambridge, Mass., 1977) 695–696.

24. Most of Leskov's Christmas stories are found in *Polnoe sobranie sochinenii N. S. Leskova,* vols. 18–19 (St. Petersburg, 1903).

25. In spite of their diversity, and the frequent thinness of their connections to the Christmas season—as discussed by McLean—the stories exhibit an underlying pattern. In almost all cases, the plot involves a "changing" or "removal of masks."

26. For a comparison of Chekhov's and Leskov's holiday tales, see B. I. Esin, *Chekhov-zhurnalist* (Moscow, 1977) 80–87.

27. These came out as a separate volume during the 1890s. Most are reprinted in D. N. Mamin-Sibiriak, *Polnoe sobranie sochinenii,* vol. 12 (Petrograd, 1917) 122–190.

28. Holiday tales offered tempting opportunities for reading and misreading. In his "Dva slova o kur'eze s 'Al'bigoitsem'," Aleksandr Amfiteatrov offers an anecdote concerning an attack by a clergyman on his 1902 story "Al'bigoets. (Legenda 1208 goda)." This piece, about the destruction of the Albigensians and the cruelty of the Catholic church, was taken by a Fr. M. Rozov as an allegory of the Orthodox church's relations with Tolstoi. Amfiteatrov wittily claims that this was quite incorrect. See A. Amfiteatrov, *Legendy publitsista* (St. Petersburg, 1905) 221–225. ("Al'bigoets" is reprinted in this collection, pp. 55–61.)

29. Sergei Iablonovskii, "Pochti rozhdestvenskoe," *Russkoe slovo,* no. 330, 25 December 1905 (7 January 1906), 3.

30. O. L. D'Or [Iosif Orsher], "Kak nado pisat' rozhdestvenskie rasskazy. (Rukovodstvo dlia molodykh pisatelei)," *Rech': Besplatnoe prilozhenie,* no. 354, 25 December 1909 (7 January 1910), 2.

31. "Mir i blagovolenie," *Novosti i birzhevaia gazeta,* no. 357, 25 December 1900, 2.

32. These included A. Khir'iakov's "V poiskakh za starukhoi," R. Antropov's "Mig," K. L-ch's "Tainstvennyi posetitel'," Diogen's "Chort," and L. Ruskin's "Pesn' pastyrei."

33. A particularly moving appeal is the unsigned editorial "Ves' khristianskii mir prazdnuet nyne . . . ," *Severnyi krai,* no. 130, 18 (30) April 1899, 1. This newspaper was quite left-wing, for a time publishing contributions by Bolshevik authors.

34. "Весь славянский мир всколыхнется до глубин души своей, и взоры всех братьев наших устремятся вместе с нами на Далекий Восток, откуда со светом Светлого праздника идет на нас из "страны восходящего солнца" желтая гроза." "Khristos Voskrese!" *Rus',* no. 106, 28 March (10 April) 1904, 1.

35. A. Chapygin, "V prazdnik (nabrosok)," *Nasha zhizn',* no. 50, 25 December 1904 (7 January 1905), 3.

36. S. Gusev-Orenburgskii, "Koshmar"; F. Sologub, "Palochka-pogonialochka i

shapochka-mnogodumochka," *Nasha zhizn',* no. 50, 25 December 1904 (7 January 1905).

37. For example, "Na paskhal'nye temy," *Severnyi krai,* no. 102, 17 April 1905, 1.

38. The Black Hundred newspaper *Den'* (Moscow) not only praised the troops that had suppressed the revolt, but published anecdotes of how true patriots react to treason. In one, a peasant is horrified by his son, a worker who returns from the city stuffed with socialist ideas. At night, while the son is sleeping, the old man beheads him with an axe and explains "Я не мог его оставить в живых . . . он мог испортить много народа." Another story deals with the revolt proper: "Один студент предательски убил солдата и был за это застрелен патрулем. После этого в один из участков явился отец студента и просил передать благодарность солдатам за то, что они избавили страну от изменника. Семье солдата, убитого студентом, он передал тысячу рублей, взять же тело отказался. 'Он мне не сын, он изменил Царю и России',—прибавил несчастный отец." "Russkaia liubov' k rodine," *Den',* no. 327, 25 December 1905, 1.

39. "Sochel'nik," *Moskovskie vedomosti,* no. 332, 25 December 1905 (7 January 1906), 3.

40. Aleksandr Astaf'ev, "Kroshka Bobik. Rozhdestvenskii ėtiud," *Moskovskie vedomosti,* no. 332, 25 December 1905 (7 January 1906), 3.

41. All these in *Novoe vremia,* no. 10697, 25 December 1905 (7 January 1906), 2–5. The issue also featured more conventional works, such as I. Golovin's weak vampire tale, "Na iavu ili vo sne. (Sviatochnyi rasskaz)."

42. Ia (pseudonym of I. I. Iasinskii), "Na temy dnia. Traur," *Birzhevye vedomosti,* even. ed., no. 9147, 24 December 1905, 3.

43. *Russkie vedomosti* was closed 23–31 December by the order of the St. Petersburg Governor-General.

44. Demokrat, "Kakaia gazeta nuzhna narodu?" *Sibirskaia zhizn',* no. 261, 25 December 1905, 2.

45. "И только Ирод-царь враг свободы/ Престол боявшись свой потерять,/ В порыве дикой, безумной злобы,/ Велел младенцев всех избивать." See E. Bakharev, "Khristos rodilsia v peshchere tesnoi," *Sibirskaia zhizn',* no. 261, 2). The prose tale, "Elka (iz rozhdestvenskikh skazok)," is published on the same page. A connection with the apolitical holiday tradition is kept by the publication of a translation from a Jean Grenier story, "V noch' pered Rozhdestvom," 2–3, an updating of the Scrooge story in an American setting.

46. *Rech',* no. 38, 2 (15) April 1906, 1. This piece was actually the second of the opening articles in the issue. The lead story discussed the difficulty of accepting the message of love and forgiveness, associated with the drama of Easter, in a country that had experienced such suffering in the last several months. The article concluded by referring to the forthcoming Duma and by calling for an amnesty for political prisoners: "Если нельзя вернуть жизни казненным, если не воскресить безжалостно загубленных, пусть живые вернутся к жизни, пусть раскроются двери тюрьмы, и крепостей."

47. "Paskha nadezhdy," *Dvadtsatyi vek,* no. 9, 2 (15) April 1906, 2. Cf. also "воскрес Христос—воскреснет и Россия!" See "Prazdnik vysshei pravdy," *Strana,* no. 37, 2 [15] April 1906, 1.

48. He himself was the author of holiday tales, such as "Golodnyi i Golodrigo," "Poidem k nim! . . . ," "Kto on?" and "Fatum." See his *Prizraki* (Moscow, 1897).

49. P. Krushevan, "Glumlen'e nad zhizn'iu," *Drug,* no. 86, 2 (15) April 1906, 2.

50. T. Shchepkina-Kupernik, "V paskhal'nuiu noch'," *Rech',* no. 38, 2 (15) April 1906, 2.

51. *Dvadtsatyi vek,* no. 9, 2 (15) April 1906, 4.

52. Vladimir Tikhonov (Mordvin), "Kum"; A. Zenger, "Uchitel' i uchenik," *Dvadtsatyi vek,* no. 9, 2 (15) April 1906, 4.

53. V. Ia., "Ozhidanie. Rasskaz," *Rech',* no. 38, 2 (15) April 1906, 3. A similar treatment of the inability of the upper classes to withstand their fears of revolutionary changes, and particularly of dealing with the masses, is found in a story by P. Boborykin, "Ne perenes!" *Russkie vedomosti,* no. 90, 2 (15) April 1906, 2. Its subject is a millionaire factory owner who is forced to flee a meeting with his workers. The humiliation leads him to feel that his old liberal self has died, and he completes this process by committing suicide.

54. Fedor Chebotarev, "Kak v detstve," *Russkaia zemlia* (Moscow), no. 22, 2 April 1906, 2–4.

55. "V rozhdestvenskii den' . . . ," *Birzhevye vedomosti,* morn. ed., no. 9663, 25 December 1906 (7 January 1907), 2.

56. Cf. another editorial: "Позволительно надеяться, что казенная военно-полевая юстиция прекратит хотя бы на эти дни священных воспоминаний свою деятельность, которая конечно вызвала бы горестные слезы на глазах Небесного Младенца в вифлеемских яслях." "Tesnymi vratami k miru," *Rus',* no. 86, 25 December 1906 (7 January 1907), 1.

57. N. Rakhmanov, "Krug vechnosti," *Tovarishch,* no. 149, 25 December 1906 (7 January 1907), 4.

58. Kaz. Barantsevich, "'Slava Bogu'," *Russkie vedomosti,* no. 313, 25 December 1906 (7 January 1907), 4.

59. This statement applies much less to publications at both ends of the political spectrum, particularly on the left, where political holiday fiction continued to appear. A story such as "Telegramma" by Shchepkina-Kupernik (*Rech',* no. 95, 22 April [5 May] 1907, 2–3), involving an émigré lured back to Russia for Easter by the police, is far more rare than in the period 1905–1906.

60. "Tol'ko dva goda proshlo . . . ," *Rech',* no. 89, 13 (26) April 1908, 1.

61. "Voskreseniia dveri," *Rus',* no. 103, 13 (26) April 1908, 2. The editorial closes with expressions of hope for a future true Easter, that can embrace the nation—"minus the oligarchy."

62. "S kazhdym novym dnem . . . ," *Rossiia,* no. 732, 13 (26) April 1908, 1.

63. Aleksandr Benois, "Khudozhestvennye pis'ma. Koe-chto o elke," *Rech',* no. 318, 25 December 1908 (7 January 1908), 2. Also in *Sovremennoe slovo,* no. 402, 3.

64. On literature during Easter 1917, following the February Revolution, see Henryk Baran, "Paskha 1917 g.: Akhmatova i drugie v russkikh gazetakh," in *Akhmatovskii sbornik. Vypusk 1,* comp. S. Dedulin and G. Superfin (Paris, 1989) 53–75.

65. "Внутреннего мира в России нет, давно нет. Идет внутри у нас борьба светлых и темных сил. Мы сказали бы, что слишком много развелось у нас Иродов, жаждущих крови. Ведь только душа Ирода могла отразиться в тех,

240 HENRYK BARAN

кто, при помощи 'кровавых наветов' на людей, созданных по образу и подобию Божьему, хотят нового избиения, новых кровавых гекатомб, новых вакханалий зверств и изуверства." "Rozhdestvo," *Rech'*, no. 354, 25 December 1911 (7 January 1912), 2.

66. "Самозакланный; во спасенье/ Всех, кто приидет ко Христу,/ Он на Земле свое служенье/ Вметнул как светоч в темноту,/ Средь обреченных на мученье,/ Что верны на своем посту.// . . . . . .// . . . . . .// Кто скажет "Нет", в том хитрость Змея,/ Возжаждет поздно—молвить "Да"./ Пребудем—сердцем не скудея,/ Мы—здесь; нас призовут—Туда./ Несть Эллина, ни Иудея,/ Есть Вифлеемская звезда!"

67. "V glubine Rossii," *Rech'*, no. 83, 25 March (7 April) 1912, 2.

68. *Rech'*, no. 86, 29 March (11 April) 1909, 1. See also "Ves' khristianskii mir prazdnuet Paskhu . . . ," *Rech'*, no. 106, 18 April (1 May) 1910, 1.

69. *Rech'*, no. 304, 25 December 1907 (7 January 1908), 4.

70. *Rech'*, no. 86, 29 March (11 April) 1909, 3.

71. O. L. D'Or, "Rozhdestvenskie peredovitsy," *Utro Rossii*, no. 67–34, 25 December 1909, 3.

72. A. A. Izmailov, *Krivoe zerkalo: parodii i sharzhi*, 2d ed. (St. Petersburg, 1910) 157–159.

73. Izmailov's parodic note: "*) Вставка цензора." (*Krivoe zerkalo* 159).

74. *Krivoe zerkalo* 161.

75. The conflict was a factor for serious writers, with intellectual and aesthetic integrity, and not for hacks, who would produce holiday texts by following one of a number of common formats.

76. Aleksandr Amfiteatrov, "Paskhal'nye pamiatki," *Rech'*, no. 89, 13 (26) April 1908, 3.

77. A. Amfiteatrov, "Ne vri!" *Rech'*, no. 304, 25 December 1907 (7 January 1908), 3. Reprinted in A. V. Amfiteatrov, *Sobranie sochinenii*, vol. 27, *Ėzopov lik* (St. Petersburg, n.d.) 310–325. The volume contains several of his parodies.

78. *Ibid.*

79. Fedor Sologub, *Stikhotvoreniia* ed. M. I. Dikman (Leningrad, 1975) 210. The poem was written in August 1898, but published in the journal *Zhivopisnoe obozrenie*, no. 15 (Easter), 14 April 1902.

80. Sologub, *Stikhotvoreniia* 246. The poem was published in the periodical *Peterburgskaia zhizn'*, no. 796, 25 December 1904.

81. Garmodii [pseud. of Briusov], "Rozhdestvenskie rasskazy v gazetakh," *Pribaltiiskii krai*, no. 8, 10 January 1902, 1–2. The article reviews Christmas issues of several Moscow newspapers, criticizes most of the published texts for their weakness and banality, and singles out for praise works by L. Andreev and A. Budishchev.

82. Subsequently included in the collection *Zemnaia os'*, where its original subtitle, "Sviatochnyi rasskaz," was changed to "Iz arkhiva psikhiatra." The volume and most other prose works referred to below are reprinted in V. Ia. Briusov, *Rasskazy i povesti* (=Slavische Propyläen, Texte in Neu- und Nachdrucken, 49) (Munich, 1970).

83. *Rasskazy i povesti* 18.

84. Briusov does not always avoid the supernatural. "Zashchita" (1903) is a more

conventional story involving a possible sighting of a ghost (or the protagonist's imagination).

85. Sologub, *Stikhotvoreniia* 319, 331.

86. Rpt. in Fedor Sologub, *Rasskazy,* ed. and intro. Evelyn Bristol (Berkeley, 1979) 225–239.

87. A. Gornfel'd, "Literaturnye besedy. XXX. Torzhestvo pobeditelei." *Tovarishch,* no. 352, 23 August (5 September) 1907, 4. Cf. L. Voitolovskii, *Tekushchii moment i tekushchaia literatura. (K psikhologii obshchestvennykh nastroenii)* (St. Petersburg, 1908) 12.

88. For example, Christmas 1911: "Zoloto korolevy" (*Odesskie novosti*); "Loèngrin" (*Rech'*); "Loèngrin. Rasskaz" (*Sovremennoe slovo*); "Potselui nerozhdennogo" (*Utro Rossii*).

89. The order of what follows is not chronological; the period in question was too brief—lasting until the end of 1917 inside Russia, though continuing, in an attenuated form, in émigré literature—and different approaches to holiday literature overlapped.

90. K. M. Fofanov, a regular contributor to *Novoe vremia,* was perhaps the best known of the lot. For a number of years, T. Shchepkina-Kupernik published sentimental poems in holiday issues.

91. For example, "Этот звон колокольный, сиянье огней,/ Эти звуки молитв, это стройное пенье/ Оживленные радостью сердца людей/ Вновь меня взволновали до слез умиленья./ Этот дым голубой от душистых курений,/ Что волнами повис над толпой в вышине,/ Этот храм—точно чудные грезы во сне . . ./ В вечно-памятный день—день рожденья Христова/ Самым светлым мечтам я во власть отдаюсь,—/ И витают предо мною картины былого,/ И я верю опять и по-детски молюсь . . ./ Хорошо бы по-детски так верить всегда,/ Да со многим давно уже ум не мирится/ Впечатленья не те уж, не те и года . . ." See M. Kuznetsov, "V Khrame," *Birzhevye vedomosti,* no. 353, 25 December 1889, 1.

92. For example, Garol'd, "Sviatochnaia fantaziia," *Kievskoe slovo,* no. 4298, 25 December 1899, 2–3 (the text is a parodic conversation between Faust and Mephistopheles, loaded with literary reminiscences). The poet Ol'ga Chiumina (pseudonym "Boi-Kot") was the author of many similar works.

93. Aleksandr Blok, *Sobranie sochinenii v vos'mi tomakh* (Moscow–Leningrad, 1960) 2:20–21.

94. Blok, *Sobranie sochinenii* 3:68.

95. *Rech'. Besplatnoe prilozhenie,* no. 354, 25 December 1909 (7 January 1910), 4. The poem was slightly reworked in 1912. See Blok, *Sobranie sochinenii* 3:164.

96. Blok, *Sobranie sochinenii* 3:269–270.

97. V. Briusov, "Na pliazhe," *Rech',* no. 354, 25 December 1910 (7 January 1911), 3. Among Briusov's poems, a text that would fit into the holiday norm is quite rare. One such work is "Zerno," which explores the theme of the cycle of death and life in nature. See *Rech'. Besplatnoe prilozhenie,* no. 354, 25 December 1909 (7 January 1910), 2. Khodasevich's poem appeared in *Russkaia molva,* no. 17, 25 December 1912 (7 January 1913), 3.

98. *Utro Rossii,* no. 101, 10 April 1916, 2.

99. *Rech'. Besplatnoe prilozhenie,* no. 106, 18 April (1 May) 1910, 2.

100. *Russkoe slovo,* no. 67, 22 March (4 April) 1915, 3. Other poems published here are Ivanov's "Peremyshl'" and "Chasha sviatoi Sofii," Bal'mont's "Bei v baraban," and Sergei Mamontov's "V drevnem Galiche."

101. One exception is M. N. Al'bov's "Poslednii den' Iudy. Paskhal'nyi rasskaz. (Iz apokrificheskikh tolkovanii)" (1898), in *Sochineniia M. N. Al'bova,* vol. 5 (St. Petersburg, n.d.) 305–317. Leskov's reworkings of the *Prolog* appeared outside the framework of holiday issues.

102. This count is based on the unpublished bibliography of Remizov's works by Alex M. Shane. I am grateful to him for the opportunity to use it, as well as for his generosity in sharing his collection of Remizoviana.

103. Only in 1911 does Remizov begin to publish regularly original fiction in holiday issues, though even then works derived from folklore play a major role.

104. They, and several other apocryphal works published in holiday issues, are reprinted in Aleksei Remizov, *Sochineniia* 7 (=*Otrechennye povesti*) (St. Petersburg, 1910–1912).

105. *Russkoe slovo,* no. 296, 25 December 1909 (7 January 1910), 2.

106. *Russkoe slovo,* no. 297, 25 December 1914 (7 January 1915), 6.

107. Reprinted in *Dokuka i balagur'e* (St. Petersburg, [1914]).

108. "Chudesnye bashmachki" has a slightly ambiguous ending. These stories, and similar folklore-based texts, are later grouped into larger wholes. Thus, "Krasnaia sosenka" as well as the stories "Obrechennaia" (1912), "Otchaiannaia" (1912), "Otgadchitsa" (1913), "Poperechnaia" (1913), and "Serdechnaia" (1913), are part of "Russkie zhenshchiny"—a gallery of individual portraits and fates, not all happy, which sometimes carry a Christian message, but which are more closely linked with the world of the magical, the demonic. See *Dokuka i balagur'e* 13–91.

109. Sologub, *Rasskazy* 314–327.

110. Fedor Sologub, "Ocharovanie pechali. Sentimental'naia novella," *Rech',* no. 89, 13 (26) April 1908, 3.

111. *Rech',* no. 354, 25 December 1912 (7 January 1913), 4.

112. *Rech',* no. 354, 25 December 1910 (7 January 1911), 4. Sadovskoi's holiday publications also include "Dedovskie chasy," *Russkaia molva,* no. 17, 25 December 1912 (7 January 1913), 3.

113. *Utro Rossii,* no. 101, 10 April 1916, 4–5.

114. *Rus',* no. 346, 25 December 1907 (7 January 1908), 3.

115. *Rech',* no. 354, 25 December 1910 (7 January 1911), 3.

116. F. Zelinskii, "Prazdnik sveta i spaseniia," *Rech',* no. 353, 25 December 1913 (7 January 1914), 4.

117. *Rech',* no. 354, 25 December 1910 (7 January 1911), 2–3; *Rech',* no. 98, 10 (23) April 1911, 2–3.

118. *Rech'. Besplatnoe prilozhenie,* no. 354, 25 December 1909 (7 January 1910), 4. Another of Auslender's holiday publications is the story "Vesennie dni," *Russkaia molva,* no. 123, 14 (27) April 1913, 3.

119. *Utro Rossii,* no. 87, 14 April 1913, 2–3.

120. According to Jewish tradition, the name of Adam's first wife.

121. Published in *Utro Rossii* and reprinted in Sologub, *Rasskazy,* 337–356. A parody of this story was published a few days later, under the title "Sologubaia

gost'ia," by Otshel'nik (pseud.), "Rozhdestvenskaia proza. (Druzheskie parodii)," *Utro Rossii,* no. 68–35, 29 December 1909, 3. The parodist uses the vampire's Jewish name to play with motifs relating to the Black Hundreds, and has the hero saved by a Black Hundred activist, rather than a heavenly being. The publication also contains parodies of Bunin and Barantsevich.

122. *Rech',* no. 318, 25 December 1908 (7 January 1909), 4–5.

123. See A. M. Remizov, *Izbrannoe* (Moscow, 1978) 80–87.

124. A. Remizov, "Galstuk. Rasskaz," *Rech',* no. 98, 10 (23) April 1911, 3–4. Reprinted in Remizov, *Sochineniia* 5:195–210.

125. *Rech',* no. 354, 25 December 1911 (7 January 1912), 2–3. Reprinted in Aleksei Remizov, *Vesennee porosh'e* (St. Petersburg, n.d. [1915]) 209–228.

126. See *Vesennee porosh'e* 229–256.

127. *Birzhevye vedomosti* [morn. ed., no. 15290, 25 December 1915 (7 January 1916), 2–3. Reprinted in Aleksei Remizov, *Sredi mur'ia. Rasskazy* (Moscow, 1917) 45–56.

128. *Sredi mur'ia* 54.

129. *Russkoe slovo,* no. 82, 10 (23) April 1911, 4–5 (chapters "Kontsert," "Kazanka").

130. Both published in *Rech',* no. 94, 6 (19) April 1914, 3–4.

131. Andrei Belyi, "Otryvki iz detskikh vpechatlenii," *Russkie vedomosti,* no. 298, 25 December 1916, 3–4.

132. *Utro Rossii,* no. 296/7, 25 December 1913, 5–6. The stories are N. Petrovskaia, "Zabvennye"; E. Nagrodskaia, "Rokovaia mogila"; Z. Gippius, "Poliubi menia belen'kim"; A. Krandievskaia, "Golubye tsvety."

133. *Russkoe slovo,* no. 71, 25 March (7 April) 1912, 3–6. The final article in the issue, "Cherty bessmertiia," explores the motif of Herzen's immortality, thus putting the Easter theme to special use. Easter motifs are also used in discussions of Herzen's life in the St. Petersburg *Gazeta-kopeika* as well as in *Utro Rossii.* See A. Vladimirov, "Gordyi iubilei," *Gazeta-kopeika,* no. 71/938, 25 March 1912, 3; V. Ermilov, "Blagovest' russkogo 'Kolokola,'" *Utro Rossii,* no. 71, 25 March 1912, 5–6.

134. Tolstoi "Chem liudi zhivy," with illustrations by N. Gė, was published in the supplement to *Utro Rossii,* no. 297, 25 December 1911, 2–8.

135. See for example, the *Paskhal'nyi al'manakh* (St. Petersburg, 1910), which included works by Chekhov, Gor'kii, V. Bonch-Bruevich, Merezhkovskii, Blok, Remizov, and others.

136. "Poprygun'ia-strekoza," *Russkoe slovo,* no. 298, 25 December 1910 (7 January 1911), 4.

137. *Rech',* no. 83, 25 March (7 April) 1912, 3.

138. "Pustynia d'iavola," *Russkoe slovo,* no. 296, 25 December 1909 (7 January 1910), 3; *Russkoe slovo,* no. 297, 25 December 1912 (7 January 1913), 4.

139. *Rech',* no. 102, 14 (27) April 1913, 2.

140. *Russkoe slovo,* no. 297, 25 December 1914 (7 January 1915), 3.

141. *Rech',* no. 102, 14 (27) April 1913, 3. Other stories by Shmelev include "V nenast'e" (1912), "Po prikhodu" (1913) and "V usad'be" (1914).

142. *Rech',* no. 98, 10 (23) April 1911, 3.

143. *Rech',* no. 354, 25 December 1912 (7 January 1913), 5–6.

144. *Russkoe slovo,* no. 89, 18 April (1 May) 1910, 4.

145. "Olen'," *Rech'. Besplatnoe prilozhenie,* no. 106, 18 April (1 May) 1910, 2–3.

146. *Russkoe slovo,* no. 297, 25 December 1911 (7 January 1912), 6.

147. *Russkoe slovo,* no. 89, 18 April (1 May) 1910, 4. Kulich, newly married, is employed by a merchant who doesn't hire married people. He is telephoned constantly by his jealous wife and pretends to others in the office that other women are calling him. In the end, he is fired because of his supposedly immoral conduct, and his wife is informed of his "depravity."

Русская Греция, русский Рим

BORIS GASPAROV

1. Противопоставленность православного и римско-католического мира является одной из доминантных тем в истории русской культуры. На протяжении многих столетий эта тема принимала все новые исторические формы; ее присутствие оставило свой отпечаток — иногда явный, иногда более опосредованный — на самых различных явлениях русской политической и культурной истории. Дуалистическая картина мира, основанная на противопоставлении православия и католичества, представляет собой не однозначную оппозицию, но культурную парадигму. Она формируется на пересечении и слиянии нескольких различных культурно-исторических концептов, связанных между собой отношениями частичного сходства и смежности.

Так, дуалистическое разделение христианского мира может осмысляться как противопоставление между славянским миром (единство которого должно быть восстановлено в идеальном будущем), с одной стороны, и «западным» романо-германским миром, с другой. Другая конфигурация описываемой парадигмы может строиться на противопоставлении России исключительно католическому «Западу» (эта модель, в частности, актуализируется в периоды обостренного культурного и политического антагонизма с Францией и Польшей); в этом случае, «русская идея» в большей или меньшей степени сходится с образом германского мира (Германии, Англии, Скандинавии), в его противостоянии романско-католическому миру. Эта модель может принимать и чисто анти-французскую вариацию, при которой даже романские католические страны (Италия, Испания) солидаризируются (хотя бы частично) с «русским» полюсом, в его противопоставленности галлизированному образу «Запада».[1] И наконец, в отдельные периоды идея о противостоянии «России» и «Запада» принимает наиболее категорическую форму, при которой весь не-православный (в сущности, весь не-русский) христианский мир сливается в единый образ, помещаемый на противоположном, по отношению к «русскому», полюсе оппозиции.

Во всех конфигурациях, которые описанная культурная модель может принимать в различные эпохи, в руках представителей разных идеологических течений и в связи с разными конкретными культурными задачами, сохраняется ее общая ценностная шкала, протягивающаяся между двумя противоположными полюсами. Важнейшим свойством, на котором строится образ позитивного полюса, в его противопоставленности негативному, является органическое «единство». Данная категория отличается многозначностью и пластичностью, позволяющей адаптировать ее к многоразличным конкретным целям и обстоятельствам. Она может интерпретироваться как непрерывность исторической традиции (связь с «корнями», или «почвой»), — в противоположность подражательности и поверхностной «моде»; как «богатое» единство разнообразных форм и голосов, естественно переплетающихся между собой, — в противоположность искусственному единообразию; как «динамическое» единство, основанное на пластическом взаимодействии всех компонентов, — в противоположность статическому, застывшему, рационалистически негибкому построению; как стремление к синтезу и «гармонии» (в частности, гармонии идеального и чувственного), — в противоположность разорванности духовного и материального начала и одностороннему преобладанию то одного, то другого из них; как гармоническое «соборное» равновесие между индивидуальным и общим, между творческой волей и «хоровым», или «диалогическим» ее воплощением, — в противоположность разрыву между личностью и средой, между индивидуализмом и урбанистической безличностью; как качественно самодостаточное целое, — в противоположность ограниченной идее, стремящейся к бесконечному количественному распространению.

Идеальные образы «России» и «Запада» (в той или иной их конфигурации) занимают полярно противоположные точки на этой шкале; они как бы отсчитываются друг от друга с обратным знаком. Как правило, Россия занимает полюс «органического единства», ее оппонент — противоположный полюс. Но в некоторые исторические моменты данная модель выступает в инверсированной форме, при которой «Россия» и «Запад» меняются ролями, при полном сохранении, однако, основных параметров каждой из этих ролей; наиболее ярким примером такого феномена являются «Lettres sur la philosophie de l'historie» (так называемые «Философические письма») Чаадаева.

Одним из важных культурных инструментов, при помощи которого строится и применяется к различным историческим ситуациям эта модель, является проекция ее в дохристианский античный мир. В этом случае, в образе античного мира оказывается подчеркнута противопоставленность «греческой» и «римской» античности как двух различных ценностных полюсов. Соответственно, православный и католический мир, «Россия» и «Запад» осмысляются как прямые наследники этих двух образов античности.

Идеальный образ античного «востока» и «запада» обладает такой же подвижностью и множественностью, так же может менять свои очертания и граничные линии, в зависимости от идеологических обстоятельств, как и современная модель национального самосознания, проекцией которой этот образ является. Образ «Рима», в качестве негативного ценностного полюса, может ограничиваться пределами имперского Рима, в его противопоставлении «классической» (греческой и римской республиканской) античности; еще большим сужением является выделение Рима в качестве столицы Западной империи, давшей начало католическому миру, — Рима эпохи «вульгарной латыни»; наконец, возможно разделение образов «Рима», как имперской метрополии, и «Италии», при котором последняя, в качестве страны романтической «гармонии», перемещается на полюс, противоположный идее имперского «запада». Однако во всех этих случаях, образ «Греции» (во всех возможных его интерпретациях) всегда выступает в качестве эпицентра и духовной родины позитивных ценностей, унаследованных и развиваемых на русской почве. Образ Греции как воплощения классической пластичности и гармонии, со всей широко разработанной в европейской традиции системой художественных ассоциаций, эстетических, филологических, исторических идей, инкорпорируется в состав русской культурно-исторической парадигмы. Это сообщает «русской идее» и различным конкретным ее проявлениям огромный потенциал идейных, жанровых, образных ресурсов. Более того, сам факт такого включения знаменует собой глубину культурных корней — от античной Греции, через Византию к церковнославянскому языку и современной русской культуре. Эта преемственность может изображаться либо как непрерывный процесс, составляющий «органическое» единство на всем его историческом протяжении, либо как диалектическая смена полярных фазисов в европейской истории: от изначальной гармонии — к потере ее и утверждению «римского» начала — и затем к восстановлению-синтезу в нарождающейся «русской идее».

Проекция национального самосознания в античность как сферу абсолютного идеала свойственна отнюдь не только русской культуре. Не говоря уже о значении такого феномена для итальянского Ренессанса, можно вспомнить ту огромную роль, которую «открытие» античного

мира сыграло в формировании немецкого романтизма, его культурно-
исторической философии, филологии и эстетики и его художественной
практики. Высвобождение античности от «искусственной» оболочки, в
которой она представала в традиции французского классицизма, послу-
жило важнейшим инструментом в формировании немецкого (романтического) самосознания и эмансипации его от французской (классицис-
тической) культурной гегемонии.[2] Это направление, начало которому
было положено в середине XVIII столетия И. Винкельманом, получило
мощное развитие на рубеже XIX века в творчестве Гете, в философии
и эстетике Йенских романтиков (круга «Атенеума»), в создании срав-
нительного «индо-германского» языкознания (в основу которого легло
сделанное Р. Раском и Ф. Боппом открытие родства между германскими и классическими языками, а затем и санскритом).

Немецкий образ античности (ориентированный, преимущественно, на
греческую античность) как колыбели идеальной гармонии, и его проекция на немецкий романтизм как наследник органических ценностей, в
противопоставлении рационализму французского классицизма, несомненно оказал большое влияние на соответствующие направления русской мысли, от первых культурно-философских идей 1820-х годов до
нео-романтических течений начала XX века. Немецкий опыт открытия
«истинной» античности позволил ассимилировать огромное культурное
содержание, разработанное романтиками; но это содержание усваива-
лось, адаптируясь к задачам и ходам мышления, типичным для русской
ситуации.

В частности, одной из характерных черт античной проекции на русской почве являлось гораздо более явное педалирование дуализма
античного мира. Граничная линия между «истинной» и «ложной» клас-
сикой проводится не столько во времени, сколько в культурном про-
странстве; противопоставляются не столько первоначальные ценности
и их последующее (в эпоху «ложного классицизма») искажение, сколько
изначально существующие два полюса, кристаллизующиеся вокруг идеи
античного «востока» и «запада», восточного и западного христианства,
греко-славянского и латино-романского мира.

Дуалистический образ античности, в качестве одного из параметров
культурного самосознания, имел особенно большие последствия для
русской филологической мысли. В развитии различных отраслей европейской филологии нового времени — лингвистики, теории жанров и
стилей, теории поэтического слова, стихосложения — основополага-
ющую роль неизменно играла классическая традиция: аристотелевская

поэтика и риторика, античное стихосложение, первые античные грамматики, наконец, теории языкового знака, идущие от Платона и Аристотеля к Августину и схоластикам. В европейской культуре нового времени развитие соответствующих областей строилось на основе фундаментальных понятий, унаследованных от античности, и различной их интерпретации. Начиная с середины XVIII века, аналогичные задачи возникли перед русским обществом. В этом случае, потенциальное разделение античного мира на два полюса и вытекающий из этого дуализм в отношении к различным элементам классической традиции, то есть осмысление их как «своих» либо «чужих», «истинных» либо «ложных», оказывали существенное влияние на то, как протекали процессы становления и развития филологической культуры на русской почве.

Ассоциативное слияние образа православия, в его противопоставлении католическому миру, и образа классической Греции, в его противопоставлении Римской империи, составило идеологический и образный конгломерат, обладавший мощным творческими потенциалом. Возводимый на классическом фундаменте корпус словесной культуры встраивался в параметры религиозной традиции и мессианистического национального самосознания. Процессы становления различных литературных направлений и филологических идей и борьба между ними проецировались в мир идеальных культурно-исторических ценностей и заряжались мессианистическим подтекстом. Присутствие этого субстрата ощущается на различных этапах развития русской литературы, русской филологической мысли и тесно с ними связанной философии национального самосознания.

2. Реформа русского стихосложения, осуществленная Тредиаковским и Ломоносовым в 1730–50-е годы, в короткий срок произвела радикальный переворот всей поэтической традиции, к этому времени уже насчитывавшей более ста лет. Каковы бы ни были чисто эстетические и технические основания для перехода с силлабического стихосложения к силлабо-тоническому,[3] замечательна та необыкновенная скорость и полная безусловность, с которой новое направление одержало победу.[4]

Одной из причин этого явления следует признать тот факт, что реформа стихосложения направлялась не только эстетическими или языковыми соображениями; она явилась культурным «жестом», несшим в себе символический заряд. Признание силлабического стиха несоответствующим «духу» русской просодии означало эмансипацию от непосредственного польского и более опосредованного французского образца. Вместо этой отвергнутой модели, реформа Тредиаковского/Ломоносова строила русский стих по образцу немецкой силлабо-тонической поэзии.[5] Примечательно, однако, что авторы реформы в своих теоретических положениях ориентировались не столько на этот реальный пример, сколько на идеальный, символически значимый образец; таким образцом послужил для них классический античный, и прежде всего греческий («гомеровский» и «пиндаровский») квантитативный стих.

Как известно, основная идея Тредиаковского заключалась в том, что он применил к русской метрике стопы классического стиха, заменив в них признак долготы признаком ударности гласного (вернее, обозначив ударные гласные как «долгие» и безударные как «краткие»). Тредиаковский реализовал свою идею в два этапа, которым соответствовали два издания его трактата «Новый и краткий способ к сложению Российских стихов с определениями до сего надлежащих званий» (1735 и 1752). В первом варианте он еще ищет компромисс, который обеспечил бы историческую преемственность с силлабической традицией. Лишь во втором, радикально переработанном издании, написанном после появления трактата и поэтических опытов Ломоносова, Тредиаковский более решительно заявил о силлабо-тонике как о принципиально новой системе и с пренебрежением отозвался о попытке «иностранца» (Кантемира) найти компромисс между двумя системами. Но даже в этой версии, более полно проникнутой пафосом коренной перестройки, Тредиаковский лишь спорадически дает почувствовать символический подтекст своего деяния;[6] в основном, он выдерживает свою прямую роль ученого филолога, оставаясь в рамках технических и историко-литературных проблем.

Иную позицию занимает с самого начала в своей реформаторской деятельности Ломоносов. Его теоретическое сочинение («Письмо о правилах Российского стихотворства», 1739), которым он сопроводил свою первую оду, исполнено мессианистического пафоса. Ломоносов трактует силлабическую метрику как знак уклонения от «истинного» античного образца, произошедшего в католическом мире. Соответственно, немецкий и новый русский стих изображается им как возрождение истинной античной традиции:

> Французы, которые во всем хотят натурально поступать, однако почти всегда противно своему намерению чинят, нам в том, что до стоп надлежит, примером быть не могут: понеже, надеясь на свою фантазию, а не на правила, толь криво и косо в своих стихах слова склеивают, что ни прозой, ни стихами назвать нельзя. <...> Неосновательное оное употребление, которое в Московские школы из Польши принесено, никакого нашему стихосложению закона и правил дать не может. <...>

Я не могу о том нарадоваться, что Российский наш язык не токмо бодростию и героическим звоном греческому, латинскому и немецкому не уступает, но подобную оным, а себе купно природную и свойственную версификацию иметь может.[7]

В чисто техническом отношении трактат Ломоносова, в сущности, лежал на линии, основное направление которой было уже намечено Тредиаковским. Полемика его с Тредиаковским касалась только частностей новой системы. Однако, в отличие от Тредиаковского, Ломоносов с полной отчетливостью и огромной энергией очертил символическую проекцию, стоявшую за реформой русского стиха. Реформа стихосложения была им возведена в ранг мессианистического культурного акта: русский стих освобождался от «ложного догмата» католического мира (разоблачаемого как продукт произвольной «фантазии») и, подобно немецкому стиху, возвращался к «правильному» устройству. Вся филологическая работа последовательно подчиняется этой идеальной цели. Даже периферийные технические новшества, относительно которых Ломоносов ведет полемику с Тредиаковским (в частности, вопрос о допущении чередующейся мужской и женской рифмы), диктуются стремлением максимально противопоставить русский стих французскому и польскому и сблизить его — реально с немецким, а в идеале с классическим образцом.[8]

Эта тема звучит еще сильнее в позднем филологическом сочинении Ломоносова — «Предисловии о пользе книг церковных в Российском языке» (1758), посвященном нормализации стилистической иерархии русского литературного языка. Важнейшей пружиной стилистической реформы Ломоносова является идея о том, что русский (разговорный, секулярный) и церковнославянский (книжный, сакральный) языковой материал образуют слитное и неразрывное целое. «Богатство», неоднородное единство этого целого признается его важнейшим качеством и служит основанием для иерархического расслоения языка на различные стили. То обстоятельство, что русский язык впитал в себя культуру церковных книг, делает его прямым наследником, и даже как бы новейшим воплощением, не только церковнославянского, но и греческого языка, и шире — античной классической культуры;[9] в идеальном образе последней, как он нарисован Ломоносовым, классическая древность сливается с временами первохристианства. В этом своем качестве русский язык отличается от языковой судьбы народов, употреблявших на протяжении столетий латынь в качестве своего культурного языка — то есть, прежде всего, от народов католического мира.

Отменная красота, важность и сила Эллинского слова коль высоко почитаются, о том довольно свидетельствуют словесных наук любители. На нем, кроме древних Гомеров, Пиндаров, Демосфенов и других в Эллинском языке героев, витийствовали великие христианския церкви учители и творцы, возвышая древнее красноречие высокими богословскими догматами и парением усердного пения к Богу. Ясно сие видеть можно вникнувшим в книги церковные на Славенском языке, коль много мы от переводу Ветхаго и Новаго Завета, поучений отеческих, духовных песней Дамаскиновых и других творцев канонов видим в Славенском языке греческого изобилия и оттуду умножаем довольство Российского слова, которое и собственным своим достатком велико и к приятию Греческих красот посредством Славенского сродно. <...>

Поляки, преклонясь издавна в католицкую веру, отправляют службу по своему обряду на Латинском языке, на котором их стихи и молитвы сочинены во времена варварские и по большей части от худых авторов, и потому ни от Греции, ни от Рима не могли снискать подобных преимуществ, каковы в нашем языке от Греческого приобретены. Немецкой язык по то время был убог, прост и бессилен, пока в служении употреблялся язык Латинской. Но как Немецкой народ стал священные книги читать и службу слушать на своем языке, тогда богатство его умножилось, и произошли искусные писатели. Напротив того, в католицких областях, где только одну латынь, и то варварскую, в служении употребляют, подобного успеха в чистоте Немецкого языка не находим.[10]

В мире символических ценностей, построенном Ломоносовым, «греческий» язык одновременно воплощает в себе абсолютную чистоту классических ценностей и первохристианства. Этот идеальный образ мыслится Ломоносовым в исторической и генетической непрерывности, от древнейших времен до современности: он симультанно включает в себя язык Гомера, классический древний греческий, язык Евангелий, язык византийских авторов, церковнославянский и, наконец, современный русский (реформированный) язык.[11]

Для Ломоносова — человека классического образования, пользовавшегося латынью (наряду с немецким языком) как средством международного научного общения, латинская культура не могла занимать чисто негативный ценностный полюс. Чтобы разрешить эту проблему в рамках своей дуалистической филологической модели, Ломоносов противопоставляет классическую и вульгарную латынь, характеризуя последнюю как язык «варварских времен» и «худых авторов». Первая принадлежит, вместе с греческим языком, к идеальному веку классической и первохристианской античности; вторая являет собой отклонение, произошедшее в католическом мире. В построенной Ломоносовым парадигме Греция и «истинный» Рим (Рим классических времен) противостоят ложной ново-римской традиции, основанной на вульгарной латыни и связанной с разделением православного и католического мира. Новейшее развитие литературного языка и стихосложения Ломоносов видит как освобождение от влияния этой позднейшей традиции и восстановление первоначальных абсолютных ценностей, то есть, в сущности, как акт, сходный с Реформацией. В этом состоит для него смысл параллели между русским и немецким языком и стихом.

Символическая мессианистическая аура, в которую облекалась филологическая реформа, способствовала тому, что последующая традиция закрепила в абсолютной, идеальной роли реформатора русского языка и стиха именно Ломоносова, а не Тредиаковского и не Сумарокова, которые нередко первыми приходили к тому, что в памяти последующих поколений безраздельно приписывалось Ломоносову. Тредиаковский и Сумароков действовали как ученый филолог и профессиональный литератор — Ломоносов выступал в своей деятельности и самосознании как культурный демиург, исполнитель сакральной миссии.[12] Этот подтекст сообщал деятельности Ломоносова значение не столько языковой и эстетической реформы, сколько «обновления», придавал ей бескомпромиссность и пафос, которым заряжалась последующая историческая традиция.

3. Формирование романтической философии истории и национального самосознания, возникновение романтического движения в литературе и полемика романтиков с адептами классицизма составляли основное содержание культурной жизни 1800–1820-х годов во всех странах Европы. В России и ход этой борьбы, и ее конечные результаты несли в себе ряд специфических черт; одним из факторов, определивших своеобразие русской культурной сцены в эту эпоху, явился идеальный образ Греции в ее отношении к современной русской культуре.

Французский классицизм XVII–XVIII веков апеллировал к условному образу античности, в котором специфические черты Греции и Рима, по сути дела, не дифференцировались. Но на рубеже XVIII — XIX вв. во Франции поднялась новая волна классицистического искусства, вызванная революцией; «героический классицизм» эпохи Республики и Империи нес на себе ярко выраженную *римскую* окраску. Эстетика Французской революции ориентировалась первоначально на суровую простоту и гражданственный пафос римско-республиканских символов, а впоследствии, в эпоху наполеоновского «ампира» — на монументальность имперского Рима.[13]

В 1810-е годы борьба младших последователей Карамзина против защитников классицизма наложилась на патриотические чувства, связанные с войной с Наполеоном и ниспровержением наполеоновской империи. В этом контексте «псевдоклассицизм», с которым вела борьбу русская «новая школа», осмыслялся как классицизм по преимуществу «римский». Последнее понятие объединяло в себе образ древнего Рима и французский классицизм, и в частности и в особенности, то его новейшее воплощение, которое он получил в эстетике наполеоновской эпохи. Этот «римский» классицизм получает трактовку как ложномонументальное искажение истинной классической традиции, носителем которой была Греция и современным воплощением которой выступает Россия, и одновременно — как «идолатрия» языческой (антихристианской, антиправославной) империи, которой противостоит апостольский мессианизм. В связи с этим, важным обертоном самосознания «новой школы» в 1810-е годы становится возрождение «греческого» классического элемента. Образ античной Греции, несмотря на его ярко выраженную «классичность», осмысляется как оружие в борьбе против «ложного» классицизма.

Характерным проявлением этой тенденции может служить история русского гекзаметра. Попытку ввести гекзаметр на русской почве предпринял еще Тредиаковский: эта попытка естественным образом вытекала из «греческого» характера нового русского стиха. Однако тот негативный образ, который закрепился за Тредиаковским в последующей культурной традиции, способствовал дискредитации всех его начинаний. До 1810-х годов гекзаметр осмыслялся как комически-неудачный эксперимент, «тредиаковщина». Адекватным воплощением высоких эпических жанров считался александрийский стих — вернее, его силлабо-тоническая адаптация (шестистопный ямб с цезурой). В 1807 году Н. И. Гнедич начинает свой перевод «Илиады», используя для этого александрийский стих. Однако к середине 1810-х годов ситуация изменилась. В журналах открылась дискуссия о русском гекзаметре. Его адептами, защищавшими гекзаметр и утверждавшими его преимущество перед александрийским стихом, были представители арзамасского круга — С. С. Уваров и А. Ф. Воейков.[14] Последний, в послании к Уварову, написанном гекзаметром («Вестник Европы», 1819, ч. 101), выразил настроение эпохи, связав утверждение нового размера с патриотически-воинственным духом, направленным против «галломании»:

Пусть говорят галломаны, что мы не имеем спондеев!
Мы их найдем, исчисляя подробно деяния Россов:
Галл, Перс, Прусс, Хин, Швед, Венгр, Турок, Сармат и Саксонец, —
Всех победили мы, всех мы спасли, и всех охраняем.

В 1811 году Гнедич начинает новый вариант перевода «Илиады», перейдя с александрийского стиха на гекзаметр; позднее Жуковский переводит гекзаметром «Одиссею». Когда в 1830 году Гнедич завершил свой перевод, Пушкин посвятил этому событию дистих, в котором в афористической форме была выражена идея о «воскрешении» гомеровской поэтической речи на русской почве: «Слышу умолкнувший звук божественной эллинской речи.// Старца великого тень чую смущенной душой».

Миф о «воскрешении» Гомера на русской почве развил впоследствии Гоголь в заметке по поводу перевода «Одиссеи» Жуковским (1846; включена в «Выбранные места из переписки с друзьями»). Гоголь рисует «Одиссею» как идеальный художественный синтез, который «захватывает весь древний мир» и служит «неиссякаемым колодцем» для всех поэтов нового времени. Однако в западной европейской культуре «Одиссея» была «забыта»; теперь (в полном соответствии со схемой диалектического синтеза) происходит возрождение этого произведения, наивысшим образом воплощающего в себе синтезирующую способность искусства, — возрождение на русском языке. Причина этого заключается в том, что только русский язык, в отличие от западноевропейских, способен воплотить в себе свойства «эллинской речи»:

Участь «Одиссеи» странна: в Европе ее не оценили; виной этого <...> недостаток [т.е. 'отсутствие' — Б.Г.] языка, в такой степени богатого и полного, на котором отразились бы все бесчисленные, неуловимые красоты как самого Гомера, так и вообще эллинской речи. <...> Теперь перевод первейшего поэтического творения производится на языке, полнейшем и богатейшем всех европейских языков.[15]

Таким образом, перевод Жуковского оказывается актом «воскресения» Гомера. Гоголь искусно обыгрывает ассоциации слова «воскресение», определяя язык русского Гомера как «слово живо». Слияние «истинной» античной (греческой) и «истинной» христианской (православной) традиции, сообщающее филологическим понятиям сакральную и мессианистическую ауру, воплощается Гоголем с такой же энергией на языке романтической (немецкой) эстетики, с какой это делал Ломоносов — на языке высокой ораторской (немецкой протестантской) традиции:

Вот скольким условиям нужно было выполниться, чтобы перевод «Одиссеи» вышел не рабская передача, но послышалось бы в нем *слово живо*, и вся Россия приняла бы Гомера, как родного! Зато вышло что-то чудное. Это не перевод, но скорей воссоздание, восстановление, воскресение Гомера. (Ibid., стр. 204–205; курсив Гоголя)

Другим проявлением «греческого фактора» в описываемую эпоху следует признать то выдающееся место, которое в поэтической культуре русского «Золотого века» заняла «анакреонтическая» струя. В 1820 г. Уваров опубликовал брошюру «О греческой антологии», к которой были приложены переводы греческих поэтов, выполненные Батюшковым. Это издание отразило интерес к классически окрашенному образу лирической поэзии, который был характерен для поэтов арзамасского круга. Во второй половине 1810-х и в 1820-х гг. данное направление получило яркое воплощение в поэзии Батюшкова, анакреонтических стихах Пушкина, любовной лирике молодого Баратынского и Языкова, творчестве Дельвига. Среди второстепенных явлений сходного характера, следует отметить таких поэтов, близких к арзамасскому кругу, как Д. В. Дашков, А. С. Норов, П. А. Плетнев.

В своей борьбе против архаистов, адепты карамзинской школы сознавали себя в такой же степени романтиками, как истинными, или эллинскими, классиками. Их символическим противником был не классицизм как таковой, но «имперский» классицизм: римско-французский по своему происхождению, напыщенно-монументальный по характеру. Эта новая окраска карамзинской школы существенно отличалась от ее первоначального направления в 1790–1800-е годы, для которого была характерна в первую очередь ориентация на французскую салонную культуру.[16] Римская империя в противопоставлении Греции и первохристианству, католицизм в противопоставлении православию (а также германскому протестантизму), наполеоновская Франция в противопоставлении России — все эти культурно-исторические символы выстраивались в единую парадигму, во многом определившую самосознание арзамасского круга в эту эпоху. В этой символической проекции, античная эллинская аура, окружавшая весь творческий образ Батюшкова, естественно соседствовала с германскими «оссиановскими» романтическими мотивами; германский (или англо-германский) по преимуществу облик музы Жуковского отнюдь не противоречил его культурной роли переводчика «Одиссеи»; Дельвиг наглядно воплощал в себе слияние античного духа, германского происхождения и русской культуры («Кто славянин молодой, грек духом, а родом германец?», — согласно поэтической формуле Пушкина); «байронизм» молодого Пушкина и Баратынского естественно сочетался с анакреонтическими тенденциями в их лирике; в творчестве Языкова сливались анакреонтические мотивы, русские фольклорные элементы и стилистика немецкой студенческой («буршевской») поэзии (Дерптский университет, где преподавал Воейков и учился Языков, получил в рамках этой мифологии наименование «северных Афин»).

В русской общественной жизни конца 1810 — начала 1820-х годов данный смысловой обертон приобретал еще один оттенок, связанный с официозным культом Александра, после победы его над Наполеоном и учреждения Священного Союза, как «Августа», осенившего вселенную «вечным миром». В этом контексте, анти-монументальная «греческая» направленность новой школы сополагалась с ее установкой на аристократическую обособленность и независимость поведения, салонную и кружковую замкнутость. В «античной» проекции, эти черты осмыслялись как нарочитый «провинциализм» (в масштабах империи) и «анакреонтическая» интимность. Книжка «О греческой антологии» была издана анонимно; в предисловии рукопись шутливо атрибуцировалась двум безымянным арзамасским жителям, чьи бумаги попали в руки «арзамасского трактирщика». Эта литературная игра полностью соответствовала духу «Общества арзамасских безвестных людей», в его противопоставлении помпезности «Беседы любителей русского слова».

В начале 1820-х гг. тема анти-имперского «провинциализма» получила дальнейшее развитие в той поэтической мифологии, которой Пушкин окружил образ своей бессарабской ссылки. Аналогия с судьбой Овидия позволяет ему строить свой образ как поэта, сосланного «Августом».[17] (В этом случае Овидий выступает на позитивном полюсе символических ценностей, вопреки своему «римскому» происхождению; основанием для такого осмысления служит тот факт, что Овидий оказывается жертвой римского императора).

Другой образной проекцией южной ссылки служит у Пушкина образ первоапостола, преследуемого гонениями со стороны империи; в этой проекции Александр получает наименование «Тиберия». Ожидание революции, которая ниспровергнет власть «Августа/Тиберия», образно оформляется как провозглашение Нового Завета, противостоящего власти языческого императора. Это настроение еще более усилилось с началом греческого восстания весной 1821 года, которое бурно переживалось в Бессарабии. Восстание Греции осмысляется одновременно как революционное ниспровержение деспотической империи, как восстановление славы античной Греции и как возрождение греческого православия.[18]

Характерным эпизодом, в котором отразился «эллинский» субстрат русской новой школы, явилось отношение Пушкина и его круга к поэзии Андре («Андрея») Шенье. Характерной чертой этого поэта, казненного в год якобинского террора, собрание стихов которого вышло в свет в 1819 году, была тесная связь всего его личностного и творческого облика с Грецией и духом греческой античности (мать Шенье была гречанка, греческий язык был его вторым родным языком, с детства он был воспитан на античной греческой поэзии). Проникнутые духом античной «гармонии», стихи Шенье были далеки как от духа современного ему неоклассицизма Французской революции, так и от устремлений новейших романтических школ посленаполеоновского времени. И сама греческая — подчеркнуто не римская, не «латинская» — аура, окружавшая облик Шенье, и факт его гибели в годы Французской революции, делали этого «классика» важным фактором в русском антиклассицистическом движении в той специфической ситуации, которая сложилась на русской культурной сцене после победы над Наполеоном. Поэзия Шенье являла собой воплощенный образ «другого» классицизма, принятие которого было для первого поколения русских романтиков так же важно, как и отрицание «ложного» классицизма.

Пушкин неоднократно обращался к образу Андре Шенье — в посвященной ему обширной элегии, многочисленных переложениях его стихов, неоконченной критической заметке, письмах.[19] В пушкинском символическом пантеоне противопоставление эллинского классицизма Шенье и ложноклассической монументальности приобретает особенную остроту в связи с тем, что оно олицетворяется в фигурах двух братьев — Андре и Мари Жозефа Шенье. Последний был автором популярнейших в 1790–1800-е годы неоклассических трагедий; предание приписывало ему роковую роль в аресте и гибели его брата. Пушкин неоднократно отзывается о М. Ж. Шенье и его творчестве с крайним презрением, а трагедию французского классицизма объявляет «самым неправдоподобным» из всех литературных жанров (заметка «О трагедии», 1825).

Таким образом, в поэтическом мире Пушкина начала 1820-х годов романтические и революционные темы и мотивы, типичные для европейской литературы нового времени, приобретают специфические оттенки, связанные с присутствием «греческого» начала. Байронический образ поэта-романтика, удаляющегося от людей (весьма близкий творческому самосознанию Пушкина периода Южных поэм) сочетается с чувством сродства с поэтом-классиком («истинным классиком»), павшим жертвой ложноклассической империи. Революционные устремления оформляются не в римско-республиканские символы, но в образы возрождающейся Греции (античной и православной) и первоапостольского Завета, противостоящего «идолатрии» вселенского императора.

Присутствие эллинистической струи в творчестве и самосознании Пушкина и его круга сыграло свою роль в том, что романтические тенденции, под знаком которых этот круг выступил на рубеже 1820-х годов, так и не развились с полной последовательностью. Поэтика «Золотого века» оказалась явлением смешанным по своему характеру: черты новейшей романтической школы сочетались в ней с салонной традицией прошлого века, антиклассицизм — с апелляцией к гармонической классичности; мессианистические революционные устремления облекались в «греческие» классические и христианские символы и противополагались «наполеоновскому» образу революционности; самосознание адептов «новой школы» сочеталось с идеей провинциализма, в символической проекции которой выступали образы апостольского братства и аристократически замкнутого кружка «немногих».

4. Мы видим, какую роль играл «греческий элемент» в том направлении, которое приняла карамзинская школа в 1810-20-е годы. Однако не меньшее значение имел эллинистический подтекст для движения оппонентов арзамасского круга в эту эпоху — младших архаистов.

Интересное явление в этом плане представляют собой эстетические взгляды Кюхельбекера, и в частности, та позиция, которую он занял в своей критике поэтов «новой школы» — Жуковского, Баратынского, Пушкина.

Еще в 1810-е годы Кюхельбекер-лицеист был увлечен идеями о «русском гекзаметре» и русском языке как наследнике греческого.[20] Позднее, в 1820 г., в рецензии на «Греческую антологию», он восторженно приветствовал переводы Батюшкова как акт «пересадки сих душистых, прекрасных греческих цветов на русскую землю».[21]

Переход Кюхельбекера на младо-архаистические позиции в начале 1820-х годов обратил его против поэзии арзамасского круга, но не изменил про-греческой (и анти-латинской) эстетической ориентации. В символическом образе «Греции» оказались изменены лишь смысловые акценты — изменены в таком направлении, которое позволило использовать этот образ для защиты традиций русского классицизма и в полемике против «элегической» поэзии арзамасцев.

Выше мы видели, что Ломоносов, очерчивая признаки высокого стиля, подчеркнул его связь с традицией торжественного пения — «парения усердного пения к Богу». В нарисованном им идеальном образе этой традиции в одном ряду выступали и гимнический стиль Пиндара, и поэтика псалмов, и византийское и церковнославянское витийство, и эстетика немецкого барокко века Реформации. За это отклонение от классицистического канона ясности и уравновешенности Ломоносова критиковал Сумароков, видевший в «пиитическом восторге» ломоносовских од варварскую невразумительность и отсутствие вкуса.[22] Эти своеобразные черты русской оды позволили впоследствии Державину назвать оду «лирическим жанром» («Рассуждение о лирической поэзии, или об оде», 1811–15). Державин, вслед за Ломоносовым, признает определяющей чертой одической поэтики высокое «пение», традицию которого он возводит к Пиндару. В этой проекции, греческий первоисточник русской оды в такой же мере противополагался латинской (горацианской) оде, в какой русский классицизм уклонялся от канона, кодифицированного в эстетике Буало.

Этот дуалистический подход к истории поэтических жанров энергично развивает Кюхельбекер в своей центральной критической статье «О направлении нашей поэзии, особенно лирической, в последнее десятилетие» (1824); статья вызвала широкий отклик в современной литературной жизни и оказала сильное (хотя и не прямое) влияние на Пушкина в его творческой эволюции в середине 1820-х гг.[23]

Взгляд Кюхельбекера на данный предмет отличается предельной решительностью. Во всей мировой поэзии он видит только одно принципиальное разделение — на поэзию «истинную» и «ложную»; такое разделение рассекает все традиционно сложившиеся границы между жанрами, литературными направлениями и эпохами. Неотъемлемым свойством истинной поэзии является «сила, свобода, вдохновение» (характерная формула «триединства», в подтексте которой Символ веры сливается с девизом Французской революции). Поэзию, удовлетворяющую этому условию, он называет «лирической», следуя в этом Державину, то есть понимая под лиризмом «парение» в смысле греко-русской оды:

Сила, свобода, вдохновение — необходимое свойство всякой поэзии. Лирическая поэзия вообще не иное что, как необыкновенное, то есть сильное, свободное, вдохновенное изложение чувств самого писателя. <...> Всем требованиям, которые предполагает сие определение, вполне удовлетворяет одна ода, а посему, без сомнения, занимает первое место в лирической поэзии, или, лучше сказать, одна совершенно заслуживает название поэзии лирической. (Кюхельбекер, стр. 454)

«Свобода» истинной, или лирической, поэзии означает отсутствие каких-либо барьеров и ограничений, пренебрежение искусственным единообразием, диктуемым «правилами». С другой стороны, атрибутами неистинной (или не лирической) поэзии является рассудочность и однообразие, которые ведут к «вялости» и поверхностной неискренности чувства. Прообразом такой поэзии для Кюхельбекера является прежде всего латинская (горацианская) элегия: ·

Элегия почти никогда не окрыляется, не ликует: она должна быть тиха, плавна, обдуманна. <...> Удел элегии — умеренность, посредственность (Горациева aurea mediocritas). (Ibid.)

Итак, мир античности последовательно разделяется на мир греческой и латинской поэзии: на «исполина между исполинами Гомера и — ученика его Виргилия; роскошного громкого Пиндара и — прозаического стихотворителя Горация» (стр. 458). Латинская традиция, в свою очередь, дает начало «ложному» французскому классицизму:

Родоначальники сей мнимой классической поэзии более римляне, нежели греки. Она изобилует стихотворцами — не поэтами. <...> Во Франции сие вялое племя долго господствовало. (Ibid., стр. 457)

Позитивной альтернативой «мнимому» французскому классицизму в европейской литературе нового времени для Кюхельбекера является Шекспир — этот излюбленный романтический символ художественной «свободы» и независимости от классицистического догмата. Подобно тому как «истинные классики» Гомер и Пиндар были противопоставлены Виргилию и Горацию, так Шекспир противостоит Вольтеру.

Из этого биполярного разделения всей мировой поэзии вытекает отношение Кюхельбекера к современной литературной сцене: отношение, которое может показаться противоречивым и парадоксальным, если не учитывать лежащую в его основе культурную модель. Противопоставление «романтиков» и «классиков», центральное для литературной борьбы этого времени как в Европе, так и в России, для Кюхельбекера фактически не существует; вернее, он использует эти наименования, но вкладывает в них содержание, весьма далекое от идеи двух борющихся литературных эпох. Историческая перспектива Кюхельбекера панхронична; идея исторической последовательности заменена в ней идеей тотального противостояния двух полярных ценностных систем, восходящих к Греции и Риму: «лирической» и «рассудочной» поэзии, «оды» и «элегии» (в обобщенном, эмблематическом понимании этих жанров), всеобъемлющего свободного «парения» — и ограниченного, стесненного шаблоном единообразия, полноты выражения национальной жизни — и «подражательной» универсальности.

С этой позиции Кюхельбекер равным образом отрицательно оценивает современных «ложных классиков» и «ложных романтиков». Под первыми он разумеет адептов неоклассицистической эстетики, разбуженной духом Французской революции, — таких как Шиллер. Под вторыми — представителей «унылой» или «неистовой» поэзии, которых он объединяет под родовым названием «элегических» поэтов; к ним равным образом относятся «неистовый» Байрон, «вялый» Ламартин, английские и немецкие представители «кладбищенского» романтизма, а также, конечно, их русские последователи, от Жуковского до Баратынского и (частично) Пушкина. И в той и в другой противоположной крайности Кюхельбекер видит односторонность, чуждую истинной «лирической» поэзии.

Позитивным противовесом «ложным классикам» и «ложным романтикам» для Кюхельбекера служат такие поэты, которые способны сочетать в равновесии классическое и романтическое начало; у которых устремленность к «высокому» не ведет к абстрактности и рационализму, а лирическое начало не обращается в индивидуалистическое «бешенство». Иначе говоря, это такие поэты, которые способны следовать линии Пиндара-Гомера, Данте-Шекспира, Ломоносова-Державина. Таких поэтов Кюхельбекер, как кажется, готов равным образом считать «истинными классиками» и «истинными романтиками». Эмфаза в его определениях и оценках явно лежит на «истинности» и «ложности», и потому различие между «классиками» и «романтиками» как бы стирается. Наивысшим примером такого синтезирующего поэта нового времени (истинного классика и романтика в одно и то же время) для Кюхельбекера служит Гете. На русской сцене он усматривает «великие надежды» в Пушкине — но тем строже предостерегает его от влияния «элегического направления». Пока же образцовым сочинением для него служит поэма П. А. Ширинского-Шихматова «Петр Великий», в которой он видит продолжение «пиндаровско-ломоносовской» традиции высокого «пения».[24]

Сходную перспективу во взгляде на «классиков» и «романтиков» выстраивает другой представитель младо-архаистического движения, также оказавший заметное влияние на Пушкина, — П. А. Катенин.[25] Цикл статей «Размышления и разборы», писавшийся Катениным во второй половине 1820-х годов (опубликованы в 1830 г.), также исходит из дуалистического противопоставления греческой и латинской поэтической традиции:

> Греки были прекраснейшим из народов; из этого естественно последовало превосходство их скульптуры и поэзии. <...> Римляне далеко не имели той врожденной склонности и способности к изящным искусствам, какими природа одарила греков. <...> Вся словесность латинская состоит из подражаний.[26]

«Естественное» совершенство греческого искусства, в его противопоставлении «подражательному» латинскому, становится изначальным символом, который Катенин, подобно Кюхельбекеру, кладет в основу как исторического обзора европейской поэзии, так и оценки современных литературных явлений. Для Кюхельбекера эпицентром его ценностной системы служил жанр оды и образ «Пиндара» и его последователей; для Катенина таким универсальным символом оказывается жанр эпической поэмы, олицетворенный в образе «Гомера», в его противоположении «Виргилию». Соответственно, говоря об исторических корнях современной европейской литературы, Катенин выдвигает на первое место не Шекспира, как это делал Кюхельбекер, а Данте (впрочем, оба этих эмблематических имени «родоначальников» литературы нового времени фигурируют у обоих критиков; различие состоит лишь в степени разработанности каждого из этих образов). Катенин трактует итальянский Ренессанс как освобождение от эстетического догмата римского «Золотого века» (в подтексте такого понимания лежит, конечно, и современный романтический образ Италии, в его противопоставлении наполеоновской Франции). В этой исторической перспективе, заслугой Данте оказывается освобождение от латинского стиха. Главное творение Данте как бы перешагивает через «Энеиду» Виргилия (которую Катенин оценивает как искусное подражание и переработку «Илиады» и «Одиссеи») и становится непосредственно рядом с Гомером:

> Данте определил место своего ада с таким же тщанием и точностью, как Гомер. <...> Виргилий, по моему мнению, далеко отстал <...> Говорят, что Виргилий списывал, что показывали посвящаемым в таинства: очень верю, но потому и дурно. («О поэзии Итальянской», *Размышления и разборы,* стр. 90, 91.)

В соответствии с логикой дуалистической модели, у Данте должна быть негативная антитеза; в этой роли у Катенина выступает Петрарка:

> Буде кто заслуживает имя классика в обидном значении слова — это Петрарка. Почтение его к древним, труды, предпринятые для отыскания и издания сокровенных дотоле рукописей, весьма похвальны; но страсть писать латинские стихи, точно как Виргилий, латинскую прозу слово в слово как Цицерон, пренебрежение к языку народному, уже прекрасному, <...> весьма предосудительны; надежда же его на восстановление Рима в виде республики, обладающей вселенною, <...> и потом собственное его испытание и производство в чин поэта, и венчание лавром на Капитолии доказывают, что голова его была не совсем здорова. <...> Петрарка <...> весь свой век играл роль, важничал и людей морочил; все его поездки, посольства, несносно длинные послания, заказная любовь отзываются мелким тщеславием и в привычку обращенным жеманством. (Ibid., стр. 95)

В этой тираде примечательна символическая насыщенность всех тех признаков, которыми Катенин наделяет создаваемый им негативный образ. Подражание латинским авторам (Виргилию и Цицерону); мечта о вселенском господстве Рима; наконец, иконографический образ поэта, увенчиваемого «лавром на Капитолии», — все эти знаки в совокупности ассоциируют фигуру Петрарки с Римом времен Цезаря — Августа. Петрарка назван классиком — но «в обидном значении слова»; это определение симультанно отсылает к образу римского и французского «ложного классицизма». И действительно, последняя часть суждения Катенина о Петрарке насыщена знаками, которые в романтической критике с почти эмблематической обязательностью связывались с образом Вольтера («игра», «мелкое тщеславие», «жеманство» и т.д.).[27] И наконец, указание на «похвальные», но малопродуктивные «труды», как кажется, отсылает к образу Тредиаковского, в качестве эмблемы «ложно-классического» направления на русской почве; в этой проекции, неспособность Петрарки оценить творение Данте и пренебрежение к обогащенному Данте «народному языку» потенциально указывают на «педантическое» непонимание Тредиаковским поэзии и языковой реформы Ломоносова.

Таким образом, Катенин, подобно Кюхельбекеру, мыслит борьбу направлений в современной литературе в терминах не «романтизма» и «классицизма», но «истинного» и «ложного» искусства. Катенин — более убежденный и последовательный «классик», чем Кюхельбекер. Он не признает «истинного романтизма» — романтизм для него существует лишь как отрицательное понятие. Однако это не делает Катенина автоматическим защитником классицизма. Филиппики этого «классика» против ложного классицизма полностью совпадают с романтической антиклассицистической критикой — и в выборе эмблематических фигур, служащих символом ложного «псевдо-классического» искусства (в античности — Вергилий и Гораций, в век классицизма — Вольтер,[28] на русской почве — Тредиаковский[29]), и в характере предъявляемых им обвинений («педантическое» непонимание живого искусства, подражательность, неискренность, «жеманная» холодность). Противопоставление «греческого» и «римского» начала выстраивается в панхроническую парадигму; понятие «старого» и «нового» утрачивает историческую, временную значимость, перекрываясь понятием «истинного» и «ложного» искусства. «Классик» Катенин говорит в один голос с «романтиками» в своих суждениях о «ложном классицизме»; но и в «новой школе» он видит *устарелое* «жеманство». Вообще, всякий ложный феномен в этой системе ценностей всегда оказывается одновременно и «новым» (в том смысле, что он уклоняется от изначального «естественно прекрасного» образца), и, вместе с тем, «устарелым» — в силу его подражательного характера.

Все рассмотренные выше концепции приходили к трактовке общепринятых эстетических категорий с позиций нарождающейся идеи русской культурно-исторической самобытности. Типично романтическая концепция национального духа претворяется на русской почве в идею «народности», которая естественным образом включала в себя «классический» элемент. Нарождающаяся русская национальная идея являет собой не только новейший этап в развитии мировой истории, но вместе с тем восстановление, или «воскрешение» древнейшего гармонического идеала. Эта модель объединяла различные, нередко сталкивавшиеся между собой явления в русской культуре 1820-х годов. Ее след виден и в поисках путей, по которым должна идти «истинная» новая поэзия, и в культурно-исторических и эстетических идеях любомудров (И. В. Киреевского, В. И. Одоевского и др.[30]). Во всех этих случаях, истинная, или гармоническая классика оказывалась необходимым компонентом в развитии национальной культуры (в романтическом ее понимании). В учении любомудров немецкая романтическая философия истории, апелляция к русским национальным традициям и классическая ориентация сочетались с такой же легкостью, как в анакреонтической поэзии Батюшкова — Дельвига — Языкова или в историко-эстетических построениях Кюхельбекера.

Прямой антитезой философии национальной самобытности России
явилась в 1820–30-е годы историко-культурная концепция П. Я. Чаадаева. Чаадаев трактует русскую «самобытность» как величайшее зло —
результат исторической обособленности России от «христианского
мира» Западной Европы (духовно объединенного вокруг Рима), неизбеж-
ным следствием которого должен стать тупик и «небытие». Мысль
Чаадаева диаметрально противоположна идеям Кюхельбекера и Катенина, Киреевского и Аксаковых, Пушкина 1830-х годов и Гоголя —
всем тем, кто разными путями и в различной степени приходил к ро-
мантически окрашенной историко-философской и эстетической идее
«народности». Однако эта мысль апеллирует к тому же культурно-
историческому субстрату, использует те же символы — придавая им
противоположный ценностный знак.

Ценностная система Чаадаева организуется вокруг тех же полярных
категорий, которые разрабатывались и применялись его оппонентами.
Ее позитивным идеалом является «единство»; уделом негативного полюса является разорванность и обособленность, и как следствие этого —
«пустота», отсутствие «силы и энергии», статичность (неспособность к
развитию), «тусклое и мрачное» однообразие, и в то же время неуравно-
вешенность («хаотическое брожение»). Разумеется, в этом случае носителем негативного начала выступает Россия, обобщенный образ которой
Чаадаев рисует в первом из своих «Философических писем» при помощи
всех приведенных выше определений.[31]

Чаадаев полностью сохраняет идею о противоположности Греции и
Рима (и преемственности этого противоположения от античной эпохи к
христианскому миру), на основе которой формировалась «почвенниче-
ская» философия и эстетика. У Чаадаева, как и у его оппонентов, Россия
выступает наследницей античной и христианской Греции, в ее противоположении античному и христианскому Риму, — но только в этом случае
данное обстоятельство ведет к негативному результату, поскольку Рим
и латинский язык являют собой символ «единства» западного христианства:

> Все европейские народы шли вперед в веках рука об руку; <...> Вспом-
> ните, что в течение пятнадцати веков у них был один язык для обраще-
> ния к Богу, одна духовная власть и одно убеждение. (стр. 120–121)

Чаадаев настаивает на единстве романского и германского мира, скре-
пленного Священной Римской империей. Духовным символом этого
единства для него служит собор Святого Петра, в архитектуре кото-

рого он усматривает ближайшее родство с готикой (письмо Четвертое; стр. 174).

В противоположность этому, Россия разделила с Византией удел «отпадения» от единства:

> Повинуясь нашей злой судьбе, мы обратились к жалкой, глубоко презираемой этими народами Византии <...> Волею одного честолюбца, эта семья народов только что была отторгнута от всемирного братства, и мы восприняли, следовательно, идею, искаженную человеческою страстью. (стр. 118)

Это противоположение проецируется затем в античную эпоху. Здесь также, античная Греция выступает в качестве негативного начала. Основанием к этому для Чаадаева служит тот самый феномен, в котором его оппоненты усматривали корень позитивного начала, — тот факт, что Греция является родиной наивысших достижений искусства: «Вы знаете, что искусство сделалось одной из величайших идей человеческого ума благодаря грекам. Посмотрим же, в чем состоит это великолепное создание их гения» (письмо Третье; стр. 156). В искусстве Чаадаев усматривает перевес материального над духовным, приводящий к «извращению законного порядка», «хаотическому смешению всех нравственных элементов». Размышляя об идеальном будущем, Чаадаев рисует его как время, когда «своего рода бесчестие покроет, может быть, великое имя Гомера», «могучие умы не дадут себя увлечь чувственным внушениям Платона», и слава Греции померкнет «почти совсем» (стр. 133, 136). Среди современников Чаадаева, Гомер чаще всего выступает в качестве наивысшего воплощения позитивного образа Греции; соответственно, у Чаадаева Гомер оказывается корнем мирового зла — «Тифоном и Ариманом», наследие которого перешло на русскую почву:

> <...> гибельный героизм страстей, грязный идеал красоты, необузданное пристрастие к земле, — все это заимствовано нами у него. <...> Мы учимся жить не у народов, описанных Цезарем и Тацитом, а у тех, которые составляли мир Гомера. (стр. 168–169)

«Органический» и «пластический» идеал, воплощенный в Гомере и Платоне, предстает у Чаадаева в травестийном виде, оборачиваясь своей негативной стороной. Соответственно, «римское» начало становится положительной альтернативой; воплощенный в именах «Цезаря и Тацита», римский «рационализм» (негативной эмблемой которого для адептов идеи «народности» служили Цицерон, Виргилий, Гораций) предстает в позитивном ракурсе.

Выше мы видели, что перевод Гомера на русский язык, возникновение «любомудрия» и т.п. трактовались как знаки «пересадки» и «возрождения» духа Греции на русской почве. Чаадаев разделяет идею «пересадки», но трактует ее в негативную сторону. Для этой цели он находит свой собственный, негативно окрашенный словесный символ: Москва, в качестве места отправления «Писем», получает греческое наименование Nécropolis.

Одним из важнейших атрибутов позитивного полюса в дуалистической культурной модели является его «изначальный», и следовательно более «древний» характер; негативный полюс всегда предстает в виде антитезиса, как результат позднейшего «искажения» и «подражания». У адептов почвеннического направления эта схема естественным образом воплощалась в указании на вторичность римского, и вслед за ним французского классицистического искусства по отношению к изначальному греческому идеалу. Совершенная Чаадаевым инверсия символических ролей лишила его этого аргумента, но не отменила необходимости возвести позитивный полюс к изначальному «корню». Чаадаев разрешает эту дилемму тем, что сополагает «римско-тевтонский» мир с древне-египетской культурой. В письме Четвертом («О зодчестве») он говорит о египетской архитектуре как «несомненно старейшей в мире». Выработанный ею пирамидальный тип противоположен горизонтальной симметрии греческого храма, но родственен готической архитектуре (к которой, как мы уже упоминали, Чаадаев присоединяет — не без некоторого замешательства — и собор св. Петра):

> В греческом стиле <...> вы откроете чувство оседлости, домовитости, привязанности к земле и ее утехам, в египетском и готическом — монументальность, мысль, порыв к небу и его блаженству. <...> С полным правом можно утверждать, что египетские памятники содержат в себе первообразы архитектонической красоты и первые элементы искусства вообще. Таким образом, египетское искусство и готическое искусство действительно стоят на обоих концах пути, пройденного человечеством. (стр. 173)

Греция теряет, вместе с позитивным статусом, свое изначальное положение на исторической шкале и превращается в антитезис по отношению к египетскому «первообразу красоты»; соответственно, роль «синтеза» переходит к романо-германскому миру, представленному, конечно, не своей негативной эмблемой (французский классицизм), но позитивной эмблемой (готика). Все те качества «римского» мира, которые, в их негативном эмблематическом воплощении, представали как средоточие отрицательного начала, предстают теперь, в позитивном своем воплощении, в противоположном свете: монументальность из символа статичности превращается в образ величия (устремленности к небу), рационализм превращается в «мысль», и т. д. И напротив, традиционные черты символического образа Греции оборачиваются негативной стороной: «органичность» предстает как бездуховность («привязанность к земле и ее утехам»), пластичность и гармония — как господство чувственного начала над мыслью, естественность и анти-монументальность — как мещанская «домовитость». Символы, в которых воплощается «русская идея» (в ее историко-философском и эстетическом смысле), как будто предстают у Чаадаева в другом освещении и ракурсе, — но и сами эти символы, и связанная с ними система ценностей остаются все те же. Полная противоположность выводов и оценок, к которым приходит Чаадаев и его оппоненты, лишь оттеняет общность символической системы, лежащей в основе их философских и эстетических взглядов, — системы, центральным стержнем которой является противопоставление «Греции» и «Рима».

5. Проведенный обзор различных явлений русской эстетической и философской мысли 1820-х годов показывает, что образы «русской Греции» и «русского Рима» выступают в качестве символической реальности, соответствие которой реальности культурно-исторической сохраняется лишь в той степени, в какой это служит взглядам и целям пишущих. Как всякий образ, эти концепты отличаются подвижностью, летучестью границ и ракурсов; они далеки от чисто «географического» (или исторического) буквализма. Сталкиваясь с феноменом, историческая принадлежность которого не соответствует его сущностной оценке, пишущие стремятся обойти это противоречие с помощью тех или иных переносов буквального значения

Так, образ Аристотеля, как правило, не вызывает симпатий у людей романтического века. Поэтому адепты «русской Греции» зачастую наделяют Аристотеля «римскими» чертами, в силу тесной связи его имени с средневековой схоластикой; с другой стороны, Чаадаев с удовольствием упоминает Аристотеля в числе греческих лже-мудрецов и предсказывает, что в идеальном будущем имя Стагирита «будет произноситься не иначе, как с известным омерзением» (Чаадаев, стр. 133).

Безоговорочно осуждая «мнимый» классицизм, многие авторы предпочитают ссылаться на имена Вольтера, Буало, либо второстепенных авторов — но при этом стремятся переместить из негативного эпицентра Расина. Так, Кюхельбекер оправдывает Расина тем, что он подчинялся рационалистическому догмату против воли, вопреки своему «гармоническому» поэтическому инстинкту. Весьма характерно также следующее высказывание Пушкина по поводу автора «Федры»:

> Кстати о гадости — читал я «Федру» Лобанова — хотел писать на нее критику, не ради Лобанова, а ради маркиза Расина — перо вывалилось из рук. <...> «Voulez-vous découvrir la trace de ses pas» — «надеешься найти Тезея жаркой след иль темные пути» — мать его в рифму! вот как все переведено. А чем же и держится Иван Иванович Расин, как не стихами, полными смысла, точности и гармонии! (Письмо к Л. С. Пушкину, январь-февраль 1824, Пушкин, т. 10, стр. 80)

Характерна в этой филиппике шутливая «руссификация» Расина; этот риторический прием, в сочетании с «греческой» аурой его трагедии, служит должным фоном для оценки Расина как воплощения «гармонии». В этом контексте, монументально-неуклюжий архаистический русский перевод осмысляется как «мнимая» трагедия («Федра Лобанова»). Не менее характерным образом подчеркнут аристократизм «маркиза» Расина — с подразумеваемым противопоставлением неоклассическому «республиканизму».

Аналогичным образом, в позитивном образе А. Шенье подчеркивается тот факт, что он «погиб жертвою Французской революции» (Пушкин, неоконченная заметка «Об Андрее Шенье») и его греческое происхождение; самое имя его подается в заметке и стихах Пушкина в «греко-русской», а не французской огласовке.

В стихотворении «Андрей Шенье» Пушкин прибег к специальному риторическому приему, позволившему поставить рядом образы Шенье и Расина. В примечаниях к стихотворению он цитирует свидетельство, согласно которому Шенье и его друг в последние минуты перед казнью читали друг другу Расина:

> «Racine fut l'objet de leur entretien et de leur dernière admiration. Ils voulurent réciter ses vers. Ils choisirent la première scène d'Andromaque». (Пушкин, т. 10, стр. 264)

«Маркиз Расин» как бы оказывается союзником поэта, казнимого Республикой, воплощающей в себе дух «римского» классицизма.

Сама настойчивость, с которой различные авторы стремятся адаптировать реальность к своим критическим построениям, перекраивая «буквальные» факты при помощи более или менее сложных риторических приемов, показывает, в какой степени их историческое ви́дение нуждается в перспективе, задаваемой оппозицией «Греции» и «Рима». Идеальный образ «Эллады» варьируется под пером разных авторов, в нем акценти-руются различные имена и признаки; эмблематическим воплощением этого образа становится то «всеобъемлющий» Гомер, то «парящий» Пиндар, то анти-монументальная и непретенциозная в своей «гармонич-ности» анакреонтическая лирика, то «динамичная» греческая скульпту-ра,[32] то периклавы Афины с их Академией и народным собранием. Но все эти конфигурации в совокупности образуют парадигму признаков, притя-гивающихся к ценностному полюсу органичного, свободного (сложного по своему составу), нескованного догмой «единства».

Не будет преувеличением сказать, что в эпоху 1810–30-х годов — эпоху, имевшую первостепенное значение для становления русской литературы и национального самосознания, — противопоставление «греческого» и «римского» начала играло более важную роль, чем различия между «классиками» и «романтиками», адептами «старого» и «нового» в лите-ратуре и языке, консервативными и радикальными политическими иде-ями, наконец, между почвенническим патриотизмом и просвещенным космополитизмом. Различные деятели этой эпохи, в своем стремлении сформулировать собственные идеи и оспорить оппонента, то и дело апеллировали к конвенциональным понятиям, широко известным из по-литических и литературных дебатов на европейской сцене. Но содер-жание этих понятий пересекалось и перекрывалось стоявшей за ними дуалистической проекцией, которая ко всем этим понятиям, в сущности, не имела прямого отношения. Внешним предметом споров служила кон-фронтация эстетических и политических эпох, борьба «старины» и «но-визны» — весь арсенал ценностей, в которых на европейской сцене осмы-слялся перелом XVIII и XIX века. Но эти исторические конфликты пере-водились на язык символов, имевших принципиально внеисторическое, универсальное, вневременное значение.

Характерной особенностью культурного мифа о «русской Греции» яв-ляется его чуждость идее исторического прогресса в смысле поступатель-ного движения во времени. Возрождение «греческого начала» знаменует собой одновременно и движение к новой цели, и возвращение к пер-воисточнику, освобождение его от позднейших наслоений. Актуальные проблемы трансформируются в панхронические символы, исторический конфликт преображается в утопическое устремление к всеобъемлющему «синтезу», будущее проецируется как возрождение изначального идеала.

Движение, окрашенное этим культурным обертоном, сочетает в себе мессианистическую устремленность и ретроспективность, самосознание первооткрывателей и нарочитую провинциальность. Общепринятые категории «старого» и «нового» (в эстетике, в отношении к языку, в сфере политических идей) переплетаются, смешиваются в амальгаму, в которой всякий «истинно» новый феномен по необходимости заключает в себе черты «истинной» старины. Апелляция к символическому образу Греции рассекает традиционные границы «архаистических» и «новаторских» литературных и политических партий, придавая их взаимодействию и борьбе сложный, смешанный характер. В этой культурной амальгаме становятся возможны духовные схождения и расхождения, на первый взгляд полностью противоречащие логике сложившихся партий и идеологических позиций. Эта неоднородность идеологической и культурной сцены, фузия и трансформация многих общеизвестных в европейском контексте (и усваиваемых на русской почве) категорий представляется важнейшим фактором, который необходимо иметь в виду при изучении истории русской культуры первой трети XIX столетия.

6. В заключение, в качестве послесловия, укажем некоторые важные смысловые линии, по которым парадигма «русской Греции» развивалась в последующие эпохи в истории русской филологической мысли.

Идея о русском языке как продолжении греческого получила своеобразное развитие во второй половине XIX века в трудах филологов и теоретиков грамматики почвеннического направления, более или менее тесно связанных с славянофильской идеологией. Одной из центральных тем «славянофильской лингвистики» 1850–70-х гг. (в лице таких ее представителей как К. С. Аксаков, В. И. Даль, Н. П. Некрасов и другие) становится стремление освободить русскую грамматику (а в конечном счете, и сам язык, этой грамматикой описываемый) от диктата «ложных» догм, противоречащих внутренней сущности русского языка. Под последними понималась римская и средневековая грамматическая традиция, возникшая из практики описания латинского языка, и ее новейшее воплощение — западноевропейская (прежде всего немецкая) лингвистика. Аргументы филологов славянофильского направления строились на идее о том, что по своему строю русский язык резко отличается от структуры латинского и западноевропейских языков, применительно к которой был разработан общепринятый канон грамматического описания. Такие черты русского языка, как исключительная свобода в употреблении временных форм, наличие категории вида, обилие частиц, широкое распространение бессубъектных (безличных) предложений, служили основным материалом, на котором основывалась данная аргументация.[33] В ряде случаев, лингвисты-славянофилы апеллировали к строю древнегреческого языка и к первым греческим грамматикам как к альтернативной модели, противопоставляя ее латинско-немецкому канону (Ф. Корш, Некрасов, Н. Богородицкий).

Интересным продолжением этого направления явилась книга Антонина Добиаша (чешского филолога, бывшего профессором в Киеве) «Синтаксис Аполлония Дискола» (1891). Добиаш отвергает идею о том, что грамматический субъект и предикат образуют вместе ядро предложения, как позднейшее искажение античной грамматической мысли на позднеримской почве. В его интерпретации, грамматика Дискола (I в.) исходит из глагола как центрального компонента, на котором основывается построение предложения; этот «динамический» (подчеркивающий роль глагола) подход был впоследствии вытеснен латинским (присциановским) каноном, согласно которому центром предложения объявлялось — по образцу логического суждения — соединение субъекта и предиката. Опираясь на авторитет Дискола, Добиаш отвергает эту логизированную модель и объявляет субъект переменным (необязательным) компонентом предложения. Исходя из этого, он предлагает разделить все предложения на два разряда: предложения имеющие два главных члена либо только один главный член (предикат). Добиаш особо подчеркивает удобство такого подхода для описания славянских языков, в силу изобилия у последних различных типов бессубъектных предложений. Эта идея получила впоследствии реализацию в монументальном «Синтаксисе русского языка» А. А. Шахматова (1910-е гг.; первое изд.: 1926–27), влияние которого в значительной мере сохраняется и в современных грамматиках русского языка. Все описание русского синтаксиса у Шахматова строится на центральном противопоставлении «односоставных» и «двусоставных» предложений.

Другой важнейший культурный очаг, для которого парадигма «русской Греции» имела существенное значение, связан с эпохой символизма и постсимволизма.

В эту эпоху романтический образ Греции как страны идеальной гармонии — образ «открытый» Винкельманом и разработанный в романтической философии и эстетике — сменяется модернистическим образом Греции, «открытым» Ницше и включившим в себя стихийное, «дионисийское» начало. В эстетике и культурной философии русских символистов традиционная идея «эллинизма» русской культуры вбирает в себя этот новый аспект; это позволяет по-новому высветить противопоставление России западному («латинскому») миру. В мире символических ценностей русского модернизма, латинизированный Запад по-прежнему выступает в качестве рационалистического, статичного, бесплодно-догматического начала; но этому негативному полюсу противостоит теперь не абсолютная «гармония», а сочетание гармонии и стихийности, порядка и хаоса, созидательной и разрушительной силы. Идея «богатого», или неоднородного единства как необходимого условия истинно творческого начала приобретает значительно более острый характер, по сравнению с романтической эпохой; то, что для Гоголя и Киреевского было всеобъемлющим синтезом, становится для В. Иванова и А. Белого ареной катастрофической борьбы контрастных сил. Эстетической эмблемой этого нового концепта оказывается не Гомер или Пиндар, не греческая статуя, — но греческая трагедия и музыка. «Камням» Рима противостоит «музыка» дионисийских мистерий и трагедийного хора (своеобразная новая реализация знаменитого определения архитектуры как «застывшей музыки», принадлежащего Гете), «римскому» пафосу церковного строительства — «варварское» восточное христианство, вместившее в себя языческий элемент (последний фактор определил интерес символистов к народной религиозности, к старообрядчеству и сектам).

В рамках настоящей статьи нет возможности, да и необходимости описывать всю ту концептуальную и образную инфраструктуру, в которую реализовались намеченные выше основные категории в культуре 1900–1910-х гг. Я ограничусь лишь единичными примерами, из сферы эстетических теорий и литературного творчества.[34]

Идея «русской Греции», в символистическом ее выражении, получила развернутое воплощение в романе А. Белого «Серебряный голубь» (1909). Герой романа видит Россию в образе, в котором проступает его греческий первоисточник-прототип:

> <...> снилось ему, будто в глубине родного ему народа бьется народу родная и еще не пережитая старинная старина — древняя Греция. Новый он видел свет, свет еще и в свершении в жизни обрядов греко-российской церкви. В православии, и в отсталых именно понятьях православного (то есть, по его мнению, язычествующего) мужичка видел он новый светоч в Мире грядущего Грека. (Гл. Третья, «Кто же Дарьяльский?»)

И родство (или, вернее, родственный симбиоз) России и Греции, и непрерывность православной традиции как важнейший параметр этого родства, — все это темы, уходящие глубоко в историю русской культурно-исторической мысли XIX и XVIII столетий. Однако Белый находит новый поворот традиционной идеи, высвечивая в идиллическом образе Греции ницшеанский компонент. Образ Греции вмещает в себя и картины «блаженной жизни райской, кущ тенистых, и медвяных лугов легковейных с играми на них и плясками хоровыми» (их воплощением служит для Дарьяльского идиллия Феокрита) — и «серные бездны, выпускающие злую саранчу»; «божественная эллинская речь» оказывается одновременно «магией и медом» (Гл. Третья, «Две»); «обряды греко-российской» церкви оказываются неотделимы от «язычествующего» начала народной религиозности и сектантства. Этот новый образ «единства» (единства не гармонически-синтезирующего, но взрывчатого и конфликтного) противостоит искусственному, «кукольному», плоско-рационалистическому миру, к которому принадлежит невеста Дарьяльского; эмблемой этого последнего, вполне предсказуемым образом, оказывается французский классицизм и век Просвещения:

> И иные здесь были портреты: екатерининская фрейлина с собачкой на подушке и с бриллиантовым шифром на плече, пейзаж с объясненьем в любви и с низко повисшей радугой, над которой Амур розовую пролил гирлянду; были и горы, каких нет в Гуголеве, и развалины замков; <...> тут был и шкаф, резной, неизвестно откуда попавший; из пыльного стекла тускло мрачными — Флориан, Поп, Дидерот, и отсыревшие корешки Эккартгаузена — «Ключ к объяснению тайн природы». Катя стояла, склонясь над роялью с томиком Расина в руках; она воспитывалась на французских классиках. (Гл. Третья, «Катя»)

Одним из главных создателей модернистического образа «русской Греции» выступил в 1900-е годы Вяч. Иванов. Он обосновывал особую близость современной русской духовности к дионисийской стихии, используя аргументы, представлявшие собой своеобразное продолжение традиционного тезиса о «генетической» связи России и Греции. Иванов подчеркивал «фракийское» происхождение Диониса — в противоположность чисто «эллинскому» характеру Аполлона; это обстоятельство, по Иванову, делало Диониса божеством, изначально принадлежащим к славяно-балканскому миру:

> Великая стихия не-эллинства, варварства, живет отдельною жизнью рядом с миром стихии эллинской. Оба мира относятся один к другому, <...> как Аполлон и Дионис — фракийский бог Забалканья, претворенный, пластически выявленный и укрощенный, обезвреженный эллинами, но все же самою стихией своей — наш, варварский, наш, славянский, бог.[35]

Идея «русской Греции» приобретает здесь самое крайнее выражение: своим дионисийским компонентом Греция оказывается обязана праславянскому миру «Забалканья». «Пластический» образ Греции, идеализированный романтиками, перемещается на негативный полюс, в качестве выхолощенного антитезиса; образ «эллинизированной» Греции как бы сливается с Римом, в его противопоставлении архаическому «дионисийскому» миру, который оказывается пра-греческим и пра-славянским в одно и то же время. В проекции русской истории, это смещение смысловых акцентов получает воплощение в символистическом образе Петербурга. В качестве «города Петра», символизирующего «строительное» начало, Петербург воплощает в себе идею Рима. Однако вместе с тем, в качестве «города Александра» (Пушкина)[36], Петербург оказывается новой «Александрией», то есть воплощает в себе идею «эллинизма». В обоих этих качествах, Петербург взрывается вырвавшимися на поверхность силами первозданного хаоса («Петербург» А. Белого).

На рубеже 1910-х годов этим идеям противостоял круг «Аполлона», из которого кристаллизовалось акмеистическое движение. В этом случае, как и в рассматривавшейся выше полемике 1820-х годов, оппоненты использовали ту же систему образов, придавая им, однако, противоположный ценностный знак. Образ Петербурга как «Александрии» и связанный с ним эллинистический облик петербургской культуры формируется в качестве позитивного концепта, играющего значительную роль в поэтической мифологии Кузмина, Анненского и ранних акмеистов. У Кузмина, в его полемике с Ивановым, «латинское» и «эллинистическое» начало сливаются в качестве позитивного идеала. В программной статье «О прекрасной ясности» («Аполлон», январь 1910) Кузмин рисует эстетический идеал «кларизма» в образе «маяков», которым угрожает «нашествие варваров» и «напор разрушительного прибоя» (стр. 5, — весьма прозрачная аллюзия Римской империи, с одной стороны, и мифологии петербургского наводнения и «Медного всадника», с другой). В последующем развертывании своего тезиса Кузмин прямо (и с откровенным вызовом) связывает свой идеал с «романским» и «латинским» локусом:

> <...> колыбелью новеллы и романа были романские страны, где более, чем где бы то ни было, развит *аполлонический* взгляд на искусство: разделяющий, формирующий, точный и стройный. И образцы рассказа и романа <...> нужно искать, конечно, в латинских землях. (стр. 7; выделено Кузминым)

Следующий закономерный этап в развитии этой культурной мифологии явили собой статьи Мандельштама 1910-х гг. Для понимания позиции

Мандельштама следует иметь в виду, что хотя номинально он выступает как адепт акмеистической школы (и значит, оппонент символистов), создаваемая им система образов-концептов оказывается, скорее, «пост-акмеистическим» синтезом, в котором обе противоположные системы сливаются в единое целое.

Мандельштам сохраняет усвоенный у Белого «романский» образ века Просвещения, в котором «кукольная» искусственность рококо соединена с сухим рационализмом философии, эстетики и морали XVIII столетия. Эти свойства эпохи недвусмысленно объясняются утратой связи с «подлинной» (греческой) античностью и с господством «римского» начала; последнее выступает во всей своей исторической непрерывности — от античного Рима, через век схоластики к французскому классицизму и Просвещению:

> Восемнадцатый век похож на озеро с высохшим дном: ни глубины, ни влаги, — все подводное оказалось на поверхности. <...> Этот век, который вынужден был ходить по морскому дну как по паркету <...> XVIII век утратил прямую связь с нравственным сознанием античного мира. Золотой шар уже не звучал сам по себе. Из него извлекали звуки исхищренными приемами, соображеньями о пользе приятного и о приятности полезного. Опустошенное сознание никак не могло выкормить идею долга, и она явилась в образе «la Vertu romaine», более подходящей для поддержания плохих трагедий, чем для управления душевной жизнью человека. Да, связь с античностью подлинной для XVIII века была потеряна, и гораздо сильнее была связь с омертвевшими формами схоластической казуистики, так что век Разума является прямым наследником схоластики. («Заметки о Шенье»)[37]

А. Шенье изображен «беглецом» из этого бесплодного мира, в поэзии которого обнаруживается «предчувствие девятнадцатого века» (то есть, века романтизма). Характерно, что Мандельштам избрал в качестве эмблематической фигуры поэта, образ которого, как мы видели выше, играл значительную роль в творческой эволюции Пушкина и нащупывании принципов «истинного романтизма» в русской литературной жизни 1820-х гг. Заметка Мандельштама (задуманная и, быть может, вчерне написанная в середине 1910-х гг., опубликованная в 1928 г.) явила собой пример связи «через столетие» с пушкинской эпохой, составлявшей важную черту творческого самосознания «Серебряного века».

Итак, мир романской «ясности» оказывается на негативном полюсе — в этом Мандельштам следует Белому и Иванову и расходится с Кузминым. С символизмом его сближает также мотив включения в образ Греции дионисийского начала. Данный мотив с особенной явственностью проявился в статье «Пушкин и Скрябин» (1915?). Скрябин выступает в качестве воплощения «русского эллинства» в его модернистическом, дионисийском воплощении:

> Огромная ценность Скрябина для России и для христианства обусловлена тем, что он *безумствующий эллин*. Через него Эллада породнилась с русскими раскольниками, сожигавшими себя в гробах. («Пушкин и Скрябин», стр. 314; курсив Мандельштама)

В полифонизме и атональности музыки Скрябина «возродился» дух античного трагедийного хора и архаических (античных и средневековых) ладов. Этот новый синтез перешагнул, как через антитезис, через век европейской «чистой» музыки, построенной на принципах гармонии и инструментального интонирования. «Строительное» начало симфонической музыки и ее абстрактность представлены в образе «белого мрамора» — этом иконографическом символе римской скульптуры и «имперской» архитектуры. Гармония Девятой симфонии определяется как «католическая радость Бетховена»; она символизирует собой торжество римско-католического начала — «белый мрамор синайской славы». Музыка Скрябина означает конец «католической» эпохи и возвращает в мир архаический симбиоз язычества и раннего христианства.

Однако Мандельштам не просто следует символистскому образу «дионисийской» Греции-России. Одновременно с этим, он в полной мере сохраняет позитивный образ классической Греции («эллинизма») и его проекции в петербургскую культуру, разработанный кругом «Аполлона». Две противоположные версии «русской Греции», служившие орудием в полемике символистов и акмеистов, сочетаются у Мандельштама в качестве двух взаимнонеобходимых компонентов синтеза.

Для Иванова и Белого стихийное начало выступало в качестве архаического пра-мира, который лишь позднее оказывается «приручен» (по Иванову, выхолощен) окультуривающей работой эллинизма. Мандельштам, для того чтобы вернуть образу гармонической «Эллады» позитивную ценность, совершает хронологическую инверсию этот системы. Он возвращается к романтической идее «эллинства» как царства изначальной гармонии; этот «гомеровский» мир получает затем «оплодотворение» стихийным началом, воплощенным в греческой трагедии. Образ Эллады движется не от дионисийских мистерий и Эсхила — к перикловым Афинам и Александрии, как это было у символистов, но в противоположном направлении: от Гомера — к последующему пробуждению дионисийского духа в трагедии. Такой прием позволяет сохранить романтический идеальный образ Эллады, и в то же время включить в него модернистический компонент. «Золотой» и «Серебряный» век, акмеизм и символизм, «Аполлон» и «башня» Иванова, эллинизированный образ Петербурга и Царского села и дух русской революции и «раскольников, сожигающих себя в гробах» не противостоят и не отрицают друг друга, но находят свое закономерное соотношение в этой синтезирующей системе образов-символов. Более того, этот прием позволяет Мандельштаму вывести противопоставление «Греции» и «Рима» на новый уровень; спецификой римского начала оказывается его неспособность воспринять дионисийский элемент:

Семя смерти, упав на почву Эллады, чудесно расцвело: вся наша культура выросла из этого семени, мы ведем летоисчисление с того момента, как его приняла земля Эллады. Все римское бесплодно, потому что почва Рима камениста, потому что Рим это — Эллада, лишенная благодати. («Пушкин и Скрябин»; стр. 318)

Созданная Мандельштамом образная модель хронологических слоев развития греческого духовного начала позволила ему символически осмыслить соотношение пушкинского века и новой эпохи русской культуры. В этой модели, Пушкинская эпоха предстает как век изначальной «аполлонической» гармонии, который должен быть впоследствии оплодотворен дионисийским элементом. В образном мире Мандельштама, Пушкин и Скрябин выступают как олицетворения этих двух закономерно сменяющих друг друга фаз возрождения «эллинства» на русской почве — своего рода «русский Аполлон» и «русский Дионис»:

Скрябин — следующая после Пушкина ступень русского эллинизма, дальнейшее закономерное раскрытие эллинистической природы русского духа. (Ibid., стр. 314)

Было бы интересно проследить, как модернистическая парадигма «русской Греции» трансформировалась после революции. Можно указать, в частности, на ту важную роль, которую сыграло в этом процессе символическое освоение образа Армении сначала у Белого («Армения», 1928), а затем у Мандельштама («Путешествие в Армению» и стихи начала 1930-х гг.). Однако рассмотрение этих более отдаленных отголосков темы выходит за рамки настоящей статьи.

Проведенный обзор позволяет с уверенностью утверждать, что в истории русской культуры противоположение Греции и Рима было важным образным инструментом, игравшим заметную роль в оформлении национального исторического, языкового и эстетического самосознания. На протяжении многих поколений эта образная парадигма реализовывалась в непрерывном развитии, в ходе которого ее контуры и смысловые импликации изменялись, перестраивались, вступали во взаимодействие с другими компонентами культурной мифологии. В настоящей работе намечены лишь основные точки, через которые проходило это развитие. Изучение поставленной проблемы в качестве целостной культурной традиции является задачей на будущее. Постановка такой задачи добавляет к истории русской словесной культуры важный и постоянный для нее аспект, присутствие которого необходимо учитывать при рассмотрении многих конкретных и внешне совершенно не сходных между собой явлений.

Примечания

1. См. о развитии романтического образа Италии в качестве анти-французской антитезы в эпоху после наполеоновских войн: Рита Джулиани, «П. А. Катенин и итальянская литература». В кн.: *Le romantisme russe et les littératures néo-latines,* publ. par Jean Bonamour & Michele Colucci (Firenze, 1987), стр. 89–120; Nina Kauchtschischwili, «La prose romantique russe et l'Italie», ibid., стр. 121–142.

2. См. анализ данного феномена на немецкой почве, от его зарождения во второй половине XVIII века до эпохи модернизма, в работе: С. С. Аверинцев. «Образ античности в западноевропейской культуре XX в. Некоторые замечания». В кн.: *Новое в современной классической филологии,* под ред. С. С. Аверинцева (Москва, 1979), стр. 5–40.

3. Сами реформаторы русского стиха рассматривали тоническую систему как более соответствующую «духу» русской просодии. Эта идея сохраняет свою силу вплоть до многих современных работ, рассматривающих соотношение структуры языка и стиха. См., например: Б. В. Томашевский, *Стих и язык. Филологические очерки* (Москва-Ленинград, 1959), стр. 98–101; В. Е. Холшевников, *Основы стиховедения. Русское стихосложение* (Ленинград, 1972), стр. 17–18. Более опосредованный взгляд на проблему, раскрывающий культурно-исторические пружины реформы, развит в работе: М. Л. Гаспаров, *Очерк истории русского стиха* (Москва, 1984), стр. 31 и след.

4. Победа силлабо-тонического стихосложения была абсолютной: в короткий срок с русской литературной сцены были вытеснены не только силлабические стихи, но и попытки некоторых авторов (таких, как А. Кантемир и сам Тредиаковский на первых этапах своей реформы) найти компромисс между двумя системами. См. М. Л. Гаспаров, стр. 37–40.

5. К. Ф. Тарановский, «Ранние русские ямбы и их немецкие образцы». В кн.: *Русская литература XVIII века и ее международные связи* (Ленинград, 1977), стр. 31–38.

6. Например, в том случае, когда он говорит о своей новой системе как о синтезе античной стопы и «древнего» (фольклорного) русского стиха, построенного на «тонической» основе. Этот синтез сменяет собой «среднее» (силлабическое)

стихосложение, выступающее в данной модели в качестве антитезы изначального («древнего») состояния (трактат «О древнем, среднем и новом стихотворении Российском», 1755).

7. Цитируется по изданию: М.В. Ломоносов, *Полное собрание сочинений*, т. 7. *Труды по филологии* (Москва-Ленинград), 1952, стр. 13.

8. Ср. формулировку М. Л. Гаспарова: «Тредиаковский подходил к традиционному стиху как реформатор-эволюционист, Ломоносов — как ниспровергатель-революционер». [М. Л. Гаспаров. «Ломоносов и Тредиаковский — два исторических типа новаторов стиха». В кн.: *М. В. Ломоносов и русская культура* (Тарту, 1986), стр. 28.

9. Общим местом грамматик и риторик эпохи классицизма было противопоставление классических языков «варварским» языкам нового времени. На этом фоне, тезис Ломоносова о «древности» русского языка и о его непосредственной связи (а не противопоставленности) с древнегреческим приобретал дополнительную эмфазу. См. В. М. Живов, «Богатство русского языка в концепции Ломоносова, его современников и последователей». В кн.: *М. В. Ломоносов и русская культура* (Тарту, 1986), стр. 79–82.

10. См. Ломоносов, стр. 587, 588.

11. В 1760-е годы весьма сходную позицию занял и Тредиаковский. В предисловии к «Тилемахиде» (1766) он утверждает сродство «славенороссийского» языка с классическими языками и противопоставляет его «изобилие» — «скудости и тесноте Французской». В этот период своей деятельности Тредиаковский даже получил ироническое прозвище «грековера». См. Б. А. Успенский. *Из истории русского литературного языка XVIII — начала XIX века* (Москва, 1985), стр. 165, 169. Но было уже поздно: символическая роль Ломоносова как идеального «преобразователя» русского языка уже прочно сформировалась после его смерти.

12. Культурная мифология, окружающая роли Тредиаковского и Ломоносова, исследуется в Irina Reyfman, *Vasilii Trediakovsky: The Fool of the «New» Russian Literature* (Stanford, 1990).

13. Яркое описание эстетических и бытовых мод начала века, отразивших этот «римский» образ, дал в своих мемуарах Ф. Ф. Вигель:

<...> новые Бруты и Тимолеоны захотели, наконец, восстановить у себя образцовую для них древность: пудра брошена с презрением, головы завились а-ла-Титюс и а-ла-Каракала, и если бы республика не скоро начала дохнуть в руках Бонапарте, то показались бы тоги, сандалии и латиклавы. Что касается до женщин, то все они хотели казаться древними статуями, с пьедестала сошедшими: которая оделась Корнелией, которая Аспазией. <...> Все делалось а л'антик (открытие Помпеи и Геркуланума чрезвычайно тому способствовало).

(Ф. Ф. Вигель, *Записки*, под ред. С. Я. Штрайха (Москва, 1928), т. 1, стр. 177)

14. Письмо Уварова к Гнедичу, открывшее полемику, и ответ Гнедича были опубликованы в 13 выпуске «Чтений в Беседе любителей русского слова» (1813). Последующая дискуссия велась в основном на страницах «Вестника Европы». См. об этом эпизоде в истории русского стихосложения и его отношении к поэтике «Золотого века»: М. Л. Гаспаров, *Очерк истории русского стиха* (Москва, 1984), стр. 125–127; С. М. Бонди, «Пушкин и русский гекзаметр», в его кн.: *О Пушкине. Статьи и исследования* (Москва, 1978), стр. 310–371.

15. Цитируется по изданию: Н. В. Гоголь, *Собрание сочинений в семи томах*, т. 6 (Москва, 1978), стр. 204.

16. Эту дифференциацию поколений карамзинской школы не учитывает Живов в своей характеристике карамзинистов как движения, представлявшего собой реакцию на идею «древности» славяно-русского языка, восходящую к русскому классицизму (В. М. Живов, стр. 82). Проницательные замечания Живова об отношении карамзинистов к идее «древности» русского языка и связи его с греческим в полной мере справедливы для начального этапа полемики с сторонниками «старого слога»; однако в дальнейшем, сначала в рамках «Арзамаса», а затем в пушкинском круге 1820-х гг., представители среднего и младшего поколений карамзинистов (за исключением, пожалуй, Вяземского) проходят существенную эволюцию. Направление этой эволюции во многом сближало их с новыми архаистическими течениями, окрашенными в романтические почвеннические тона.

17. См. о роли поэзии Овидия и его образа в бессарабский период творчества Пушкина: А. И. Малеин, «Пушкин и Овидий». *Пушкин и его современники*, вып. 23–24 (Петроград, 1916), стр. 45–66; Вл. Ванслов, «Пушкин о 'золотом веке' римской литературы». *Ученые записки Калининского педагогического института*, т. 36 (Калинин, 1963), стр. 3–47; Boris Gasparov, «Encounter of Two Poets in the Desert: Pushkin's Myth». In: *Myth in Literature* (Columbus, Ohio, 1985), pp. 124–153.

18. В марте 1821 года, под свежим впечатлением от известия о выступлении Александра Ипсиланти, Пушкин пишет восторженное письмо (адресованное, по-видимому, В. Л. Давыдову: сохранился лишь его черновой отрывок), в полной мере отразившем эту идеологическую амальгаму:

Греки стали стекаться толпами под его трое знамен, из которых одно трехцветно, на другом развевается крест, обвитый лаврами, с текстом *сим знаменем победиши*, на третьем изображен возрождающийся Феникс. (Здесь и далее Пушкин цитируется по изд.: А. С. Пушкин, *Полное собрание сочинений в 10 томах*, под ред. Б. В. Томашевского [Москва-Ленинград, 1949], т. 10, стр. 22–23.)

«Три знамени», составляющие симультанный символ греческого восстания, воплощают в себе греческую мифологию, эмблему Французской революции и образ торжества христианства и конца языческого Рима (крест Константина).

19. См. о различных аспектах использования образа и поэзии Шенье в творчестве Пушкина: Б. Г. Реизов, «Воспоминание из Андрея Шенье у Пушкина». В кн.: *Поэтика и стилистика русской литературы. Памяти академика Виктора Владимировича Виноградова* (Ленинград, 1971), стр. 127–133; В. Б. Сандомирская, «Андрей Шенье». В кн.: *Стихотворения Пушкина 1820–1830-х годов. История создания и идейно-художественная проблематика*, под ред. Н. В. Измайлова (Ленинград, 1974), стр. 8–34; André Markowicz, Quelques notes sur Puškin et les poètes français. In: *Le romantisme russe* стр. 181–204.

20. Красноречивым свидетельством юношеских взглядов Кюхельбекера и той культурной атмосферы, в которой эти взгляды возникли, служат письма к нему Г. А. Глинки — мужа его сестры, бывшего профессором русской словесности в Дерпте. Глинка предостерегает своего корреспондента от слишком прямолинейного отождествления русского языка и стиха с греческим:

Что ж принадлежит до содержащихся в письме твоем <мыслей> о близком свойстве русского языка к древнегреческому, о греческом экзаметре и проч., то мне кажется, что суждения твои о сих материях не совсем основательны; самые же ошибки твои приписываю или поверхностному твоему о них сведению, или пристрастию, со стороны в тебя вложенному. (Письмо от 10 июня 1814)

См.: А. В. Архипова, «Отзвуки литературной полемики 1810-х годов в письмах Г. А. Глинки к К. В. Кюхельбекеру». *Пушкин. Исследования и материалы*, т. 8 (Ленинград, 1978), стр. 149.

21. Цитируется по изданию: В. К. Кюхельбекер, *Путешествие. Дневник. Статьи* (Ленинград, 1979) стр. 451.

По-видимому, этот образ в статье Кюхельбекера послужил источником для Пушкина в его полушутливом дружеском поэтическом портрете Дельвига (1829): «Кто на снегах возрастил Феокритовы нежные розы?» Присутствие в этом образе подтекста, восходящего к Кюхельбекеру, как бы скрепляет «братство» всех трех лицейских поэтов. Эта деталь служит еще одним свидетельством того внимания, с которым Пушкин относился (при всей внешней иронии) к высказываниям «Кюхли».

22. См. о критических взглядах Сумарокова и его «Одах вздорных», пародировавших импульсивность ломоносовского стиля: П. Н. Берков, *Ломоносов и литературная полемика его времени, 1750–1765* (Москва-Ленинград, 1936), гл. 5–6. Различие в трактовке классицизма у Ломоносова и Сумарокова очерчено в статье Ю. Н. Тынянова «Ода как ораторский жанр» (в его книге *Архаисты и новаторы* (Ленинград, 1929), стр. 48–86). О «барочной» струе ломоносовской оды см.: Dmitrij Chizhevskij, *History of Russian Literature from the Eleventh Century to the End of the Baroque* (s'Gravenhage, 1962), стр. 393–428.

23. См. о взаимоотношении Пушкина и Кюхельбекера в середине 1820-х гг.: Ю. Н. Тынянов, «Пушкин и Кюхельбекер». В кн.: Ю. Н. Тынянов *Пушкин и его современники* (Москва, 1969), стр. 233–294); Б. М. Гаспаров, *Поэтический язык Пушкина* (Vienna, 1992), Введение, гл. II.

24. Конечно, Кюхельбекер безмерно переоценивал значение Шихматова; однако причины такой оценки вполне ясны в контексте развиваемых им идей. Поэтический стиль Шихматова (одного из ведущих авторов круга «Беседы любителей Русского слова», высоко ценимого А. С. Шишковым) являл собой интересное сочетание лирического и эпического элемента, архаистического словаря и эзотерических новаторских поэтических приемов. См. подробнее: М. Г. Альтшуллер, *Предтечи славянофильства в русской литературе (Общество «Беседа любителей русского слова»)* (Ann Arbor, 1984), стр. 106–136.

25. См. о взаимоотношениях Пушкина и Катенина: Ю. Н. Тынянов, «Архаисты и Пушкин». В его кн.: *Архаисты и новаторы* (Ленинград, 1929), стр. 120–163.

26. Статьи «О поэзии Греческой» и «О поэзии Латинской». Цитируется по изданию: П. А. Катенин, *Размышления и разборы* (Москва, 1981), стр. 53 и 70.

27. Катенин прямо сопоставляет Петрарку с Вольтером в письмах к Н. И. Бахтину; см. об этом: Рита Джулиани, «П. А. Катенин и итальянская литература». В кн.: *Le romantisme russe* стр. 89–119 (см. в особенности стр. 101).

28. Портрет Горация в статье «О поэзии Латинской» несет в себе аллюзионные черты образа Вольтера; осуждение Горацием «грубой старины» и пренебрежение Гомером явно отсылают к знаменитой оценке Шекспира Вольтером, ставшей своего рода негативным «паролем» романтической критики:

<...> он один из приятнейших лириков, умный и веселый сатирик; только вкуса его в суждениях над другими безусловно похвалить не могу: я вижу в нем какое-то светское педантство, самодовольное пренебрежение к *грубой* старине и поверхностное понятие о многом, даже о всем известном отце стихов, Гомере: ни его, ни божественного Ахилла его Гораций не принимал. (стр. 80; курсив Катенина.)

29. Впрочем, безусловно осуждая «галантное» направление раннего Тредиаковского, Катенин высоко оценил «Тилемахиду». В письме к Н. И. Бахтину (28 апреля 1829) он воздает должное попытке Тредиаковского ввести на русской почве гекзаметр, и особо отмечает, что «он пишет греческие имена, как должно» (стр. 291). Пересмотр традиционного отношения к Тредиаковскому происходил у Катенина, быть может, не без влияния того факта, что в журнальной полемике конца 1820-х годов его противники (в частности, Н. И. Греч) сопоставляли его самого с Тредиаковским — в качестве «педантического» и малоодаренного критика «новой школы». Характерно, что «реабилитация» Тредиаковского воплощается под пером Катенина в знаки, отождествляющие его с «греческим» началом.

30. См. об этом «парадоксе» историко-культурного мышления любомудров: Alexander Bourmeyster, "Les *Ljubomudry* et l'héritage de la culture antique," *Revue des études slaves,* t. 46 (1967), 81–97; его же, "Les *Ljubomudry*: Culture classique et culture pseudo-classique." In: *Le romantisme russe,* стр. 15–26.

31. «Философические письма» цитируются (в русском переводе) по изданию: *Сочинения и письма П. Я. Чаадаева,* под ред. М. О. Гершензона, т. 2 (Москва, 1914), стр. 111, 112, 117.

32. Характерным примером могут служить два дистиха Пушкина — «На статую играющего в бабки» и «На статую играющего в свайку», в которых скульптурный образ «русской удалой игры», насыщенный динамизмом, сопоставляется со статуей Дискобола. Антитезой этому «греко-русскому» скульптурному образу могут служить стихи Пушкина «К бюсту завоевателя», посвященные бюсту Александра работы Торвальдсена, выдержанному в духе триумфального портрета римского императора; созданный Пушкиным образ подчеркивает «мраморную» неподвижность и холодный блеск статуи, изобличающие лживость оригинала.

33. См. подробнее: Boris Gasparov, «The Language Situation and the Linguistic Polemic in Mid-Nineteenth-Century Russia». In: *Aspects of the Slavic Language Question,* ed. Riccardo Picchio & Harvey Goldblatt, vol. 2. *East Slavic* (New Haven, 1984), стр. 297–334.

34. Я не буду касаться в этой статье более широких вопросов о роли «греческой» парадигмы в философских, историко-культурных, религиозных концепциях данной эпохи (в трудах С. Н. Трубецкого, Ф. Ф. Зелинского, Л. П. Карсавина и др.).

35. Статья «О веселом ремесле и умном веселии» (1907); цитируется по изд.: Вячеслав Иванов, *Собрание сочинений,* под ред. Д. В. Иванова и О. Дешарт, т. 3 (Брюссель, 1979), стр. 20. См. анализ полемики Иванова с Кузминым вокруг этого тезиса в работе: John A. Barnstead, «Mikhail Kuzmin's 'On Beautiful Clarity' and Viacheslav Ivanov: A Reconsideration». *Canadian Slavonic Papers,* Vol. 24, No. 1 (March 1982), 1–10.

36. См. о мифологии Петербурга как «города Александра»: И. А. Паперно. «Пушкин в жизни человека Серебряного века». In: *Cultural Mythologies of Russian Modernism: From the Golden Age to the Silver Age,* ed. Boris Gasparov, Robert P. Hughes, and Irina Paperno (Berkeley, 1992).

37. Статьи Мандельштама цитируются по изданию: Осип Мандельштам, *Собрание сочинений,* под ред. Г. П. Струве и Б. А. Филиппова, изд. второе, т. 2 (New York, 1971) стр. 293–294.

Boris Gasparov/Summary: Russian Greece and Russian Rome

One of the features inherited by post-Petrine Russia from the Muscovite epoch was its view of itself as the direct heir and successor of Greece. This view was founded, among other factors, on a perception of Church Slavic as a Greek language "transplanted" to Slavic soil. This gave rise to the idea of an un-interrupted succession from Ancient (Homeric) Greek, through the Greek of the New Testament and patristic writings, through Old Church Slavic, to the Russian language of modern times. The other side of this symbolic special relation with Greece was an opposition to the Roman world and its modern successors (the Catholic lands in general, and France in particular).

This idea played an important role at critical junctions in the development of Russian literature and literary language. It was voiced by Lomonosov as a basis for his reform of the Russian stylistic system and prosody, as well as by Russian neo-classical writers and Romantics of the nineteeth century—from A. Shishkov and V. Kiukhel'beker to Pushkin and Gogol'. Opposition between a "true" (i.e., Greek) and "false" (Roman) classicism superseded, on Russian soil, the opposition betwen the Classics and Romantics, thus imparting peculiar features to the Romantic movement in Russia. This cultural pattern reemerged also at the beginning of the twentieth century, where it played an instrumental role in shaping some of the trends of Russian modernism.

On the Nature of the Word

Theological Sources of Mandelshtam's
Dialogue with the Symbolists

IRINA PAPERNO

A close interaction between religious and aesthetic spheres was characteristic of Russian culture at the beginning of the twentieth century. The foundation for this tradition was laid by Vladimir Solov'ev, with his conception of the religious nature of art. Inspired by Solov'ev's teaching, the Symbolists projected theological notions into diverse regions of aesthetics and philology.[1] This tendency found expression first and foremost in the Symbolist theory of the poetic word which was built on the metaphorical identification of poetic language and the divine Logos. In this framework theological notions became applicable to the explication of philological problems. In their aspiration to construct a poetics based on a new understanding of the nature of the word, the Acmeists were also guided by ideas, concepts, and images borrowed from theological doctrines. This study will analyze the theological projections and subtexts of Mandelshtam's dialogue with the Symbolists regarding the nature of the poetic word.

The Symbolists viewed poetry as a religious act—a magical act of creation and subjugation of reality in which the poet comes into contact with the divine ("theurgy"). The poetic word (or poetic language) was seen as possessing sacred properties: magic (*magichnost'*), energy, and creative force (*deistvennaia sila*). According to Viacheslav Ivanov's programmatic article, "The Testaments of Symbolism" (*Zavety simvolizma,* 1910), Symbolism posed the problem of language's dual nature: to the ordinary word or linguistic sign (the "word-concept"), the "word-symbol" was added, thus satisfying the demand for the other language, the language of "sacred poetry" (123).[2] "Symbolism in the new poetry appears as the vague initial recollections of the sacred language of magicians and sorcerers, those who once brought a special secret significance to the words of a national language . . . . They knew the names of gods and demons, people and things, which were different from those used by the general populace, and it was on the basis of their knowledge of

the true names that they claimed power over nature" (127). According to
Ivanov, the concept of the "language of the gods" had been applied to
poetry as far back as the ancient Greeks. He saw the model of such an
"other tongue" in the poetic language developed by contemporary Russian
Symbolism, a movement that created the "ritual art" and uncovered "the
nature of the word as symbol" (135). Symbolism was seen as "an anticipation . . . of the religious epoch [in the life] of language" (129). "The word-
symbol promised to become a sacred revelation . . . . It remained for artists
to integrally embody in their lives and work . . . the Weltanschauung of
mystical realism . . ." (136–137).

Andrei Belyi also distinguished the two types of the word: the "word-
term" or abstract concept, the word with logical or terminological meaning,
as it exists in common language; and the "word-symbol," the poetic word
(Belyi's views found their clearest expression in the essay "The Magic of
Words" ["Magiia slov"], 1909).[3] In Belyi's words, the word-term is a "dead
word" whereas the poetic word-symbol is a "living word," or a "word-made-
flesh." Poetic nomination establishes such a link between the object and
sound, which expresses the object's secret essence. In this very act Belyi saw
a confirmation of the existence of the object. Thus, artistic creation was
equivalent to the creation of the world. Moreover, the act of naming united
the thinking "I" with the outside world: only in the process of naming the
object could the thinking "I" become mystically one with the world, with the
true essence of things. Thus, neither the thinking subject nor the world itself
could exist outside of the act of naming. Belyi likened the "living speech" of
poetry, which gave the poet magical power over the natural world, to a
"sacred tongue," the language "in which humankind received its greatest
revelations" (432). "Living speech" involved "communication with divinity
itself" (431).

In Belyi's theory theological concepts were combined with principles of
nomination traceable to the philological doctrines of Aleksandr Afanas'ie-
vich Potebnia (1835–1891) in whom Belyi saw a precursor of the Symbolists.[4] According to Potebnia, all names have been initially motivated; that is,
any word is, metaphorically speaking, linked with the "essence" of the object
or phenomenon it designates. The word is made up of the combination of
three elements: the external form of meaning, i.e., sound; the internal (or
inner) form (the "representation," "image," or "symbol" of meaning); and
the meaning itself (the "content" or "idea"). The internal form is the original
root meaning or *etymon,* understood as the direct motivation for naming.
(For example, *oko* (eye) is the internal form of the word *okno* (window);

whereas for the word *stol* (table) the internal form is *stlat'* (to spread), and for *zashchita* (defense) the internal form is *shchit* (shield).) In the course of a word's life its internal form usually wears away. But a word with "living representation" ("*s zhivym predstavleniem,*" Potebnia's term) has a special status and unique potential; it is the embryonic form of poetry and myth. Moreover, according to Potebnia, the structure of the trope and the structure of the poetic work are analogous to the structure of the word.

In "The Meaning of Art" (*Smysl iskusstva,* 1907) Belyi rewrote the schema proposed by Potebnia in theological terms. He proposed the following model for the process of nomination or "symbolization." For Belyi symbolization is an indivisible unity made up of three elements: (1) the image (flesh); (2) the idea (word); (3) the living link, which predetermines both the idea and the image (word made flesh). In "The Magic of Words" Belyi developed Potebnia's ideas on the nature of the trope. He maintained that the mythological notion of existence follows from the idea of resemblance inherent in the internal form of the word. The internal image, or symbol, is perceived as an actual, living reason for the object or phenomenon; the image becomes invested with ontological being. In metaphorical terms, "the symbol becomes an incarnation; it comes to live and act independently." For instance, a poet says "white-horned moon," and a white horn of the moon "becomes" the white horn of a mythical creature. In this manner verbal creation (poetry) is transformed into myth; it turns into the religious creation of life.

Potebnia compared his conception of the poetic word with religious beliefs positing the existence of a secret connection between the word and the object it denotes. As examples of such beliefs, Potebnia cited myths that deify the word, including the doctrine of the divine word (Logos) of the Greeks and Hebrews.[5]

Following Potebnia, Belyi saw an analogy between the process of symbolization in poetry and the mystical doctrines concerning the magical power of the word, from the ancient Indian, Egyptian, and Orphic traditions to the Hellenistic tradition. Belyi accorded a central place among such analogies to the rapprochement between the Symbolist conception of the word and the "doctrine of the Logos in Christian mysticism."[6] Within the scientifically-based arguments of Potebnia, he found a positive foundation for the Symbolist principle of "mystical realism."

Such, in short, was the methodological and metaphorical vocabulary inherited from Symbolism by the aesthetic schools of the 1910s and 1920s. Major doctrines in the philosophy of language grew out of this cultural context. The ideas of Pavel Florenskii, Sergei Bulgakov, A. F. Losev, and,

to a certain degree, Mikhail Bakhtin had their basis in theology.[7] Such
metaphors as "the living word," "the word made flesh," "the resurrection of
the word," became inseparable parts of the language of the Acmeists,
Futurists, and Formalists.[8]

Imiaslavie and Aesthetic Debates in the 1910s

The symbolist views on the nature of the poetic word were formulated by
Ivanov and Belyi in the period 1907–1909 (the publication of their works
dates from 1910). In this same period the question of the name of God
became an issue of interpretation for Russian theologians. The problem was
raised in connection with the movement in the Russian Orthodox monasteries of Mount Athos known as *imiaslavie* (name-glorification). (Its proponents, who called themselves *imiaslavtsy,* were also known as *imiabozhtsy*.)
These debates began between 1907 and 1910, and reached a climax in the
years 1912–1913.[9] The question of the essence of the God's name grew out
of the hesychast tradition and the mystical "Jesus prayer" ("wisdom-act"
[*umnoe delanie*], or the "internal prayer," also called the "art" or the "art of
arts"). The prayer, which constitutes one of the central elements of Orthodox spiritual life, is performed by constantly repeting the name "Jesus." As
one enters into the mystical state, the name loses its "external" form, its
linguistic encasement, and ceases to be pronounced aloud. "Merging with the
breath," it enters the heart of the supplicant where it dwells in silence. This
act is to bring one into communion with God through his name. Pronounc-
ing the word "Jesus," the subject would inevitably enter into a real relationship with the object; that is, the supplicant enters into a real relationship
with the hypostasis of the God-man.[10]

The *imiaslavtsy,* the group of uneducated Athonian monks of peasant origin, developed these ideas further. From the idea of Christ's direct, mystical
presence in his name they drew conclusions concerning the divine nature of
the name "Jesus" itself. They advanced the new dogma that "the name of
God is God himself." As the name of God came to be venerated, special
place was accorded to the commandment against taking God's name in vain.

Opponents of *imiaslavie,* the educated clergy, argued from a rationalist
position, emphasizing the earthly nature of the name "Jesus" and equating
the God's name with a "human word," a "nominal appelation." The divine
name, they argued, should be understood as a common linguistic phenomenon, a simple proper name. From the point of view of *imiaslavie,* this was
the heresy of *imiaborchestvo* (onomatoclasm), a direct continuation of the
iconoclastic heresy, a product of "nihilism" and "positivism."

At the heart of the controversy over the divine name lies the general philosophical problem of the nature of the sign. Theologians who participated in the debates saw them as a continuation of the struggle between realism and nominalism in medieval theology, and, in the context of the time, a manifestation of the confrontation between materialism and idealism, between rationalism and mysticism. As M. Muretov, a professor at the Moscow Theological Academy, wrote, the question raised on Mount Athos afforded an occasion to resolve the fundamental dispute between "idealism-realism-mysticism" and "materialism-nominalism-rationalism," antagonism between which "one finds in art—painting, music, literature—and on the whole in all things in one form or another."[11]

Both extremes, *imiaslavie* (name-glorification) and *imiaborchestvo* (onomatoclasm), were criticized by the Orthodox church. The position of the Orthodox church rested on patristic tradition, the fourth-century controversy between the heretic Eunomius on one side, and Basil the Great and Gregory of Nyssa on the other. Eunomius divided names into two sorts: "things named by people" or "invented names," which were signals or nicknames for things, human names, "only words"; and superhuman names reflecting the very essence of things and, for that reason, immutably linked with things. The latter were divine names (*sofiinye imena*), given to human beings by God. According to Basil the Great's criticism of Eunomius, no single name could convey the essence of God. Gregory of Nyssa argued that the connection between names and objects was "free and creative" and was established "by the power of reason." The name of God was not equivalent to the divine essence; any linguistic concept of God, therefore, was an idol, a deceptive image. The only name that could convey the divine essence was silence of the soul immersed in a reflection of the ineffable image of the Divinity. The response from the Orthodox church was to maintain the "apotheosis of ineffability" (*pafos neizrechennosti*).[12]

The events on Mount Athos drew a wide response from authors close to Symbolism, such as Sergei Bulgakov, Pavel Florenskii, Vladimir Ern, Sergei Askol'dov, and Nikolai Berdiaev, who sympathized with the *imiaslavie* movement.[13] For them the question of the name of God constituted a direct analogy to the issue of the poetic word as posed by Symbolism. It is noteworthy that the very subject of the "Jesus prayer" appeared as a metaphor for poetry in Symbolist writings even before the *imiaslavie* movement. Thus, Viacheslav Ivanov in his "Athena's Spear" (*Kop'e Afiny*, 1904) maintained that the psychology of art (of mystical, monastic [*keleinoe*] art, as was Symbolism) is the psychology of the inward prayer (*"molitvennogo dela-*

niia").[14] The two paradigms converged: on one hand, concepts associated with the Symbolist theories of the word were adapted to the theological dispute over the name of God; on the other, concepts that took shape during the discussion of this theological issue came to be actively employed in later discussions on the nature of the poetic word.

Debates around *imiaslavie* reached their peak in the period 1912–1913, in the wake of Symbolism's decline, as new artistic concepts and movements, most notably Acmeism and Futurism, gained momentum. Though they stood in opposition to Symbolism, the Acmeists acknowledged their dependence on its legacy. In the Acmeist manifesto, "Acmeism and the Legacy of Symbolism," also known as "Acmeism and the Testaments of Symbolism" (*Nasledie simvolizma i akmeizm,* or *Zavety simvolizma i akmeizm,* 1913), the movement's ideologue, Gumilev, wrote that "clearly, the cognition of God, Theology, the beautiful lady, shall remain on her throne; but the Acmeists want neither to lower her to the level of literature nor to take literature into her adamantine coldness."[15] Symbolism's legacy prompted the Acmeists to the active use of theological metaphors. The confrontation between Symbolism and Acmeism on the nature of the poetic word was perceived as a battle between the position of "Orthodox aesthetics" and "aesthetic heresy." From the standpoint of the Symbolists' "profession of aesthetic faith," Acmeism represented an "aesthetic heresy." From the point of view of the Acmeist Guild of Poets (*Tsekh poetov*), Symbolism was a heresy which the Acmeists were called to combat.[16]

Mandelshtam's position was inconsistent. According to Gumilev, "even after the foundation of the Guild of Poets, Mandelshtam 'long persisted in the symbolist heresy.'"[17] An early poem "The Heart Dressed in a Cloud" (*Kak oblakom serdtse odeto,* 1909–1910), which was not included in the collection *Kamen',* is essentially a profession of the Symbolist faith. In this poem Mandelshtam described poetic creation as an act of making the word flesh: "Even signs demand a body, and words participate in the flesh" (и признаки требуют тела, / и плоти причастны слова). The poet's divine calling is to give the "thirsting objects" their hidden names (*zavetnye imena*). While the name given by the poet was described as living flesh, all that lay outside of the creative poetic act was accorded the metaphor "stone": "And flesh pretended to be a stone until the calling of the poet should be revealed to him by the Lord" (И камнем прикинулась плоть / Пока назначенье поэта / Ему не откроет Господь). Mandelshtam equated the act of poetic creation with a sacrament: "And the mystery of marriage breathes in the simple combination of words" (И дышит таинственность брака / В простом сочетании слов).

John Malmstad has shown that one of Mandelshtam's first retorts in the dialogue with Symbolism on the nature of the poetic word was the 1910 poem known by the title "Silentium," which it was given only in 1913 upon publication in *Kamen'*. According to Malmstad's convincing analysis, "Silentium" was Mandelshtam's response to Ivanov's lecture, "On the New Literary Groups" (*O novykh literaturnykh gruppirovkakh*), presented in March 1910 at a meeting of the Society of Free Aesthetics (*Obshchestvo svobodnoi éstetiki*); this lecture formed the basis of "The Testaments of Symbolism."[18]

Ivanov's speech presented variations on a theme from Tiutchev's well-known poem "Silentium": "A spoken thought is a lie." According to Ivanov, Tiutchev was "the true progenitor of our true Symbolism," the parodox of Tiutchev lay in the realization that the word had ceased to be true to the internal experience. Tiutchev posed the problem of the need for a "different poetic language," a different word (123). This, Ivanov maintained, led to the epoch in Russian art of the "religious reaction of our national genius against the tide of iconoclastic materialism" (133), that is, to Symbolism. The newest school of Symbolism sought to satisfy the need for a word (poetic language) that would serve "as mediary between man and the world of divine essences" (131). The school created the magical word-symbol, capable of "restoring truth to the 'spoken thought'" (133).

In "The Magic of Words," which was presented as a paper at a meeting of the Society of Free Aesthetics in 1909, Belyi also touched on the theme of "Silentium." His opening thesis is Tiutchev's famous formula. "'A spoken thought is a lie,' said Tiutchev, and he was correct, if by the word 'thought' he understood an idea expressed in a series of terminological concepts" (429). Belyi offered to replace the word-concept with the "other word," the word-symbol, or a "living word," which is the "music of the ineffable." He claimed that "the spoken living word is not a lie. It is the expression of the sacral essence of my nature; and insofar as my nature is nature in general, the word is an expression of the most sacred mysteries of nature" (429).

When one examines Mandelshtam's "Silentium" in this context, it becomes clear that he did not accept the amendment to Tiutchev proposed by Ivanov and Belyi. Mandelshtam envisioned not the "other word," but pure music, the word unspoken, or silence.

In the context of the period's theological controversy, Mandelshtam's dialogue with the Symbolists parallels the argument between the proponents of *imiaslavie* and their Orthodox adversaries concerning the Jesus prayer and the name of God. The ideas of Ivanov and Belyi are analogous to Eunomius's notion of the existence of two types of words, or names, the human and the divine, the second of which conveys the true essence of things. Mandelshtam's position is comparable to that of Orthodoxy (in particular to that of Gregory of Nyssa): it is the apotheosis of silence, of the ineffable.

Mandelshtam made an obvious and direct reference to the Mount Athos heresy in his 1915 poem, "On Athos Even Now" (*I ponyne na Afone*):

> И поныне на Афоне
> Древо чудное растет,
> На крутом зеленом склоне
> Имя Божие поет.
>
> В каждой радуются келье
> Имябожцы-мужики:
> Слово — чистое веселье,
> Исцеленье от тоски!
>
> Всенародно, громогласно
> Чернецы осуждены,
> Но от ереси прекрасной
> Мы спасаться не должны.
>
> Каждый раз, когда мы любим,
> Мы в нее впадает вновь,
> Безимянную мы губим,
> Вместе с именем, любовь.

> (Even now on Athos,
> the miracle tree grows,
> on the steep green slope
> the divine name sings.
>
> They rejoice in every cell,
> *imiabozhtsy,* peasants:
> the word is pure merriment,
> the cure for melancholy!
>
> Loudly throughout the populace
> the monks have been condemned,
> but from the beautiful heresy
> we ought not to save ourselves.
>
> Each time we love
> we fall into it anew;
> the nameless [love] we destroy
> together with the name [we give it], love.)

Mandelshtam equates faith with love, the divine name with the name of the beloved and maintains that faith/love is nameless and that the heretical pronunciation of the divine/beloved's name is ruinous, both for the speaker and for the object.[19]

Another poem connected with *imiaslavie* is "Your Precarious and Agonizing Image" (*Obraz tvoi, muchitel'nyi i zybkii*, April 1912).[20]

> Образ твой, мучительный и зыбкий,
> Я не мог в тумане осязать.
> «Господи!» — сказал я по ошибке,
> Сам того не думая сказать.
> Божье имя, как большая птица,
> Вылетело из моей груди.
> Впереди густой туман клубится,
> И пустая клетка позади.

> (Your image, agonizing and precarious,
> I could not feel in the fog.
> "Lord!" I said by mistake,
> without myself thinking to say it.
> The name of God, like a great bird,
> flew out from my chest.
> Ahead a thick fog swirls,
> and an empty cage behind.)

A variation on several elements of the theme of the Jesus prayer, this poem presents a lyrical "I" who, striving for the direct, sensory contact with the image of God (*osiazanie*),[21] "by accident" invocates the divine name. The name of God is represented in the poem as an independent being, a living force—a bird that dwelt in the heart of the man (in the "cage" of the chest), then left the body. We can interpret this image as a representation of death (the bird flying out from the cage-body is an established symbol of the departing soul). In this Mandelshtam follows a Judaic teaching, according to which the one who utters the name of God dies. The proponents of *imiaslavie* viewed this rabbinical prohibition as stemming from the original belief in the divine nature and independent value of the name itself.[22]

The images employed by Mandelshtam in this poem echo those introduced by Ivanov in "The Testaments of Symbolism." Thus, lamenting the destiny of the "dead words" of the common language, as opposed to the "living words" of the Symbolist poetic language, Ivanov wrote that the "the attempt to 'utter' such a word serves only to destroy it further, and he who hears such a word spoken takes into his soul not life but rather the dead coverings of life departed (*otletevshei zhizni*)" (121–122). Mandelshtam's images form a different picture: the attempt to utter a "living word" (a word-symbol) serves to destroy the speaker, while his soul flies away with the word, leaving behind the dead coverings (the empty chest).

In this poem Mandelshtam responds to Symbolism not only by means of its images but also by the specific poetic device he employs. Behind this poem lies a concrete text, the proverb, "The word is not a sparrow; if it flies out, you'll not catch it" (Слово не воробей, вылетит не поймаешь). This proverb serves as motivation for both the bird image of the word and for the text as a whole. Thus, the poem unfolds as it develops the semantic potential contained within the proverb.

It is likely that Mandelshtam came up with the idea of using this proverb as well as with the strategy of constructing the meaning of the poem on the basis of the proverb from his reading of Potebnia's *From Notes on the Theory of Literature* (*Iz zapisok po teorii slovesnosti*). Discussing popular beliefs in that the word is the thing itself, Potebnia cited as evidence the folk saying "The word is not a sparrow; once you've let it go, you shall not catch it."[23] In the same work he described creation of the poem as a process parallel to that of word derivation. The meaning of the poem is derived from the meaning of an "image" (its "inner form"), and a ready-made verbal formula, an idiom or a proverb, can fulfill the role of such inner form.[24] This description applies to the poem "Obraz tvoi," for which the proverb "The word is not a sparrow . . ." served as the inner form. In a later essay, "Culture and the Word" (*Slovo i kul'tura,* 1921), Mandelshtam described poetic creation in terms that clearly refer to these ideas of Potebnia: "A poem lives through its inner image, that sonorous mould of a form, which anticipates the written verse. Not a single word yet exists, yet the poem is already resonating. This is its inner form that resonates, and this is what the poet's hearing discerns" (226–227).[25] Further on, Mandelshtam maintained that such a strategy was basically different from these employed by the Symbolist poets. (This question will be addressed below.)

It becomes clear from the preceding analysis that, along with "Silentium," "Obraz tvoi" is a metaliterary poem. It alludes to the theological problem of God's name and to the aesthetic problem of the poetic word raised by the Symbolists. As the poem demonstrates, Mandelshtam's position in relation to Symbolism was not unambiguous. (This was precisely the conclusion drawn by John Malmstad upon a close analysis of "Silentium.") Mandelshtam is operating with the concepts and images derived from the debates around *imiaslavie* and with the Symbolist notions that stand behind them. However, he tranforms their meaning. Moreover, by evoking the Judaic notion of the destructive consequences of uttering God's name, he calls into question the Symbolist idea of replacing the word of the common language with the "living word," the symbol.

Mandelshtam developed his idea of a "wordless" appeal to God in the poems devoted to Protestantism, "The Lutheran" (*Liuteranin*) (1912) and "Bach" (1913). Like "Silentium," "The Lutheran" was a response to a Tiutchev poem, "I Love the Lutheran Service" (*Ia Liuteran liubliu bogosluzhen'e*).[26] In it Mandelshtam reflects on the advantages of oratorical practices that are not viewed as divinely inspired:

> И думал я: витийствовать не надо.
> Мы не пророки, даже не предтечи
>
> (And I thought: no need to orate.
> We are not prophets, not even precursors.)

Parallel to this theme runs the theme of refusing to reproduce God's image in an icon, which appears in the poem "Bach":

> Здесь прихожане — дети праха
> И доски вместо образов,
> Где мелом, Себастьяна Баха,
> Лишь цифры значатся псалмов.
>
> (Parishioners here are children of dust,
> and boards replace the icons,
> where, in chalk, only the numbers
> of Sebastian Bach's psalms are designated.)

The chalk board with its human scribblings in a Lutheran church is set in opposition to the venerated icons in the Orthodox church, while a sound, such as the sound of organ music, compared to a bird's song, is opposed to the word. Thus, the Protestant poems exhibit Mandelshtam's "onomoclastic" and iconoclastic tendencies.

According to Boris Uspenskii, also connected to the theological debates on the name of God is the poem written in 1920, "I Joined the Round Dance of Shadows That Trampled a Tender Meadow" (*Ia v khorovod tenei, toptavshikh nezhnyi lug*), in which Mandelshtam describes the evolution of his thought concerning the nature of the poetic word:

> Сначала думал я, что имя — серафим,
> И тела легкого дичился,
> Немного дней прошло, и я смешался с ним
> И в милой тени растворился.

(I first thought the name was a seraph,
and I avoided the delicate body.
Not many days passed, and I blended with it,
and in the darling shadow [I] dissolved.)[27]

A new and extremely important theme appears in this poem: the corporeal
nature of the word.

Theology and Philology in Mandelshtam's Essays of the 1920s

The evolution of Mandelshtam's views on the nature of the poetic word is
clearly represented in his philological essays published around 1920. In "The
Morning of Acmeism" (*Utro Akmeizma*), published in 1919 (though written
apparently between 1912 and 1913 as an Acmeist manifesto), Mandelshtam
put forward the concept of a new, Acmeist word, the "word as such" (*slovo,
kak takovoe*). Unlike the Symbolist word, to which symbolic significance is
assigned in verse (according to Ivanov such a word is "the image and likeness of higher realities"), the Acmeist "word as such" carries ordinary meaning, the meaning assigned to it in everyday usage.

For Mandelshtam the word itself was a "reality" of poetry; the word was
the "material" from which the poetic word was "constructed." Consequently,
the process of poetic creation was understood as an organization of linguistic material (the sound and meaning of the words), rather than a mystical
act of theurgy. In opposition to the Symbolists' notion of the word-as-flesh,
Mandelshtam introduced the metaphor of the word-stone, the material in
the hands of the poet-craftsman. (Mandelshtam traced this image, as well as
that of the word-as-music, to Tiutchev.)

The polemics with the Symbolists is further developed in Mandelshtam's
later, post-revolutionary essays, "Word and Culture" (*Slovo i kul'tura*, 1921)
and "On the Nature of the Word" (*O prirode slova*, 1922). Here Mandelshtam's
conception of the word changes to a considerable extent.

In "On the Nature of the Word" Mandelshtam claims that the Symbolists
equated the word's poetic sense with its figurative, metaphoric, or symbolic
meaning. The Symbolist is interested in the word not in and of itself but only
as a likeness or "correspondence": "For the Symbolist . . . a rose is a likeness
of the sun . . . . Acmeism grew from a repudiation: 'Down with Symbolism.
Long live the living rose!'—such was its initial slogan" (256). Thus the
denotative, direct meaning of the word becomes effaced in verse, while the
word's symbolic meaning is promoted as "absolute," that is, as its true and only
meaning. The word is torn away from the object in the external world that it

denotes and is related primarily to the "higher reality" that it symbolizes. Mandelshtam describes this situation in metaphorical terms: the words of Symbolism are not "utensils" but rather objects intended "exclusively for liturgical use." Furthermore, he argues that

> The Symbolists sealed the meanings of all words and images and designated them solely for liturgical use. This turned out to be very inconvenient—one cannot get by or stand up or sit down. You cannot eat on the table because it is not just a table. You cannot kindle a fire because that might turn out to mean something that you will not be pleased about later.
>
> Man is no longer master in his own house. He has to live either in a church or in a sacred druidic grove . . . . (255)

At the opposite extreme lies what Mandelshtam describes as the firm attachment of the word to the thing or object that it denotes: "What is the nature of the word's attachment to its meaning? Can it be a serf-like dependence? The word after all is not a thing" (255). Mandelshtam takes his departure from the slogan of realism, "the word is the thing itself." (Potebnia quoted this formula discussing popular mythological realism.) Mandelshtam, however, reads it as a metaphor. As becomes clear from his later arguments, Mandelshtam understands the claim "the word is the thing" not as identification of the word with the object that it denotes, but rather as limiting the meaning of the word in verse to its denotative meaning (in Russian linguistic terminology, *predmetnoe znachenie,* or "objective" meaning). In "Word and Culture" Mandelshtam writes,

> Do not demand particular substantiveness, concreteness, or materiality from poetry. That's today's revolutionary hunger. It's Thomas's doubt. Why is it so necessary to touch it with your fingers? And most of all, why identify the word with the thing, the grass, the object it denotes?
>
> Is the thing master of the word? The word is Psyche. The living word does not denote an object but rather freely chooses this or that objective significance, substance, nice body, as if seeking a dwelling place. Around the object the word wanders freely, like a soul around a body it has quit but not forgotten ("Word and Culture" 226)[28]

Thus for Mandelshtam the word has, as it were, a dual nature. Its meaning cannot be limited either to the symbolic or to the direct, denotative meaning. In metaphorical terms the word's nature is neither "absolute" nor "substantial," "material," or "corporeal."

Mandelshtam sought synthesis in a "scientific" understanding of the word: "The most convenient and, in a scholarly sense, correct approach is to view the word as an image, that is, as a verbal representation" ("On the Nature of the

Word" 255–256). This claim is clearly a reference to Potebnia's conception of the "internal image," or "inner form."

In referring to Potebnia, Mandelshtam consciously followed the lead provided by the Symbolists, in particular, by the theories of Ivanov and Belyi.[29] Mandelshtam, however, interprets Potebnia's conception in a different manner. Belyi understood Potebnia's notion of the inner image (form) primarily as an affirmation of the oneness of word and "idea," or sound and meaning, and consequently, as the philological basis of realism. Mandelshtam, in contrast, sees inner form as a guarantee of the oneness of the symbolic and denotative meanings of the word. It is revealing that in "On the Nature of the Word" he should insist that the notion of the reality of the word as such is a kind of "Russian nominalism."[30] According to Mandelshtam, the Symbolists fell into the sin "against the language that creates images according to human needs"; their "sin" derived from their overlooking the figurative, symbolic meaning that the word contains already in its direct, "substantative" meaning, that is, the meaning it has in everyday usage. Mandelshtam stated emphatically that "there is essentially no difference between a word and an image" (254). The word is already an image, that is, the word in and of itself (*slovo, kak takovoe*) is a symbol. He asks, "Do we need, therefore, any particular intentional symbolism in Russian poetry?" (254). From this he derives his appeal to write "imageless verse" (*bezòbraznye stikhi*) ("Word and Culture," 226).[31] From this point of view Russian Symbolism appeared as "false-symbolism" (*lzhe-simvolizm*).

Mandelshtam seems to be suggesting the following creative strategy: a poem develops not by ascribing secondary symbolic meanings to a word (the move from "rose" to "sun") but by unfolding the semantic potentials already contained within the word. Working with sense turns out to be much the same as working with sound: in the first case, one deals with the development of the internal form (the original root meaning) while in the second, what is at issue is the development of a word's external (sound) form.[32] Such a technique applied to a poem as a whole involves the use of a ready-made verbal formula ("the word") in the capacity of an image that anticipates the poem itself (described above in connection with the poem *"Obraz tvoi..."*).

By applying the "scientific" conception of the word derived from the positivist philologist Potebnia, Mandelshtam arrived at a notion of the word which reaffirms the union of its two natures, that is, the word as thing, the word in its denotative meaning, and the word as symbol, the word in its metaphorical or symbolic meaning. Without ceasing to be a thing, without losing its denotative meaning, the word also functions as a symbol.

The issue, however, is not exhausted by its "scientific" side. Mandelshtam constantly resorts to theological metaphors in his essays. "The word as such" is described as a "living word," a "word-flesh," a "word-Eucharist" (226). The epigraph to "On the Nature of the Word," taken from Gumilev's poem "The Word" (*Slovo*) (from the text by an Acmeist), contains a direct reference to the idea of the Word as God: "In the Gospel of John it is said that the word is God" (И в Евангелии от Иоанна / Сказано, что слово — это Бог).

I would like to suggest that the problem of the word's poetic nature is resolved in Mandelshtam's essays in accordance with Christological doctrine and the Chalcedonian creed. The Council of Chalcedon marked the victory of Orthodoxy over two extreme tendencies, one that emphasized mysticism, undervaluing Christ's humanity, and one that emphasized rationality, de-emphasizing Christ's divinity. The Chalcedonian creed maintains the oneness of Christ's two natures, the human and the divine. This oneness in no way diminishes the distinction between the two natures united within the one figure of Christ. In the person of Christ (the Word made flesh) human nature, in no way lessened, is united with the divine. In a similar manner, Mandelshtam's "word as such" represents a unity of the word's denotative ("common") and symbolic meanings.

To summarize, in his essays of the early 1920s Mandelshtam repudiated the initial premise of Ivanov and Belyi—that the poetic word was of a fundamentally different nature than the word of the common language. For Mandelshtam a common, human word, a word of natural language or the Acmeistic "word as such," in and by itself proves to be the "word-symbol," or the "Word-God," "living word," "word-made-flesh."

Mandelshtam connected his new conception of the poetic word, the sacralization of the "word as such," with the Russian Revolution. He maintained in "Word and Culture" that with the Revolution a new era in the life of the word began. Social upheaval led to a transformation of the word's nature—the word became flesh. "A heroic era in the life of the word has begun. The Word is flesh and bread" (225). Mandelshtam's argument ran as follows: the sacralization of the word was a part of the sacralization of culture, itself the result of the secularization of the state that came with the Revolution. He described the situation in contemporary social terms: "Culture has become the church. The church-culture has become separated from the state" (223).[33] With the Revolution sacralization spread through all spheres of human life: "Worldly life no longer concerns us; we no longer eat; we partake of a monastic meal-sharing (*u nas ne eda, a trapeza*); we have not rooms but cells (*ne komnata, a kel'ia*), not clothes but vestments (*ne odezhda, a odeianie*) . . . . We drink water from clay vessels as if it were wine . . . . Apples, bread, potatoes quench not only physical hunger but spiritual as well" (223). Here Mandelshtam metaphorically equates the concept of culture with that of "Christianity": "any cultured person is now a Christian" (223). The final metaphor in this chain is the "word made flesh": "the word is flesh for him [any cultured person] and the simple loaf is joy and mystery" (223).

One of the principal sources for these metaphors and ideas is F. F. Zelinskii's conception of Hellenism. Zelinskii's book *The Religion of Hellenism* (*Religiia éllinizma*) was not published until 1922; however, the book was based on his university lectures, and its basic ideas were apparently widely known in artistic circles at an earlier time.[34] Zelinskii viewed the interrelation between the processes of secularization and sacralization which encompassed diverse aspects of life (art, science, daily routine) as the major dynamic forces of Hellenism. According to Zelinskii, Hellenistic culture endowed an individual's bed (*lozhe*) and dining table (*trapeza*) with sacred significance. He concluded this argument with discussion of the magic of the word, which at the beginning of the Hellenistic period spread throughout Persia and Egypt and was taken up by the mediators between these two cultures, the Jews. The magi of Egypt, Zelinskii wrote, "plumed themselves on knowing the true names of all the demons . . . . They were the true *'imiaslavtsy.'*"[35] Zelinskii maintained that the interrelation and struggle between secularization and sacralization prepared the way for the genesis of the new Christian religion in the bosom of the Hellenistic culture: "Christianity could arise only in such times when the creative forces of sacralized culture reached their peak."[36]

It appears that in his essays of the early 1920s Mandelshtam equated the Russian Revolution with the era of the rise of Christianity, that is, with the epoch of the "incarnation of the word," as Zelinskii described it. In the framework of this metaphor Mandelshtam attributed a Hellenistic spirit to contemporary Russian culture and reflected on the "Hellenistic nature" of the Russian language. By "Hellenistic nature" he apparently understood the tendency of the word in a common language (the Russian language) towards incarnation: "The Russian language is a Hellenistic language. By virtue of an entire array of historical conditions, the living powers of Hellenistic culture . . . headed into the bosom of Russian speech, endowing it with the self-confident mystery of the Hellenistic world view, a mystery of free incarnation; *for this reason the Russian language became speaking and resonating flesh* ("On the Nature of the Word" 245).

By claiming, in his "Word and Culture," that "a heroic epoch had begun in the life of the word," Mandelshtam apparently responded to an earlier declaration made by Ivanov in "The Testaments of Symbolism." "Symbolism," wrote Ivanov, "seemed to be the anticipation of a hypothetically conceivable, truly religious epoch of language," when language would embrace the two distinct modes of discourse (discourse about empirical reality and discourse "about objects and relations of another order") (129). Mandelshtam claimed that a religious epoch of language arrived with the Revolution and with the new, Acmeist poetics. The new poetic word, the Acmeist "word as such," a unity of the two distinct natures, is the word-God.

This general metaphor—the epoch of the new poetics as an epoch of Christianity—provides a framework for interpreting the metaphoric images in Mandelshtam's philological essays of the 1920s. To clarify their meaning, however, we must briefly turn our attention to other sources on the history of Christianity Mandelshtam could have consulted. I would like to suggest that Mandelshtam derived many of his ideas on the rise of Christianity from Sergei Trubetskoi's *Doctrines of Logos in its History* (*Uchenie o Logose v ego istorii,* 1900), a book that was widely known and highly regarded in artistic circles. Trubetskoi equated the concept of Christianity with the "doctrine of the Logos." The birth of Christianity was seen, therefore, as the act of the incarnation of the Word. In historical perspective, the appearance of Christianity was possible thanks to the "meeting of Greece and Judea" within Hellenistic culture. This meeting, according to Trubetskoi, meant the unification of the Greek philosophical ("abstract") concept of Logos with the concrete Judaic notion of a living god. This union of two cultural paradigms was itself an act of incarnation of the word: it posited the "word" in the form of the living god, Christ.

Trubetskoi took as his starting point Vladimir Solov'ev's claim that Judaic thought was characterized by a marked tendency toward materializing the divine principle; it was this materialistic tendency, claimed Solov'ev, that led to the appearance of the notion of the word "incarnate."[37] Likewise, Trubetskoi in his *Doctrine of Logos* accorded an important place in the history of Christianity to Judaic thought.

Central to Trubetskoi's argument is a claim for the positive, rational nature of Christian doctrine. Christianity or, in his words, "the revelation of the word's human face," rendered the word a tangible reality, an object of actual experience rather than abstract speculation. He insisted that the Christian doctrine of Logos constituted a weltanschauung of "well-grounded idealism" or, in other words, a "materialization and humanization of idealism." In this as well Trubetskoi followed Solov'ev, who saw the main significance of Christianity in its "positive" idea of incarnate divinity and godmanhood.

Trubetskoi's theories throw light on several aspects of Mandelshtam's argument. Among them are references to Henri Bergson. Mandelshtam connected to Bergson's neo-vitalistic philosophy the concept of culture's evolutionary process, the interpretation of Hellenism, and a view of the word as an intricate matrix of phenomena, as a link or "system" (256). The content of Bergson's philosophy was subjected in Mandelshtam's hands to the same metaphorical reworking as are so many other concepts advanced in these essays. In Bergson's thought Mandelshtam espied the manifestation of a "Judaic mind," the representative of monotheistic consciousness. He wrote that "contemporary philosophy in the person of Bergson, whose profoundly Judaic mind is obsessed by the persistent necessity of a practical monotheism, proposes to us the doctrine of a system of phenomena" (242). Appealing to Bergson must have strengthened the metaphoric identification of contemporary Russian culture with the culture of Hellenism at the time of the birth of Christianity. Following Trubetskoi's conception, Mandelshtam accorded to Bergson's philosophy a role equivalent to the Judaic element in the formation of Christian doctrine.

It is conceivable that Trubetskoi's conception encouraged Mandelshtam's tendency toward "materializing" and "humanizing" the symbolistic theory of the word. Mandelshtam's conception of the word contrasted sharply with the Symbolists' "mystical idealism." The "positive" nature of the poetic word, its "reality," "substantiveness," "corporeality," were of primary importance to Mandelshtam, particularly at the beginning of the 1920s. His position, however, was not the positivism of materialist philosophy but the positivism of Orthodox Christianity as interpreted by such religious philosophers as Vladimir Solov'ev and Sergei Trubetskoi.

In summary, Mandelshtam's views on the nature of the word evolved in the following manner. In the essays of the 1920s Mandelshtam accepted (more accurately, expropriated) the Symbolist concept of the poetic word as the equivalent of the divine Logos. However, Mandelshtam found fault with the Symbolists for not giving full value to the "human," "corporeal," "material" nature of the word. In philological terms, Mandelshtam's "word as such" is a word that, without losing its qualities as an element of natural language or losing its direct, denotative meaning, became a poetic word-symbol possessing the properties of energy and creative power attributed to it by the Symbolists. In theological terms, the "word as such," without losing its corporeal or material nature, "was God." Mandelshtam's conception was directed against the Symbolist principle of language's dual nature. He resolved the problem of dualism of the word in accordance with Chalcedonian dogma. Thus, Mandelshtam assumed the position of "Orthodoxy," which triumphs over Symbolism's mystical heresy.

I must add in conclusion that Mandelshtam's views on the nature of the poetic word should be seen as an intricate array of metaphoric notions, an evolving poetic text, rather than as a full-fledged theory.

Notes

I wish to thank Russell Valentino who translated this article from Russian. A preprint of this article (in Russian) appeared in *Literaturnoe obozrenie,* no. 1, 1991.

1. Thus, for instance, the problem of the relationship between man and poet (or life and work), one of central importance to Pushkin studies of the first quarter of the twentieth century, was resolved in accordance with the Christological model. See my articles, "Pushkin v zhizni cheloveka Serebrianogo veka," in *Cultural Mythologies of Russian Modernism: From the Golden Age to the Silver Age,* ed. Boris Gasparov, Robert P. Hughes, and Irina Paperno (Berkeley, 1992) 19–51; and "Nietzscheanism and the Return of Pushkin in Twentieth-Century Culture (1899–1937)," in *Nietzsche's Influence on Soviet Culture,* ed. Bernice Glatzer Rosenthal (forthcoming).

2. V. Ivanov, "Zavety simvolizma," *Borozdy i mezhi* (Moscow, 1910). All page references to this essay are provided in the text. It should be noted that in early medieval theology the concept of the symbol had a different meaning than in contemporary usage. According to Adolph Harnack, the author to whom Belyi refers in "Magiia slov," "at that time 'symbol' denoted a thing which, in some kind of way, really is what it signifies." See *History of Dogma* (London, 1910) 2:144.

3. A. Belyi, "Magiia slov," *Simvolizm: kniga statei* (Moscow, 1910). All page references to this essay are provided in the text. On Belyi's theory of the poetic word, see Steven Cassedy, "Bely's Theory of Symbolism as Formal Iconics of Meaning" and "Bely the Thinker," in *Andrey Bely: Spirit of Symbolism,* ed. John E. Malmstad (Ithaca, 1987).

4. In his "'Mysl' i iazyk': filosofiia iazyka A. A. Potebni," Belyi wrote of Potebnia, "The Symbolist Verlaine speaks to us, not a professor from Khar'kov" ("Logos" [1910], bk. 2, p. 246). On Potebnia's influence on Belyi, see Cassedy 292–293 and 324–331; see also E. Bel'kind, "A. Belyi i A. A. Potebnia (k istorii voprosa)," *Tezisy I Vsesoiuznoi konferentsii "Tvorchestvo A. A. Bloka i russkaia kul'tura XX veka"* (Tartu, 1975) 160–164.

5. In *Mysl' i iazyk;* quoted from A. A. Potebnia, *Èstetika i poètika* (Moscow, 1976) 173.

6. See Belyi's commentaries to "Magiia slov," *Simvolizm* 619–624.

7. For analysis of the connections between theology and the philosophy of language, see Naftali Prat, "Orthodox Philosophy of Language in Russia," *Studies in Soviet Thought* 20 (1979): 1–21.

Among the central achievements of the "Orthodox philosophy of language" are the works of Pavel Florenskii, such as "Sviashchennoe pereimenovanie" (1907), "Mysl' i iazyk," "Imena" (the early 1920s). For a description of these works and a bibliography,

see A. S. Trubachev and N. K. Bonetskaia's foreword to P. A. Florenskii's "O literature," in *Voprosy literatury,* no. 1 (1988): 150–152. Also important are: S. N. Bulgakov,
Filosofiia imeni (Paris, 1953 [written in the 1920s]), and A. F. Losev's *Filosofiia imeni*
(Moscow, 1927). Both these works were written under the influence of Florenskii, and
both Bulgakov and Losev trace their conceptions of the word to philosophical realism.
Of a more complex nature is the philosophical position of Mikhail Bakhtin, who also
uses theological categories. According to Clark and Holquist, "unlike Florensky,
Bakhtin succeeded in translating his theological concerns into a philosophy of dis-
course." See Katerina Clark and Michael Holquist, *Mikhail Bakhtin* (Cambridge,
Mass., 1984) 137.

8. See the manifestos of A. Kruchenykh and V. Khlebnikov: the unpublished drafts
on *"slovo, kak takovoe"* and *"bukva, kak takovaia"* (1913), *"Deklaratsiia slova, kak
takovogo"* (1913), "Novye puti slova" (1913). See *Manifesty i programmy russkikh futu-
ristov* (Munich, 1967); and V. Shklovskii's "Voskreshenie slova" (1914).

9. *Imiaslavie* can be traced to the monk Ilarion's book *Na gorakh Kavkaza. Beseda
dvukh startsev podvizhnikov o vnutrennem edinenii s Gospodom nashikh serdets cherez
molitvu Iisus Khristovu* (1st ed., Batallashinsk, 1907; 2d ed., rev. 1910; 3d ed., Kievo-
Pecherskaia Lavra, 1912). Ilarion reflects in his book on the presence of God in the
Jesus prayer and identifies the name of Jesus as "God Himself." Soon after the appearance of the book, the journal *Russkii inok* published a review written by the monk
Khrisanf (I. I. Minaev), in which the author repudiated the doctrine of Ilarion, calling
it heretical. In the second edition of his book Ilarion included a reply to this review.
The Holy Synod in a decree of 27 August 1913 declared the movement a heresy. The
movement was interpreted as an anti-government revolt, and its proponents were subdued by military force. All of these events continued to be widely discussed in print up
until 1917. For a bibliography on the subject, see G. Florovskii, *Puti russkogo bogoslo-
viia* (Paris, 1937) 571–572. Prat has indicated the importance of the movement for the
development of the "Orthodox philosophy of language" (2).

10. The formulations of the theologian M. Muretov, author of *Filosofiia Filona
Alesandriiskogo v otnoshenii k ucheniiu Ioanna Bogoslova o Logose* (Moscow, 1885);
quoted from Ieroskhimonakh Antonii (A. K. Bulatovich), "Moia bor'ba s imiabor-
tsami na Sviatoi gore," *Istoricheskii vestnik* (October 1916): 166.

11. Quoted from Antonii, "Moia bor'ba" 164–165.

12. The formulation of G. Florovskii. See his *Vostochnye ottsy IV veka* (Paris, 1931)
143. On the views of Gregory of Nyssa, see pp. 135–143. The source for these ideas was
Plato's *Cratylus;* on this subject see Naftali Prat.

13. See P. A. Florenskii's preface ("Ot redaktsii") to Antonii's (A. K. Bulatovich)
Apologiia very vo imia Bozhie i vo imia Iisusa (Moscow, 1913). The outline of Florenskii's *Mysl' i iazyk* included the section "Magichnost' slova. *Imiaslavie* kak filosofskaia
predposylka." See P. A. Florenskii, *Mnimosti v geometrii* (Moscow, 1922) 68–69. See
also S. N. Bulgakov, "Afonskoe delo," *Russkaia mysl'* (September 1912); V. Ern,
Razbor poslaniia Sviatogo Sinoda ob imeni Bozh'em (Moscow, 1917); S. Askol'dov, "O
pustynnikakh Kavkaza," *Russkaia mysl'* (May 1916). Sergei Bulgakov served as secretary for the subcommittee of the Moscow Council, which was convened in 1917 and
planned to review the problem of *imiaslavie.* For Bulgakov *imiaslavie* served as the

point of departure for his *Filosofiia imeni,* in which he analyzed the issue of the name of God (in Bulgakov's terminology, "the development of the doctrine of Logos") as a part of the general philosophical problem of the nature of language. Bulgakov drew an analogy between "human naming" (general linguistic and poetic naming) and the divine act of the incarnation of the word: "Human naming exists in the image and likeness of divine" (178). The product of such naming is the word-symbol (Bulgakov referred to the concept introduced by Viacheslav Ivanov). The symbol is a word "not in the nihilistic sense of a sign invented by man, as claimed by *imiabortsy* and iconoclasts (*ikonobortsy*), but in the sense of a unification of two beings, and thus of force and depth" (192). Bulgakov employs the following metaphors for the word-symbol: the word as holy water, as Eucharist, as the holy blessed bread; the word as icon, temple, altar, shrine (192).

14. V. Ivanov, "Kop'e Afiny," *Po zvezdam* (St. Petersburg, 1909) 47–48, 50–51. The metaphor of culture as prayer (*"umnoe delanie"*) is also found in Ivanov's "O veselom remesle i umnom veselii" (1907, included in *Po zvezdam*). See also Belyi's comment: "Ivanov priznaet za tvorchestvom—obuslovlivaiushchee iavlenie molitvu (bogodelanie, teurgiiu)." *Vesy,* no. 5 (1908): 61.

15. N. S. Gumilev, "Nasledie simvolizma i akmeizm," in *Sobranie sochinenii v 4 tt.,* ed. G. P. Struve and B. A. Filippov (Washington, 1968) 4:175.

16. Ivanov uses the expressions "correct aesthetic profession" (as applied to the heart of the Symbolist movement) and "aesthetic heresies" in his "Ekskurs: o sekte i dogmate" (1914), *Borozdy i mezhi* 160–164.

17. N. Gumilev, "Pis'ma o russkoi poezii," *Apollon,* no. 1 (1914) and no. 1 (1915); see also L. Ginzburg, *Literatura v poiskakh real'nosti* (Leningrad, 1987) 157.

18. John Malmstad, "Mandelshtam's 'Silentium': A Poet's Response to Ivanov," in *Vyacheslav Ivanov: Poet, Critic and Philosopher,* ed. Robert Louis Jackson and Lowry Nelson, Jr. (New Haven, 1986) 236–252.

19. In metrico-rhythmical form and imagery the poem "I ponyne na Afone" follows Russian religious verse (the genre known as *dukhovnyi stikh*), in which such images as the bird singing out "cherubic verse" from the branches of a "sacred" or "miraculous tree" (*chudnoe drevo*) growing "on a steep hill" (*na krutoi gore*) abound. Another possible source is the book by Monk Ilarion (a peasant-monk), *Na gorakh Kavkaza* (see note 9), in which the image of the tree appears as a symbol of Jesus prayer. See *Na gorakh Kavkaza* (Kiev, 1912) 76, 94.

On Mandelshtam's treatment of the name of God and of the name in love, see Omry Ronen, *An Approach to Mandelshtam* (Jerusalem, 1983) 90, 202–203.

20. Boris Uspenskii noted the connection between the poem "Obraz tvoi" and *imia-slavie* in "Semiotics of the Icon (An Interview)," *PTL. A Journal for Descriptive Poetics and Theory of Literature* 3 (1978): 537–539. See also Gregory Freidin, *A Coat of Many Colors: Osip Mandelshtam and His Mythologies of Self-Representation* (Berkeley, 1987) 356, n. 124. Uspenskii considers *imiaslavie* the source of the motif of the "blessed, senseless word" (*blazhennoe, bessmyslennoe slovo*) and draws connections between the movement and a wide range of Mandelshtam's poems; Freidin also treats the image of the "blessed, senseless word" (from the poem "V Peterburge my soidemsia snova," 1920) as directly linked to *imiaslavie* (181). I believe that the theme of the magical word,

which is central for Mandelshtam's verse, and the image of the "blessed, senseless word" have meanings traceable to various sources and not only to the *imiaslavie* movement. Ronen has shown that the images of the magical word in the poetry of the 1920s can be divided into two different groups—the proper name and *"zaum'"* (trans-sense) (6). I find it more plausible that the image of the "blessed, senseless word," as well as other images of senseless words, are connected with Khlebnikov's concept of the mystical glossalalia, or the "language of the gods," the language of charms and spells, that is, in Khlebnikov's words, "the sacred language of paganism." See V. Khlebnikov, "O stikhakh" (1920); on this topic see Ronald Vroon, *Velimir Xlebnikov's Shorter Poems: A Key to the Coinages* (Ann Arbor, 1983) 188–192. Among the poems connected to *imiaslavie* Freidin mentions "Imiabozhtsy" (1915); Mandelshtam has no such poem.

21. The image of touch (*osiazanie*) is found in the writings of *imiaslavtsy:* "He who recites the Jesus prayer comes into real contact (*real'no soprikasaetsia s*) with God Jesus himself—like Thomas, touches (*osiazaet*) him spiritually" (*Istoricheskii vestnik,* October 1916, 167). The image of Thomas also appears in Mandelshtam's "Grifel'naia oda," where his outstretched fingers reach into the words of the poem as if into Christ's flesh, seemingly in an attempt to feel the concreteness of the poetic word.

22. See Antonii (A. K. Bulatovich), *Apologiia* 66.

23. A. A. Potebnia, *Iz zapisok po teorii slovesnosti* (Khar'kov, 1905) 452.

24. Examples cited by Potebnia in this regard include Tiutchev's "Слезы людские":

Слезы людские, о слезы людские,
Льетесь вы ранней и поздней порой,
Льетесь безвестные, льетесь незримые,
Неистощимые, неисчислимые,
Льетесь, как льются струи дождевые
В осень глухую ночною порой.

(Human tears, oh, human tears,
You pour at late and early times,
You pour unknown, you pour unseen,
Sourceless, countless,
You pour as the streams of rainfall
Into the muffled autumn at night time.)

According to Potebnia, one of this poem's premises is a ready-made verbal formula—a comparison of rain to tears. Another component is the set of direct impressions that the poet received on the evening of the poem's creation, among which are the return home during a rainy night in an open carriage (77). Compare this with Gumilev's assertion, in his review of the second edition of Mandelshtam's collection *Kamen'* (*Apollon,* no. 1 [1916]), that the "inspiring agent" for Mandelshtam is "only the Russian language," whereas phenomena of the external human world serve as a "pretext" for creating poetry. As an example Gumilev mentions "a Bach concert [and] a newspaper article on *imiabozhtsy.*"

The motif of "accidental" utterance of the name of God might also be traced to Potebnia's *Iz zapisok po teorii slovesnosti:*

At various times there has been and continues to be a belief that the word serves only as a mediary between the supplicant and God; but this cannot be the general basis for the belief under consideration. The word becomes a deed not only in prayer but also when it is pronounced accidently and without intention; that is, not only when it is assumed that an evil deity lurks in wait for an individual's mistakes in order to turn them to his harm, but also when there is no thought whatsoever about some outside being or entity beside the word itself. This belief is premised on the notion that the word is itself a being (454).

25. Here and elsewhere in the text all references to Mandelshtam's essays are to Osip Mandelshtam, *Sobranie sochinenii*, ed. G. P. Struve and B. A. Filippov, 2d ed., vol. 2 (Munich, 1971). On the connections between this idea in Mandelshtam and Potebnia, see Freidin 162. The first scholar to note the connection was A. Bem in his review of "O prirode slova" (*Volia Rossii* [Prague] nos. 6–7 [1923]: 159–160).

26. Ronen 281, n. 88.

27. Uspenskii 539. Beside the theological, there is yet another level in "Ia v khorovod tenei": the poem is saturated with allusions to Pushkin. These are such characteristic elements of Pushkin's poetic lexicon as *milaia ten'* ("для милой тени / Не нахожу ни слез ни пени"), *"revnost',"* *"ugol',"* (the last two referring to Pushkin's *"Prorok"* with its theme of the poet-prophet, who possesses a living and acting word). Pushkin's voice resonates also in the syntactic and rhetorical structure of the lines "И богохульствует, и сам себя клянет, / И угли ревности глотает" (cf. "Я трепещу и проклинаю, / И горько жалуюсь, и горько слезы лью" [Pushkin, "Vospominanie"]). Finally, the lines "Земли девической упругие холмы / Лежат спеленатые туго" refer to Pushkin's "Gavriiliada" ("двух девственных холмов / Под полотном упругое движенье") This subtext serves as the motivation for the verb *"bogokhul'stvuet."* The resulting impression is that Pushkin's voice, or his "shadow," is present in Mandelshtam's poem. It would seem that the "dear shadow" (*milaia ten'*) and the "secret image" (*tainyi obraz*) refer to Pushkin. It is characteristic that Pushkin's name should remain unstated in the poem. According to my observations, not once does Mandelshtam refer to Pushkin by name in his verse though he cites him constantly; this is in marked contrast to the practice of his contemporaries (Blok, Kuzmin, Akhmatova). Mandelshtam, it would seem, follows a self-imposed prohibition against reference to Pushkin's name. (Several of the Pushkin associations were pointed out to me by Boris Gasparov.)

I would like to suggest an additional motivation for making a connection between the theme of the name of God and Pushkin. The main apologists of *imiaslavie*, Ieroskhimonakh Antonii (A. K. Bulatovich) and Skhimonakh Ilarion (Zelepukin, Bulatovich's former servant-companion), in the years preceding their monastic careers, participated in military expeditions to Ethiopia, which were described in Bulatovich's widely read book *S voiskami Menelika II. Dnevnik pokhoda iz Efiopii k ozeru Rudol'fa* (St. Petersburg, 1900). It was suggested that the idea of the divine nature of the name of God was prompted to Bulatovich and Zelepukin by liturgical practices of the "Black Christians" in Ethiopia (see "Afonskaia smuta," *Rech'* [22 May 1913]. This connection between *imiaslavie* and Ethiopia, the birthplace of Pushkin's ancestor Hannibal, could have prompted Mandelshtam to draw a symbolic connection between the theme of the name of God and the Pushkin theme.

28. According to P. Nerler, the notion that the word is "free" to move from one "thing" to the other can be traced to Bergson's *Evolution creatrice;* see the commentary to O. Mandelshtam, *Slovo i kul'tura* (Moscow, 1987) 279. The image of a soul wandering around the body it has quit comes from Tiutchev's "Ona sidela na polu." Kiril Taranovskii notes this in his *Essays on Mandelstam* (Cambridge, Mass., 1976) 158.

29. The phrase "the word as such," used by Mandelshtam to indentify the Acmeist word (and also employed by Futurists in their manifestos; see note 12) was introduced by Belyi in his article on Potebnia ("Mysl' i iazyk: Filosofiia iazyka A. A. Potebni," *Logos* 2 [1910]. On this subject see Cassedy 325–328.

30. Freidin (172–173) suggests a different interpretation of the concept of "nominalism" in Mandelshtam's work.

31. E. A. Toddes links these notions of Mandelshtam to the philological ideas of OPOIAZ (in Mandelshtam's words, "the Russian science of poetry, brought to life by Potebnia and Andrei Belyi"). According to Toddes, in the ideas advanced by OPOIAZ in the late 1910s—early 1920s, Mandelshtam could have found a confirmation of ideas he himself had put forth in "Utro akmeizma"; this is particularly true of Shklovskii's "O poezii i zaumnom iazyke," where Shklovskii treats the notion of the internal sound speech (*vnutrenniaia zvukorech'*) that precedes a poem. See E. A. Toddes, "Mandel'shtam i opoiazovskaia filologiia," *Tynianovskii sbornik. Vtorye tynianovskie chteniia* (Riga, 1986) 79, 81. Futurist attempts, in particular those of Khlebnikov, to reformulate the Symbolist notion of the poetic word, were quite important for Mandelshtam.

32. As Ronen has shown, in actual poetic practice Mandelshtam constantly employs the device of unfolding the text by playing on the sound components or etymological meanings of key words (See Omry Ronen, "Leksicheskii povtor, podtekst i smysl v poetike Osipa Mandel'shtama." *Slavic Poetics: Essays in Honor of Kiril Taranovsky,* ed. Roman Jakobson, C. H. van Schooneveld, Dean S. Worth (The Hague and Paris, 1973). Freidin (162–165) also cites examples of etymological play with words in Mandelshtam's verse. The device of "subtext," described by Kiril Taranovskii and Omry Ronen, is essentially part of the same Potebnian strategy of working with "internal form": the subtext can be seen as a "word" that anticipates and motivates the text.

33. Freidin understands these metaphors literally, pointing to them as evidence that "Mandelshtam combined his 'nominalism' with an insistence on the social significance of art for the revolution" (175; see also p. 178).

34. K. F. Taranovskii, in his *Essays on Mandelstam* (146), introduces other examples of Mandelshtam's use of Zelinskii's ideas. Taranovskii maintains that Zelinskii served as the basic source of Mandelshtam's "Hellenism." On Mandelshtam's Hellenism, see also Victor Terras, "Classical Motives in the Poetry of Mandelstam," *The Slavic and East European Journal* 10, no. 3 (1966): 252–253.

35. F. F. Zelinskii, *Religiia ellinizma* (Prague, 1922) 105–106, 107.

36. Ibid., 108.

37. This theory is proposed by Vladimir Solov'ev in his *Evreistvo i khristianskii vopros* (1884). On this subject, see Nikita Struve, *Ossip Mandelstam* (Paris, 1982) 135. Struve suggests that there is a connection between Mandelshtam's essays and the ideas of Solov'ev, and he presents the arguments for interpreting Bergson's philosophy as a product of Judaic thought.

Icon and Logos

The Role of Orthodox Theology
in Modern Language Theory and Literary Criticism

STEVEN CASSEDY

No one will dispute the claim that twentieth-century literary criticism in the West has been obsessed with language. From formalism to structuralism, from phenomenology to poststructuralism, from Cleanth Brooks to Jacques Derrida, language has been the object of a continuing obsession. Literary criticism and linguistics, the "science" of language, have been so closely intertwined at moments in the modern age as to be indistinguishable.

Traditional historical accounts of modern criticism focus largely on Western European thinkers as the sources of this preoccupation with language. The linguistic orientation of structuralist criticism, for instance, can be readily traced back to Ferdinand de Saussure. The skeptical view of language we find in Paul de Man and Derrida can be traced back to Heidegger and ultimately Nietzsche.

The last thing we would think of as a source of modern literary and linguistic theory would be anything Russian. Russian *religious* thought would be completely out of the question. But should it be? Consider the structuralist movement, which swept American literary criticism in the 1960s and early 1970s, making French departments the most revered and feared of the literature departments at so many American institutions. The person who takes credit for inventing the "structural method" in literary studies and poetics was not French at all, but Russian. He was also not, strictly speaking, a literary critic, but a linguist. It was Roman Jakobson, who in 1929, at the first Congress of Slavists in Prague, proposed new modes of poetic analysis and, to use his expression, "christened" them the structural method.[1]

The standard account of Jakobson's role in the rise of structuralism is like the account of most modern literary criticism, focusing exclusively on Western European models and predecessors. Saussure is mentioned as a major influence on the young Jakobson, and Jakobson's early critique of the Swiss linguist is mentioned as proof of this influence. But in fact neither Saussure nor

Jakobson's response to him was the source of Jakobson's poetic or linguistic theory. If we can believe Jakobson himself, the impulse to his pioneering work in various fields came from some rather surprising quarters: for his new direction in language studies he credits artists like Picasso, Joyce, Braque, Stravinsky, Khlebnikov, and Le Corbusier (*SW* 1:631–632); for the analysis of language "in its means and functions" he credits the poetry of Khlebnikov (*SW* 1:633); and for the analytic study of verse he credits the essays of Andrei Bely (*SW* 5:569). Jakobson's early work in the area of poetics shows above all his debt to the language theories of formalist critics like Shklovsky and *zaum'* poets like Khlebnikov and Kruchenykh.

Thus if theory of language and literary criticism are intimately connected, if Jakobson played the role he claims to have played in the rise of this one style of modern criticism, then we cannot help acknowledging that there is a strong indigenous Russian element in the theory of language that was to lead to structuralism. If we look at the implicit and explicit theories of language of the various figures that worked in this field at the time that Jakobson was beginning his scholarly career—some of them included in Jakobson's own accounts of his intellectual sources—we find a very different picture from the one we get in most histories of modern criticism. Instead of sober, formalistic, "scientific" theories of language, we find a strong religious current. It appears overtly in some thinkers, who unashamedly examine language from a Russian Orthodox theological perspective. It appears in disguise in others, who present their theories as the fruit of rigorous, scientific labor. But it leaves its mark on almost everyone.

As it happens, religious language philosophy underwent a revival in the early years of the twentieth century in Russia. Naftali Prat investigated this trend in an article published in 1979.[2] The movement includes such early twentieth-century figures as Pavel Florensky, Sergei Bulgakov, Gustav Shpet, Aleksei Fedorovich Losev, Andrei Bely, even "Voloshinov," whom Prat discusses as the author of *Marxism and the Philosophy of Language* (*Marksizm i filosofiia iazyka*). Prat identifies several sources for this trend: Platonism, as it traditionally dominates Orthodox theology, German idealism, Husserlian phenomenology, and Russian poets. But the dominant tradition, the one that follows Russian religious thinking in general through the ages, long before the revival that Prat speaks of, is Platonism, which means the doctrine of the Logos.[3]

In the Russian tradition, as Prat points out, Logos has to do with the unity of thought and language and the notion of adequately expressing a thought by means of the word. It is as though the Russians had got from Plato's *Cratylus* not the part about the conventionality of language, but rather the part that acknowledges that at least some measure of a name is given by nature. And when names express their named objects in a way that is given by nature, they do so by means of the essence, or *eidos* of that object.

But Logos, of course, has a Christian religious meaning, too, and while this meaning derives in part from a Platonic tradition, it contains other elements as well. Many of these other elements are Greek, but they are uniquely Christian in their combination. Credit for working out the doctrine of the Logos that has become standard in subsequent Christian theology must go to the third-century Church Father Origen, who in the *First Principles* (ca. 225 A.D.) both identifies God the Son with the Logos (something that was not new with him) and subordinates the Son to the Father (something that was to prove immensely controversial afterwards). In Christian theology Logos thus comes to be synonymous with the Son of God and thus has to do with the Incarnation. The Son of God comes into being when the Word of God (Logos) becomes Flesh. Theologians refer to this act of God as an act of condescension, or (as the Russians are fond of calling it) humiliation (*unizhenie*). The Greek is *kenosis,* which means an "emptying," because in the New Testament passage that describes this act, Christ is said (in Greek) to have "emptied himself" (that is, of his divinity) in order to assume the form of a man (Phil. 2:7).

God's Word, or the Logos, thus has a peculiar ontological status. As the Son of God, the Logos, to use the theological phrase, has two Natures in one Person. Christ is both human and divine. To the extent that he is human, other fleshly creatures can partake of his experience and thus approximate—but not attain—his divinity. From the perspective of the fleshly creature, Christ's divinity resides in him as an invisible and immeasurable essence that we can contemplate but never apprehend. Origen refers to Christ as the "image of the invisible God," hoping in this way to show Christ's divine nature as it coexists with the fleshly side that is accessible to sentient beings. "Our Saviour is therefore the image of the invisible God, the Father, being the truth, when considered in relation to the Father himself, and the image, when considered in relation to us, to whom he reveals the Father."[4] Even if the Son enjoys the same divine status as the Father, however, he is clearly subordinate to him. "We, therefore, having been made according to the image, have the Son, the original, as the truth of the noble qualities that are within us. And what we are to the Son, such is the Son to the Father, who is the truth."[5] The Son's existence springs from the Father's, and the Son is of the same goodness as the Father, but he is described as the "image of [God's] goodness," since he is born from that goodness.[6]

The doctrine of Incarnation has wide ramifications in Christian, and especially in Orthodox Christian theology. The principal area in which it shows up is iconology. It would not be extravagant to say that the theology of icons forms the basis of Russian language philosophy. The definitive formulation of this theology belongs to the eighth-century Syrian theologian Saint John of Damascus. The eighth century was the time of the great controversy over iconoclasm, and it was Saint John who resolved the controversy by providing what was to become the authoritative theology in support of the veneration of icons in the Eastern Christian churches.

The iconoclasts had charged that venerating icons meant worshiping false gods. When we bow before an icon, they argued, we are showing reverence for a mere piece of wood, an idol. In his treatise *On the Divine Images,* John responded that when we venerate an icon, our veneration goes not to the material icon itself, but to the prototype.[7] The prototype of an icon is the invisible and infinite essence that is incarnate in the icon. That invisible and infinite essence is God. Since God is the prototype of an icon, when we venerate an icon we are worshiping God, not a mere piece of wood with paints and lacquers on it.[8] Icons are thus like the Word made Flesh in that they come about as a result of an act of divine condescension. Like Christ, an icon has a dual nature: it is a material object, but it contains within it an invisible and infinite essence that we can only approximate through our experience of its material dimension.

There is a certain epistemology implicit in the account of icons that we find in Saint John of Damascus and also in the Christian notion of the Logos. The icon contains its reference to an invisible prototype. The Logos contains its invisible essence or idea. Both require a peculiar act of "seeing," one that strives to go beyond the physical object towards an immaterial essence, an idea, or grace. When we venerate an icon, we are aware that the ultimate object of our attention is something ideal that we cannot perceive. When we seek to participate in the experience of Christ, we are aware that what we seek is something that we cannot experience. Icon and Logos thus come together in the notion of idealism. Neither concept can exist without the ultimately Platonic sense that the physical thing stands for or points to something purely ideal.

This kind of essentialism will be the trademark of Russian language philosophy. It will manifest itself in various ways, but the constant factor will be the notion that the words of language contain ideal essences that allow them to perform their signifying function in a way that is motivated and necessary, rather than conventional and arbitrary. Words behave like icons or like the

Logos, and a great many Russian thinkers will wittingly or unwittingly exploit the natural confusion between the word *slovo* in its everyday sense as a unit of discourse and the word *Slovo* in its sense as the Word of God. Andrei Bely is a perfect example. In "The Emblematics of Meaning," he attempts a theory of symbolism, something that naturally involves words and language. But when he comes to talk at length of words it is in a passage having to do with the Johannine Logos, the Incarnation, and icons. The context of his discussion would suggest to the reader that "Word" should be read only as synonymous with "second person of the Trinity," but since the principal subject is the nature of symbols, it is difficult to overlook the meaning of "Word" that has to do with language.[9]

There are two doctrines in early modern Russian language theory that serve to perpetuate the idealism and essentialism I have described. The first is the doctrine of inner form, and the second is the doctrine of the poetry-prose distinction, that is, the doctrine that poetic language is intrinsically different from "ordinary" language. Both doctrines were given currency in Russian thought by the Ukrainian-born philologist Aleksandr Afanas'evich Potebnia, who also showed that they were intimately connected.

The concept of inner form had originated with the German philologist, Wilhelm von Humboldt, for whom this almost mystical notion was the secret to his dynamic conception of language. Language was a form of ceaseless activity, or *energeia,* for Humboldt, something always being creatively generated by the collective folk imagination of its speakers.[10] Inner form is what mediates between objective reality and the subjective inwardness of the speaker.[11] Potebnia altered this doctrine in a most significant way. In *Thought and Language (Mysl' i iazyk,* 1862), he defines inner form as the "closest etymological meaning" of a word, by which he meant quite simply the etymological root. Thus the closest etymological meaning of the Russian word *stol* (table) is the Slavic root /stl/, which carries the meaning "to spread."[12] The term "inner form" serves Potebnia because he believes in a surviving, essential core of meaning in words that is passed on from one generation of speakers to the next and that stays the same in spite of the numerous mutations a language undergoes.

What does this have to do with Platonic idealism? Potebnia has taken a romantic, dynamic conception of language from his German predecessor and replaced the most characteristic feature of it with something that is fixed and eternal. Where inner form in Humboldt was a force that guided the living language through its constantly present state of flux, for Potebnia it became the essence of the word, safely and immutably settled in a distant, mythical, and changeless past. There is no attempt on Potebnia's part to account for the source of the Slavic root /stl/; it simply exists, frozen in a timeless state as the origin and inner form of future words. Inner form is thus a kind of essence, a kind of *eidos* or idea that lies behind the word but is incarnate in it.

And this leads to the other concept, namely the poetry-prose distinction. For Potebnia there is language whose inner form is in evidence, and there is language whose inner form is not. The first kind of language is poetic, and the second is prosaic. To be poetic, says Potebnia, language must be symbolic, by which he means that its meaning must be directly accessible. Inner form is precisely what allows the meaning of language to be directly accessible. Thus poeticity (*poėtichnost'*), as Potebnia puts it, is the "symbolism" of language.[13]

Potebnia did not come up with the idea of the poetry-prose distinction by himself. It was an age-old idea. But two things are curious about his formulation of it. First, he attempted to give it a scientific underpinning by founding it on the concept of inner form. Second, his use of the inner form concept merely shows him to be the Platonist and idealist that he was. The secret to poetic language, this quality called *poėtichnost'*, is something that allows poetic language to signify by nature (*physei,* to use Plato's term), and that something is a fixed, eternal essence. Poetic language for Potebnia is thus iconic in the sense that the listener or reader, like one who venerates icons, must see the essence, or inner form, through the material dimension, or "outer form," of the word.

It is difficult to say whether we can safely characterize Potebnia's thought as Orthodox in the sense of being founded on Orthodox Christian faith.[14] But there is no doubt that it is Orthodox in its underlying iconic essentialism and idealism. And there is certainly no doubt that it found fertile ground in the work of later thinkers, and many of these used Orthodox religion either overtly or covertly in their theoretical writings.

Andrei Bely is an example of one who used it covertly. In 1909 he wrote, among many other things, "The Emblematics of Meaning" (*Ėmblematika smysla*) and "The magic of words" (*Magiia slov*). He also reread Potebnia and wrote a critical review of Potebnia's *Mysl' i iazyk*. After criticizing Potebnia's mysticism in the review, Bely then went on to appropriate Potebnia's ideas and terminology in his own essay, which he titled "The Magic of Words." The title and the style of this essay suggest that Bely has adopted a form of mysticism of his own, but the basic characteristic of "The Magic of Words" is its essentialism. It is all about the poetry-prose distinction, and, in one of its most heavily borrowed passages, Bely accordingly makes use of the concept of inner form (*SE* 105). He is discussing various tropes, which he calls "forms of representation." He closely adheres to the Potebnian notion that poetic language consists of three parts: the sound or outer form, the image or inner form, and the meaning or content. Bely says this:

> One thing is common among the various forms of representation: the tendency to expand the verbal presentation of the image in question, to make its boundaries unstable, to give rise to a new cycle of verbal creation, that is, to give the customary presentation an impetus in the word, to impart motion to its inner form. A change in the inner form of a word leads to the creation of a new content in an image. And thus full sway is given to our creative perception of reality.[15]

Bely's essentialism is far more obvious than just his use of the expression "inner form" (and the correlative idea that poetic language is intrinsically and essentially distinct from ordinary language). Bely, without ever saying so, relied heavily on the Russian Orthodox theology of icons in his approach to questions of aesthetics and meaning. In fact, it is no exaggeration to say that iconology is the key to the way Bely thought, and nowhere is this more evident than in "The Emblematics of Meaning," which Bely wrote in the same year as "The Magic of Words." Here the whole notion of the symbol, which Bely understands broadly as any signifying object, is based entirely on a framework of Orthodox iconology and logology. The eternal essence of symbols for Bely is something he calls "Value," but it is clear from his scheme that "Value" is just Bely's formalist substitution for "prototype," or "God."[16] For Bely, the act of perceiving a poetic word (since a poetic word is a symbol) involves an act of seeking an invisible essence incarnate (*voploshchennyi,* a word Bely uses frequently) in the word.

Viktor Shklovsky is another example of an early twentieth-century figure whose thinking is essentialist and who was interested in Potebnia. In fact, he and Bely appropriated some of the very same material from Potebnia. One of Shklovsky's earliest articles was a critique of Potebnia, in which the young formalist reproached his Ukrainian predecessor for ignoring outer form (presumably in favor of inner form, a charge that anyone familiar with Potebnia would immediately recognize as completely unfounded).[17] But Shklovsky had a fairly powerful devotion to *inner* form himself, as he showed in another of his earliest articles, "The Resurrection of the Word" (*Voskreshenie slova*). In a passage that shows extensive borrowings from

Potebnia, Shklovsky talks about the central, vivid element in a word that becomes lost as the word is subjected to continued use. The name he uses for that element is "inner form."[18]

The whole cast of Shklovsky's thought in "The Resurrection of the Word" (*Voskreshenie slova*) is theological. The title is not an arbitrary choice of metaphors. *Voskreshenie slova* means literally the "raising of the word" in the sense of the "raising" of Lazarus (*voskreshenie Lazaria* in Russian). The idea expressed throughout the article is the same as in Bely's "The Magic of Words" and the same as in Potebnia. Poetic language is intrinsically different from ordinary language, and the reason is that the poetic word contains an essence that is lost to perception the more that word is used. Words are thus more poetic just after they have been created. "Today," Shklovsky says, "words are dead, and language resembles a cemetery, whereas the word that had just come into being was imaginal and full of life [*zhivo obrazno*]. Every word in its basis [*osnova*] is a trope. . . . And often, when one succeeds in reaching the image that had formed the basis [*osnova*] of a word but that has been lost, obliterated, one is amazed at its beauty, a beauty that once was but is no more."[19] To "resurrect" the word is to reestablish contact with its essence. The analogy to icon and Logos could not be more pronounced, since the "raising" or "resurrection" signals the presence of the divinity, and icons and the Logos, properly speaking, contain the divinity incarnate.

There are thinkers in the early twentieth century who write about language from an overtly theological perspective. The most prominent of these is Sergei Bulgakov (1871–1944). His principal work in this field is called *Philosophy of the Name* (*Filosofiia imeni*), a work that was written in 1919 but not published until 1953, after Bulgakov's death.[20] Bulgakov makes no excuses for his Orthodox thinking and makes no attempt to disguise the theological and iconological structure of his philosophy. For him, the (everyday) word is inseparable from the Word (of God). Just as the Word of God was made incarnate and thus contains within it the essence of the divinity, the everyday word contains a Platonic idea, or *eidos*. Bulgakov equates this *eidos* with what he calls the "inner word" (*FI* 21). Icons and names are virtually identical concepts for Bulgakov. "Every icon," he says, "is a name that has taken root and sprouted" (*FI* 182). God's name is a "verbal icon of the Godhead" (*FI* 184).

Bulgakov even had some things to say about poetic language that place him squarely in the tradition I have been discussing. After asserting that there are not words, only *the* word, not *logoi*, only *the logos*, Bulgakov invokes what sounds like the standard Formalist-Futurist doctrine of the poetry-prose distinction. The word in poetry, says Bulgakov, is distinguished from the word in prose because "in poetry the life of the word itself is felt," "the word itself is the end, not the means, as it is in prose" (*FI* 144). In Formalist and Futurist theories of poetic language, the poetic word always called attention to itself "as such" (*kak takovoe*), and this always had to do with its ideal signifying power, something that in writers like Shklovsky was linked with inner form.

Since Bulgakov's principal work on language was published so late and since he was forced into exile in 1922, his role in the history of modern language philosophy is difficult to assess. I mention him largely as an example of a thinker whose ideas on language were manifestly derived from Orthodox theology.

The truly pivotal figure in our story, however, is Roman Jakobson, whose period of exile (most of his life), proved so enormously fruitful and influential in the West. I spoke earlier of Jakobson's debt to various poets and artists. His earliest work, written when he still lived in Russia, is cast in a Formalist-Futurist mold and sounds like an odd combination of early Shklovsky and Khlebnikov dressed up in the slightly more respectable fashion of then-current linguistics. But the clothes do not make the man in this case; they hide him. Underneath, there is an unremitting Platonic idealist still entirely in the grip of the traditional Russian myths about language.

Later on, especially after he came to the United States, Jakobson was intent on establishing his identity as a scientist; it was all part of the effort to claim legitimacy for the "science" of language whose most famous spokesman he was. But he was a poetician in addition to being a linguist, and poetics was the thing that always brought out the man of faith in Jakobson throughout his career. "Modern Russian poetry" (*Noveishaia russkaia poèziia*), Jakobson's early article on Khlebnikov, is full of talk about the poetry-prose distinction. Uncritically accepting Khlebnikov's own idea about the self-valued, or self-spun word (*samovitoe slovo*) Jakobson says that "poetry," "is the formation of a self-valued, 'self-spun' word" (*SW* 5:305). Poetic language differs from ordinary language because in poetic language "linguistic representations (both phonetic and semantic) focus more attention on themselves" (*SW* 5:304). He unabashedly uses Shklovsky's notion of the petrification of language and the need to invigorate it by creating words that call attention to themselves "as such." "The form of words in practical language," he says, "easily ceases to be consciously felt, it dies away, becomes petrified, whereas the perception of the form of a poetic neologism, a form given *in statu nascendi,* is absolutely compulsory" (*SW* 5:333). "Poetry is language in its aesthetic function," he says in another place in the essay (*SW* 5:305). It is in this context that he issues perhaps the most famous sentence of his study on Khlebnikov. What allows poetic language to have an "aesthetic function" is the distinctive quality of such language, and that quality Jakobson calls *literaturnost'*, which he defines as "what makes a given work a literary work" (*SW* 5:305).

At one moment he invokes the doctrine of inner form so casually and un-critically as to suggest that there can be no dispute about its scientific validity (*SW* 5:354). He is speaking of Khlebnikov's neologisms and how they appear to be "seeking out a meaning for themselves." The word in Khlebnikov's poetry, he says, "loses its object-quality [*predmetnost'*], then its inner and finally even its outer form" (*SW* 5:354). Everywhere there is the sense that poetic language contains a hidden essence, some ideal core that clearly distinguishes it from ordinary language but that is never susceptible to any kind of serious, scientific characterization.

"What is Poetry?" is a question that Jakobson continued to ask himself throughout his career, even years after he wrote the article that bears the question (in Czech) as its title. And the answer always had to do with essences. In "What is Poetry?"—which Jakobson wrote in the early 1930s—there is still talk of inner form and of an abstract quality called *poètichnost'* (the same word that Potebnia had used some eighty years earlier) that inheres in poetic language and makes it poetic rather than ordinary. "Poeticity," Jakobson says, "is present when the word is felt as a word and not a mere representation of the object being named or an outburst of emotion, when words and their composition, their meaning, their external and inner form acquire a weight and value of their own instead of referring indifferently to reality" (*SW* 3:750). Both *poètichnost'* and *literaturnost'* are deeply essentialist, almost mystical terms, as Elmar Holenstein, who has written about Jakobson's connection with both the phenomenological and the structuralist movements, has pointed out.[21]

The fact is that Jakobson, this man of science, was never entirely comfor-table with the skeptical idea that language is an arbitrary system of signs. In 1965 he published an article called "Quest for the Essence of Language," in which he referred to Saussure's doctrine of *l'arbitraire du signe* and then went on to list instances in language where the sign appears *not* to be arbitrary. For example, in the phrase *veni, vidi, vici* there is a "diagrammatic resemblance" between sign and signified because the order of the words corresponds to the order of the actions they relate. And in most cases the length of words corre-sponds to concepts of degree and number: superlatives are usually longer than comparatives, comparatives are usually longer than positives, and, with the notable exception of zero-ending genitive plurals in Russian, plurals are usually longer than singulars.[22]

Jakobson went back and forth on the question of the arbitrariness of the sign, apparently without realizing it. For instance, in his 1958 article, "On Linguistic Aspects of Translation," he asserted that there is no *signatum* without a *signum,* no signified thing without a sign to signify it. This statement is based on a view of language that is the very opposite of the mystical and essentialist view Jakobson adopts in other places. Here language is a closed system that generates its own objects and that has no need of an independently existing world of objects to signify. As Jakobson explicitly says, those objects do not exist outside language; a *signatum* comes into being only when there is a *signum.* Jakobson's essentialist view of language, by contrast, will always insist on an independent world of objects, real or imaginary, to which the *essential* nature of the sign-signified relationship allows signs to refer in an ideal way.

But whenever Jakobson came to speak of poetic language, his essentialism returned full force. No matter what he said about the arbitrariness of the sign in language in general, poetic language appeared to retain its claim to the "by nature" (*physei*) sign-signified relation. In "Quest for the Essence of Language" Jakobson discusses various factual similarities between signifier and signified. Certain sounds in language actually show a resemblance to the things they refer to in the real world, Jakobson says. The resemblance is particularly noticeable in poetic language, which thus, more than any other type of language, defies the skeptical, "modern" theory of arbitrariness. In an article titled "Vers une science de l'art poétique," Jakobson finds himself making the same extraordinary claim for poetic language. His choice of words here is telling. He says that in poetic language there is "an essential change in the relation between the signifier and the signified" (*SW* 5:542). The implied change in relation he refers to is a change from a relation between signifier and signified that is purely arbitrary to one (in poetry) that is not. Jakobson wrote this article in 1965, a half-century after Shklovsky and others had written in the thinly disguised Platonic style that shaped Jakobson's youthful—and later—thinking.

How does Jakobson's essentialist faith in poetic language bear on the structuralist movement? A primary factor in the elaboration of his structural methods was the insight that language is a system that exists "as an evolution." The notion that language is a system is something he had encountered in Saussure;

the notion that the system of language evolves over time is something he felt was missing in Saussure. In 1928 he and Tynianov made this proclamation: "An analysis of the structural laws of language and literature and their evolution inevitably leads to the establishment of a limited series of actually existing structural types (types of structural evolution)."[23] From the very beginning, the principal idea in the new, structuralist theory was that careful inspection would reveal in language not only a relational network evolving over time, but also, hidden inside that network, certain invariant factors. Thus there was an epistemology involved in the examination of language that was not unlike the epistemology called for in the veneration of icons. Just as the Orthodox worshiper is meant to "see" through and beyond the icon to an essence that is not visible to earthly senses, the structuralist observer looks through and beyond language to see abstract structures and invariant factors.

We find an analogous principle at work when Jakobson turns his attention much later to an individual poem. Without doubt his most famous contribution to the structuralist movement is the study of Baudelaire's "Les Chats" that he coauthored with Lévi-Strauss in 1962. The study is so fundamentally structuralist as to be almost a caricature of itself. The authors first submit Baudelaire's text to an intricate grammatical analysis and then use the results of that analysis to construct a system of diagrammatic schemas representing anything from verb functions to rhyme. The one thing that is clear above all else is that the ultimate goal of the project is to *replace* the poem with an object other than the poem itself. The authors explicitly say this, once the analytic phase of their study is complete: "As we now reassemble the pieces of our analysis, let's try to show how the different levels on which we've situated ourselves blend together, complete each other, or combine, thus giving the poem the character of an absolute object."[24] This "absolute object" is a strange mathematical-grammatical nexus of relations, a system, or structure.

And isn't this the same iconic impulse all over again? Doesn't one need to believe, before embarking on an enterprise like this, that in the poetic object, just as in language, there inheres an essence, something invisible and immeasurable (in this case simply because it is entirely abstract), something whose presence we are aware of, something we can speak of (as we can speak of God) but can never see or touch? Thus whether Jakobson is playing the mystic, seeing truths in poetic language that are not there in ordinary language, or playing the structuralist, seeing structures in language, especially poetic language, that others cannot see, his vision is always iconic and essentialist. The fundamental activity of the structuralist poetician is the activity of penetrating behind the concrete wall of language to an impalpable and invisible essence—call it structure, call it the non-arbitrary power of poetic language to signify—that lies beyond.

This is the important point of contact between Russian religious philosophy in the twentieth century and modern literary criticism and theory in the West. In spite of its other roots in mathematics and a number of different fields, structuralism would never be what it was in literary studies without Jakobson. But we have seen that Jakobson, when he is viewed in his native context, occupies a place in a long tradition of language philosophy that is ultimately religious either overtly or only in its tendency towards Platonic essentialism. So "without Jakobson" means without this Russian tradition. That is the true place of Russian religious thought in modern literary and linguistic theory in the West.

Notes

1. Jakobson tells this story in the "Retrospect" to the first volume of his *Selected Writings* (The Hague, 1971) 633. References to this edition will be abbreviated in the text as *SW*.

2. "Orthodox Philosophy of Language in Russia," *Studies in Soviet Thought* 20 (1979): 1–21.

3. Ibid., 2.

4. *Origen on First Principles*, trans. G. W. Butterworth (London, 1936) 19–20.

5. Ibid., 20.

6. Ibid., 27.

7. Saint John of Damascus, *On the Divine Images: Three Apologies against Those Who Attack the Divine Images*, trans. David Anderson (Crestwood, 1980) 40.

8. Ibid., 40.

9. See Andrei Belyi, *Simvolizm* (Moscow, 1910; rpt. Munich, 1969) 94–95. English translation in *Selected Essays of Andrey Bely*, ed. and trans. Steven Cassedy (Berkeley, 1985) 153–154. Subsequent references to *Selected Essays* will be abbreviated *SE* and cited within the text.

10. Wilhelm von Humboldt, *Gesammelte Schriften*, ed. Albert Leitzmann (Berlin, 1907; rpt., 1968) 7:44–46.

11. Ibid., 7:86.

12. A. A. Potebnia, *Mysl' i iazyk* (Khar'kov, 1862; rpt. Kiev, 1926) 77.

13. Ibid., 134.

14. The most thorough discussion of Potebnia in English is John Fizer, *Alexander A. Potebnja's Psycholinguistic Theory of Literature: A Metacritical Inquiry* (Cambridge, Mass., 1986). Fizer does not see the religious element that I have described. His analysis could probably best be described as phenomenological.

15. *Simvolizm* 442; *Selected Essays* 105.

16. I have developed this point at length in *Selected Essays* 40–42, 46–48.

17. Viktor Shklovskii, "Potebnia," first published in *Birzhevye vedomosti*, 30 Decem-

ber 1916; reprinted in *Poètika: Sborniki po teorii poèticheskogo iazyka* (Petrograd, 1919) 3–6. The quoted words appear on p. 4.

18. Viktor Shklovskii, "Voskreshenie slova," first published as a brochure (Petersburg, 1914); reprinted in Jurij Striedter, ed., *Texte der russischen Formalisten* (Munich, 1969–1972) 2:2–17. See pp. 3, 5, for the expression "inner form."

19. Striedter, *Texte der russischen Formalisten* 2:3.

20. Sergii Bulgakov, *Filosofiia imeni* [Philosophy of the name] (Paris, 1953). Abbreviated in the text as *FI*.

21. See Elmar Holenstein, "Jakobson and Husserl: A Contribution to the Genealogy of Structuralism," *Human Context* 7 (1975): 61–83. Holenstein discusses "poeticity," "literaricity" (his rendering of *literaturnost'*), and essentialism on p. 75.

22. "Quest for the Essence of Language," *SW* 2:345–359.

23. Roman Jakobson and Iurii Tynianov, "Problemy izucheniia literatury i iazyka," *Novyi Lef* 12 (1928): 36–37. The translation I have used appears in Ladislav Matejka and Krystyna Pomorska, eds., *Readings in Russian Poetics* (Cambridge, Mass., 1971) 79–81.

24. Roman Jakobson and Claude Lévi-Strauss, "Les chats de Charles Baudelaire," *L'Homme* 2 (1962): 5–21; and in *Questions de poétique,* ed. Tzvetan Todorov (Paris, 1973) 401–419. The quoted phrase appears on p. 414 of *Questions de poétique.* My translation.

Notes on the Contributors

Stephen L. Baehr is Professor of Russian at Virginia Polytechnic Institute and State University. He is the author of *The Paradise Myth in Eighteenth-Century Russia: Utopian Patterns in Early Secular Russian Literature and Culture* (Stanford, 1991) and is currently working on a book entitled *The Machine and its Enemies in Nineteenth- and Twentieth-Century Russian Literature and Culture.*

Henryk Baran is Professor of Slavic Languages and Literatures at the State University of New York at Albany. He is the author of several studies of Velimir Khlebnikov and the editor of *Semiotics and Structuralism: Readings from the Soviet Union* (White Plains, 1974).

Stephen K. Batalden is Professor of History at Arizona State University. He is the author of several studies on the history of the modern Russian Bible and *Catherine II's Greek Prelate: Eugenios Voulgaris in Russia, 1771–1806* (New York, 1982).

Steven Cassedy is Professor of Slavic and Comparative Literature at the University of California, San Diego. He has published *Selected Essays of Andrey Bely* (Berkeley, 1985) and *Flight from Eden: The Origins of Modern Literary Criticism and Theory* (Berkeley, 1990).

Johanna Renate Döring-Smirnov is Professor of Russian at the University of Munich, Germany. She is the author of *Die Lyrik Pasternaks in den Jahren 1928–1934* (Munich, 1973) and co-editor of *Text, Symbol, Weltmodell, Johannes Holthusen zum 60. Geburtstag* (Munich, 1984) and *Velimir Chlebnikov 1885–1985* (Munich, 1986).

Michael S. Flier is Oleksandr Potebnja Professor of Ukrainian Philology at Harvard University. He is the author of *Aspects of Nominal Determination in Old Church Slavic* (The Hague, 1974). Among volumes he has co-edited are *Medieval Russian Culture* [with Henryk Birnbaum] (Berkeley, 1984), *The Scope of Slavic Aspect* [with Alan Timberlake] (Columbus, 1985), and *Language, Literature, Linguistics* [with Simon Karlinsky] (Berkeley, 1987).

Boris Gasparov is Professor of Slavic Languages and Literatures at Columbia University. His latest book-length studies are *Poėtika "Slova o polku Igoreve"*

[Poetics of "The Song of Igor's Campaign"] (Vienna, 1984) and *Poéticheskii iazyk Pushkina kak fakt istorii russkogo literaturnogo iazyka* [Pushkin's poetic language as a fact in the history of the Russian literary language] (Vienna, 1993).

Gary Marker is Professor of History at the State University of New York at Stony Brook. He is the author of *Publishing, Printing, and the Origins of Intellectual Life in Russia, 1700–1800* (Princeton, 1985) and a forthcoming monograph entitled *Reading and Literacy in Early-Modern Russia (1649–1801)*.

Olga Matich is Professor of Slavic Languages and Literatures at the University of California, Berkeley. She is the author of *Paradox in the Religious Poetry of Zinaida Gippius* (Munich, 1972) and co-editor of *The Third Wave: Russian Literature in Emigration* (Ann Arbor, 1983).

Hugh McLean is Professor of Slavic Languages and Literatures at the University of California, Berkeley. He is the author of *Nikolai Leskov: The Man and His Art* (Harvard, 1977) and editor of *In the Shade of the Giant: Essays on Tolstoy* (Berkeley, 1989).

Irina Paperno is Professor of Slavic Languages and Literatures at the University of California, Berkeley. Her main work is *Chernyshevsky and the Age of Realism: A Study in the Semiotics of Behavior* (Stanford, 1988).

Bernice Glatzer Rosenthal is Professor of History at Fordham University, Bronx, New York. She is the author of *D. S. Merezhkovsky and the Silver Age: The Development of a Revolutionary Mentality* (The Hague, 1975), editor of and contributor to *Nietzsche in Russia* (Princeton, 1986), and co-editor, with Martha Bohachevsky-Chomiak, of *A Revolution of the Spirit: Crisis of Values in Russia, 1890–1924* (New York, 1990).

William Mills Todd III is Professor of Russian Literature at Harvard University. He is author of *The Familiar Letter as a Literary Genre in the Age of Pushkin* (Princeton, 1976) and *Fiction and Society in the Age of Pushkin: Ideology, Institutions, and Narrative* (Cambridge, Mass., 1986), and the editor of *Literature and Society in Imperial Russia: 1800–1914* (Stanford, 1978) and *Soviet Sociology of Literature: Conceptions of a Changing World* (Armonk, 1989).

Ronald Vroon is Professor of Slavic Languages and Literatures at the University of California, Los Angeles. He is the author of *Velimir Khlebnikov's Shorter Poems: A Key to the Coinages* (Ann Arbor, 1983) and *Velimir Khlebnikov's* Krysa: *A Commentary* (Stanford, 1989).

Reginald E. Zelnik is Professor of History at the University of California, Berkeley. He is the author of *Labor and Society in Tsarist Russia: The Factory Workers of St. Petersburg, 1855–1870* (Stanford, 1971), and editor and translator of *A Radical Worker in Tsarist Russia: The Autobiography of Semën Ivanovich Kanatchikov* (Stanford, 1986). He is currently completing a book on the Kreenholm strike of 1872 and writing a study of workers' autobiographies.

INDEX

334   INDEX

Teilhard de Chardin, Pierre, 139
Terras, Victor, 125
Theocritus, 275
Theodosius, Metropolitan, 33
Tikhomirov, Lev, 66, 69–71, 81n
Tikhon of Zadonsk *see* Tikhon Zadon-
skii
Tikhon Zadonskii, 125, 132n
Tiutchev, F. I., 293, 297, 298, 309n
Toddes, E. A., 310n
Tolstoi, A. N., 233
Tolstoi, Dmitrii, 52, 62, 76n, 78n
Tolstoi, L. N., 103–121, 121n, 123n,
124–126, 135, 137, 138, 144, 159,
161, 216, 232, 235n
Ton, Konstantin, 27
Trediakovskii, V. K., 249–251, 253,
254, 264, 265, 280n, 281n, 284n
Tretiakov, P. M., 109
Troitskii, S. M., 3
Trotskii-Siniutovich, 61, 62, 63
Trubetskoi, S. N., 135, 303–304
Twain, Mark, 205
Tynianov, Iu. N., 283n, 322

Ushinskii, K. D., 55, 65
Uspenskii, B. A., 4, 5, 19n, 101n, 174,
187, 189n, 297, 307n
Uvarov, S. S., 254, 256

Viazemskii, P. A., 282n
Viebig, Clara, 205
Vinogradov, Sergei, 80n
Virgil (Publius Vergilius Maro), 261,
263–265, 267
Vladimir I (Sviatoslavich), Prince of
Kiev, 95–97, 99, 100n
Voeikov, A. F., 254
Vogt, Karl, 105
Volkov, Semën, 68
Voloshin, M. A., 179, 181–183, 221,
228
Voltaire, 261, 264, 265,
270, 283n
Volynskii, Akim, 170n

Wagner, Richard, 138, 149, 151

Zaitsev, B. K., 232
Zaozerskii, Filipp, 66, 70, 81n
Zelinskii, F. F., 228, 302, 310n
Zenkovskii, V. V., 153n
Zhidkov, pastor, 87
Zhivov, V. M., 282
Zhukovskii, V. A., 255–256, 259, 262
Zieliński, Tadeusz, *see* Zelinskii, F. F.
Zlobin, Vladimir, 170n
Zola, Émile, 205

Compositor: Berkeley Slavic Specialites
Text: 10/13 Monotype Times New Roman
Display: Monotype Times New Roman

CPSIA information can be obtained
at www.ICGtesting.com
Printed in the USA
BVHW070849041019
560256BV00001B/99/P